Proposal Planning & Writing

Proposal Planning & Writing
Fifth Edition

Jeremy T. Miner and Lynn E. Miner

 GREENWOOD

AN IMPRINT OF ABC-CLIO, LLC
Santa Barbara, California • Denver, Colorado • Oxford, England

Library of Congress Cataloging-in-Publication Data

Miner, Jeremy T.
  Proposal planning & writing / Jeremy T. Miner and Lynn E. Miner. — Fifth edition.
    pages cm
  Includes bibliographical references and index.
  ISBN 978-1-4408-2967-3 (hardcover : alk. paper) — ISBN 978-1-4408-2969-7
  (paperback : alk. paper) — ISBN 978-1-4408-2968-0 (ebook)
1. Proposal writing for grants—United States.   I. Miner, Lynn E. II. Title.
  HG177.5.U6M56   2013
  658.15'224—dc23   2013016400

ISBN: 978-1-4408-2967-3 (case)
       978-1-4408-2969-7 (pbk)
EISBN: 978-1-4408-2968-0

17 16 15 14 13   1 2 3 4 5

This book is also available on the World Wide Web as an eBook.
Visit www.abc-clio.com for details.

Greenwood
An Imprint of ABC-CLIO, LLC

ABC-CLIO, LLC
130 Cremona Drive, P.O. Box 1911
Santa Barbara, California 93116-1911

This book is printed on acid-free paper ∞
Manufactured in the United States of America

Contents

Preface

He from whose lips divine persuasion flows.
—Alexander Pope

The fifth edition of *Proposal Planning & Writing*, like previous editions, is a comprehensive reference source for grantseekers. It covers the essentials: finding public and private funds, picking the "best fit" funders, writing all proposal components persuasively, polishing your drafts through creative editing strategies, and utilizing appropriate follow-up techniques. It leads you step-by-step through the process of planning and writing successful proposals.

WHY GRANTS FAIL

A central question that every successful grantseeker must understand is: Why do grant applications fail?

Over the years, we have asked this question of grantmakers, grant reviewers, and grantseekers. Interestingly, responses vary with perspective.

When public and private grantmakers are asked about application failings, their responses are immediate and nearly identical. Program officers consistently identify "failure to follow the application guidelines" as the most common reason why proposals are turned down. Examples include:

1. Applicant ineligible to apply.
2. Project inconsistent with stated priorities.
3. Narrative exceeds page limitations.
4. Failure to include all required documents.
5. Budget requests support for prohibited expenses.
6. Missed the submission deadline date.

Grant reviewers, on the other hand, often respond with the following:

1. No documented need statement.
2. Lack of measurable objectives.
3. Methods not well thought out.
4. Weak evaluation approach.
5. Inexperienced project director.
6. No plan for sustainability.

And when we pose this question to grantseekers in our proposal writing workshops, we hear these frequent answers:

1. Bad ideas.
2. Good ideas poorly presented.
3. Insufficient preproposal contact.
4. Outcomes are not significant.
5. Target populations not clearly identified.
6. Asking for too much money.

What do you think is the most common reason why grant proposals are not funded? Which one of these dozen-and-a-half possibilities would you pick as the top reason?

Our answer?

None of the above.

While all of the 18 reasons listed above certainly weaken a proposal and may result in its declination, the biggest reason that grants fail is lack of money.

That's right. Grantmakers simply receive more quality proposals than they are able to fund. Consequently, they have to turn down strong proposals simply due to insufficient funding.

Because grantseeking today is extremely competitive, your responsibility, as a proposal writer, is to persuasively present great ideas that are well documented, whose objectives are expressed in measurable terms that implement innovative methods to targeted audiences, with the resulting outcomes rigorously evaluated and widely disseminated to other stakeholders. All of this will be done under the leadership of a strong project director who is well credentialed and has talked with program officers, past grant winners, and past grant reviewers prior to actual writing. In this book, you will find hundreds of tips to help you meet your responsibility.

The content of this book is based on our grantseeking experiences over the past four decades in writing successful proposals, conducting grant workshops nationwide, reviewing government and foundation proposals, and critiquing application guidelines for grantmakers. We don't just talk in abstract terms about grants; we share the practical tips that have enabled us to write winning grants for years.

We practice what we teach.

NEW TO THIS EDITION

While the fifth edition retains the essential features of previous editions for planning and writing successful proposals, the following additions are designed to better meet the emerging needs of today's grantseekers in an era of increased competition for limited resources.

New Chapter on Sustainability

It's one of the questions that many grant writers dread: "How will your project be sustained beyond the granting period?" Application guidelines may approach sustainability in different ways, but sponsors all want to know the same thing—"What's next?" Providing evidence that you have considered the issue of future funding and have a tentative plan in mind can make your proposal stand out from other grant applications. In this fifth edition, we add a new chapter that examines different types of sustainability, includes sample proposal language that can easily be adapted to multiple situations, and presents common proposal rejection reasons based on inadequate sustainability plans.

Expanded Presentation of Logic Models

Assessment and evaluation are instrumental to project success; they pinpoint what is really happening in your project and allow you to be accountable to sponsors. Logic models are graphical displays that illustrate the relationship between a current situation, processes, and resulting outputs and outcomes. Logic models demonstrate, often in one page, the depth of your project planning, implementation, evaluation, and reporting. New to this edition are more sample logic models, which can be easily adapted to most grant projects.

Advanced Writing Tips

An unintended consequence of public and private sponsors who accept applications electronically is the changing of how grant reviewers read proposals. Reviewers may read proposals on their computers and mobile devices, skimming at first and then circling back

as necessary. They use technology to their advantage. An enhanced presentation of writing and editing techniques includes advanced tips that consider differences in your proposal content and organization and proposal design based on whether proposals are submitted electronically as attached word-processed or Portable Document Format (PDF) files, online text boxes, web-based fillable forms, or combinations thereof.

More Examples and Annotated Examples

Our book readers and workshop participants repeatedly tell us they want more examples—and we've listened. In addition to increasing the number of examples by 75 percent, at the end of every chapter in Part III: Writing Government Proposals (Chapters 7–15), a new section has been added called "Grant Gaffes." The exhibit presents a common but flawed response that is often included in proposals. These negative examples highlight mistakes others have made, ones that you'll want to avoid. We annotate key dimensions of the response in call-out thought bubbles, drawing attention to what went right, where the narrative veered off course, and what might be done to rescue the passage.

Beyond these significant updates, readers will find enhancements in this fifth edition that address, many for the first time, the following topics:

- International grantseeking opportunities
- Justifying the need for basic science research
- Coordinating budgets and proposal narratives
- Overcoming writer's block
- Collaborative writing
- A model for resubmission proposals

One additional enhancement: starter sentences. A big challenge in writing any proposal section is overcoming inertia, getting started. Once the first few sentences are written, then the rest of the section seems to flow more easily. To help jump-start your grant writing, in each of the proposal writing chapters we've included ten starter sentences to help speed up your writing process.

TARGET AUDIENCES

This fifth edition will be of value for grantseekers wishing a concrete guide through the fundamentals of proposal planning and writing. Based on our 20 years of experience with this text, users represent the following disciplines:

- **Economic Development**: City planning, land use, urban revitalization, workforce development, job creation.

- **Education**: Day care programs, adult education, public and private schools, special education departments, colleges and universities, English as a foreign language programs, libraries.
- **First Responders**: Police, fire, emergency medical services.
- **Government**: Local, state, and federal agencies; courts, human services, parks and recreation.
- **Health Care**: Hospitals, nursing homes, public health organizations, Veterans Administration, International Health, families, maternal and child health.
- **Philanthropy**: Foundations, charitable organizations, service clubs.
- **Religions**: Churches, synagogues, mosques, and other houses of worship; faith-based organizations, religious education.
- **Social Services**: Community development, rehabilitation, mental health, welfare, senior citizens.
- **Other**: Fine and performing arts, senior citizens' advocates and agencies, and special interest groups.

STRUCTURE AND CONTENT

Proposal Planning & Writing is organized to lead you through the grantseeking process. Seventeen chapters and a bibliography are arranged in a logical order.

Part I: Finding Sponsors and Planning Proposals presents four chapters with information on print and electronic sources to identify and qualify the tens of thousands of grantmakers that award more than $300 billion in philanthropic funds annually.

Part II: Writing Private Foundation and Corporate Proposals contains two chapters that give you a time-tested template to write proposals for private foundations and corporations; nine complete proposals show how the template can be used in different grant writing situations.

Part III: Writing Government Proposals dissects the longer federal grant proposals and presents many examples for each section. Nine chapters address: problem statements; goals, objectives, and outcomes; methods; evaluation; dissemination; budgets; sustainability; appendixes; and abstracts.

Part IV: The Final Steps includes two chapters that take you from your initial draft through the process of rigorous editing to produce a highly persuasive proposal that appeals to the mindset of your grant reviewers.

Readers have shared with us the various ways they find and use information in this book, insights that may be beneficial to you as well.

- **Education.** They read the entire book cover-to-cover as an educational exercise before they begin writing a grant proposal. They highlight, underline, and circle points of interest. They write notes in the margins. They flag and dog-ear pages they wish to return to later.
- **Information.** They focus on reading the 10 successful proposals presented in the book. Armed with this information, they consider ways these template samples can be adapted to their specific situation. With a generic model in mind, they springboard to their own writing.
- **Persuasion.** They use the table of contents and index to identify precise topics for which they are seeking a helpful tip. This approach helps them focus on a particular task, increasing the persuasiveness of their proposals one section, one paragraph, one sentence, one word at a time.

In short, successful grantseekers are individuals who are so dedicated to their ideas that they will find the means to carry them out with or without outside support. Sponsors have clear objectives and expectations that they hope to realize by providing financial support to such dedicated persons. A persuasively written grant proposal is the link between them. This book helps you forge that link.

Let's begin planning your best grant ever!

PART I
Finding Sponsors
and Planning Proposals

OVERVIEW OF PART I

Tens of thousands of grantmakers give away more than $300 billion annually. How do you find those sponsors who would fund your projects?

Part I gives you the basic print and electronic information sources to identify a list of public and private sponsors who might fund your projects. With a little research time, you can narrow down that initial suspect list and identify those grantmakers who have a high probability of funding your organization.

Chapter 1 helps you get ready to begin your grantseeking journey. It examines the individual and organizational attitudes held by successful grantseekers. It offers an overview of the grantseeking process—from start to finish. It recognizes that you probably have other work responsibilities besides writing grants and suggests some effective time management strategies so you can write more grants in less time. Finally, it suggests some ways in which you can help build your own internal infrastructure for successful grantseeking.

In Chapter 2, the focus is on finding public grants from federal and state agencies. Most federal grantmaking agencies provide online information that is readily accessible—so much so, in fact, that an Internet search can be overwhelming. We present some efficient ways of identifying federal grant dollars. State agencies, on the other hand, lag behind many federal

agencies in making grant information available. Accordingly, we offer some strategies for ferreting out state-level grant funds.

With Chapter 3, our attention turns to finding private funds from foundations and corporations. We identify five different types of foundations and suggest how approaches to them might differ. Presently, there are approximately 100,000 private foundations that award grants. Information about private foundation funding priorities and past grant support is generally accessible, and we point to multiple print and electronic sources that will help you select likely sponsors of your projects. In contrast, information about corporations is less accessible, and successful grantseekers must be especially resourceful in their quests for funding. We show you the tips that the professionals use when seeking corporate funding.

By the time you have completed your search of public and private funding sources, you have a list of potential "suspects" who might fund your proposal—but you don't know for sure. In Chapter 4, we prescribe a four-step process to convert these "suspects" to "prospects" by talking with program officers, past grant winners, and past grant reviewers *before* you start to write your next proposal. Engaging in preproposal contact substantially increases your likelihood of getting funded.

CHAPTER 1
Introduction to Grantseeking

*There is nothing more uncertain in its success than to take
the lead in the introduction of a new order of things*
—Machiavelli

Grantseeking is a multibillion-dollar-a-year business—
and growing annually!

Following a 500-year-old Machiavellian maxim,
your challenge, as a grantseeker, is to introduce a new
order of things without guarantees of outcomes. In
Chapter 1, you will learn the following:

- The grantseeking landscape
- Common attitudes about grantseeking
- Five steps for getting started
- Strategies for effective time management

THE GRANTSEEKING LANDSCAPE

According to the National Center for Charitable
Statistics, approximately 1.5 million nonprofit organizations are applying for the more than $300 billion
given away annually in grants. If those funds were
distributed evenly, each organization would receive a
grant of $200,000 per year. Of course, averages can be
deceptive, and in reality some organizations receive
multimillions in grants while others receive token
amounts—or even none.

Grantseeking is always a competitive process,
and even more so in tough economic times as organizational needs outstrip resources and groups turn
to grants as a means of strengthening their financial
footing while pursuing their missions. Grant writing
is a skill that becomes the financial lifeblood of many
nonprofits. Making collective use of the grant-writing
tips throughout this book will significantly increase
your success rate.

ATTITUDES ABOUT GRANTSEEKING

Grantseekers often wonder if it is really worthwhile to
write grants. Certainly the organizations that receive
collectively billions of grant dollars annually think so.
To find out how you can access those dollars and answer
many questions along the way, we begin by looking at
some attitudes—and misconceptions—about grants.

Individual Attitudes

What does the word *grants* mean to you? Frankly, for
some people the term generates negative reactions,
such as "professional begging," "futility," "risk-taking,"
"mystique," "hustle," or "con job." To such people, pursuing grants is risky because positive outcomes aren't
guaranteed. These people steer clear of grants for
many pessimistic reasons: lack of motivation, lack of
skills, lack of confidence, fear of failure, fear of change,
fear of success, lack of time, unrealistic expectations,
and laziness. Such individuals who are a "quart low
on attitude" are destined to fail if they pursue grants.
Skeptics will say, "Grants, why bother?" Successful
grant winners, on the other hand, will answer, "For
many reasons." People write grants to:

1. Earn money.
2. Finance crucial projects.
3. Gain job security.
4. Achieve recognition and build reputations.
5. Break the regular job routine.
6. Solve problems creatively.
7. Have fun.

What brings you job satisfaction? Certainly, money—a decent salary and the security it produces—is an extremely important factor on the job. While employee satisfaction fluctuates with the circumstances in each organization, most job satisfaction studies show that employees desire (1) interesting work, (2) recognition for work performed, and (3) a feeling of being "in" on things. Grantseeking can satisfy all three components of a rewarding job. If you are responsible for mustering grant support from others on your staff, you must show how grants will meet these basic psychological needs.

Perhaps the most critical element in your ability to pursue grants successfully is your sense of self-worth—the picture you have of yourself in your mental photo album, your self-esteem. Those with high self-esteem have a feeling of competence and believe in their ability to cope with the challenges of life. The value you place on yourself strongly influences how you perform on the job.

If you approach proposal planning and writing with a positive attitude and are willing to persist, you will succeed. If you doubt success from the start, you will fail. The applicable behavioral principle is the notion of the "self-fulfilling prophesy." In essence, it says, "What you believe will happen." Many like you have already mastered the grants process. We believe you too can be a successful grantseeker.

Organizational Attitudes

Many grantseeking organizations harbor misconceptions about grantseeking that serve as formidable internal barriers to winning grants. Some common myths that need to be debunked include the following.

Myth: People will fund my needs. Sponsors fund their needs, not yours. When writing proposals, you must show you can become a change agent to solve a problem important to them. For example, as a school official you may want a new computer laboratory. Sponsors are apt to be much less interested in your perceived needs than an opportunity to support a project that will train children in reading, mathematics, and science for the 21st century. Put differently, in this example sponsors care more about innovative ways to teach children than they do about buying computers. More broadly, the principle is this: Grantmakers prefer to fund people, not "things."

Myth: You can run a program on grants forever. Sustained grant support over many years is difficult to obtain. Start-up project support is the easiest to find and operating support is the most difficult. While project support can be successfully parlayed over many years,

it is usually segmented into different phases or is periodically redefined if it is to be sustained. The grant principle is this: Sustainability is the key feature in many grants because funders want to know what will happen when the grant funds end.

Myth: Use the weasel words that people want to hear. There are no magic buzzwords to sprinkle in your proposal. "In" words today go "out" tomorrow. Don't be concerned about using vogue words. The simple, honest, direct approach is best. The grant principle is this: Persuasive proposals are written to the level of expertise of the reviewer and are expressed in direct and clear language.

Organizational Benefits. Organizations pursue grants for many financial and programmatic reasons. For instance, grants will provide budget relief through the direct and the indirect costs they provide. Often, grant money can be leveraged to attract additional funds from other sources. Beyond these fiscal considerations, receiving grants can launch new program initiatives that may have real public relations value for your organization. This, in turn, can bring zest to your recruitment program, making it easier to attract new talent to your organization.

Organizational Barriers. Agencies entering the grants arena must recognize and respond to a fundamental principle of behavior, namely, *organization prevents reorganization*. This means the very fact that you are organized one way makes it difficult to organize another way. Grandma said it best: "You can't teach an old dog new tricks." And yet, commitment to a successful grants program means that organizational priorities may need to change. Time and resources will be allocated differently. New systems and procedures will be implemented, as discussed below.

Resistance to change is natural and can be minimized by showing individuals how their job satisfaction will increase. Perhaps the best motivators for employees are the achievement, the recognition, the work itself, and the responsibility. One of people's greatest needs is the ability to achieve, and through achievement, they experience psychological growth. Your task is to control and increase the effectiveness of the motivators within your organization that induce growth. Grants enable you to do things that you would not otherwise be able to do within your organization, or at least not as quickly.

Coping with Change. At its most basic level, grants produce change. Something needs to be changed, and that is one reason why people pursue grants. Nevertheless, some people resist change because it is threatening in some way. As grant writers work with others in developing grant proposals, they will undoubtedly run into some common forms of resistance:

- *Self-interest*—Change may make it difficult or impossible to satisfy personal needs and desires at work. *"I was hired to do important other things besides writing grants."*
- *Fear of the unknown*—Not knowing or lacking a basis to predict the outcomes of change creates an atmosphere of fear. *"What's in it for me?"*
- *General mistrust*—Lack of confidence in leadership, not understanding the need for change, and feeling that past performance is being questioned undermine confidence that change is good or even needed. *"My workload is already too heavy and now they want me to do more; why should I?"*
- *Fear of failure*—Change means altering the way people do their jobs and run their programs. Change creates discomfort and concerns about meeting new demands. *"Don't talk to me about grants. I tried it once and struck out—a total waste of time."*
- *Differing perceptions and goals*—Seldom do different people see things the same way, and this would be true of change. Individuals set goals for themselves and their work; as a result, change is often seen as disruptive. *"No matter what they say, getting grants doesn't get you any benefits around here."*
- *Peer pressure*—Persons who are not directly affected by the change may resist it nonetheless, in order to protect the interests and needs of coworkers and friends. Persons who champion the change may feel pressure from peers to resist it. *"Nobody else around here chases grants, why should I?"*
- *Bureaucratic inertia*—Stemming from rigid rules and standardized procedures, bureaucracy fosters lack of initiative and flexibility on the part of staff and employees. *"Sure, I'll write a grant just as soon as they give me some reassigned time and some decent institutional grant support."*

To overcome resistance to change, the emphasis must be on planned change that arises from a compelling need while recognizing the psychosocial dynamics of change that must occur over time and be guided by change agents.

Motivating Others. To be a successful grantseeker, you need to engage others within your organization to help in various ways. Follow the old adage: "Work smarter, not harder." Encourage others to join your grantseeking activities. These suggestions will help you secure "buy-in" from your colleagues.

- Communicate clearly grantseeking expectations in job descriptions and interviews.
- Promulgate written policies that affirm the organizational importance of grantseeking.
- Give people time, resources, and training to write grants.
- Secure seed funding for pilot projects.
- Recognize and reward grant activities within the organization.
- Use the in-house newsletter or letters from a central administrator to praise grant writers on their efforts.
- Share your grant knowledge with others in your organization since enthusiasm is contagious.
- Start small and build; pick a few people to become the in-house grant experts and gradually expand.

As you work with colleagues in your organization, help them build realistic expectations about grantseeking; otherwise, their false expectations will produce disappointments and disincentives for pursuing grants. For instance, supervisors must recognize that it takes approximately six to nine months to find out whether a federal grant has been funded. If bosses expect a decision soon after submitting a proposal, they will be needlessly disappointed.

Sponsor Attitudes

Grantmakers—also called "sponsors" and "funders"—are vitally concerned about specific problems, injustices, or inequities they see in their world. They are so concerned that they commit their money to solve these problems. In essence, they see a gap between what is and what ought to be. Their mission is to close this gap. Another name for "gap" in grant parlance is "need," perhaps the most crucial section of your proposal; see Chapter 7 for further details. The gap represents their view of the problems that deeply concerns them.

Successful grant writers understand the sponsor's view and express that view in proposals. Too often, proposal writers focus on their own need for funds instead of matching their project's goals with a sponsor's priorities. You should select sponsors that share your view of the world and tailor proposals to them. (See Chapter 4 for specifics.) Sponsors view grants as investments in an improved future. Proposals are funded when they express the priorities shared by the sponsor. Projects are rejected when they do not match a sponsor's priorities.

GETTING STARTED

Do you have all of your "ducks in a row"? Do you have the essential infrastructure in place to begin grant writing? Your infrastructure roadmap includes clearly defined administrative structures and personnel roles. It requires key personnel with the skills and tools to assemble competitive proposals. In short, it's all about credibility—credibility of the individual leading the project, the organization that individual represents, and the grant idea. With an infrastructure in place, we'll next guide you through the five main steps to become a successful grantseeker.

1. **Select your grant ideas.** Look internally to your staff and volunteers for suggestions. Hold brainstorming sessions. Ask colleagues, "If we had a million dollars, what would we do with it?" Look externally to citizens, clients, and advisory boards. What suggestions would they have? For now, compile your list of grant ideas. Don't worry about which ones are the most fundable; that'll come later (Chapter 4).

2. **Identify possible funding sources.** Examine print and electronic funding sources for both public (Chapter 2) and private (Chapter 3) grants. When finished, you'll have a list of sponsors who *may* be interested in funding your projects.

3. **Conduct preproposal contacts.** Following the four-step process in Chapter 4, you will find out which sponsors are most likely to fund your proposals. Grantseeking is a contact sport. You will want to contact program officers, past grant winners, and past grant reviewers—all before you decide *if* and *what* you should write.

4. **Write your initial proposal draft.** Following the application guidelines and reviewer's evaluation form, quickly write your first draft. Remember: the first draft is for getting down, not for getting good. Experienced grantseekers spend approximately 25 percent of their time writing the first draft and 75 percent of their time rewriting and editing— your next step. (Chapters 5–15).

5. **Edit your initial proposal draft.** Cycle through your draft many times, continually looking for one feature to improve at a time (Chapter 16). Examples: make sure you provide all of the requested information, check for spelling and grammar errors, and design a visually appealing document.

TIME MANAGEMENT: WRITING MORE PROPOSALS IN LESS TIME WITH GREATER EFFICIENCY

Why do we all complain about the lack of that precious commodity—time? Effective time management enables you to feel in control, be productive, and enjoy what you do.

Very few people have grant writing as their only job responsibility. Usually it is one of many tasks that includes such things as project administration, training, research, advising, public relations, other fundraising, personnel management, budgeting, phone answering, envelope stuffing—and the list goes on.

We all know the basics of effective time management, but we need periodic reminders about such things as the following:

1. Set priorities daily.
2. Do first things first.
3. Remember, you don't "find" time, you "make" time.
4. Recognize there is always time for important things.
5. Recall long-term goals while doing small tasks.
6. Eliminate unproductive activities quickly.
7. Focus on one thing at a time.
8. Establish deadlines for yourself and others.
9. Delegate whenever possible.
10. Handle each piece of paper only once.
11. Keep things organized.
12. Don't fret when time is spent on activities beyond your control.

Of the many good books on time management, our favorite is *How to Get Control of Your Time and Your Life* by Alan Lakein.

Beyond these common sense suggestions, successful grantseekers adhere closely to their "To Do List," avoid a huge time robber—interruptions—and use efficient office procedures.

To Do List

Consider your "To Do" list inviolate. If you write it down, it shall get done. Set "tickler" reminders on your calendar for the most important tasks so they don't drop down too far as new "to do" items get added to the list. Examples:

- Identify possible federal and state funding sources.
- Review guidelines.
- Call program officer to get copy of reviewer's evaluation form.
- Talk with past grant winner.
- Outline proposal.
- Draft three pages.
- Conduct a primary literature review.
- Find documenting statistics.
- Collect samples of successful proposals.

Avoid Interruptions

Take control of your time. Examples:

- Tell colleagues that a closed door or a "Do Not Disturb" sign means business.
- Don't check your e-mail and voicemail frequently; schedule communication checks several times a day.
- Postpone the interrupters by asking them if you could talk later; then, set up a time.
- Jot down an agenda to use when you want to talk with them: it will hasten your meeting.

Using Efficient Procedures

Use your time effectively. Examples:

- Return calls during lunch hour that require only a short answer or when you're posing a simple question. Many people will be away from their desks, and you'll reach voicemail. Be specific in your call. This way they can leave you a complete, detailed answer.
- "Power Block" your time in intervals where you do nothing except what you schedule yourself to do. Make appointments with yourself to work on your proposal.
- Use color coding with your online calendar. For example, proposal due dates can be flagged in red, and reminders one week in advance of the due date can be flagged in yellow. In instances where the sponsor indicates a date by which funding decisions will be made, list that date to your calendar in green.
- To get people off the phone, warn them your time is limited by saying, "It sounds interesting, but I've got to leave in five minutes," or "Since I really can't spend a lot of time on the phone, let's make plans to meet for lunch instead."
- Voicemail can receive calls while you're not there. Callers are now accustomed to it, but change your messages frequently to update callers on your schedule.
- When you leave a voicemail message for someone, state a time you will be available in order to avoid phone tag, e.g., "John, I'll be at my desk between 2:00 and 4:00 p.m. this afternoon," or "Sara, please call me tomorrow morning between 8:00 and 10:00 a.m."
- Leave some free time on your appointment calendar to provide you with the flexibility you need to deal with distractions, delays, and emergencies while avoiding stress.

- Sort the mail into six categories:

  1. To toss: go through the mail stack quickly, tossing or deleting things that aren't worth opening.
  2. To ask about: attach sticky notes to remind yourself what to ask about or drag into a "Query" file.
  3. To file: if you don't need it now, it can be filed.
  4. To call: handle quicker than by letter or e-mail response.
  5. To do: things that require action.
  6. To read: be selective.

Tame the time robbers so they don't tame you.

CLIP FILES AS A PREMIER TIME MANAGEMENT TOOL

Successful grantseekers have effective systems and procedures in place to save time when hunting for and organizing information. If you could cut down the amount of time you spend managing information, you could write more proposals or work on other responsibilities. We recommend using clip files for organizing and managing grant information. With them, you "chunk" the grant process into small, manageable units and distribute your information into those categories.

The clip file theme runs throughout the book. We'll cite some examples below to get you started; additional tips are found at the end of each chapter. To begin, create a system of file folders, notebooks, or electronic files that contain the following labels.

Clip File Labels	Clip File Labels
Developing Grant Ideas (Chapter 1)	Methods (Chapter 9)
Refining Grant Ideas (Chapter 1)	Evaluation (Chapter 10)
Uniqueness (Chapter 1)	Dissemination (Chapter 11)
Advocates (Chapter 1)	Budget (Chapter 12)
Finding Public Funds (Chapter 2)	Sustainability (Chapter 13)
Finding Private Funds (Chapter 3)	Appendixes (Chapter 14)
Preproposal Contacts (Chapter 4)	Abstracts (Chapter 15)
Problem Statement (Chapter 7)	Complete Proposals (Chapter 16)
Goals, Objectives, Outcomes (Chapter 8)	Grant Review & Funding Decisions (Chapter 17)

We'll give examples of the first four clip files here to familiarize you with the concept; the remaining topics are discussed in appropriate chapters as indicated in parentheses. Whenever you see the following symbol, get out your kitchen (or electronic) scissors, clip the action item, and add it to your *clip* file; you'll *save* time when you write your next grant. Just like people clip grocery coupons to save money, look for the *clip and save* symbol in this book to save you valuable grant writing time.

Clip File Action Item # 1
Developing Grant Ideas

Assemble your wish lists of organizational needs. Beyond the strategies cited above for motivating others, where else can you get grant ideas? Consider reports from commissions or government offices citing pertinent needs, consultant reports, grant idea worksheets, lists of recently funded grants, and lists of requests for proposals. Every time someone says, "We ought to do this—if we had the money," write "this" on a piece of paper and add it to your clip file. There is no need to evaluate the ideas at this point; that comes later. For now, just brainstorm. Think so far outside of the box that you can't even see it. To illustrate, a brainstormed list of ideas to overcome obesity might include the following: make exercise activities more accessible; reward land owners who protect open space outside the city; add more bike-safe lanes on the road; give employees an extra half hour to walk during their lunch break; once a week, turn off the TV and walk around the block—twice; pick a partner with whom to exercise; rotate between eating new fruits one week and new vegetables the next; plan meals to get away from processed food by making a double batch and freezing half. Experienced grantseekers have found they can often combine single ideas and craft them into a bigger—and more fundable—idea.

Clip File Action Item # 2
Refining Grant Ideas

The more ways you can describe your grant ideas, the better chance you have of getting funded. Why? Because different sponsors fund different types of projects serving different populations in different locations. You have four different options to redefine your project. You can identify alternative:

- Subject matter areas
- Project locations
- Constituency groups served
- Types of grants

Assume you work for an inner-city elementary school. How else might you describe your school? A model school for language immersion? A demonstration center for parental involvement in education? A cross-cultural community center? A school/industry partnership location? Each description presents your school in a different light and could attract different sponsors.

As another example, assume you work for a rural health care agency. How else might you describe yourself? A regional one-stop health shopping service? A countywide multispecialty health clinic? A rural life-care health center? A federal health demonstration center? Again, different focus points could appeal to different sponsors.

Each variable—subject matter, location, constituency, grant type—gives you some choices about the way you might describe your project. For example, suppose you wanted to create an information clearinghouse for the homeless. You might redefine your project as follows.

Subject Matter Area

In broad terms, your project might be described as one dealing with "education," "social welfare," or "social justice." In more narrow terms, keyword phraseology might include "low-cost housing," "information dissemination," or perhaps, "minority education." As further examples, keyword terms in the broad area of medical diseases might include the following: "accidents," "AIDS," "Alzheimer's Disease," "asthma," "breast cancer," "cardiovascular diseases," "cystic fibrosis," "diabetes," "mental health," "HIV infection," "Parkinson's Disease," and "Sudden Infant Death syndrome," among many.

Project Location

Your project impact area could range from the "neighborhood" to the "city," "region," "county," "state," "national," or even "international" level, depending upon the scope of your efforts.

Constituency Groups Served

While you might want to make your information clearinghouse available to all those who need its service, you might wish to specialize in serving the needs of one or more populations, e.g., "minorities," "aged," "disadvantaged," "single parents with low income," or "poor families." Other target groups might include the following: "children and youth," "handicapped," "refugees," "veterans," and "women."

Type of Grant

Keywords for different types of grants include the following: "service delivery," "capacity building," "research," "equipment," "exhibition," "workshops," and "travel." Since many different types of grants are available, you might choose to cast your information clearinghouse for the homeless project to emphasize any of these categories.

- A low-cost housing dissemination project for minorities in your city.
- A housing demonstration information project for the disadvantaged poor in the Midwest.
- A housing training project for the aged in the state.
- A seed project for an information clearinghouse on housing in the region.

Use creative thinking to identify different ways to appeal to potential sponsors. What can you adapt, modify, magnify, minify, substitute, rearrange, reverse, or combine to come up with a distinctive project?

Clip File Action Item # 3
Uniqueness

Include the following in your clip file: your mission statement, mission statements from other organizations like yours enabling you to identify your distinctive differences, endorsements from experts, bibliographies, résumés, and organizational self-assessment tools.

One starting point in identifying your uniqueness is to examine (or brush off the dust and reexamine) your organizational mission statement. It is a brief, clear summary of your organization's goals. Ideally, it contains no more than one hundred words. It provides a context for the specific grant activities that you will pursue.

One hospital identified its unique characteristics as follows: the only self-sufficient laboratory in the state with administrative support for the project, strong community reputation, centralized location, solid partnership program with physicians, open-heart surgery center, and active research program.

Consider this mission statement from an alcoholism rehabilitation agency named Return:

The mission of Return is to help individuals regain an active, productive life without the use of alcohol. Recovery comes through rehabilitative support and a self-desired change rather than from prescription. Return is a hospital-based program that emphasizes keeping the alcoholic in contact with family, employer, church, community, recreation, and cultural activities during the recovery process. (56 words)

Still having trouble determining your organizational uniqueness? Ask yourself and answer these questions:

1. What is your agency "known" for?
2. What are you recognized as being "the best" at?
3. What will make you more unique in the future?
4. What separates you from your grant competition in the eyes of grantmakers?
5. What do the leading grantmakers say about your agency?

We once worked with an organization that initially could identify only a dozen "brag points," features that differentiated themselves from peer organizations. We encouraged others to contribute to this initial list, which now stands at 184 unique items. When writing proposals, they review the current list and select those items that would be most persuasive to the proposal reviewers.

Clip File Action Item # 4
Advocates

List the types of services that your organization needs but is unable to provide with internal staff, e.g., legal, financial, management, or personnel; contact external service providers who know your organization and may be able to advocate on your behalf. List specific services you might use but lack access to, e.g., telephone credit card, data entry, desktop publishing, and travel; perhaps your organizational friendraising can identify people who can assist with these services.

To help build your clip files, invoke the aid of your colleagues. Have staff members, for example, bring one addition to your clip file at each staff meeting. Further, make full use of so-called idle moments. Whether you are reading the evening newspaper, waiting in a doctor's office, or scanning the in-flight magazine while flying, develop a habit of continually being on the lookout for printed ideas that may be useful someday in developing a proposal.

What about politicians? Are they good advocates? Should you use them to help get grants? Like Thanksgiving Dinner, "Yes," but in moderation. Local, county, state, and federal government officials can be of some help in getting grants. Among the appropriate ways to network with politicians:

1. Keep them posted on your grant priorities.
2. Meet periodically with staffers in charge of congressional liaison in your specialty area, education, health, social services, environment.
3. Invite them to share new reports with you (for your clip file).
4. Write draft support letters you'd like to receive from them for major (not all) proposals you submit, if the sponsor would see value in it. Unsure? Ask as a part of your preproposal contact (Chapter 4).
5. Invite them to visit your organization and see for themselves the good work you are doing.

CHAPTER 2
Finding Public Funds

The art of government consists in taking as much money as possible from one class of citizens to give to the other.
—Voltaire

OVERVIEW OF PUBLIC FUNDING

Consistent with the 200-year-old Voltaire observation, federal and state governments award billions of grant dollars each year. This chapter focuses on finding public grant funds at the national and state levels. In Chapter 2, you will learn the following:

- Three different types of government funding.
- Basic reference tools for finding federal government grants.
- Basic reference tools for finding state government grants.
- Tips for conducting grant information searches.

Although no one single source of information covers all government grants, many agencies have some type of grantmaking program, usually found on a Web site or in an agency publication. Because so much information is available on the Web, we begin by looking first at the interagency references and then focus on agency-specific print and electronic sources of information regarding federal and state government grants.

TYPES OF FEDERAL GOVERNMENT FUNDING

The federal government uses three different types of funding mechanisms to support or stimulate activities. Congress passed the Federal Grant and Cooperative Agreement Act of 1977 to distinguish between and establish criteria for using grants, cooperative agreements, and contracts. In practical terms:

1. A **grant** is a financial award from a federal sponsor that expects modest involvement from its program officers.
2. A **cooperative agreement** is awarded by a federal sponsor when it expects substantial involvement from its program officers.
3. A **contract** is a financial award from a federal sponsor wherein specific services are performed for a set fee.

The table on the following page highlights some of the differences among these three funding mechanisms.

Feature	Grants	Cooperative Agreements	Contracts
Funding idea initiated by . . .	Project Director	Project Director or Sponsor	Sponsor
Project announcement . . .	Unsolicited	Solicited	Competitive bidding
Direction determined by . . .	Project Director	Project Director and Sponsor jointly	Sponsor
Level of oversight by sponsor . . .	Minimal	Substantial	Substantial
Payment plan . . .	Drawdown scheduled	Variable	Drawdown after expenditures
Purchased equipment belongs to . . .	Applicant institution	Applicant institution	Sponsor (sometimes)

Recognizing that the federal government uses three different mechanisms (grants, cooperative agreements, and contracts) to award funds, we next discuss the tools available to identify funding opportunity announcements.

FEDERAL GOVERNMENT INFORMATION SOURCES

Grants.gov

Grants.gov was created in 2002 to be your "one-stop shopping" source to find and apply for billions in federal government grants. Through the use of a common Web site, www.grants.gov, you can find and apply for grant funds online, thereby simplifying grants management and eliminating redundancies. All federal agencies are required to post competitive grant and cooperative agreement opportunities at grants.gov. The top five issuing agencies include Department of Health and Human Services, Department of the Interior, Department of Agriculture, Department of Education, and Department of Justice. The federal agencies that award grants and cooperative agreements have developed common data elements, electronic processes, and uniform administrative rules—all to be accessible through a single portal.

Begin your search for funding opportunities by visiting the grants.gov home page as illustrated in Exhibit 1.

Next, to find specific federal grants, you can search by keyword, funding opportunity number, catalog of federal domestic assistance number, broad category designation (e.g., health, education, or environment), name of grantmaking agency (e.g., Department of Health and Human Services, Department of Education, or Environmental Protection Agency). Further, an advanced search feature enables you to combine their individual search parameters. Exhibit 2 shows an example of a keyword search for "obesity" grants.

Finally, once you have entered your search terms, you will be presented with a list of pertinent grant opportunities. The results of the keyword search for obesity grant opportunities are shown in Exhibit 3. Each hit is a hotlink that will open up information that can be viewed in either summary or detailed form.

Submitting Applications via Grants.gov. If you only want to find grant opportunities, you do not need to register with grants.gov. However, to apply for federal funding via grants.gov, you must register once before using. Follow the five-step process listed under the "Get Registered" tab, which includes: (1) obtaining a Data Universal Numbering System (DUNS) number; (2) registering with Systems Award Management (SAM); (3) entering a username and password; (4) identifying

GRANTS.GOV HOME PAGE

EXHIBIT 1

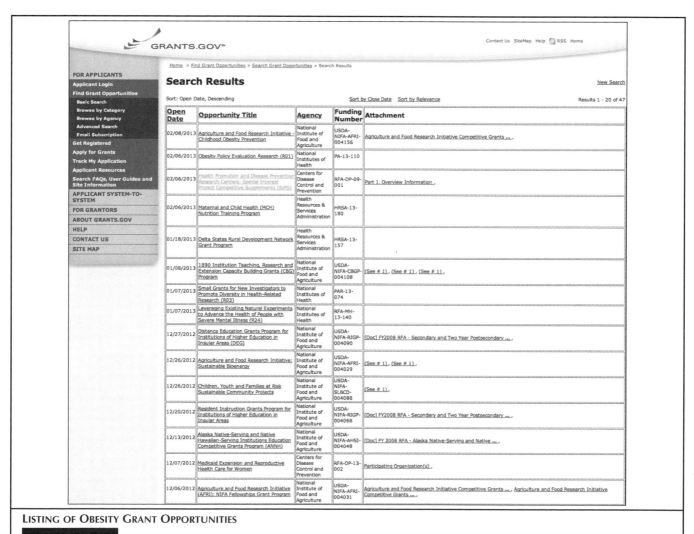

KEYWORD SEARCH FOR OBESITY GRANT OPPORTUNITIES()

EXHIBIT 2

LISTING OF OBESITY GRANT OPPORTUNITIES

EXHIBIT 3

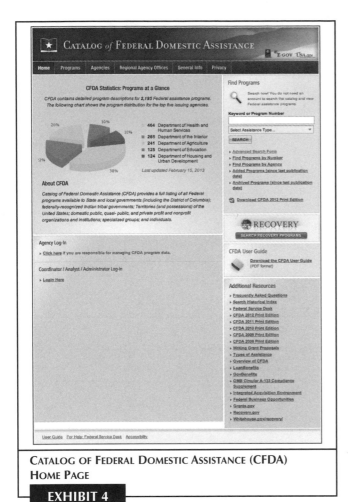

CATALOG OF FEDERAL DOMESTIC ASSISTANCE (CFDA) HOME PAGE

EXHIBIT 4

an Authorized Organization Representative (AOR); and (5) tracking the AOR status. The grants.gov registration process takes business days to complete, but once completed your organization can apply for more than 1,000 grant programs offered by 26 different federal agencies.

Catalog of Federal Domestic Assistance

To many grantseekers, the *Catalog of Federal Domestic Assistance* (CFDA) represents a "Christmas Wish Book" of grant possibilities and includes more than 3,000 pages of federal grant programs. The CFDA is published annually in the spring with a fall supplement. It is available at a nominal charge from the Superintendent of Documents, Washington, DC, 20402 or free at www.cfda.gov.

The CFDA contains useful browsing features that will save you time in identifying potential grant opportunities. Experienced grantseekers find four tools particularly useful: Agency index, which lists grant opportunities by agency name; Applicant Eligibility index, which categorizes grant opportunities by type of applicant; Deadline index, which lists grants by their due dates; and, Functional Codes index, which classifies federal grant programs into broad categories ranging from agriculture, consumer protection, education, and health, to transportation. Many grant programs are cross-listed under multiple functional areas.

In exhibit 4 you will find the home page for the CFDA. Type your keywords in the search box on the right-hand side or click on "Advanced Search" for additional search options.

CFDA Search Tips. Follow these tips when searching the CFDA:

1. Begin searching by using narrow terms and broaden them on subsequent searches until acceptable hits are found. For example, if you are seeking funding for a youth violence prevention program, begin with narrow terms like "youth crimes" and, if that search is unsuccessful, use broader terms like "juvenile justice," "dispute resolution," "gangs," and "anticrime."
2. Select some terms from the Functional Browser to begin your search. More than likely, you'll come up with too many options, and some won't be relevant to your situation. It's time to narrow your search.
3. Skim read several relevant grant programs identified in step two. Look for the keywords used in those grant descriptions and use them to search further. For example, we were once looking for funds for a "community development" project. Use of the phrase "community development" revealed very few hits. Conclusion: our search was too narrow. Looking for broader terminology, we read some grant descriptions and saw repeated use of the phrase "economic revitalization." When that phrase was entered into the search engine, it yielded the types of grant programs we were seeking.
4. When using phrases, enclose them in quotation marks; otherwise, the search engine might retrieve occurrences of each word singularly rather than the literal string phrase.
5. To further narrow your search you can use Boolean Operators, words like AND, OR, NOT (all in capital letters). Named after a famous British mathematician, George Boole, these operators allow you to string words and phrases together. Examples follow:
   - "highway construction" AND noise
   - "drug abuse" AND "battered women"

- "dispute resolution" AND NOT international
- "community development" OR "economic revitalization"

Phrases—but not single words—should be enclosed in quotation marks.

6. Use "wild cards," the asterisk symbol (*) or percent sign (%), for root words. For instance, a search for *bio** or *bio%* will return items such as *biodiesel, bioenergy, bioinformatics, biomass, biomedical, biotechnology,* and *bioterrorism.*

7. Remember, the CFDA is not only a source of information about federal funds, it also identifies state-level sources via flow-through dollars. Use the Applicant Eligibility index to identify those grants that state governments are eligible to receive. Contact the federal program officer to identify precisely where those funds end up in your state government.

Federal Register

The *Federal Register* is the government's "daily newspaper." Among other things, it lists rules, regulations, and application deadlines for new grant programs from federal agencies. Like the *Catalog of Federal Domestic Assistance,* the *Federal Register* is available in both print (for a subscription fee) and electronic (for free) formats. Exhibit 5 shows the *Federal Register* home

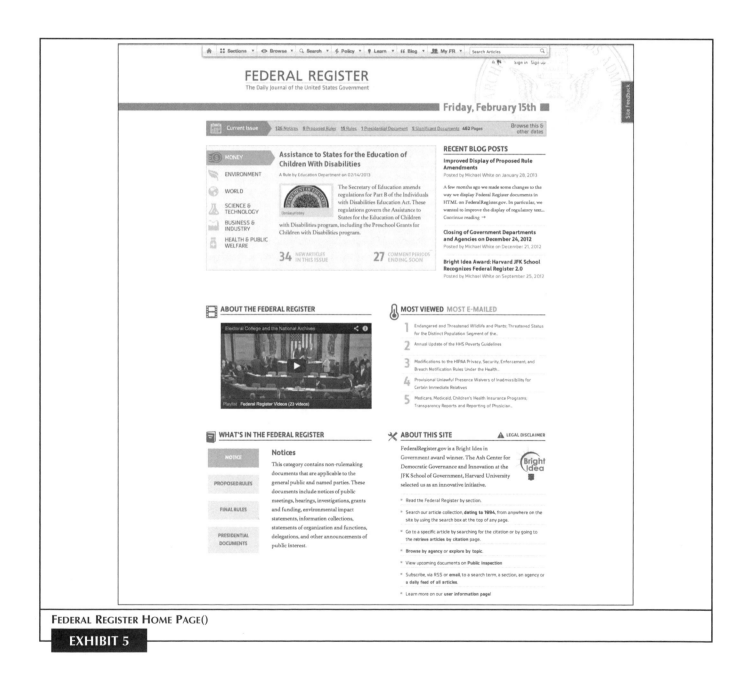

FEDERAL REGISTER HOME PAGE()

EXHIBIT 5

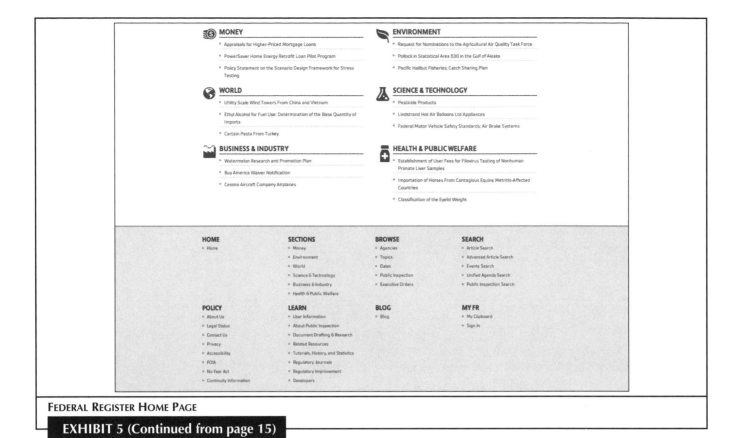

MONEY
- Appraisals for Higher-Priced Mortgage Loans
- PowerSaver Home Energy Retrofit Loan Pilot Program
- Policy Statement on the Scenario Design Framework for Stress Testing

WORLD
- Utility Scale Wind Towers From China and Vietnam
- Ethyl Alcohol for Fuel Use: Determination of the Base Quantity of Imports
- Certain Pasta From Turkey

BUSINESS & INDUSTRY
- Watermelon Research and Promotion Plan
- Buy America Waiver Notification
- Cessna Aircraft Company Airplanes

ENVIRONMENT
- Request for Nominations to the Agricultural Air Quality Task Force
- Pollock in Statistical Area 630 in the Gulf of Alaska
- Pacific Halibut Fisheries; Catch Sharing Plan

SCIENCE & TECHNOLOGY
- Pesticide Products
- Lindstrand Hot Air Balloons Ltd Appliances
- Federal Motor Vehicle Safety Standards; Air Brake Systems

HEALTH & PUBLIC WELFARE
- Establishment of User Fees for Filovirus Testing of Nonhuman Primate Liver Samples
- Importation of Horses From Contagious Equine Metritis-Affected Countries
- Classification of the Eyelid Weight

HOME
- Home

SECTIONS
- Money
- Environment
- World
- Science & Technology
- Business & Industry
- Health & Public Welfare

BROWSE
- Agencies
- Topics
- Dates
- Public Inspection
- Executive Orders

SEARCH
- Article Search
- Advanced Article Search
- Events Search
- Unified Agenda Search
- Public Inspection Search

POLICY
- About Us
- Legal Status
- Contact Us
- Privacy
- Accessibility
- FOIA
- No Fear Act
- Continuity Information

LEARN
- User Information
- About Public Inspection
- Document Drafting & Research
- Related Resources
- Tutorials, History, and Statistics
- Regulatory Journals
- Regulatory Improvement
- Developers

BLOG
- Blog

MY FR
- My Clipboard
- Sign In

FEDERAL REGISTER HOME PAGE

EXHIBIT 5 (Continued from page 15)

EXHIBIT 5 (Continued from page 15)

page at www.federalregister.gov. The "Current Issue" toolbar allows you to quickly locate notices, proposed rules, rules, and significant documents.

Grants.gov, *Catalog of Federal Domestic Assistance*, and the *Federal Register* all provide information about federal *grants* and *cooperative agreements*. In addition, there are also opportunities for *contract* dollars.

FedBizOpps

FedBizOpps (www.fbo.gov) is the single source for federal government contract opportunities that exceed $25,000. It is maintained by the U.S. General Services administration. All federal agencies must use FedBizOpps to tell the public about these contract opportunities.

On a typical federal workday, the government publishes Uncle Sam's official shopping list of 500–1000 procurement notices. More precisely, federal agencies use FedBizOpps to post any and all relevant procurement information on the Internet, including procurement notices, solicitations, drawings, and amendments. Grantseekers can sign up to automatically receive procurement information by solicitation number, se-

lected organizations, and product service classifications. A visit to the FedBizOpps home page reveals the screen as seen in Exhibit 6.

A little filtering moxie will get you the information you seek.

- What timeframe do you want to search: Today only? The past week? The past month? Select your search timeframe from the dropdown menu on "Posted Date."
- Are you looking for regular competitive bidding opportunities or are you looking for special set-asides, e.g., small business, women-owned, historically black colleges and universities, veterans only? Select the appropriate category from the "Set-Aside Code" dropdown menu.
- If you are looking for contract opportunities in a particular geographic location, select the appropriate choice from the "Place of Performance" dropdown menu.
- Do you have flexibility to perform a variety of projects on a specific subject matter? Enter keywords in the "Keyword/Solicitation #" box. You may use Boolean operators (AND, OR, NOT, "+," and "−") to join keywords in the search.

FEDBIZOPPS HOME PAGE

EXHIBIT 6

- If you wish to limit your search to a particular agency, e.g., Health and Human Services, enter the agency name in the "Agency" box.

If you do a global search without any filtering, you will end up with a lot of irrelevant contract opportunities. On the other hand, if you apply the above database filters, you will quickly identify contract opportunities within your area of interest and expertise.

As you review a contract solicitation, you may wonder if it is truly open for competition; that is, does someone else already have the "inside track?" It's possible they do. One way to tell is to look at the length of the announcement. The longer the announcement, the greater the likelihood it is "wired." If it refers to prior work conducted by another organization, that group may have an advantage on the bidding.

If you are interested in a solicitation, begin your preproposal contacts (as described in Chapter 4). Tell your program officer about you, your organization, and the kind of projects that you are interested in. Through your preproposal contacts, you will be able to judge whether you want to do business with this agency. One caution: contract support is relatively

complex and certainly not for the uninitiated. Often it requires two proposals: a technical proposal and a business proposal.

GOVERNMENT-SPONSORED FEDERAL AGENCY WEB SITES

Nearly all federal agencies maintain their own individual Web sites in addition to posting funding opportunities on grants.gov and FedBizOpps. For convenience, the common federal Web sites are listed on the inside back cover of this book. As you would expect, these Web addresses are quick and easy reference tools for identifying grant opportunities and deadlines. However, these Web sites contain many other types of information as well, as the 16 examples in column two, Exhibit 7, exemplify.

Obviously, not all agencies provide the information in column two. However, the trend is to expand. As a result, the future will see more agencies providing more detailed information.

Staying Connected with Federal Grant Opportunities

All of the public grant sources discussed so far have one thing in common—you must proactively seek the funding information. An alternative exists: you can let the information come to you. Many of these sites, agencies, and programs allow you to subscribe to have information alerts sent to you directly. For instance, you can register with grants.gov to receive free e-mail notifications of new grant postings (www.grants.gov /search/subscribeAll.do). The advantage to this, of course, is that you don't have to spend valuable time searching for grant information. The disadvantage is that you may get too much irrelevant information, such that "e-mail" becomes "eeek mail," and your time is spent sorting through it all.

In addition to hosting Web sites, all 26 federal agencies have a social media presence on Facebook, Twitter, and YouTube at a minimum. Some agencies also include social media tools like RSS feeds and Flickr. The National Institutes of Health and the National Science Foundation are the most common posters of grant information, which is not surprising because they tend to be federal agency leaders in many technological applications. To date, only limited amounts of grant information is posted on such topics such as application guidelines, deadlines, current priorities, grant funding, available grants, types

Agency Name	Type of Information	Web Address*
Administration on Aging	Agency Press Releases	www.aoa.gov/AoARoot/Press_Room/For_The_Press/pr/index.aspx
Center for Medicare and Medicaid Services	How to Write a Final Report	www.cms.gov/Research-Statistics-Data-and-Systems/Research/ResearchDemoGrantsOpt/Downloads/authorsguidelines.pdf
National Endowment for Democracy	Home Pages of Grantees	www.ned.org/where-we-work
National Endowment for the Humanities	Grant Deadlines	www.neh.gov/grants
National Endowment for the Humanities	List of Recent Grant Awards	www.neh.gov/news/recentawards.html
National Historical Publications and Records Commission	What We Do/Don't Fund	www.archives.gov/nhprc/apply/eligibility.html
National Institutes of Health	Names of Current Reviewers	www.csr.nih.gov/Committees/rosterindex.asp
National Institutes of Health	Abstracts of Awards	projectreporter.nih.gov/reporter.cfm
National Institutes of Health	Sample Funded Proposal	www.niaid.nih.gov/ncn/grants/app/default.htm
National Science Foundation	Video of NSF Mission Statement & Overview	www.nsf.gov/about/
National Science Foundation	Staff directory	www.nsf.gov/staff/
U.S. Department of Education	Prior Grant Awards	www2.ed.gov/fund/data/award/grntawd.html
U.S. Department of Health and Human Services	Organizational Chart	www.hhs.gov/about/orgchart.html
U.S. Department of Justice	Application review process	www.ojp.usdoj.gov/grants101/applicationreview.htm
U.S. Department of Transportation	Fast Lane Blog	fastlane.dot.gov/
White House	Faith-Based and Neighborhood Partnerships	www.whitehouse.gov/administration/eop/ofbnp

*These Web addresses go directly to the type of information cited, which may or may not be on the home page of the agency.

TYPES OF WEB-BASED GOVERNMENT GRANT INFORMATION()

EXHIBIT 7

of grants, grant writing tips, and review protocols. Nevertheless, it is worthwhile to monitor grantmaker communications every so often for the purpose of "tuning in" to their values because they post messages that are important to them.

PRIVATE-SPONSORED FEDERAL AGENCY GRANT INFORMATION

Beyond the print and electronic newsletters and bulletins published free by federal agencies, a few commercial firms also provide grant information for a fee. To remain competitive, all are expanding the services they provide. Brief descriptions follow of seven commercial vendors, along with Web addresses to seek additional information.

The Grant Advisor Plus

The Grant Advisor Plus publishes electronic information about grant and fellowship opportunities, especially targeted for faculty in U.S. institutions of higher education. An online newsletter covers grant opportunities from federal agencies (except the National Institutes of Health) as well as many independent organizations and foundations. Published monthly (except July), each issue contains 20–25 program reviews with descriptions, eligibility requirements, special criteria, funding amounts, and contact information (including phone and fax numbers, e-mail and Web addresses). The remainder of the newsletter comprises the Deadline Memo with more than 300 listings of grant and fellowship programs for the coming four months, organized into eight academic divisions: fine arts, humanities, sciences, social sciences, education, international, health related, unrestricted/other. For more details, visit www.grantadvisor.com.

Grant Forward

Grant Forward is an improved, commercially licensed version of the University of Illinois Research Information System (IRIS) at the Urbana-Champaign Library. The Grant Forward Database of funding opportunities contains records on 10,000 federal and private funding opportunities in the 46 different subject matter areas ranging from agriculture to zoology. The Grant Forward Database is updated regularly and is available on the Web to subscribers. In addition to the database, the Grant Forward office also maintains an alert service and an expertise service. The alert service allows users at subscribing institutions to create personal search profiles and receive funding alerts automatically. The expertise service enables faculty members to create detailed electronic CVs ("biosketches") and post them on the Web for viewing by colleagues at other institutions, program officers at federal and private funding agencies, and private companies. For details, visit http://grantforward.com. A free trial is available.

Federal and Foundation Assistance Monitor

The **Federal and Foundation Assistance Monitor** features a comprehensive review of federal funding announcements, private grants, and legislative actions affecting community programs, including education, economic development, housing, children and youth services, substance abuse, and health care. Each grant notice is categorized by subject matter. For foundations, it indicates areas of interest and projected grant awards, as well as funding priorities for both national and regional organizations. In addition, each issue contains proposal-writing tips to help grant coordinators and development professionals write more successful applications. Finally, it also offers advice from grant officials on exactly what funders are looking for, and details key points from fundraising workshops sponsored by public and private agencies. Visit their Web site for a free trial: www.cdpublications.com.

InfoEd Global

InfoEd Global is a comprehensive grant management software firm that helps you prepare, submit, and manage proposals and awards through the entire grants lifecycle in a single integrated solution. Among its capabilities, you can quickly locate government and private funding opportunities; develop proposals prepopulated with grant and sponsor data; submit, track, and report on proposals postsubmission; manage revisions; monitor awards; track deliverables; and integrate financial data with institutional accounting systems. The funding opportunity database contains over 40,000 grant opportunities from more than 10,000 sponsors, worldwide. Other software provisions enable you to post and search biosketches and receive automated alerts that match grant and contract announcements with your interests. Further details exist at http://infoedglobal.com.

Pivot

Pivot is the next-generation information source for what was previously known as the Community of Science (COS). Pivot provides rapid access to information about the funding of science. It is a global registry designed to provide accurate, timely, easy-to-access information about what new funding opportunities exist, and who is working on what subject, and where. Visit their Web site at http://pivot.cos.com.

BIG Online America

BIG Online is a comprehensive source of fundraising information, opportunities, and resources for charities and nonprofits. Database information includes details on many U.S. foundations, their granting history, geographic giving analyses, searchable 990s, and graphic portrayal of data. Their Web site is www.bigdatabase.com. A free online tour is available.

GrantStation

GrantStation offers nonprofit organizations, educational institutions, and government agencies the opportunity to identify potential funding sources for their programs or projects as well as resources to mentor these organizations through the grantseeking process. GrantStation provides access to a searchable database of more than 6,000 private grantmakers that accept inquiries and proposals from a variety of organizations; federal deadlines, which are updated twice a week; links to state funding agencies; and a growing database of international grantmakers. In addition, GrantStation publishes two e-newsletters highlighting upcoming funding opportunities: the weekly *GrantStation Insider,* which focuses on grant opportunities for U.S. nonprofit organizations; and the monthly *GrantStation International Insider,* which focuses on international funding opportunities. For more details, visit www.GrantStation.com.

INTERNATIONAL GRANT OPPORTUNITIES

While the reference tools cited in this chapter focus primarily on grant opportunities within the United States, some contain information on international approaches. Among the federal agencies providing international-based grants are the U.S. Department of State, U.S. Agency for International Development, U.S. Information Agency, National Institutes of Health Fogarty International Center, and the National Science Foundation Office of International Science and Engineering. All of the private sponsored federal agency grant information sources cited above contain select international references. The Pivot database contains, for example, multiple international grant opportunities in the health arena. In Chapter 3, we discuss the many more international grant opportunities that exist in the private sector.

STATE GOVERNMENT FUNDING

The discussion so far has focused primarily on federal grants, cooperative agreements, and contracts, although some state dollars can be identified by use of the Applicant Eligibility browser in the *Catalog of Federal Domestic Assistance.* These funds are essentially federal "pass-through" dollars targeted for state distribution. Unfortunately, no state-level equivalent of the CFDA exists. Generally, states have some basic grant information online, even though it is still sparse for many of them. As a result, specific state-level funding opportunities must be searched out through electronic sources and personal contacts, as opposed to comprehensive print directories.

Electronic Information Sources

As a starting point to find state grant information, visit the generic address www.state.gov, inserting the name of your state as one word or using the two-letter postal abbreviation. For instance, if you live in Minnesota, you would visit www.minnesota.gov or www.mn.gov. It would take you to the state government home page for Minnesota, as Exhibit 8 reveals. Enter "grant" into the search engine to identify state-level grants or find reports of prior grants, which suggest agencies and programs that you may wish to approach.

Some states have specific Web sites announcing state grants, as Exhibit 9 from North Carolina illustrates.

North Carolina grants (www.ncopenbook.gov/NCOpenBook/GrantsHome.jsp) can be searched by state funding agency, grant program keyword, or location of grantee.

For a directory of official state, county, and local government Web sites, visit www.statelocalgov.net. This Internet directory provides convenient one-stop access to the Web sites of thousands of state agencies and city and county governments. Use the drop-down menus on the left to view directory pages for states, topics, and local borough, counties, and parishes with cities, towns, townships, and villages. A sample Web page is indicated in Exhibit 10.

Human Information Sources

Legislative Officials Your state legislative officials can help identify pathways to grant programs, if you let them know your interests. To identify your legislative officials at both the state and federal levels, visit www.congress.org. One main job of legislators, of course, is to provide constituency services. As one of their constituents, it is appropriate for you to request their assistance, especially since they have access to comprehensive information networks and a support staff to help "dig" for information.

Agency Mission Statements Review the mission statements from those state agencies whose broad interests match your needs. The Department of Health and Social Services might be interested in your approach to adolescent pregnancy prevention. The Department of Transportation might be interested in your ideas on improving highway resurfacing. The Department of Public Instruction might welcome your ideas on teaching geometry to middle school students. A few persistent phone calls or a walk down a few corridors in the state capitol building should identify existing grant opportunities in your area of interest, whether it is in education, health, social services, or technology development.

SAMPLE STATE GOVERNMENT HOME PAGE: MINNESOTA()

EXHIBIT 8

SAMPLE HOME PAGE FOR STATE GRANTS: NORTH CAROLINA

EXHIBIT 9

DIRECTORY OF STATE AND LOCAL GOVERNMENTS ON THE INTERNET()

EXHIBIT 10

 Clip File Action Item # 5
Finding Public Funds

Build your Finding Public Funds clip file, by including such information as the following:

- Copies of pertinent grants.gov, *Catalog of Federal Domestic Assistance*, *Federal Register*, and FedBizOpps pages.
- Lists of past grant winners, found on Web sites or available from program officers.
- Model letters requesting application forms and guidelines.
- Web pages from federal and state grantmaking programs.

- Copies of successful public grant proposals, available under the Freedom of Information Act.
- Sign up to receive all new postings on rants.gov.

 Clip File Action Item # 6
Finding Public Funds

Set aside five minutes each day and explore the government Web sites listed on the inside back cover of this book. When you find sponsors who might fund your projects, copy that information and paste it in your Finding Public Funds clip file.

CHAPTER 3
Finding Private Funds

The impersonal hand of government can never replace the
helping hand of a neighbor.

—Hubert H. Humphrey

OVERVIEW OF PRIVATE FUNDING

Vice President Humphrey recognized the importance of private philanthropy more than 100 years ago: non-governmental philanthropy is crucial to support the nonprofit world. Private grant funding comes primarily from foundations and corporations. Although wealthy individuals also provide private funding, those dollars are seldom available for competitive grants since they are usually given at the sole discretion of the philanthropist. (Some information sources for seeking individual philanthropy are found in the Bibliography). Accordingly, this chapter restricts itself to finding foundation and corporation grants. In Chapter 3, you will learn the following:

- The different roles that foundations fulfill.
- Five different types of foundations.
- Basic reference tools for finding private foundation and corporate grants.
- How to analyze foundation tax records.
- Perspectives on corporate philanthropy.

The Web addresses in this chapter and on the back inside cover of this book will help you find private funding sources for your projects.

In comparison with public grants, private grants are usually shorter in length, and less background information is available for prospect research. Private funds sometimes provide support in areas not extensively funded in the public sector, e.g., religion. Private proposals may take less time to prepare and, in many instances, offer quicker funding decisions. However, your choice is not necessarily between public or private funding; often, both can and should be solicited.

This chapter begins with a general discussion of foundations and their self-images. Next, it describes the five different foundation categories and their outlooks on giving: national foundations, community foundations, family foundations, special purpose foundations, and corporate foundations. While the corporate foundation is legally an independent tax-exempt organization, it conducts business more like a corporation than a foundation. Sources of print and electronic information about finding funds are presented. The chapter concludes with a discussion of corporations: their cultures, funding options, and reference sources.

Basic Foundation Characteristics

A private foundation is a tax-exempt philanthropic organization concerned about injustices or inequities. In 2013, approximately 100,000 private foundations were registered in the United States. Annually, they award more than $46 billion. While the figures vary slightly from year to year, the 10,000 largest foundations typically have 90 percent of the assets and make 80 percent of the awards. By federal law, foundations must give away 5 percent of their market value assets or interest income each year, whichever is greater. Consider what this 5 percent rule means to Bill and Melinda Gates. Not widely known, they control two foundations: the Bill and Melinda Gates Foundation had 2010 assets of $37 billion; the Bill and Melinda Gates Foundation Trust had assets of $36 billion. Collectively their $73 billion in assets means they must award $3.6 billion annually. Foundations are required to follow the 5 percent rule or risk losing their tax-exempt status.

Foundation Roles

Foundations see themselves in multiple roles; five are identified below, along with sample language you might use in a proposal to reflect these differing values.

As **grantmakers,** foundations provide direct financial resources that target immediate or emerging concerns.

> As a grantmaker, you perform an incalculable service by helping groups and individuals foster lasting improvement in the human condition.

As **catalysts,** foundations help mobilize leaders and constituencies.

> An extraordinary convergence of community need and immediate opportunity motivates us to seek your investment in triggering an overdue change—the primary reason for our special request. From a broader perspective, this proposal is a catalytic change agent to impact the lives of a vulnerable population through fierce dedication and warm compassion.

As **community resources,** foundations provide services to donors, nonprofit organizations, and the community-at-large.

> Our proposal concentrates on helping people build just and caring communities that nurture people, spur enterprise, bridge differences, foster fairness, and promote civility.

As **resource developers,** foundations build a permanent, unrestricted endowment.

> This proposal develops crucial resources to build better futures that more effectively meet the needs of today's vulnerable children and families. The project outcomes will strengthen the support services, social networks, physical infrastructure, employment, self-determination, and economic vitality of our target community.

As **stewards,** foundations receive and distribute community resources.

> You and I share something in common—a profound stewardship responsibility to the local community. Accordingly, this proposal invites your shared partnership in making a difference.

To help determine which roles your target foundation deems most important, read their "About Us" description on their Web site, mission statement in their annual report, or recent giving history (See Analyzing Tax Records later in this chapter). Next, use your preproposal contacts (Chapter 4) to validate your first impressions and base your appeals on those roles, since they represent the psychological needs of foundations.

With these orienting perspectives on foundations, we next present examples of the five different types of foundations.

TYPES OF FOUNDATIONS

Foundations vary considerably in market assets, staff size, funding priorities, review protocols, geographic giving patterns, and preferred approach. Some are eager to share information about themselves; others take a very constrained approach to information dissemination. Approximately 100,000 private foundations existed in 2013. The intuitive approach is to start looking for private foundation grant information on the Web. Unfortunately for grantseekers, most foundations do not have Web sites. Of the roughly 10 percent of private foundations that do have Web sites, they tend to be the larger ones that have adequate staffing. To see whether a particular foundation has a Web site, you can check the Foundation Directory Online (discussed later in this chapter) or query Google.

As you search for private foundation funding sources, it is essential to understand the five different types of foundations. Each type has its own "values glasses," and successful grantseekers must reflect those ideals in their proposals. For each type, we describe their broad focus, list some specific names, include an exemplary Web site, and indicate sample grant awards.

National Foundations

National foundations are the largest and most familiar funding sources because they control a significant percentage of the philanthropic assets and make roughly 15 percent of all foundation awards. Ten of the larger national foundations are listed below:

1. Bill and Melinda Gates Foundation: www.gatesfoundation.org
2. David and Lucile Packard Foundation: www.packard.org
3. Lilly Endowment, Inc.: www.lillyendowment.org
4. J. Paul Getty Trust: www.getty.edu/grant
5. Rockefeller Foundation: www.rockefellerfoundation.org
6. Pew Charitable Trusts: www.pewtrusts.org

FORD FOUNDATION HOME PAGE (COURTESY OF THE FORD FOUNDATION)

EXHIBIT 11

7. W. K. Kellogg Foundation: www.wkkf.org
8. John D. and Catherine T. MacArthur Foundation: www.macfdn.org
9. Andrew W. Mellon Foundation: www.mellon.org
10. Ford Foundation: www.fordfoundation.org

Because they are national in scope, national foundations prefer impact programs with high visibility. They are not good sources of requests for operating support or grants to extend old projects into new areas. "New ideas with national impact" are the watchwords for attracting national foundation dollars. Their roles as grantmakers and catalysts are especially important. Fortunately, in-

formation about national foundations is generally quite accessible. For example, a visit to the Ford Foundation Web site reveals the home page in Exhibit 11.

Each year, the Ford Foundation receives approximately 40,000 proposals and funds 1,400 (3.5%) of them. Three sample Ford Foundation awards are shown in Exhibit 12.

National foundations are looking for projects that address national needs, or at least very widespread issues. Methodologically, they are interested in unique, cost-effective approaches. Decisions are usually made by an independent board of directors.

$2,000,000 to Nonprofit Finance Fund, New York, NY, in 2011. To launch Artplace, new public/private grant-making initiative to promote role of arts and culture in building livable, sustainable communities, payable over 1 year.

$1,100,000 to Center for Land Reform, Flint, MI, in 2011. For general support to create vibrant communities through reuse of vacant, abandoned, and problem properties in American cities and towns, payable over 1 year.

$1,000,000 to Center for Responsible Lending, Durham, NC, in 2011. For general support for education and advocacy to protect homeownership and family wealth by eliminating abusive financial practices, payable over 2 years.

SAMPLE FORD FOUNDATION GRANTS: A NATIONAL FOUNDATION

EXHIBIT 12

CALIFORNIA COMMUNITY FOUNDATION HOME PAGE (COURTESY OF THE CALIFORNIA COMMUNITY FOUNDATION)

EXHIBIT 13

Community Foundations

Community foundations are the best places to go for strictly local support. Their roles as stewards and developers of community resources are especially important. They are very responsive to programs serving local or community needs. They seek creative solutions to community problems. Their focus is on long-term community betterment. They are generally available to all nonprofit organizations and are quite willing to disseminate information about their programs and priorities. Examples of community foundations include the following:

1. New York Community Trust: www.nycommunitytrust.org
2. Houston Endowment, Inc.: www.houstonendowment.org
3. Cleveland Foundation: www.clevelandfoundation.org
4. Marin Community Foundation: www.marincf.org
5. Chicago Community Trust and Affiliates: www.cct.org
6. San Francisco Foundation: www.sff.org
7. Columbus Foundation: www.columbusfoundation.org
8. Saint Paul Foundation, Inc.: www.saintpaulfoundation.org
9. California Community Foundation: www.calfund.org
10. Greater Milwaukee Foundation: www.greatermilwaukeefoundation.org

As an example, the California Community Foundation, established in 1915, was Los Angeles's first grantmaking institution and is the country's second-oldest community foundation. The foundation makes grants to organizations serving the greater Los Angeles region in the following areas: human services, children and youth, community development, civic affairs, community health, community education, arts and culture, the environment, and animal welfare. A visit to their Web site (Exhibit 13) reveals a range of useful information, including grant guidelines, a downloadable version of the foundation's grant application form, a list of recent grants, brief bios of selected donors, a list of foundation-sponsored publications, and a calendar of upcoming foundation-related events.

Exhibit 14 lists examples of three grants among many recently made by the California Community Foundation.

Contacts with community foundations are essential. If you can demonstrate credibility and project need, you can overcome the lack of prior grant experience. A board of directors representing the diversity of the community typically makes decisions.

Family Foundations

Family foundations are generally small and controlled by the donor or the donor's family. While the family foundation roles vary, many see themselves as resource developers and stewards of funds.

The special family interests determine their granting priorities. Often geographic limitations are apparent in their giving patterns. Networking through preproposal contacts (Chapter 4) discloses top funding priorities. Family foundations are the most rapidly growing type of foundation. Examples of family foundations with a Web presence include the following.

$50,000 to Chinese American Museum, Friends of the, Los Angeles, CA, in 2011, payable over 1 year.

$35,000 to Proyecto Pastoral, Los Angeles, CA, in 2011, payable over 1 year.

$32,000 to Los Angeles Community College District Foundation, Los Angeles, CA, in 2011, payable over 1 year.

SAMPLE CALIFORNIA COMMUNITY FOUNDATION GRANTS: A COMMUNITY FOUNDATION

EXHIBIT 14

1. Daniel P. Amos Family Foundation: amosfamily foundation.org
2. Duffield Family Foundation: www.maddiesfund.org
3. Henry J. Kaiser Family Foundation: www.kff.org
4. Ford Family Foundation: www.tfff.org
5. Gates Family Foundation: www.gatesfamily foundation.org
6. Walton Family Foundation: www.waltonfamilyfoun dation.org
7. Perrin Family Foundation: www.perrinfamily foundation.org
8. Jay and Rose Phillips Family Foundation: www .phillipsfnd.org
9. Helen Bader Foundation: www.hbf.org
10. William and Flora Hewlett Foundation: www .hewlett.org

Exhibit 15 presents the home page of the Milwaukee-based Helen Bader Foundation, which was founded in the name of the late Helen Bader, who, throughout her life, sought to help others as a businesswoman and social worker. Since 1992, the foundation has

HELEN BADER FOUNDATION HOME PAGE (COURTESY OF THE HELEN BADER FOUNDATION)

EXHIBIT 15

$25,000 to Marquette University, Milwaukee, WI, in 2011. For Social Entrepreneurship, payable over 2 years.

$20,000 to La Causa, Milwaukee, WI, in 2011. For La Causa Crisis Nursery and Respite Center, payable over 1 year.

$20,000 to Milwaukee Jewish Day School, Milwaukee, WI, in 2011. For Collaborative Library Expansion, payable over 1 year.

SAMPLE HELEN BADER FOUNDATION GRANTS: A FAMILY FOUNDATION

EXHIBIT 16

supported programs across the lifespan through interests in Wisconsin and Israel.

Three sample grants recently made by the Helen Bader Foundation are presented in Exhibit 16.

Special Purpose Foundations

Special purpose foundations concentrate on very focused areas of interest. They see their roles as grantmakers to support immediate or emerging concerns. For instance, the Coulter Foundation favors biomedical research. The Research Corporation supports projects primarily in the physical and life sciences. Many special purpose foundations are health-related and concentrate on specific medical conditions, e.g., cancer, heart, or lung problems. Others are more academically focused and support faculty in particular disciplines, e.g., chemistry or philosophy. Examples of special purpose foundations follow:

1. Wallace H. Coulter Foundation: www.whcf.org
2. Research Corporation: www.rescorp.org
3. American Philosophical Society: www.amphilsoc.org
4. American Chemical Society: www.acs.org

ROBERT WOOD JOHNSON FOUNDATION HOME PAGE (COURTESY OF THE ROBERT WOOD JOHNSON FOUNDATION)

EXHIBIT 17

$3,774,224 to University of Wisconsin, Madison, WI, in 2011. For technical assistance to implement County Health Roadmaps initiative to improve health outcomes in communities, payable over 3.5 years.

$3,000,000 to Rutgers, the State University of New Jersey, New Brunswick, NJ, in 2011. For research to serve New Jersey in developing effective health policy, payable over 4 years.

$199,390 to Center for State and Local Government Excellence, Washington, DC, in 2011. For research to inform public decision makers about local health departments' successful workforce strategies in the face of budget and personnel cuts, payable over 2 years.

SAMPLE ROBERT WOOD JOHNSON FOUNDATION GRANTS: A SPECIAL PURPOSE FOUNDATION

EXHIBIT 18

5. American Heart Association: www.heart.org
6. American Diabetes Association: www.diabetes.org
7. American Council for Learned Societies: www.acls.org
8. American Psychological Association: www.apa.org
9. Ronald McDonald House Charities: www.rmhc.org
10. Robert Wood Johnson Foundation: www.rwjf.org

Perhaps the best known special purpose foundation is the Robert Wood Johnson Foundation, www.rwjf.org, which specializes in funding health care (Exhibit 17). Seventy-five percent of their funds are set aside for foundation priorities and 25 percent is reserved for unsolicited proposals. The Robert Wood Johnson Foundation supports research, training, and service demonstrations. They like to field test promising ideas and evaluate the results; take proven ideas and approaches to scale; give heightened visibility to an issue, idea, or intervention; cause coalitions of like-minded or disparate individuals and groups to form and act around a problem or issue; and reach and engage organizations and institutions that would not otherwise seek philanthropic support.

Three examples of recently funded projects appear in Exhibit 18.

Your needs statement for special purpose foundations should be documented in terms of their priorities. Your methodology should be viewed as unique in this area. Networking with people who are experts is especially important. Their board of directors usually makes funding decisions after receiving input from technical specialists.

Corporate Foundation Funding

Corporate foundations represent the philanthropic arm of their corporate parents. Generally, corporate foundations are especially interested in funding programs in communities where their companies have plant operations. Often, they see their roles as stewards and providers of community resources. As a result, they are particularly responsive to the needs of their workers in those communities. To attract corporation foundation dollars, specify what you have to offer that will affect their workers, products, or corporate concerns. Networking through your contacts can help reveal funding priorities. Examples of major corporate foundations follow:

1. 3M Foundation: www.3Mgiving.com
2. Alcoa Foundation: www.alcoa.com/global/en/community/foundation.asp
3. Agilent Technologies Foundation: www.agilent.com/contributions/foundation.shtm
4. Bank of American Foundation, Inc.: www.bankofamerica.com/foundation
5. ExxonMobile Foundation: www.exxonmobile.com/Corporate/community_foundation.aspx
6. Starbucks Foundation: www.starbucks.com/responsibility/community/starbucks-foundation
7. Target Foundation: www.targetfoundation.org
8. Verizon Foundation: www.verizonfoundation.org
9. Wal-Mart Foundation: foundation.walmart.com
10. Toyota USA Foundation: www.toyota.com/foundation

An example of a corporate foundation is the Toyota USA Foundation. One of its major priorities is to build bridges that lead to improvements in mathematics and science education, as Exhibit 19 indicates.

Exhibit 20 lists three same grants awarded by the Toyota USA Foundation.

Prior grant experience is important when seeking corporate funds. Corporate foundations give money to those organizations they trust. A board of directors who are usually corporate officials as well makes funding decisions. Study the corporate culture to understand how to approach the corporate foundation.

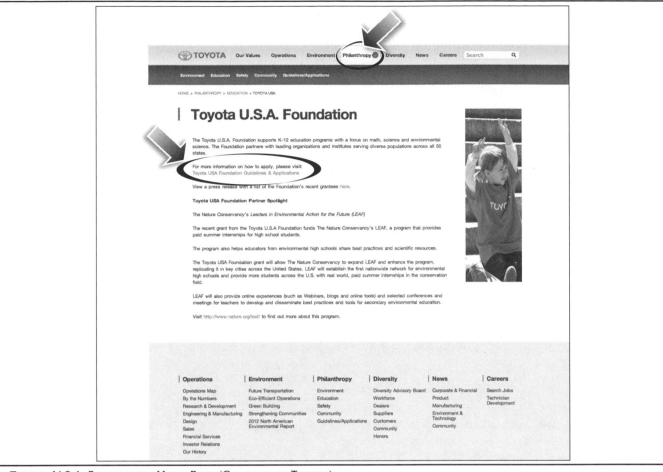

TOYOTA U.S.A. FOUNDATION HOME PAGE (COURTESY OF TOYOTA)

EXHIBIT 19

$205,000 to National Wildlife Federation, Austin, TX, in 2010. To improve science learning for students in grades K-8 within the Austin Independent School District by expanding its Schoolyard Habitats Program and increasing teachers' capacity to use these outdoor classrooms, payable over 1 year.

175,000 to Black Rock Forest Consortium, Cornwall, NY, in 2010. To develop the Digital Forest, a Web-based application that allows students to draw on data sets and mathematical models embedded in a "virtual" simulation of Black Rock Forest to analyze environmental changes over time, payable over 1 year.

$150,000 to Rochester Institute of Technology, Rochester, NY, in 2010. To enable the TPS (Toyota Production Systems) Lab to partner with WE@RIT (Women Engineers at the Rochester Institute of Technology) to provide K-12 programs focused on production, distribution, and supply chain concepts for the delivery of high-quality, cost effective products and services to over 745 girls annually, payable over 1 year.

SAMPLE TOYOTA U.S.A. FOUNDATION GRANTS: A CORPORATE FOUNDATION

EXHIBIT 20

INTERNATIONAL GRANTSEEKING OPPORTUNITIES

Listed below are private US foundations that have an established track record of providing grants to international projects and organizations.

1. Toyota USA Foundation Grants: www.toyota.com/foundation
2. Matsumae International Foundation Grants: www.mars.dti.ne.jp/~mif
3. Alcoa Foundation: www.alcoa.com/global/en/community/foundation.asp
4. AT&T Foundation: www.att.com/gen/corporate-citizenship?pid=17722
5. Carnegie Corporation: www.carnegie.org
6. Coca-Cola Foundation: www.thecoca-colacompany.com/citizenship/foundation_local.html
7. Michael and Susan Dell Foundation: www.msdf.org
8. Ford Foundation: www.fordfoundation.org
9. Bill and Melinda Gates Foundation: www.gatesfoundation.org
10. GE Foundation: www.ge.com/foundation
11. IBM International Foundation: www.ibm.com/ibm/responsibility/initiatives
12. W. K. Kellogg Foundation: www.wkkf.org
13. John D. and Catherine T. MacArthur Foundation: www.macfound.org
14. David and Lucille Packard Foundation: www.packard.org
15. Pew Charitable Trusts: www.pewtrusts.org

Grantseekers looking exclusively for information about Canadian foundations might visit http://charitycan.ca. While this is a subscription service, it does offer a 24-hour free trial.

THE FOUNDATION CENTER

The Foundation Center is an independent national organization whose mission is to disseminate information about philanthropic giving by connecting change-oriented people with existing resources. They maintain the most comprehensive database on U.S. and, increasingly, global grantmakers and their grants. It maintains five regional libraries (New York, Atlanta, Cleveland, San Francisco, and Washington, DC); 439 funding information centers located in public libraries, community foundations, and educational institutions throughout all 50 states; and 18 libraries in 18 countries. Each site offers valuable free print and electronic information resources. To find the location of the collection nearest you, call the Foundation Center toll free at 1–800–424–9836 or visit http://foundationcenter.org/collections.

VISITING FOUNDATION CENTER LIBRARIES

The starting point to drill down on private foundation information sources is to visit your nearby library foundation collection. In it, you will find invaluable print and electronic information sources and helpful reference librarians to help direct your quest for funding information.

Foundation Center Electronic Information Sources

Multiple electronic information sources exist through the Foundation Center. All are free to use at the locations where the Foundation Center has a physical presence. Some information is also available on the Internet, both free and for a fee.

Let's begin with a visit to your nearest Foundation Center or Funding Information Center. Be sure to bring a flash drive to copy valuable electronic information that can be later massaged on your office computer.

Ask the librarian to point you to the Foundation Directory Online database. It enables you to search more than 100,000 grantmaker profiles and 2.4 million records. You can search on multiple parameters. When you search for grantmakers, you can search by name, location, subject matter, types of support, geographic giving focus, names of key personnel, type of foundation, total giving, and current assets. To illustrate, if you were trying to find grantmakers in the St. Louis, Missouri, metropolitan area with assets of greater than $1 million who currently accept grant applications for projects dealing with persons with disabilities, the Foundation Directory Online database would yield seven potential funders. You would then download those foundation profiles and explore their giving histories on their tax records (990s) before preparing proposals.

The Foundation Center does have a free online Foundation Finder (http://foundationcenter.org/findfunders/foundfinder), but it only gives contact and tax record information, not information about funding priorities. Of perhaps greater use to grantseekers are the many grant statistics provided online free by the Foundation Center, including the top 100 U.S. foundations by asset size and total giving, top corporate grantmakers by asset size and total giving, largest community foundations by asset size and total giving, top grantmakers by state, international grantmakers, top foundations awarding grants by subject area (from arts to religion), top foundation awards for specific populations, and top grant recipients. The Foundation Center database "pie" is cross-cut many ways.

Foundation Center Print Information Sources

Beyond electronic information sources, a visit to one of the Foundation Center libraries contains a broad collection of grant and other nonprofit organization reference books. A few are cited below to indicate the type and range available for study. Many are published by the Foundation Center itself; reference books from other publishers are also available. Typically, grant directories are updated annually. While the content changes slightly from year to year, the type of information presented remains virtually unchanged.

Foundation Directory. The 2012 edition of the *Foundation Directory* contains key facts on the 10,000 largest US foundations, including fields of interest, contact information, financials, names of decision makers, and nearly 60,000 sample grants.

Foundation Directory: Part 2. The 2012 edition of *Foundation Directory: Part 2* presents basic information on the next 10,000 largest US foundations. It includes the same information as its companion publication above.

Foundation Directory Supplement. The 2012 edition of the *Foundation Directory Supplement* provides the latest facts on thousands of foundations in the *Foundation Directory* and *Directory: Part 2*. New insights highlight changes in foundation status, officers and trustees, contact information, and giving interests.

Guide to Funding for International and Foreign Programs. The 2012 edition of *the Guide to Funding for International and Foreign Programs* includes grantmaker portraits on over 1,900 current international funding sources, complete with addresses, financial data, giving priorities, application procedures, contact names, and key officials. Sample grant awards are listed and are easily searchable by subject field, geographic area, and type of grant.

National Directory of Corporate Giving. The 2011 edition *National Directory of Corporate Giving* cites over 3,300 corporate foundations and roughly 1,700 corporate giving programs. Company profiles include giving priorities, contact information, and Web site links.

Foundation Grants to Individuals. The 2011 edition features over 9,500 entries and current information for individual (as opposed to institutional) grantseekers. Organized alphabetically by state, *Foundation Grants to Individuals* identifies contact information, program descriptions, grant amounts, and application guidelines.

The PRI Directory: Charitable Loans & Other Program-Related Investments by Foundations. Recognizing that other funding mechanisms exist besides grants, the 2010 edition of the *PRI Directory* identifies other revenue streams (Program Related Investments: PRI) often used to support community revitalization, low-income housing, microenterprise development, historic preservation, and human services. It contains the same type of information as found in other Foundation Center directories.

The Celebrity Foundation Directory. The 2011 edition of *The Celebrity Foundation Directory*, available only in downloadable format, flags the private foundations created by VIPs in business, entertainment, politics, and sports to help underserved populations and support medical research, green technology, and countless other causes.

Foundation Reporter, 2011. The *Foundation Reporter* covers the top 1,000 private foundations in the U.S. that have at least $10 million in assets or whose annual giving totals $500,000 or more. Thirteen indexes provide easy access to needed data. Seven foundation indexes arrange funders by headquarters state, location of grant recipients, application deadline, and a master index showing all funders alphabetically by foundation name. Six biographical indexes list funding executives who influence grant decisions by name, alma mater, corporate affiliations, club affiliations, and more. Researchers can use this critical information to identify common areas of interest between the foundation decision makers and the proposed project.

Annual Register of Grant Support 2013. This guide presents more than 3,100 grant-giving organizations offering nonrepayable support. It shows you how to tap the funding potential of these sources. Organized by 11 major subject areas—with 61 specific subcategories—the *Annual Register of Grant Support 2013* is a major resource for researching and uncovering a full range of available grant sources. Not only does it direct you to traditional corporate, private, and public funding programs, it also shows you the way to little-known, nontraditional grant sources such as educational associations and unions. For each grant program, you'll find information on eligibility requirements and restrictions, application procedures and deadlines, grant size or range, and contact information.

Grants Register. The *Grants Register* is another prospect research tool that contains information about private and public funding sources. It differs from other reference works in that it contains information on international grant programs as well as those in the United States. More precisely, it provides information about (1) scholarships, fellowships, and research grants; (2) exchange opportunities and travel grants; (3) grants-in-aid; (4) grants for all kinds of artistic or scientific projects; (5) competitions, prizes, and honoraria; (6) professional and vocational awards; and (7) special awards. The 2012 edition contains information on 1,100 grantmakers from 49 different countries.

State Foundation Directories. Most states publish a directory of their private foundations. These directories customarily present the basic identifying information for all statewide foundations, small and large. This document is particularly useful when you are seeking support for local or statewide projects, because many of the small- to mid-sized foundations concentrate their support on projects that serve their locale. The Foundation Center can identify where to obtain the directory for any given state. For example, *Foundations in Wisconsin: A Directory* is available through the Marquette University Funding Information Center (www.marquette.edu/fic); the *Directory of Illinois Foundations* is available through the Donors Forum of Chicago (www.donorsforum. org); and the *Michigan Foundation Directory* is available through the Council of Michigan Foundations (www. michiganfoundations.org).

Chronicle of Philanthropy. In addition to the above book references that provide grant-related information, one biweekly newspaper publishes information about a wide range of philanthropic activities. The *Chronicle of Philanthropy* contains information about governmental, foundation, corporate, and individual grants. It describes new grant trends and changes in personnel within the philanthropic community. Because it publishes information so frequently, it is an effective way to monitor subtle changes in the philanthropic scene or to obtain early access to information about new grant opportunities. Electronic updates are posted regularly at www.philanthropy.com, which is available free to regular print subscribers.

ANALYZING TAX RETURNS

From the reference sources listed so far, you will identify several potential sponsors that might be interested in supporting your organization. An important next step is to determine precisely where these organizations have spent their money in the past. Often, past performance is a predictor of future behavior. Some foundations publish annual reports or list recent grant winners on their Web site; that information is very valuable in analyzing giving patterns. To gain additional financial and funding information about all foundations, large or small, you can review their tax records.

By law, foundations are required to submit IRS 990-AR (Annual Reports) or 990-PF (Private Foundation) returns. The 990s are the private foundation equivalents of your individual 1040 income tax records; the 990s are readily available free on the Internet, thus inviting a new era of public scrutiny. The premier site is GuideStar (www.guidestar .org). It gathers and publicizes information about nonprofit organizations that includes missions, programs, leaders, goals, accomplishments, and finances. The GuideStar home page is presented in Exhibit 21.

Once registered with GuideStar (instantaneous and free), you can review foundation tax records, paying particular attention to four important pieces of information:

1. One section will identify the net assets of the foundation. If you multiply this value by 5 percent, you will know the minimum amount of money the foundation dispersed during the reporting year.
2. A second section will list the names of key foundation personnel. Circulate that list within your organization to identify possible linkages or networks.
3. A third section will list the recipients of the grants for the reporting year. Study the list and see whether you can identify organizations similar to yours that received foundation dollars.
4. A fourth section will identify the process for submitting grant applications.

Finally, remember that the vast majority of all foundations do not have any paid staff. Even among larger foundations—those giving away more than $100,000 annually or with assets of at least $1 million—less than one in four has paid employees. As a result, the 990 serves as the *only* source of information on activities of most smaller foundations. As you analyze 990s, invariably funding patterns will become apparent to you.

GUIDESTAR: A PATHWAY TO PRIVATE FOUNDATION TAX RECORDS (COURTESY OF GUIDESTAR USA, INC., WWW.GUIDESTAR.ORG)

EXHIBIT 21

Look for trends relative to subject matter area, project location, constituency groups served, and type of grant (see Chapter 1).

PERSPECTIVES ON CORPORATE PHILANTHROPY

Overview

In larger corporations—those with net annual sales in excess of $10 million and more than 200 employees—grantseekers can usually find three different "pots of money."

Corporate Foundation Funding. Some corporations establish separate foundations for social and legal purposes. Technically, these funds are independent of the parent corporation and are legally classified as a foundation. In reality, they behave like corporations and they are best approached from the corporate perspective. Suggestions for securing corporate foundation funding were cited earlier in this chapter.

Corporate General Philanthropy Funding. Some corporations establish a pool of pretax corporate earnings to distribute for general philanthropic purposes. Depending on the health of the economy, those philanthropic dollars represent 1–3 percent of pretax profits. Usually, the grants are made to those projects for which the corporation can also benefit. Contact your local Chamber of Commerce for a list of area corporations. Call and ask to speak with the person who handles "community relations."

Corporate Research and Development (R&D) Funding. Some corporations rely on outside organizations like universities and research institutes to develop new products or services, especially in those instances when corporations lack the in-house expertise or equipment to conduct the needed R&D. Usually, strong collaborations need to be established before funding is secured. Someone who carries a title such as "Vice President of Research" is often the point of contact.

This chapter concludes by offering practical tips on the basic approaches to both general and R&D

corporate funding, including pertinent examples, and electronic and print corporate information sources.

Corporate General Philanthropy Funding

Approach to Corporate General Philanthropy Funding. Because corporations award shareholder profits as they make grants, corporate officials are particularly selective in identifying their recipients. When corporations award grants, they follow a concept of "profitable philanthropy"; that is, they often fund those projects that will bring them better products, happier or healthier employees, lower costs, or good public relations—all things from which they can benefit, the "What's in it for me" syndrome. As a corporate grantseeker, your challenge is to describe your project in terms that will benefit the corporation.

Example of Corporate General Philanthropy Funding. Organizations can attract corporate funding by making it a "win-win" situation for all. Recently, the Health Baby Agency was concerned generally about the high incidence of adolescent pregnancy in its inner city, and more specifically was alarmed at the low birth weight and poor nutrition received by the newborns. Visiting nurses reported that mothers were cutting off the end of the nipples on baby bottles so the infants could consume their nourishment faster; additionally, the nurses observed that the infant formula consisted of sugar water instead of healthy nutrients. The problem: these new mothers lacked information on the benefits of good infant nutrition. The Healthy Baby Agency went to a manufacturer of baby food formula and gained $25,000 to develop a video on infant nutrition that would be played for mothers of newborns while they were in the hospital, postdelivery. What was in it for the corporation? Two things: their products were prominently displayed during the filming of the video (but not commercially plugged) and the corporation was generously acknowledged during the credits at the end of the video. This project was so successful, in fact, that the corporation later sponsored additional videos in languages other than English.

The Healthy Baby Agency found that crucial point of "connect" with the corporation: an innovative project that underscored the importance of their corporate mission, namely, developing healthy babies. The corporation was able to secure substantial publicity from this project, letting others know what a good corporate citizen they were. What is your point of "connect" with a corporation? These organizations found "hot buttons" with corporations and were successful in obtaining philanthropic support.

- A university approached a corporation that hires many of its engineering graduates and obtained funding for minority student scholarships.
- A museum first loaned paintings to help decorate a new corporate office and then later received funding for an art restoration project.
- A hospital received corporate support for a diabetes research project from a corporation whose CEO had a family history of diabetes.

How do you find your corporate "hot button?" Through prospect research!

Corporate R&D Funding

Approach to Corporate R&D Funding. Corporations are "for-profit" firms. This descriptor pretty well sums up the major purpose of any corporation—to make money for its owners who range from the sole owner/entrepreneur of a small company simply looking to support his family, to a large, publicly traded company holding millions of shares of stock. Corporate R&D funding represents the pinnacle of profitable philanthropy. Corporations fund those projects for which they believe a long-term—but often "more immediate"—gain will be received.

Example of Corporate R&D Funding. Profitable philanthropy worked for both parties in a recent case where a university laboratory was conducting cutting-edge research on sensors and their use in liquid environments. The laboratory director approached an automobile manufacturer and explained how the sensors could detect when it was time to change the oil in an automobile; that is, instead of changing the oil automatically every 3,000 miles as most people do, the research professor gave details how his sensors could determine when the oil became dirty enough to change regardless of miles driven, thereby more efficiently reducing engine wear. The corporation supported the R&D project and now includes the sensors in all automobiles it manufactures. The research laboratory received funding for their R&D project as well as a nice revenue stream from royalty sales and patents. It was a win-win situation for both parties.

Corporate Internet References

Foundation Center. At present, few direct sources of corporate funding information reside on the Internet. The Foundation Center maintains an online database of corporate giving. This subscription-based service profiles more than 3,800 companies, 2,800 company-sponsored foundations, 1,300 direct corporate giving programs, and records of 380,000 recently awarded grants. Further details regarding *Corporate Giving Online* are available at http://foundationcenter.org/getstarted/tutorials/corporate. The online subscription databases for InfoEd Global, GrantForward, and Pivot, discussed in Chapter 2, also contain corporate sponsorship information.

ThomasNet. ThomasNet, a 100-year-old company, has established an online presence for its well-known directory. It lists nearly one million U.S. and Canadian companies that provide industrial products and services in 67,000 different categories. It also includes links to online catalogs and corporate websites. Search engines permit use of keywords and Boolean terms: AND, OR, NOT. Visit www.thomasnet.com.

How can you use ThomasNet to bolster your corporate grantseeking? First, determine what type of business might be interested in supporting your project; then use ThomasNet to find those corporations with similar commercial interests. For instance, if your project deals with infant nutrition, ThomasNet could identify for you those firms that manufacture baby food and infant for-mula. If you have a health or wellness project, consider seeking out insurance companies or HMO providers.

Corporate Web Sites. Beyond the Foundation Center and ThomasNet sites, you can explore corporate commercial sites, most of which follow the standard address: www.organizationname.com. Often, you will encounter corporate descriptions, not specific grant-related information, although there are some exceptions, as the IBM www.ibm.com/IBM/responsibility/initiatives address (Exhibit 22) reveals.

Additional sources of corporate funding include, but are not limited to the following:

1. DuPont: www2.dupont.com/Social_Commitment/en_US/outreach
2. FarmersInsurance: www.farmers.com/farmers_community.html
3. Monsanto Fund: www.monsantofund.org
4. Abbott Fund: www.abbottfund.org/grants
5. SonyCorporation: www.sony.com/SCA/corporate-responsibility/overview.shtml
6. GlaxoSmithKline: http://us.gsk.com/html/community/community-grants-corporate.html
7. Cisco Systems: csr.cisco.com/pages/support-for-community-partners

HOME PAGE OF CORPORATE GRANTMAKER: IBM (REPRINT COURTESY OF INTERNATIONAL BUSINESS MACHINES CORPORATION, © 2013 INTERNATIONAL BUSINESS MACHINES CORPORATION)

EXHIBIT 22

8. Bank of America: www.bankofamerica.com/foundation/index.cfm?template=fd_volunteergrants
9. Boeing: www.boeing.com/companyoffices/aboutus/community/cash_grants_faq.html
10. State Farm: www.statefarm.com/aboutus/community/grants/company/company.asp

SEC Information. If you are contemplating a corporate solicitation, study the Securities and Exchange Commission Web site. It'll provide very useful information about the prospect's values and financial history. Go to www.sec.gov and click on the EDGAR database to search for actual company filings with the SEC. A friendly tutorial is available to help you interpret the SEC forms.

US Patent and Trademark Office. The USPTO maintains an excellent Web site at www.uspto.gov of all patents and trademarks ever issued in this country. This database is very current, with patents typically listed in their entirety within a week of being issued. Patent information often gives another useful insight on a company's product development interests and needs. This database obviously is a good place to begin a search of a company's patent portfolio, to identify patents that the company might be asked to donate or otherwise make available at no cost to your organization. One caveat, however, is that it takes two to three years for a patent to issue after its original application. In some cases, by the time a patent issues, the company may have moved away from that technology. In such cases, a company might be willing to donate nonessential patents to your organization.

State Corporate Records Files. Most states require corporations, and in many cases, other business entities such as limited liability companies (LLCs), to file brief annual reports that list the company's registered agent and registered address at a minimum, plus other information that varies from state to state. Such information may include names of officers, names of board members, and previous names and addresses the company has used. Most often, such records are kept by a state's Secretary of State office, but sometimes the records are more difficult to locate. Some such states such as Wisconsin, California, and Georgia provide this information at no cost over the Internet to residents and nonresidents alike. To find state corporate records, go to the state home page, www.xx.gov (where xx is the name of your state with no spaces) and then look under the Secretary of State's entry.

Corporate Grant Print References

Information on government grants is quite accessible and, indeed, is backed legally by the Freedom of Information Act. Information about private foundation grants is somewhat less accessible than in the government arena, although many foundations go to considerable effort and expense to publish information about their interests. Additionally, the public accessibility of foundation tax records keeps philanthropic information flowing. Access to information becomes quite restricted in the case of corporations. As private, independent organizations, they have no obligation to disseminate information about their philanthropic activities. Corporations are responsible to their stockholders, not the general public. The stockholders have access to company finances, including philanthropic activities.

You can start gathering your corporate background information by requesting a copy of an annual report (for publicly held companies only) from the public relations office of your target corporation, if it is not available online. It will provide you with a view of the world as seen through corporate eyes. It may or may not indicate the total dollar volume contributed for philanthropic purposes. Even if such information is disclosed, you may not find the level of detail you may wish, namely, the names of grant recipients, their grant titles, and their grant amounts.

If you are having trouble getting corporate information through the usual channels, try getting the information from a stockholder—or buy one share of stock and become a stockholder yourself. As a stockholder, you will have privileged access to information about charitable corporate contributions.

If your organization doesn't have a history of attracting corporate donations, start small and request larger grants as you establish credibility. For your first approach, you may wish to request nonmonetary support, e.g., in-kind donation of a product or "borrowing" an executive. Corporations are very cost conscious; therefore, challenge grants have special appeal because corporations feel they are getting the most for their dollar. While there are nearly 2.5 million corporations, only about one-third of them make general contributions to nonprofit organizations.

Corporate Giving Directory. Unlike government and foundation grants, few reference books list corporate giving preferences. One basic reference document is the *Corporate Giving Directory*. The 33rd edition provides detailed profiles of the 1,000 largest corporate foundations and corporate direct giving programs in the United States. These funding sources represent nearly $6 billion in cash and nonmonetary support. Listings include complete contact information, giving philosophy, application procedures, restrictions, and information on specific grants given.

National Directory of Corporate Giving. The *National Directory of Corporate Giving* gives you reliable, fact-filled, and up-to-date entries on approximately 4,400 major corporations awarding grants to nonprofit organizations.

Corporate General Business References

Beyond the prospecting research tools that provide direct information about corporate grant information sources, several large business directories might be useful for grant-seeking purposes. None contain specific grant information. However, they contain contact and financial information that could point you along the right path. The following corporate business references are available in the business section of most public libraries. As you peruse these references, look for linkages, connections, and networks that can help establish a contact between your organization and the corporation.

Fortune 500 Directory. It lists the 500 largest industrial corporations and pertinent information about sales, profits, assets, market value, earnings per share, and total return to investors. Visit http://money.conn .com to see the complete list.

Fortune Magazine. The late May or early June issues list the top 500 industrial and top 500 service corporations. Read the online version at http://money.conn.com.

Forbes Market 500. Forbes ranks both industrial and nonindustrial corporations and includes information on market value, sales volume, assets, and profits.

Dun and Bradstreet's Million Dollar Database. This reference tool lists information on corporations with a net worth of over $1 million. Electronic information is available at www.mergentmddi.com.

Standard and Poor's Register of Corporations, Executives, and Industries. A good beginning point

in your search for corporate grants, the entries include corporate name, address, phone; a list of major corporate officers; sales volume; number of employees; primary bank; and description of products, including corporate trademarks.

State Manufacturing Directories. To research corporations within your state, locate your state manufacturing association directory in your public library. Most states have one that lists names of key personnel, company size and dollar volume, products manufactured, and locations of company plants. Check with the nearest Business Reference Librarian for specifics.

Business Journals. The larger metropolitan areas publish a regular business journal—a business newspaper that reports regional business information. It is a valuable source of detail about the financial and philanthropic health of business firms in your areas. To read online versions of business journals, visit www.newspapers.com.

Not all of the references cited above have online Web sites; some online references are free, while others do charge an access fee. After reviewing these basic business materials, start networking with your corporate contacts following the suggestions in Chapter 4, Preproposal Contacts.

Clip File Action Item # 7
Finding Private Funds

As you expand your Finding Private Funds clip file, consider including items like the following:

- Copies of grant opportunities from the print and electronic reference sources cited above.
- Names of past grant winners.
- Model letters requesting application forms and guidelines.
- Tax records from private foundations.
- Annual reports from foundations and corporations.
- Copies of successful proposals.
- At your next office staff meeting, identify five different types of corporations that might support your organization, and, then, seek them out in ThomasNet.

CHAPTER 4
Preproposal Contacts

Personal relationships are the fertile soil from which all advancement, all success, all achievement in real life grows.
—Ben Stein

OVERVIEW

You now have several ideas for seeking grants (Chapter 1). You've looked at public and private funding sources (Chapters 2 and 3) for your ideas. Next, you wonder which "suspects," among many, offer the best chance of getting funded; that is, which "suspects" are really the best "prospects?" It's now time to heed Ben Stein's advice and launch some new personal relationships.

This chapter details the many things you can do to increase your chances of getting funded by using preproposal contacts. In Chapter 4, you will learn the following:

- The value of engaging in preproposal contacts.
- A four-step process for picking the sponsors that have the highest probability of funding your projects.
- 100 PREP questions you can ask of program officers, past grant winners, and past grant reviewers.
- How to overcome PCJ (Preproposal Contact Jitters).
- A three-step formula for opening statement success on the telephone.

At the moment, your list of "suspects" falls into a "maybe" category: maybe they will fund you, maybe they won't. You can move those "suspects" from the "maybe" category to either a "yes" or "no" category by following the four-step process described below. The outcome will identify your real "prospects," those sponsors with a higher probability of funding your proposals.

RATIONALE

Preproposal contact is a process that helps you see the grant world from the sponsor's perspective. You already know your viewpoint. Preproposal contact lets you judge how well your needs match those of the sponsor. In essence, you are evaluating them first, before they evaluate your proposal. Ask yourself questions like these:

- "Are these the kind of people I can and want to do business with?"
- "Can my services solve their problems?"
- "Should I send them a proposal?"
- "If so, what are they looking for?"

In order to produce a win-win situation, both you and the sponsor must be satisfied with each other.

You can make successful preproposal contacts by following these four steps that will validate the information obtained from your initial funding search that identified potential public and private grantseekers:

1. Write to the program officer requesting basic application information.
2. Call a past grant winner to learn success secrets.
3. Call a past grant reviewer to learn proposal evaluation policies and procedures.
4. Call the program officer to validate prospect information.

Who should make these preproposal contacts? You should, where "you" is the person who will be leading the grant, a project director or principal investigator. Grantmakers want to talk to the person who will be in charge of the grant, if awarded, and not a grant writer or grant consultant.

After making these contacts, detailed below, you can easily decide whether you should submit a proposal to any given sponsor on your "suspect" list. If the answer is "yes," you substantially increase your likelihood of getting funded. If the answer is "no," then you have not wasted your time writing a proposal that the sponsor was likely to decline; instead, you move on to another sponsor that is a better match for your situation. This chapter explains precisely how to conduct your preproposal contacts by specifying who you should talk to, what questions you should ask, and how you can interpret their answers.

The initial tendency of beginning grantseekers is to just write, mail, and hope for the best. Frankly, we know of no better way to get turned down. In contrast, experienced grantseekers know the value of preproposal contact and typically report four benefits:

1. It is crucial in selecting a sponsor who is highly likely to fund your proposal.
2. It pinpoints what is required to put together a winning proposal.
3. You make more efficient use of your proposal development time.
4. It prepares for possible site visits, if you end up on the "short-short" list for funding.

Beginning grantseekers, on the other hand, are sometimes reluctant to contact people who can provide valuable grant information because they have a bad case of the "jitters."

OVERCOMING PREPROPOSAL CONTACT JITTERS

Making preproposal contacts, whether through calls, visits, letters, or e-mails with grant officers, is a key first step in grant writing. If you are stalled at this point, you may be suffering from Preproposal Contact Jitters (PCJ)—a common malady that strikes many grantseekers.

The typical symptoms of PCJ include fear of failure and rejection, anxiety, vacillating between making the contact and postponing it, helplessness, and lack of focus. The basic cause of PCJ is lack of preparation.

Imagine that today you get a letter saying you have been funded. Ask yourself: "What's the first thing I will do?" You can't really answer this question unless you've first anticipated and answered questions like these:

- "What do I specifically want to accomplish in this project?"
- "What have I done, up to now, to get the project started?"
- "How's it working out?"
- "What else could I do?"
- "What will happen to the project if it doesn't get funded?"

- "Exactly what are my resources (human, physical, financial) for this project?"
- "Precisely what do I want from the grantor?"
- "Have I talked with everyone involved and clearly planned the project?"
- "Does my time and task chart give me enough guidance to get started?"
- "Specifically, when, where, and how will I make the preproposal contact?"

You will think of more questions that you must answer before you make your preproposal contact, and we will list many that you'll find helpful. Most grant officers welcome contacts from well-prepared potential applicants. Knowing that you are a likely fit saves both of you time and effort.

Another manifestation of PCJ arises when beginning grantseekers wonder, "Why would the program officer want to talk to me?" The answer: program officers would much rather formally review a strong as opposed to a weak proposal. Preproposal communications afford the program officer with opportunities to strengthen the quality of proposals officially received. Since not all worthy proposals can be funded, federal program officers sometimes use the high quality of rejected proposals as a basis for seeking increased funding for the next fiscal year.

In more extreme cases of PCJ, grantseekers develop creative rationalizations to avoid making preproposal contacts. Common avoidance reasons include the following:

- "We're so small; they won't want to talk with us."
  In this case, size doesn't matter. Grantmakers are on the hunt for great ideas to solve problems that they care about. If you've done your homework and have a great idea, they'll listen.
- "They're so busy, I don't want to interrupt or intrude on them."
  These days, who isn't busy? They are never too busy for the next great idea. If you are having trouble connecting, work with a staffer to schedule an appointment to discuss your proposal plans.
- "I tried it once and struck out. Why bother?"
  Rarely do we get the rebuff at the federal level; our only rare exception has been in an instance when we ran into a "rotator," a temporary federal program officer who was two weeks away from leaving his post and returning to his "real" job in academia. Refusing to take "no" as the answer, we went up the organization chart and spoke with the division director and requested his suggestion of another individual who might be able to answer our questions. His referral opened the door to a better informant.

- "I tried this once and was told to 'Just send in your proposal.'"

We sometimes run into screeners, gatekeepers, whose job it is to protect the time of the boss. If told to "just send in the proposal," We respond by saying:

> I am not here to waste the boss's time. I understand that Ms. Bigg probably gets lots of calls, and that's one of the reasons why I'm reluctant to just send in a proposal. I don't want to waste her time and yours. You see, we have several ideas that could potentially be of value in helping centralize services to the elderly, thereby helping them save money in the process [or whatever is appropriate]. I'd like to ask Ms. Bigg a few questions first so I can submit something of real value to you.

We've found that type of response effective in dealing with gatekeepers, especially among private foundations. However, in the case of smaller foundations that lack a full- or even part-time staff, your best option in finding an informant is to explore networks and linkages with board members.

When asked about the importance of preproposal contact before submitting an application, a federal program officer recently said it best: "It's THE most important thing to do." Moreover, it sometimes yields unexpected dividends. For example, experienced grantseekers have, because of preproposal contacts:

- learned about new grant opportunities not yet announced
- heard about upcoming changes to application guidelines and administrative policies
- critiqued draft proposal application forms and guidelines
- been asked to serve as beta test sites on new computerized grantseeking ventures.

All of these outcomes provide you early access to valuable grant information.

Beginning grantseekers sometimes feel that while preproposal contacts have value, the program officers are much like sales people for their agencies, only looking out for their interests and not yours. In other words, agency staff members benefit when the number of proposals in their interest area increases. Encouragement from program officers to submit a proposal needs to be weighed carefully; their optimism and hope can sometimes mask very real barriers to funding, such as budget constraints, geographic award criteria, or changing funding priorities.

Successful grantseekers gather information from multiple sources (program officers, past grant winners, prior grant reviewers) before deciding whether to submit a proposal. Triangulate your information by questioning program officers, past grant reviewers, and past grant winners. In the following four-step process, we suggest 100 questions you might ask to validate your information and maximize your likelihood of getting funded. Do you have to ask all 100 questions? Absolutely not! Choose the ones that you think will be insightful as you decide whether to approach any given sponsor, recognizing that other questions will arise in the natural course of the conversation.

STEP ONE: INITIAL CONTACT WITH PROGRAM OFFICER

Why Do Step One?

Making initial contact with the program officer satisfies two objectives. First, you obtain the application forms and guidelines to follow should you decide to submit a proposal. When these materials arrive, study them to determine whether you have the interest and capacity to respond. Second, it is an important beginning step in relationship building with the program officer. You seek not only to gather basic information but to build a relationship with the program officer.

Who to Contact—and How

Contact the program officer who was identified from your initial prospect research. If you have no prior relationship with the program officer, send a letter, since it will help build the name recognition of your organization, in addition to securing basic grantseeking information. If you have dealt with this program officer in the past, a phone call or e-mail will suffice.

A federal program office recently offered this advice to grantseekers: "Consolidate your questions; too many e-mails can be annoying." E-mail has become too user friendly. It's too easy to fire off a question whenever you think of one. Moreover, because e-mail is so easy, we also expect realistic and immediate responses. This program officer added, "I e-mail back and forth twice, then I pick up the phone and call." Her rationale: phone calls allow for verbal clues, e.g., pauses that alert her to and allow her to clear up potential misunderstandings.

What to Request—and Why

Contact the program officer when you are ready to evaluate your funding prospects. You are seeking three pieces of information:

1. A copy of the current application forms and guidelines.
2. The names of several past grant winners.
3. The names of several past grant reviewers.

You do not need to explain your project in any detail. On the contrary, you want to know what the sponsor considers important in order to determine how you might cast your proposal. At this point, any detailed description of your proposal to the program officer is premature and should await the finding from your pre-proposal contacts.

Contacting the past grant reviewers will give you valuable insights into the review process. To submit a successful proposal, you need to know how your proposal will be reviewed, especially timeframes and points awarded for proposal sections. Learning from the experiences of past grant reviewers and knowing what they were instructed to look for in their reviews will help you decide whether to submit your proposal.

Sample Letter to Program Officer

Your letter to a program officer should do the following:

1. Introduce yourself and your organization.
2. State a benefit that appeals to them, based on your initial prospect research.
3. Explain that to deliver your potential benefits, you need more information.

The following sample letter in Exhibit 23 was used by a social service agency to seek basic information from a local private foundation. It could easily

---

Letter Requesting Grant Application Information

Today's Date

Ms. Program Officer Name
Agency Title
Agency Name
Mailing Address

Dear Ms. Program Officer:

Teen Pregnancy Services specializes in working with inner city teenage mothers in Atlanta, helping them ensure their infants receive good nutrition, while, at the same time, reducing developmental health problems. Recently, the governor of Georgia cited our work as a "role model for social service agencies throughout the state."

We have some ideas that may be of value to you and the Healthy Baby Foundation. Accordingly, we request three specific items:

_____1. A copy of your current application forms and guidelines
_____2. A list of your recent grant winners
_____3. Names of three past grant reviewers

These three items will help us understand better your current priorities to see whether our ideas would be worthwhile for you to look at in a formal proposal.

Sincerely,

Your Name
Title

Enclosure
Address Label
Self-Addressed, Stamped Envelope

LETTER REQUESTING GRANT APPLICATION INFORMATION

EXHIBIT 23

---

be modified to other types of sponsors. Be sure to use your organization's letterhead; you want the sponsor to begin to recognize your agency's name and logo.

As you review this sample letter, note, first, that the administrative assistant opening the letter reads the phrase "Letter Requesting Grant Application Information." This header phrase helps the reader determine the purpose of the letter without having to read it in detail; that is, the header provides a quick basis for referral or response. Second, the header also signals that this letter is *not* a grant application and should not be treated as such. Finally, notice the enclosures. Some sponsors have response packets already assembled in sealed envelopes. If that is the case, they appreciate your thoughtfulness in providing a gummed address label. On the other hand, if they don't have information packets preassembled, they can gather pertinent materials and put them in your large manila, self-addressed envelope bearing plenty of postage in case they have large information packets. Either way, this courtesy makes it easier for them to respond, you'll get your information much sooner, and you'll be taking an important first step in establishing your organizational efficiency.

As you prepare to make your initial approach to a program officer, do your homework. Because more and more grant information is available online, you may discover that portions of your three-part request are already in the public domain. Accordingly, you may need to modify your generic letter by, say, deleting the request for copies of the application guidelines.

In sum, Step One represents a reconnaissance, information-gathering stage. You must gather information to decide whether you should submit, and these three individuals—program officers, past winners, and past reviewers—can furnish that crucial information. Step One happens quickly: a generic letter, once on your word processor, can easily be adapted in two minutes' time—well worth the investment!

STEP TWO: CONTACT A PAST GRANT WINNER

Why Do Step Two?

You want to contact past grant winners to learn their secrets of success. Obviously, they did something right, because they were funded. Their success tips and experiences in dealing with the sponsor will help you decide whether to submit your proposal. You will not be asking their feedback on your proposal idea;

rather, you will be idea mining for those good information nuggets that might be useful as you develop your proposal. Experience is a wonderful teacher, and you can profit from their experience.

Who to Contact—and How

From the information you received in Step One, you want to contact a project director or principal investigator who received a grant from your target sponsor, preferably an organization that is similar to yours or working on a project like yours, although this is not always possible.

Government organizations are very open about identifying their grant recipients; it is one means of encouraging other grant applicants. Besides, the names of government grant winners are in the public domain and available under the Freedom of Information Act— a federal law (5 U.S.C. §552) that ensures government records are available for public inspection.

The situation is a little different with private sponsors. Some private foundations volunteer the names of their grant recipients because they like to be known for doing charitable good. About 15 percent of the private foundations publish annual reports that often include lists of recipient names. For those foundations that neither publish grant winner names nor include them in your Step One request, your fallback position is to examine the sponsor's tax records (Form 990, see Chapter 3) to learn the names of recipients; that information is public.

Corporate grant award information is less available than private foundations. If your potential corporate sponsor does not include names of past grant winners in response to your Step One letter, then a shareholder or stockbroker may be able to secure this information for you. If not, your fallback position is to ask the corporate sponsor directly for a profile of a typical grant winner: type of organization, size, and geographic location. If your profile is substantially different from their typical grant winner, then you should discuss this fact with the sponsor to see whether you should apply.

In sum, you should be able to identify the names of all past public grant winners and many (but not all) private grant winners. The preferred method of contact is by telephone: it's easier, cheaper, quicker, and most important, the informants will often say things verbally they would be reluctant to put in writing. Your telephone approach has two key parts: the opening statement and some follow-up questions. Both parts are described below.

The Opening Statement to Past Grant Winners

You want to use an attention-getting opening statement that will pique the curiosity of a past grant winner and elicit further communications. Within the first few seconds, you'll either create interest or resistance. TV advertisers, for example, have known this for years: if you don't get viewers' attention immediately, they will go channel surfing or head for the refrigerator.

Here's a three-step formula for opening statement success on the telephone. Briefly, explain the following:

1. **Who** are you? Introduce yourself and organization.
2. **Why** are you calling? State an interest-stimulating, curiosity-creating benefit that appeals to their desire to gain, or avoid loss.
3. **What**'s in it for them? Involve them in the conversation; you want to do more listening than talking. Tell them that in order to deliver potential benefits, you need to get information.

Beginning grantseekers often wonder, "Why should a past grant winner talk to me? Won't they see me as competition? Why should they share their success secrets with me?"

These are good questions that deserve solid answers! People who worry that past grant winners won't talk freely can counter those concerns by offering something of value: information exchanges, collaboration possibilities, proposals swaps. Consider these opening statements to winners of government, private foundation, and corporate grants.

Call from university history professor to a winner of a federal humanities grant:

> Dr. Maki, Fred Johnson from the National Endowment for the Humanities suggested I give you a call [Why]. I'm Bob Iacopino with the Children's History Institute at Midwest University [Who]. Like you, we're investigating the role of children in the Civil War. Fred thought since our efforts seem to overlap, it might make sense to consider some type of mutually beneficial collaboration [What]. If I've caught you at a good time, I'd like to learn more about your project, tell you what we're doing, and ask you some questions about your experiences with NEH. (95 words)

Call from a youth agency to a winner of a national foundation grant:

> Hi, Mr. Rockefeller. I'm Shandel Lear with the Why Care Agency [Who]. I understand you recently got a grant from the Ford Foundation to teach geometry to middle school children. Congratulations. We are also doing something similar in this area. I'm calling today because depending on your situation, there's a possibility we might be able to collaborate in some fashion [What]. If I've caught you at a good time, I'd like to exchange project information and discuss your experiences with Ford [Why]. (81 words)

Call from a nonprofit dental clinic to a winner of a corporate grant:

> Hello, Mr. Metal. I'm Dr. Mona Molar with Midwest Dental Associates [Who]. I understand you were recently selected as a winner of a Sullivan Community Oral Health Grant. The reason I'm call is this: depending on your priorities, there's a good chance our ideas might dovetail with your project [What]. If I've caught you at a good time, I'd like to get a brief update on your project, explore possible linkages, and learn more about your experiences with Sullivan Dental Products Company [Why]. (81 words)

These opening statements are designed to get consent to move on to the next phase, the investigating, questioning stage. These three examples can be uttered in 30–40 seconds. Write out your opening statement, verbatim, 45 seconds—max! (The average adult speaks approximately 160 words per minute.) As you gain more experience with opening statements, you will drift away from this opening script, but it gives you a secure base to start with.

Follow-up Questions to Past Grant Winners

Questioning is the foundation of preproposal contacts, getting essential background information to decide (1) whether you should submit a proposal, and (2) if you submit, how best to frame the proposal so it matches the "values glasses" of the sponsor. The list of questions that one could pose to a past grant winner is theoretically endless. Nevertheless, if you want to write a successful grant, you must PREP first, where PREP is an acronym to distinguish between four basic types of questions:

1. **Position:** What are the baseline situations, present circumstances, and basic facts?

2. **Rationale:** What are the problems, needs, and injustices that exist today?
3. **Expectation:** What are the implications for addressing these problems?
4. **Priority:** What approaches are most likely to lead to an improved situation now?

Collectively, PREP questions span a continuum of time from past actions to future intentions. Beginning grantseekers often ask too many **Position** questions and too few **Rationale-Expectation-Priority** questions. Here are some "starter questions" in each category, to which you will undoubtedly add your own.

Position Questions: The Baseline Situation. Position questions explore baseline information and relationships with the sponsor from the perspective of past grant winners and lay the foundation for more probing types of questions:

- "Did you call or go see the sponsor before writing the proposal?"
  Preproposal Contact. This question will reveal the extent to which the grantee engaged in preproposal contact.
- "What materials did you find most helpful in developing your proposals?"
  Proposal Development Materials. This answer will suggest those reference materials and tools that the grantee found valuable in writing the proposal, e.g., Web sites, government reports, primary and secondary text references.
- "Who did you find most helpful on the funding source staff?"
  Internal Advocate. This query will help identify an "in-house hero," an agency staff person who may be the best source of inside information for you.
- "Did you use any special advocates on your behalf?"
  Special Advocates. This question will indicate what role, if any, people outside of their organization (board officials, lobbyists, politicians) played in securing the grant.
- "Did the funding source review a preproposal or a proposal draft prior to final submission?"
  Review Drafts. This query identifies their receptivity to preproposal contact. Most agencies welcome this contact, given sufficient lead time. One federal program officer recently commented, "Less than 1 percent of our proposals are funded 'cold' without any preproposal contact."
- "How close was your initial budget to the awarded amount?"
  Budgets. The answer to this question identifies the extent to which budget negotiations took place.

What was cut or increased? What level of documentation was required to justify budget items?
- "What level of cost sharing, if any, did you contribute? What proportion of that was cash and what was in-kind?"
  Cost sharing. Cost sharing may not have been required by the sponsor but was included voluntarily as evidence of institutional commitment to the project. This question will help to identify the level of financial contributions, if any, that will appeal to reviewers.
- "Did the sponsor show a preference for internal or external evaluations? Or both?"
  Evaluation. The vast majority of sponsors are interested in knowing whether or not a project was successful. However, they vary widely in their preferences for evaluators who are internal or external to the institution. In one unusual instance, a federal sponsor with a preference for external evaluators prohibited a university from engaging the services of a faculty member at a sister institution located nearly 100 miles away. The sponsor's rationale: although outside of the home department and university, the faculty member belonged to the same university system and, thus, was considered to be "internal" and have a potential stake in the final evaluation results. You will want to clarify the preferences of the sponsor.
- "Did you have a site visit?"
  Site Visit. If one occurred, ask what took place; that is, was it face-to-face or virtual? Who attended? How long did it last? To whom did they speak? Were questions broad ranging or focused? Was there an opportunity to supplement the proposal with additional materials?

Rationale Questions: Problems Existing Today. Rationale questions go to the heart of sponsor giving from the perspective of past grant winners: the problems, needs, and injustices that exist today. Those problems may be either (1) in your topic area if it's the same as past grant winners, or (2) in an area different than yours, in which case, your interest is in learning about sponsor motivations in funding past grant winners' projects. Consider these questions to ask of past grant winners:

- "You got funded because the sponsor was convinced you could solve some big problems they were concerned about. What were those big problems?"
  Big Picture Problems. Look for big picture problems that really trouble the sponsor.

- "What are some of the biggest dissatisfactions with the current approaches to this problem?"
  Current Failures. Listen for sore spots and raw nerves.
- "Generally speaking, what are the disadvantages of the way these problems are being handled now?"
  Status Quo Shortcomings. Pay attention to what's wrong today and could become worse tomorrow.
- "Are there problems or difficulties in this area that are particularly challenging now?"
  Major Hurdles. Take note of priorities among complex problems: what are the top issues?
- "What kinds of problems are the biggest at the moment? Personnel problems? Financial problems? Management problems? Training problems? Reliability problems? Quality problems? Other?"
  Problem Categories. Help your informant focus on different dimensions of the problem.

Obviously, the questions are not discrete. The overlap is intentional; good interviewers know the importance of asking a question more than one way to get at the heart of an issue.

Expectation Questions: Basic Implications for Addressing Problems. Expectation questions look at the "so what?" implications of the rationale questions from the vantage point of past grant winners. These questions also identify the sponsor's outlook for changing the problem situation. Six sample questions will get you started:

- "Was there a hidden agenda to the program's guidelines?"
  Hidden Agenda. Priorities change, and what was top priority at the time the grantee's proposal was funded may have changed as you plan to submit now.
- "Given the problems you identified, what are the implications of those difficulties?"
  Implications. Get the informant talking about the consequences of existing problems.
- "What's the desired impact on these problems, balancing project breadth, depth, and financial resources available?"
  Project Balance. Proposals can be too broad or too narrow. The answer to this question helps you find a proper balance within budgetary constraints.
- "What are some other implications?"
  More Implications. One of the most revealing questions in interviewing: "What else?"
- "Among the many consequences of these problems, which ones are most significant? Reduced

self-esteem, workplace bottlenecks, lost hopes, limited aspirations, impaired health status, financial drains, personnel turnover, high training costs, lost productivity, dependency on others, higher costs, slowed down expansion, reduced output, other?"
  Implication Priorities. One final pass at "What else?"
- "What would you do differently next time?"
  Things to Change. Invariably, people learn from the positive experience of getting a grant and have concrete suggestions about things they would change to strengthen their next grant proposal.

Priority Questions: Approaches for an Improved Situation. Priority questions concentrate on identifying the top activities that will effectively and efficiently improve the conditions surrounding the identified problems, needs, and injustices that exist today, as seen by past grant winners.

- "Why did the sponsor think it important to solve the problem you identified?"
  Significance. Look for the sponsor's motivation in solving the problem.
- "How does your project really help?"
  Solution Impact. What are the key features of your proposed solution?
- "What are the benefits you see of your approach?"
  General Benefits. Look for reasons why the sponsor found this solution so useful.
- "Would this approach be useful for cost reasons or something else?"
  Economic Benefits. Narrow the general benefits to that major motivator: money.
- "Will your approach reduce the frequency or severity of the problem?"
  Programmatic Benefits. Look for the things that will change, e.g., the incidence or magnitude of the problem.
- "How were you able to convince the sponsor that your approach is sustainable?"
  Long-term Benefits. Affecting change is good, and being able to sustain that change is even better.
- "Could you clarify how this approach would help?"
  Additional Benefits. One last call for "What else?"
- "Can you recommend the names of some external evaluators who have the credentials and experience assessing the types of projects and outcomes of interest to the sponsor?"
  Evaluator Recommendations. In asking this question, it's highly likely that past grant winners are going to offer the names of the individuals who evaluated

their projects. In a sense, these individuals have already been vetted by the sponsor and have direct experience that may contribute to the successful evaluation of your project.

In the course of a 10-minute phone conversation, you will have a much better idea of how your needs mesh with those of the sponsor.

STEP THREE: CALL TO PAST GRANT REVIEWERS

Why Do Step Three?

Past grant reviewers had firsthand experience in evaluating proposals like yours. They actually measured the psychological impact—the persuasiveness—of the proposals they read. Your goal in contacting past grant reviewers is to learn about the specific process that will be followed when your proposal is reviewed. For example, if a reviewer has only three minutes to review your proposal, you will write differently than if the reviewer has three hours to review it. As another benefit of talking with past grant reviewers, you will learn about the scoring system used to review proposals; some proposal sections may be more important than others.

Who to Contact—and How

Step One should have identified the names of some past grant reviewers. They may be specialists in the field or internal staff members. Sometimes, one can find the names of federal program reviewers on agency Web sites. Private sponsors may or may not provide the names of reviewers. If not, ask your program officer for information about a typical reviewer's profile, since your proposal should be written to the level of expertise of the reviewer. Just like your contact with past grant winners in Step Two, you need both an opening statement to pique interest and information-yielding follow-up questions.

The Opening Statement to Past Grant Reviewers

These opening statements follow the same model discussed for past grant winners, although the actual content is different, as the following examples illustrate.

Call from a researcher in a local environmental protection agency to recent reviewer of a federal grant:

Hi, Dr. Beach. I'm Gary Grant with the SandCrab Agency [Who]. I understand you recently served as a reviewer for the National Institute of Seashells. We are in the process of putting together a proposal to NIS [Why]. I'm calling today to request a friendly favor. If I've caught you at a good time, I'd like to discuss your experiences with NIS so we can see whether our proposal would be of value to them [What]. (74 words)

Call from a health agency administrator to a reviewer of health care foundation proposals:

Hello, Ms. Lawson, I'm June Thompson with the Atlanta Lung Society [Who]. Dr. Barry Gimbel mentioned that you recently reviewed grant proposals for the National Breatheright Association. We are completing a proposal to the NBA, and I'm calling today wondering if we can exchange professional favors? [Why]. If I've caught you at a good time, I'd like to discuss your experiences with NBA so we can be sure that what we propose would be of value to them. In turn, I'd like to send you a copy of our proposal, if that would be of interest [What]. We've done this successfully in the past and actually ended up collaborating with our newfound friends. May I send you a proposal copy? (118 words)

Call from a fire chief to a reviewer of corporate proposals:

Hello, this is Chief John Hunkel from the Detroit Fire Department calling [Who]. The folks at Mitsubishi Communications said you recently served as a reviewer for their Emergency Communications Program. We're targeting a proposal to them for their next deadline. As you know, you won't be reviewing our proposal since they regularly rotate reviewers in each competition cycle. So I'm wondering if you can extend to us a professional courtesy [What]. If I've caught you at a good time, I'd like to get your perspectives on the proposals you reviewed [Why]. What were the typical shortcomings of the proposals you looked at? (99 words)

Follow-up Questions to Past Grant Reviewers

Again, many PREP questions could be asked; those that follow are suggestive, not prescriptive.

Position Questions: The Baseline Situation. Position questions explore baseline information and relationships with the sponsor and lay the foundation for more probing types of questions from the viewpoint of past grant reviewers:

- "How did you get to be a reviewer?"
  Selection as Reviewer. Usually you just submit a résumé and express an interest, showing how your background and expertise meshes with agency priorities. Consider being a reviewer yourself. It's an easy way to get "inside information," establish your credibility with the sponsor, and improve your success rate.
- "Did you review the proposals at the sponsor's office or at home?"
  Review Environment. The difference here is between a mail and a panel review. Mail and electronic reviews are done under more relaxed conditions but often require greater documentation, whereas a panel review is apt to be done quicker, placing a higher premium on proposal readability and scanability.
- "Did you review electronic or hard copies of the proposals?"
  Proposal Presentation. The trend, especially at the federal government level, is to review electronic copies of proposals. Some agencies have greater experience than others relative to handling electronic copies of proposals. You are especially interested in knowing whether formatting problems existed when reading electronic copies. Sometimes electronic copies are printed out for review using black and white printers; if your proposal uses color fonts or illustrations, the reviewers may not see important messages.
- "Did you follow a particular scoring system?"
  Proposal Scoring System. Invariably some portions of a proposal carry greater weight than other portions. This information will enable you to concentrate your efforts on the highest scoring portions.
- "How much time did you have to read the proposals?"
  Review Time. If the reviewers have essentially unlimited time to read a proposal (as in a mail review) then you write one way, but if they are under severe time constraints, then you write another way. One reviewer recently noted that in a panel review situation he could allow approximately 20 seconds per page to finish the review process on time. While that is not the norm for proposal review, it does suggest that one uses different proposal writing

strategies under such conditions, e.g., simple and short sentences, creative use of headings and subheadings, lots of white space, boldface for emphasis, and bulleted lists.
- "Did reviewers fill certain roles on the panel as specialists or generalists?"
  Reviewer Assignments. Program officers may fill panels with specialists, generalists, or a combination of the two. To write to the level of expertise of the reviewer, you need to know whether, for example, the panel has three members who are content specialists or who are generalists representing content, evaluation, and financial areas, respectively. Writing to generalists often means that you need to educate as well as persuade them of the significance and merits of your approach.
- "What surprised you the most about the review process?"
  Review Surprises. This question is an open-ended call for "What else?" One private foundation reviewer answered the question this way: "I was shocked at the range of quality of applications. A few rose to the top. Quite a few sank to the bottom. We spent most of our time debating the merits of the ones in the middle." A reviewer for a government program said: "We had way fewer applications this year than last year. How is it that as the economy gets tighter, the number of applications decreases? It's completely counterintuitive."

Rationale Questions: Problems Existing Today. Rationale questions go to the heart of sponsor giving from the vantage point of past grant reviewers: the problems, needs, and injustices that exist today. Whether the past grant reviewer evaluated proposals in your topic area or another area, your interest is in learning about what motivates sponsors to fund projects.

- "What were you told to look for?"
  Identification of Problems. Invariably the reviewers are told to look especially at the statement of the problem or need. Any particular "red flags" raised by the reviewers should be addressed as you develop your proposal. Sometimes, reviewers are instructed to look for elements of proposals that are not requested in the application guidelines. Your proposal should respond to all items on the application guidelines and the reviewer's evaluation form.
- "How often did you notice this problem in proposals?"

Frequency of Problems. This answer will help determine the more frequently occurring proposal problems. The problems may deal with proposal content or format. For instance, one reviewer lamented that proposals were written in 10-point type. Although this was allowable according to the guidelines, the reviewer found it very tiring to read.

- "What were the disadvantages of the way this problem area was being approached in the proposals you read?"
  General Barriers. This answer highlights the reviewers' insights into problems not being addressed in the proposals they reviewed, problems that you may be able to incorporate into your proposals.
- "What are the biggest hurdles people face in reaching their grant objectives?"
  Specific Barriers. This answer prioritizes existing problems in meeting grant objectives.
- "What difficulties linger that still are not being addressed?"
  Unanswered Issues. This answer spotlights existing problems that remain unresolved.
- "How does the existing data support this problem?"
  Need Documentation. This answer indicates data sources for quantifying existing problems.

Expectation Questions: Basic Implications for Addressing Problems. Expectation questions look at the "so what" implications of the rationale questions, as seen by past grant reviewers. They also identify the sponsor's outlook for changing the problem situation.

- "What were the most common mistakes you saw?"
  Avoiding Common Errors. The resulting answers should clearly list those errors that you want to avoid, errors like failing to number the pages or to list the résumés of project directors or consultants, or math mistakes on the budget.
- "What are the implications of those mistakes?"
  Implications of Mistakes. The answer indicates both the logical and psychological dimensions of proposal errors and suggests ways in which proposals could be improved. One grant reviewer bemoaned how a proposal confused goals, objectives, and activities—"It just doesn't make sense to have seven goals with four objectives and 27 activities."
- "What happens when those proposal problems occur?"

Consequences. This answer implies a relationship between proposal problems and their impact on reviewers.

- "How does this problem relate to the bigger picture?"
  Impact on Bigger Picture. This response places the current problems in a larger context.
- "If there were no budget limits, what should have been proposed that wasn't?"
  Overcoming Financial Barriers. Playing "what if," this answer invites creative solutions that are not fiscally constrained.
- "Of the many probable causes, which one is most significant?"
  Causation. While most problems have multiple causes, this question probes for the more significant factors.
- "Could a higher scoring proposal get bumped out in favor of a lower scoring proposal that meets other special criteria?"
  Special Criteria. This question recognizes that awards are made sometimes on a basis other than merit, e.g., geographic location of the applicant, type of organization, PI status as a novice investigator, extensive collaborative relationships, or prior relationships with the sponsor.
- "Was there a preference for projects that are path breaking or ones that take the next logical step along established research lines?"
  Supporting Safe Science. This question goes to the heart of striking the balance between projects perceived as "innovative" or "risky."
- "Was additional consideration given to projects that used an external reviewer?"
  External Reviewers. In some instances, grant reviewers impose additional review criteria beyond that specified by the sponsor: Though the guidelines simply stated that a project evaluation must be conducted, this question probes to determine whether more weight was given to proposals evaluated externally rather than internally.
- Was there a staff review following your peer review?"
  Staff versus Peer Review. This answer suggests what happens after the review process is over. You especially want to find out how much discretionary authority the program officers have over the peer review results.
- "How would you write a proposal differently now that you have been a reviewer?"
  Avoiding Reviewer Aggravation. People invariably learn from the positive experience of seeing the

inside process of awarding grants and have a number of suggestions about things they would do if they were asked to write a proposal again—something that is called "learning."

Priority Questions: Approaches for an Improved Situation. Priority questions concentrate on identifying the top activities that will effectively and efficiently improve the conditions surrounding the identified problems, needs, and injustices that exist today from the perspective of past grant reviewers.

- "What's not happening in this area that should?"
  Intervention Failure. This answer highlights areas needing intervention.
- "How would you close the gap?"
  Needed Intervention. The response suggests how to intervene.
- "Which actions are most likely to solve the problem?"
  Intervention Options. This reply implies probable intervention options.
- "What would be the key features of an ideal solution?"
  Ideal Intervention. Among various options, this answer indicates the components of an ideal solution.
- "Why would this solution be useful?"
  Intervention Justification. This query probes why the ideal solution has value.
- "What might be the benefits from this approach?"
  Intervention Benefits. The response compiles the benefits list for the intervention strategy.
- "Are there other ways this might help?"
  Other Outcomes. This question explores for other anticipated outcomes.
- "What levels of commitment to sustainability are reviewers expecting to see in proposals?"
  Project Sustainability. While application guidelines may ask for evidence of sustainability, rarely do they specify a specific number of years that projects must be sustained beyond the termination of grant funds. Past grant reviewers may be able to clarify, for example, whether grantees were promising to sustain projects in perpetuity or for an equal number of years as the granting period.

Answers to questions like these, resulting from a 10-minute phone conversation, will help shape your proposal format and content. On the other hand, if you are accumulating negative "vibes" from your discussion with a past grant winner and past grant reviewer, you may decide to start over with your preproposal contact

that focuses on a different grantmaker. If you are getting encouraging messages, continue on with Step Four.

STEP FOUR: FOLLOW-UP CONTACT WITH PROGRAM OFFICER

Why Do Step Four?

The information you gain in Steps One through Three will generate some preliminary ideas about the final scope of your proposal, along with some unanswered questions. Your follow-up contact with the program officer enables you to draw the final parameters around your proposal: what to emphasize, include, and exclude. In completing Step Four, you synthesize grant information from multiple sources to develop a highly competitive proposal, should you decide to proceed with submission.

Who to Contact—and How

You are now going back to contact the same individual you wrote to in Step One, this time with a phone call or e-mail to thank the program officer for the information you recently received. Indicate while you have studied the information carefully, you still have additional questions that were not covered in the material you received.

Early in your relationship with program officers, ask them whether they prefer phone or e-mail communications. Before you pick up the phone or send off a quick e-mail, ask yourself:

- Do I need this answered immediately?
- What other questions will I need answered?
- Can I wait a day or two to see whether I come up with any additional questions?

Consolidate as many of your questions as possible into one concise message. Include your e-mail address and phone number at the end of your e-mail message. It may be easier for the program officer to answer your questions with a two-minute phone call than type a two-page e-mail.

Once again, your phone call consists of two parts: an opening statement and follow-up questions.

The Opening Statement to a Program Officer

Note that each open statement consists of 80–90 words and takes approximately 40 seconds to present.

Call from a university researcher to federal government program officer regarding a biosensors program:

> Hello, Dr. Jones. I'm Libby Johnson with the Neuroscience Research Laboratory at Midwest Medical College [Who]. Thanks for sending the recent application materials. I'm calling today because depending on your current interests in biosensors, there's a possibility we might be able to help cut down on the time biomedical researchers spend preparing liquid phase sensors, while also increasing their accuracy and speed [What]. If I've caught you at a good time, I'd like to discuss your situation to see whether our approach is something you'd like more information on [Why]. (89 words)

Call from a school administrator to a private foundation youth violence program officer:

> Hello, Mr. Bancroft. I'm Charlie Jones, principal of the West Division High School in Cleveland [Who]. Thanks for sending the recent application materials. I'm calling about your "Cops in Schools" program that was just announced [Why]. Depending on your main interests, there's a possibility our past experiences and existing networks might be of value. If your calendar permits, I'd like to ask some questions that were not addressed in the recent materials you sent me to see whether our proposal ideas might be of value to you [What]. (85 words)

Call from a hospital administrator to a regional corporation:

> Hi, Mr. Goodwrench. I'm Evie Johnson with the Midwest Hospital [Who]. Thanks for sending the recent application materials. I'm calling today because, depending on your current commitment to serving disabled adults, there's a possibility we might be able to reduce your difficulty in hiring physically challenged individuals while at the same time increasing your staff diversity [Why]. If I've caught you at a good time, I'd like to ask a few questions that were not addressed in your materials to see whether this is something you'd like more information on [What]. (88 words)

Follow-up Questions to a Program Officer

When talking with program officers, explain that you analyzed their guidelines carefully, but still have some unanswered question that you'd like to raise to ensure that your proposal would match their agency priorities. Briefly describe your project, stressing objectives and outcomes. Then ask the following types of PREP questions.

Position Questions: The Baseline Situation. Position questions explore baseline information and relationships with the sponsor, and lay the foundation for more probing types of questions from the viewpoint of the program officer.

- "What is your current budget?"
  Program Budget Amount. This answer will tell you how much money is allocated to your grant program, a starting point for the next more crucial question.
- "How much of that money will be available for new awards as opposed to noncompeting continuation awards?"
  Program Budget New Money. This answer will tell you how much money is actually available for new projects like one you propose.
- "What is the anticipated application/award ratio?"
  Application Competitiveness. The funding odds will tell you your mathematical chances for success. Just remember that the grants business offers no guarantees. Funding odds are highly variable among grant programs and range from 5 to 50 percent.
- "Does the program provide one-time-only support or will it permit other funding opportunities?"
  Continuation Funding. This answer will let you know if you can go back with future funding requests or if you are likely only to receive one award.
- "Would you review our preproposal (two- to three-page concept paper)?"
  Preproposal Review. If they will (and many do), then you will have an important opportunity to better match your proposal with their priorities.
- "Would you review our draft proposal if we got it to you early?"
  Draft Proposal Review. Again, a favorable response will ensure a better match between your proposal and their expectations. Give them enough response time; don't expect them to do this three weeks before the program deadline.
- "Who officially reviews our final proposal?"
  Reviewer Expertise. Since proposals should be written to the expertise level of the reviewers, this answer will help determine the amount of technical detail you write.
- "How do you review proposals? Who does it? Outside experts? Board members? Staff?"

Review Procedures. This information will help you analyze your reviewer audience and the conditions under which they read proposals. To illustrate, three individuals were assigned recently to review some federal grant proposals. Because of traffic delays, one reviewer was stuck at an airport, and a backup reviewer was called in and given one hour to read a 30-page proposal and write up 10 pages of evaluation. At best, this reviewer could skim read a proposal, not read for elaborate details.

- "How are the proposals being evaluated? Against what yardstick are the proposals being measured?"
Evaluation Criteria. The response suggests in general terms how your proposal will be evaluated. Are they scored independently against the guidelines? Are they ranked against each other? Are they prioritized within sponsor funding categories? On a first come, first funded basis?

- "To what extent are the same reviewers used in subsequent review cycles?"
Resubmission Considerations. One federal agency turns over 100 percent of reviewers every year. One private foundation retains 95 percent of reviewers from year-to-year; reviewers know when an application has been resubmitted with only modest updates. In the absence of major changes, particularly to the title and opening pages of the narrative, reviewers may prejudge the proposal: "I've read this before."

- "Do you plan to offer a workshop, teleconference, webinar, technical briefing session, or a preproposal conference to explain how to prepare an application?"
Presubmission Training. Some sponsors conduct training sessions to help applicants prepare their proposals, either through group meetings or conference calls. These sessions not only help you better understand how to prepare a competitive proposal but also provide insights into people who will be guiding your proposal review process.

Rationale Questions: Problems Existing Today.
Rationale questions go to the heart of sponsor giving from the vantage point of the program officer: the problems, needs, and injustices that exist today. Rationale questions explore sponsor motivations in funding projects.

- "Why does this problem persist?"
Duration of Problem. This answer implies major barriers to problem resolution.
- "What are the major variables in this larger problem?"

Dimensions of Problem. This answer suggests the different facets of the problem you seek to address.

- "What are the biggest hurdles in this area now?"
Problematic Barriers. The response points out the bigger challenges people in the field now face.
- "Is the problem getting worse or better?"
Changes Over Time. The reply draws a verbal trend line for the severity of the problem.
- "What are the biggest sources of dissatisfaction with current approaches?"
Current Failures. This query probes to discover what hasn't worked to date.
- "Which dimensions of this problem need to be addressed next?"
Problem Priorities. This answer points to the "big impact" needs.
- "Why have you targeted your program dollars to this problem?"
Financial Priorities. This answer explains why money will solve the problem.

Expectation Questions Basic Implications for Addressing Problems. Expectation questions look at the "so what" implications of the rationale questions from the perspective of the program officer. Expectation questions also identify the sponsor's outlook for changing the problem situation.

- "Does my project fall within your current priorities?"
Matching Your Project with Sponsor Priorities. If it does, begin writing. If it doesn't, explore different objectives that might yield a better fit or ask for suggestions of other grant programs that might be interested in your project.
- "Since your average award last year was $xx,xxx dollars, do you expect that to change?"
Budget Request. This answer will help you determine the budget size you should request.
- "Will awards be made on the basis of any special criteria, e.g., geography or type of organization?"
Special Award Criteria. This answer will help reveal legal or administrative considerations in the decision-making process. For instance, they may be especially interested in receiving proposals from small organizations in the Midwest or private hospitals in the Southeast.
- "What level of cost sharing do you expect of grantees?"
Cost sharing. Even when the application guidelines do not include cost sharing as an evaluation criterion, it may be expected or "strongly encouraged" as evidence of a commitment to the sustainability

of the project. The answer to this question will identify the level of financial contributions, if any, that will appeal to reviewers.

- "Are there any unannounced programs or unsolicited funds in my area to support my project?"
"Hip Pocket" Dollars. Sometimes you will discover unobligated or uncommitted funds in the "hip pocket" of the program officer by asking this question.
- "What are the most common mistakes in proposals you receive?"
Typical Proposal Errors. Pay particular attention to the answer, for they are things you want to avoid.
- "What would you like to see addressed in a proposal that other applicants may have overlooked?"
Pet Ideas. Many program officers like to feel a partner relationship in the proposal development process. This question provides them with an opportunity to articulate their pet ideas.
- "Would you recommend a previously funded proposal for us to read for format and style?"
Getting Sample Proposals. Sometimes a model proposal is helpful to review. Either they will provide you with a copy or refer you to a source where you can get it, e.g., project director.
- "Should the proposal be written for reviewers with nontechnical backgrounds?"
Proposal Technical Writing Style. The level of technicality in your proposal should be geared to the background of your reviewers. In a federal panel of three reviewers, one was an expert in the subdiscipline and two were branch generalists. Proposals must educate the generalists as well as persuade the specialist.
- "What percentage of your awards is made in response to unsolicited proposals?"
Competitiveness of Unsolicited Proposals. If they fund few unsolicited proposals, you may be wasting your time. Responses vary among program officers. One mission-oriented agency may award less than 5 percent of its funds in response to unsolicited proposals while another may award 95 percent.
- "Can you provide me with a copy of the reviewer's evaluation form?"
Reviewer's Evaluation Form. Use this form to organize your proposal, using the same headings and subheadings, even if they differ from those in the application guidelines. Sometimes discrepancies exist between the application guidelines and reviewer's evaluation form, an agency oversight that often occurs when two different people are responsible for developing

the documents. One person prepares the guidelines while another develops the evaluation criteria. In cases of conflict, follow the reviewer's evaluation criteria.

Priority Questions: Approaches for an Improved Situation. Priority questions concentrate on identifying the top activities that will effectively and efficiently improve the conditions surrounding the identified problems, needs, and injustices that exist today in the opinion of the program officer.

- "What's essential that isn't happening now?"
Clarification of Need. The answer focuses on the key dimensions of today's problem.
- "Why solve this problem?"
Magnitude of Need. This answer identifies the scope of the problem.
- "What's needed to close the gap?"
Bridging the Gap. Another question that tells us how to narrow the discrepancy between "what is" and "what should be."
- "Would this approach produce what is needed?"
Solution Feasibility. This answer provides a "trial balloon" response to your proposed action plan.
- "How do you think this would work?"
Implementation Strategies. This answer helps map out a successful action plan to solve the problem.
- "How would this really help?"
Distinctive Features. This answer points out the distinctive benefits or payoff of your solution.
- "Is there specific evaluation data you would like to see collected to facilitate a meta-analysis of your funding portfolio?"
Evaluation Data. Inevitably, grantees must submit some type of quarterly, midyear, or annual progress report to the sponsor. Make the program officer's job easier by collecting from day one the type of data needed to justify to executive authorities the merit of the project.
- "What are the long-term benefits of this solution?"
Long-Range Payoffs. This answer describes the long-range implications of your solution.
- "To what extent do you expect the project to be institutionalized versus sustained through other sources of funding?"
Project Institutionalization. This question examines means and ends relating to sustainability. The program officer can clarify whether it is more important for the project to be institutionalized by the applicant or for the project to continue with financial support from a combination of gifts, grants, and

revenue from investments, intellectual property, and fee-for-service.

- "What combination of financial and nonfinancial commitments to sustainability are you seeing and approving in the applications you receive? *Financial and Nonfinancial Sustainability.* This question opens the door to a dialog with the program officer about ways the project will "live on" beyond the granting period as well as ways the project may be financed once grant funds terminate.
- "What outcomes do you expect from grantees?" *Program Officer Expectations.* This answer clarifies what the program officer will expect from you.

Again, a 10-minute phone call will give you a substantial competitive edge. This four-step process is one that successful grantseekers follow. After looking at the information gleaned from following it, you can see the disadvantage you would face if you **didn't** follow it.

In sum, the purpose of conducting preproposal contact is to narrow down your list of "suspects" and identify those sponsors who appear to be a good match with your organization's needs. You do not always need to go through all four steps. Sometimes, the feedback you gain in steps two or three will be sufficient for you to determine that the match is not a good one.

In that case, scratch the potential sponsor's name off of your list and move on to the next one. Doing this homework before starting to write will pay dividends later on because you will write a more competitive proposal.

Clip File Action Item # 8
Preproposal Contacts

Develop your Preproposal Contacts clip file by taking the following actions:

- Write out sample opening statements that you could use on the telephone to past grant winners, prior reviewers, and program officers; adapt the models in this chapter to your situation.
- Generate an electronic list of the four PREP question categories that can be used with past grant winners, prior reviewers, and program officers. Have the list on your computer screen when you make the calls; type in answers during the telephone conversations. Use a headset to talk so your hands are free to type in answers.
- Create a database to track your preproposal contacts, including contact information, who you talked to, date, information learned, and impressions.

PART II
Writing Private Foundation and Corporation Proposals

OVERVIEW OF PART II

Part I focused on the process of proposal planning. It identified the major print and electronic sources needed to find sponsors who might fund your proposals. Once an initial suspect pool was determined, pre-proposal contact was needed to narrow down the list of potential funders and settle on those that have the highest probably of granting you funds. A four-step model was presented to help you gain pertinent background information from program officers, past grant reviewers, and past grant winners.

In Part II and Part III, we turn our attention from proposal planning to proposal writing. Specifically, in Part II, we analyze the approach to write grant proposals to private sources. In Part III, we follow up with strategies to write grant proposals for public funding sources.

Private grantmakers—foundations and corporations—often require short proposals, typically a few pages in length. The letter proposal format is perhaps the most commonly written type of private grant. It is ideally suited for those situations where private grantmakers have no specific form to follow; they just want you to submit a brief synopsis of your pro-

ject. Accordingly, Chapter 5 presents a seven-step template to develop your own letter proposal. Those proposal elements are as follows:

- Part One: *Summary*—a one-sentence proposal overview
- Part Two: *Appeal*—rationale for approaching sponsor
- Part Three: *Problem*—description of the need or gap
- Part Four: *Solution*—method for solving the problem
- Part Five: *Capabilities*—your credentials to solve the problem
- Part Six: *Budget*—your specific request for funds
- Part Seven: *Closing*—a check-writing nudge to the sponsor

For each proposal element, we provide you with examples, ideas, and questions to help you start writing. In essence, the letter proposal is a versatile tool that can be adapted to many different circumstances.

In Chapter 6, we take the basic seven-step template presented in Chapter 5 and modify it for use in other grant situations. Specifically, we present eight different examples of complete letter proposals using this model. Further we show how it can be tailored for use with government agencies or in those situations where private grantmakers have an actual form to use in preparing your proposal.

CHAPTER 5
Letter Proposal Template

More than kisses, letters mingle souls.

—*John Donne*

OVERVIEW

A letter proposal is a short grant proposal, usually two to five pages long. As the name implies, it is written in letter form and used whenever a foundation or corporation has no specific submission guidelines to follow, hopefully for some soul mingling, as poet John Donne suggests. In Chapter 5, you will learn the following:

- The difference between letter proposals, letters of intent, and letters of inquiry.
- The seven essential ingredients of a letter proposal.
- Tips for writing each part of a letter proposal.
- The flexibility of the letter proposal.
- The letter proposal is especially useful in situations where no required application form exists.

Sometimes, private sponsors will decide whether you get funded on the basis of your brief letter proposal, regardless if you are asking for $100 or $1 million. A few private sponsors use the letter proposal as a screening device and request an expanded proposal if your idea captures their interest. In either case, final draft or screening device, you face the challenge of writing a short, clear, concise document.

The grants community is not consistent in its use of three terms: letter proposals, letters of intent, and letters of inquiry. What one sponsor may mean by the term *letter of intent,* another may mean *letter of inquiry.* Still others may use the two terms interchangeably. This chapter begins with a brief discussion of all three terms as they are used in the majority of grant opportunity announcements. As you respond to these calls for information about your grant ideas, be certain you understand what the sponsors mean by the terms they are using.

LETTER PROPOSALS, LETTERS OF INTENT, AND LETTERS OF INQUIRY

All three—letter proposals, letters of intent, and letters of inquiry—share similar characteristics: they are short and communicate to potential grantmakers information they seek. They are different in the information they transmit.

- A **Letter Proposal** is a short grant proposal written in a letter format. It contains an abridged version of the basic proposal elements: summary, need, objectives, methods, applicant credentials, and budget.
- A **Letter of Intent** alerts the sponsor of your plan to submit a formal proposal. It may contain your name and a tentative working title, but little else. Grantmakers use it as a "head count" to anticipate the number and variety of applications they might receive.
- A **Letter of Inquiry** is similar to a Letter Proposal except it is not written in a letter format. It does include the same essential grant proposal elements, but they are presented in a more formal layout that usually includes a cover page and appropriate headings and subheadings.

Consider, for example, the Carnegie Corporation's instructions for preparing a Letter of Inquiry, which is their first step in applying for a grant.

In essence, Carnegie is seeking a five-page synopsis of your project. In responding to their guidelines, your cover page (not counted in the five-page limit) would include project title, collaborators (if any), and appropriate contact information. In the five-page narrative, you would restate the major headings and subheadings implicit in their eight bulleted points. Put differently,

A letter of inquiry clearly and consistently describes the project, its aims, its significance, its duration, and the amount of funds required. The document should not exceed five pages. Please address the following points in a letter of inquiry:

- What problem does your project address? Why is this issue significant? What is the relationship of the problem/issue to the corporation's current program interests as noted in its Information Pamphlet and Web site?
- What strengths and skills does your organization and personnel bring to this project? What makes your organization the right one to conduct this project?
- Who will lead the project? Identify key personnel and attach résumés.
- What do you intend to demonstrate or prove? What means will you use? If the project is already underway, what have you accomplished so far?
- If you are requesting funding from Carnegie Corporation for a component(s) of a larger project, specify which activities you are requesting the corporation to fund and how they relate to the larger project.
- What outcomes do you expect, both immediate and long term?
- If you have requested funds from other sources (or plan to), please list those sources and note the status of your request.
- What plans do you have to disseminate information to the public about your project?

CARNEGIE CORPORATION LETTER OF INQUIRY GUIDELINES

EXHIBIT 24

your proposal outline for Carnegie might be as indicated in Exhibit 25.

The end product in Exhibit 25 is a brief document the sponsor can evaluate to determine whether you should receive an invitation to submit a full proposal. It also prevents grantmakers from spending unnecessary time assembling application materials for projects that are a fundamental mismatch with sponsor priorities and thus would ultimately be unsuccessful.

A **Letter of Intent** (LOI) is requested by sponsors in those instances when they want to get an approximate idea of how many applications to anticipate. Armed with this estimate of anticipated proposals, they can more efficiently organize the review process, e.g., determine size of staff needed to administer the reviews and respond to applicant postsubmission inquiries.

To illustrate, a recent request for a letter of intent was published by the National Institutes of Health (NIH) for their Rheumatic Diseases Research Core Centers (P30) grant opportunity. It reads as follows:

> Although a letter of intent is not required, is not binding, and does not enter into the review of a subsequent application, the information that it contains allows IC staff to estimate the potential review workload and plan the review.
>
> By the date listed in Part 1: Overview Information, prospective applicants are asked to submit a letter of intent that includes the following information:
>
> - Descriptive title of proposed research
> - Name, address, and telephone number of the PD(s)/PI(s)

- Names of other key personnel
- Participating institutions
- Number and title of this funding opportunity

This NIH request is typical of most issued by private foundations and government agencies. Corporations seldom request an LOI. Letters of intent are issued in response to a specific request for proposals; in contrast, letter proposals may be submitted in response to both solicited and unsolicited proposals. In essence, a letter of intent simply notifies the sponsor of your plan to submit a proposal, as Exhibit 26 indicates.

ELEMENTS OF LETTER PROPOSAL

In certain respects, a short **Letter Proposal** is more challenging to write than a longer full proposal, because each sentence must carry a heavy information load. Accordingly, it is helpful to segment the writing process into seven different components:

- Part One: *Summary*—a one-sentence proposal overview
- Part Two: *Appeal*—rationale for approaching the sponsor
- Part Three: *Problem*—description of the need or gap
- Part Four: *Solution*—method for solving the problem
- Part Five: *Capabilities*—your credentials to solve the problem
- Part Six: *Budget*—your specific request for funds
- Part Seven: *Closing*—a check-writing nudge to the sponsor

I. Statement of Problem

A. Significance
B. Relevance to Carnegie Priorities

II. Organizational Capacity

A. Strengths
B. Personnel and Skills
C. Uniqueness to Conduct Project

III. Key Project Personnel

A. Project Director
B. Other Key Project Personnel

IV. Project Goals and Objectives

A. Methods for Achieving Goals and Objectives
B. Project Times
C. Current Project Status

V. Carnegie Funding Request

A. From Carnegie
B. Relationship to Larger Project

VI. Project Outcomes

A. Immediate
B. Long-Term

VII. Funding from Other Sources

A. Sources and Amounts
B. Status of Requests

VIII. Dissemination

A. Target Audiences
B. Dissemination Messages
C. Dissemination Methods

OUTLINE OF INQUIRY LETTER TO CARNEGIE CORPORATION

EXHIBIT 25

In seven brief sections, you anticipate and answer the major questions that private sponsors will be asking as they read your letter proposal. These seven proposal parts are suggestive, not prescriptive. Deviate without guilt from the letter proposal format when it makes sense to do so. In the illustrations that follow, each part identifies what you are trying to accomplish as you write that section and provides some sample paragraphs to help you start writing.

PART ONE: SUMMARY

Objective: To summarize the entire proposal in one or two sentences.

Preparing to Write

Study the critical elements of the model sentence, including:

- *Self-Identification*: State your organizational name.
- *Organizational Uniqueness*: Cite a brief "claim to fame" from a mission statement that explains your reason for being.
- *Sponsor Expectation*: Explain what you want them to do.
- *Budget Request*: Identify how much money you are requesting.
- *Project Benefit*: State the major project outcome for the sponsor, not you.

Today's Date

Ms. Jerri Kurri, President
Finnish Athletic Foundation
123 Maki Drive
Helsinki, California 90120

RE: Letter of Intent
Your Proposal Title
Your Organizational Name

Dear Ms. Kurri:

This letter conveys our intent to submit a formal proposal in response to your recent initiative on dental implant research with toothless hockey players. Our 10-year history of implant research enables us to bring unique value to your programmatic goals. The collaborators for this project include the California Sports Authority, three California dental schools, and the California Dental Association. You will receive the required original and six proposal copies in advance of your October 3rd deadline. In the meantime, feel free to contact me for further information.

Sincerely,

Your Name
Your Title

LETTER OF INTENT

EXHIBIT 26

The model summary sentence takes on the following structure:

"[Identification], [uniqueness], [expectation] in a [request] that [benefits]."

Examples

As you study the following five examples, note how they all include the five critical summary elements. These examples represent a range of funding requests and can be adapted easily to your situation. An example of a complete letter proposal can be found at the end of this chapter. In Chapter 6, you will find eight additional examples of complete letter proposals. One final complete letter proposal is found in Chapter 16.

1. The basic summary sentence for a university research project seeking corporate support:
   Midwest University [identification], as Wisconsin's largest independent educational institution [uniqueness], invites the investment of the Big Gene Corporation [expectation] in a $250,000 research project [request] that builds the long-term infrastructure for scientific advancements in biomedical research [benefit]. (32 words; one sentence)

2. A welfare agency seeking foundation support for an HIV/AIDS prevention project:
   The Family Welfare Agency, the largest welfare agency in Horton County, seeks $20,000 from the Happy Family Foundation to teach HIV/AIDS prevention to urban teens. (26 words; one sentence)

3. A public school seeking foundation funding for a cultural diversity project:
   Quinkleberry High School, recently described by the governor of Minnesota as "a benchmark of public school excellence that others should strive to follow," invites your participation in a $200,000 special project to increase the multicultural learning experiences of its students. (42 words; one sentence)

4. A multispecialty medical clinic seeking corporate support to increase its service delivery:
   Advanced Healthcare Medical Clinic, the most comprehensive healthcare facility within the eastern region of the state, invites your investment in a $500,000 service project that would increase the access and improve the delivery of rural healthcare services. (37 words; one sentence)

5. A faith-based organization seeking foundation funding for a food pantry program:
   Houston Unity Church, the most centrally located church in the inner city, invites you to share

Self-Oriented Benefits	Sponsor-Oriented Benefits
Lincolnwood Fire Department, exclusively responsible for the fire safety of 85,000 residences and 12,000 businesses, invites your investment in a $750,000 grant to buy a new fire truck.	Lincolnwood Fire Department, exclusively responsible for the fire safety of 137,000 individuals and $42 million in property, invites your investment in a $750,000 grant to ensure continued community safety during a period of increased vulnerability.
The Family Welfare Agency, Atlanta's only urban family crisis intervention agency, respectfully requests a grant of $75,000 to meet its operating expenses.	The Family Welfare Agency, Atlanta's only urban family crisis intervention agency, respectfully requests a grant of $75,000 to sustain the delivery of crucial welfare services to victims of violence and abuse.
Fairview Middle School, recently recognized by the governor as a "Center for Educational Excellence," requests a $5,000 grant to pay for a guest speaker who will talk about teen bullying.	Fairview Middle School, recently recognized by the governor as a "Center for Educational Excellence," requests a $5,000 grant to help decrease bullying behavior among teens.

in a $15,000 service project to coordinate disjointed food programs for the poor. (30 words; one sentence)

As you now write your summary statement for your proposal, avoid the trap that beginning grant writers often encounter: expressing the benefit to themselves instead of to the sponsors. Contrast the example pairs of self- and sponser-oriented benefits.

In both pairs of examples, the message is clear and simple: sponsors usually give money to organizations that help other people; sponsors seldom give money to organizations that only help themselves. After you write your summary sentence, reread it and see whether it presents a self- or sponsor-oriented benefit.

PART TWO: APPEAL

Objective: To explain why you are appealing to the sponsor for their funding.

Preparing to Write

These tips will help explain why you "knock on their door":

- Conduct prospect research on the sponsor as described in Chapter 4.
- From your prospect research, identify values that the sponsor seems to cherish, e.g., high-risk projects not normally funded by the government, cutting-edge research, demonstration projects with a national impact, or low-cost/high-benefit projects.
- Summarize key funding patterns that attract you to the sponsor, e.g., "80 percent of your award dollars in the last two years have gone to support projects

like this," or "Last year, you awarded $2.5 million to private universities in support of projects on technology transfer." When you analyze a sponsor's giving history, you can usually find a pattern of giving that attracts you to them.

Examples

Six examples follow: three targeting foundations and three targeting corporations. As you write your sponsor appeal paragraph in your next letter proposal, you may wish to "cherry pick" the sentences that best fit your situation. Each sample paragraph ends with a word count; while there is no "ideal" number of words, many paragraphs will range from 80 to 150 words.

1. An Alzheimer's Research Center seeking foundation support for a neuroscience project:
   We are encouraged that the R. U. Rich Foundation supports new frontiers in the neuroscience of memory; over 75 percent of your grant dollars during the last three years have been invested in cutting-edge genetics technology research. The foundation has been an inspiration because you have supported biomedical projects over the years with absolute consistency. Clearly, your support fills a valuable niche in light of the more conservative and traditional funding offered by the federal government. This strong commitment to innovative research is shared by researchers in our Biomedical Research Institute. (90 words; four sentences)
2. An Interfaith Council seeking foundation support for an international missionary project:
   The best ideas are ones that help people. For decades, you have directed your resources to promoting the religious and educational well-being of millions. Since 1969, you have systematically

examined the increasing impact of missionary work on almost every aspect of our lives. For instance, your current list of grant awards shows over $400,000 in project support targeted for missionary service. Because of your unprecedented concern for the needs of the financially and spiritually impoverished in third-world countries as well as your position of leadership in the philanthropic community, we turn to the Big Bucks Foundation for its support of a $90,000 international missionary project. (109 words; five sentences)

3. A private university seeking foundation support for student scholarships:

We are encouraged that the George and Martha Washington Foundation has given $681,389, or 53 percent, of all its awards in the last two years to private colleges and universities. This type of recognition is essential for independent universities that are tuition-dependent and lack state financial support. Midwest University wants to attract the brightest students into our ranks: people with fresh perspectives on current issues who we can encourage to become tomorrow's top leaders. Midwest has a national reputation for providing a values-based, liberal arts education; this reputation, in turn, attracts many top-caliber applicants. Unfortunately, the number of academically talented students in all areas of study who deserve our help strains our limited scholarship funds. Your contribution will be especially important in providing vital student assistance to our nation's future leaders. (133 words; six sentences)

4. A child welfare agency seeking corporate support for a social services project:

In our shared commitment to making our community a better place to live and work, we look forward to finding avenues of mutual support. Such a partnership is particularly timely since public funding for human services and civic needs continues to decline at a dramatic rate. Because of your demonstrated concern for children as well as your position of leadership in our city, we turn to the Coffee Bucks Corporation for its support in expanding community outreach services to at-risk youth. (82 words; three sentences)

5. A health agency seeking corporate support for a community health program:

We recognize your commitment to being an outstanding corporate citizen, and we appreciate the fact that you are as concerned about the health of our community as you are with the health of your business. Indeed, it is sometimes difficult to determine where business interests end and community interests begin. Since you provide important work for the good of others, your investment in this project would contribute significantly to maintaining a community health program of the highest quality and national distinction, based here in San Antonio. Moreover, it would also serve as a standard of committed civic responsibility, inspiring others to support this important fund-raising effort. As a result, your philanthropic generosity could be leveraged to attract additional support from the business community. (124 words; five sentences)

6. A local police department seeking corporate matching funds for a juvenile justice project:

Like many communities, the Evergreen Police Department (EPD) must cope with the consequences of escalating juvenile crimes. The rising crime rate comes at a time when local government budgets are retrenching due to our dwindling tax base. Accordingly, EPD must rely on support from external sources if it is to remain financially healthy and meet community service obligations. We have been fortunate in attracting partial funding from the Department of Justice through their Community Oriented Policing program. Their matching grant will provide three years of funding to hire one juvenile justice officer, provided the community will fund a second officer. In response, the City Council has committed one-half salary for a second officer, wishing that the budget allowed full matching funds. Since your support over the years has played a catalytic role in local efforts to help nurture and challenge ideas that are locally developed, we now seek your generous support to secure this co-funding opportunity—and secure the future of our troubled youth. We hope you are able to take advantage of this opportunity to leverage your support dollars in continued partnership with the City. (185 words; eight sentences)

PART THREE: PROBLEM

Objective: To briefly summarize the current problem and its long-term implications.

Preparing to Write

Focus the problem or need statement from their perspective, not yours. Funding your project is not their end goal. You must show how funding your project can be a means for them to reach their end goal, namely, their mission.

A "need" is a gap between "what is" and "what ought to be." Document that gap with statistics, quotations, reasoning, or surveys and express it in human terms. Limit your documentation to brief but clear statements. Beware of the excessive use of statistics, which may only confuse the reader. See Chapter 7 for a fuller discussion of writing a problem statement.

Examples

Four examples follow, two each seeking foundation and corporate support. Because the need section is a crucial proposal section, it is longer and contains more detail than other proposal elements.

1. A research institute seeking foundation equipment funding:

   As you know, interdisciplinary research combined with genetic technology fuels the rapid advancements in the modern life sciences. To remain at the cutting edge of these discoveries, institute researchers must consolidate and expand the analytical methods they now use to study the expression of gene regulation. Currently, our researchers lack the capability for genomic analysis at levels of detail now possible with new technology. This lack of powerful and productive equipment inhibits our ability to use state-of-the-art methodology, to perform critical experiments, and to develop more efficient, definitive, and versatile research programs.

   There are two major consequences from this lack of modern equipment. First, it presents insurmountable barriers to scientific progress in understanding the mechanisms underlying such diseases as Alzheimer's and cancer. Neuroscience questions on the mechanisms that alter gene functions often require equipment support that extends beyond the financial boundaries of individual research projects. Maintaining state-of-the-art equipment has become prohibitive. Second, the institute has a serious responsibility to train scientists who will contribute to an ever-changing technological society in the future. To meet this challenge, our laboratories must be equipped with modern, sophisticated instrumentation. (186 words; 10 sentences)

2. A community mental health proposal to a community foundation:

   The purpose of this proposal is to initiate a psychological support service for inner-city families with teenage parents. The results of a recent Community Life Survey revealed 68 percent of the urban households in the 53206 zip code region have single mothers with an average of 2.3 children. These families—mothers, grandmothers, and great-grandmothers alike—experience a growing strain in trying to balance family and work responsibilities. In contrast, their suburban peers have support systems lacking in the urban areas. As a result, a significant and spiraling gap exists between the stress levels in urban and suburban households in our community.

   The problem is further exacerbated by the collision between service providers in the two communities. Suburban households have more financial resources and coping mechanisms to deal with stressors than what exists in corresponding urban environments. Bottom line: very few service providers have the cultural expertise or multicultural staff to be seen as credible and affordable helping agencies. Clearly, this lag in inner-city family support services is a problem that needs to be creatively addressed. (176 words; eight sentences)

3. A medical school curriculum development proposal to a pharmaceutical corporation:

   Genetics is one of the most rapidly developing areas of neuroscience. While physicians must understand genes and their function in health and disease, today's medical students receive little training in human genetics, its basic science concepts, or clinical applications.

   A recent survey of American medical schools revealed medical students receive an average of only 18 hours of genetics instruction. Now that the human genomic code has been cracked, demands for genetic testing are coming with growing demands from patients and insurance companies alike. Additionally, new issues in confidentiality, patient counseling, informed consent, and societal perceptions have added extra dimensions of complexity for medical students.

   To close the gap between rapid advances in medical science and the training received by future physicians, the need exists to develop a model course in medical genetics that could be integrated into medical school curricula nationwide. By reason of its multiplier effect, education is one of the most constructive longer-term approaches to ameliorating troubling genetics questions. (161 words; seven sentences)

4. An elder care agency seeking corporate support for consolidation of services:

The rationale for this project is driven by the demographics of aging. The elderly population is increasing in size.

- By 2020, 40 percent of our population will be over age 65.
- One-half of the elderly will be 75-plus years old.
- Elderly women will outnumber elderly men three to two.
- At age 85, there will be 4 men for every 10 women.

As a result of these demographics, there will be a marked increase in consumer demands for specialized health care services, especially among those patients with comorbid chronic health conditions, e.g., congestive heart failure and diabetes. Presently, local health services for the elderly are fragmented. Geographically, they exist in many different locations. Their disparate locations result in reduced purchasing power, ineffective case management, and duplication of records. (126 words; nine sentences)

PART FOUR: SOLUTION

Objective: To describe your approach to the problem.

Preparing to Write

Justify your selection of methodology. While most problems can be solved using multiple approaches, explain why you chose your preferred one. Summarize the outcomes that your approach will generate. Convey confidence that you can solve the problem. Use a one-page attached time and task chart (See Chapter 9) to detail your methodology.

Examples

Four examples follow, including approaches to both foundations and a corporation:

1. A day care center proposal seeking foundation support to train parents of preschool children:
   This proposal addresses a crucial service to our community—counseling and support for parents of preschool children. In recent months, we have witnessed a series of tragic cases of children who have been neglected and abused. The plight of these youngsters is dramatic evidence of the need for young parents to learn proper care and development of their children—one of the most important

responsibilities of their lives. The Blackstone Parenting Center was established to meet these needs. Its centerpiece is a theory-driven training program called STAR: Stop, Think, Assess, Respond. This four-step response to childlike behaviors is preferable to the more customary use of corporal punishment for our target population. STAR has an established track record across various culture groups and is ready for implementation here. (128 words; seven sentences)

2. A hospital seeking corporate funding for a teen smoking prevention project:
   Our intervention strategy directly addresses a major teen health hazard—smoking. The project approach will close the health hazard gap by getting at the root causes that lead to addiction. We will avoid the two primary unsuccessful techniques used in the past: (1) fear of death: too remote of a concern during the teen years; and (2) health impairment: permanent lung damage has little stimulus value to change behavior. Instead, we will initiate a five-pronged approach that is targeted at the average age of the first-time smoker: 13 years old. Our campaign, called Butt Out Now, will:
   - Develop an in-house program to fight tobacco use in middle schools.
   - Create Web sites and use social media to discourage youth smoking.
   - Empower teen smokers to quit successfully.
   - Enact peer-teaching programs to defend youth against advertising and peer pressure.
   - Remind physicians to take a proactive role.
   Our accompanying Time and Task Chart describes in detail how campaign phases interrelate. (157 words; 11 sentences)

3. A battered women's shelter organization seeking foundation funding for research on families at risk for domestic violence:
   Our approach uses both qualitative and quantitative methods. We will use interviews and questionnaires to determine responses to aggression and its impact on the family. Two key questionnaires are the Ryder Aggression Scale and the Intent to Institutionalize Scale. Both instruments will be given to a random selection of the clients at the Family Wellness Center over the next two years. To interpret the resulting scale values, focus group interviews will be conducted with the clients to better understand their perceptions of core family values. The outcome of this research has implications for the training of social welfare personnel and will be submitted for publication to

the *Journal of Domestic Tranquility*. (111 words: six sentences)

4. A collaborative university/community agency proposal seeking foundation funding for adult literacy training:

    The attached Time and Task Chart summarizes the project methodology, including major milestones, responsible personnel, and duration. The innovative aspects of the project include close supervision of tutors, emphasis on family approaches to literacy training for adults, and the inclusion of graduate students earning academic credit. Since methods of teaching reading to children are not directly transferable to adults, the method of choice is the Randolph Reading Review, which presents adult-level stimulus material in a combined phonetic and sight vocabulary approach. A 2009 study by LaCour documented the effectiveness of this technique with a similar population, when compared with other common intervention strategies. (105 words; four sentences)

PART FIVE: CAPABILITIES

Objective: To establish your credentials to carry out the project.

Preparing to Write

As you write this section, your task is to establish three types of credibility: (1) your organization, showing you work in an environment capable of supporting the project; (2) your project idea, indicating that you have identified a unique problem that you are capable of solving; and (3) your key project staff, demonstrating that you have experienced and credentialed personnel to ensure project success.

Examples

Two corporate and two foundation examples follow:

1. A pediatric hospital seeking foundation funding to work with emotionally disturbed preschoolers:
    The State Pediatric Hospital has been meeting the needs of emotionally disturbed preschoolers for 13 years. The trained staff represents over 300 years of combined experience in this specialized area. The hospital's geographic location is less than a two-hour drive for 80 percent of the state's population. The hospital is in a unique position to conduct this project for two reasons. First, veteran pediatricians and child psychiatrists with extensive national networks will conduct this project. Second, as a private institution not dependent upon public funding, it can provide a detached perspective without the constraints that publicly funded hospitals might experience. (99 words; six sentences)

2. A university biology department seeking corporate funding for genetics research:
    Here are some things you should know about us. Our biology department is uniquely suited to conduct this crucial genetics research. Stemming from the department's solid past of 30 years of doctoral studies in biological science, its faculty includes Drs. Smith, Johnson, and O'Connor. This distinguished academic core cumulatively represents 224 years of productive research experience at our university. With special focus on the molecular basis of oncogenesis, our current research uses unique systems to analyze the genetic and hormonal factors responsible for gene regulation. While these systems are not widely studied in established programs of cell biology, they are most suitable for answering the cutting-edge questions of gene expression and regulation—and our department is endowed with the intellectual talent to succeed. (124 words; seven sentences)

3. A county department of aging institute seeking foundation funding to coordinate services for the elderly:
    The Grant County Department of Aging is uniquely positioned to develop an integrated system of geriatric medical and nonhealth services. Since 1980, the department has provided quality health, education, and research services. As a result, it serves a full range of seniors' needs. The department has a 20-plus-year history of positive networking with the business community. Accordingly, this project represents a systematic continuation of prior geriatric efforts in the area where we've transformed vision into success. It organically grows out of our past activities in the area of integration of essential services. We are solidly endowed with the intellectual resources, a skilled population, and healthy attitude to successfully implement our action plan. (114 words; seven sentences)

4. An environmentally conscious agency seeking corporate funding to train volunteers:
    The Greenspace Society is similar to many other organizations that are dedicated, as our mission statement says, to environmental protection and

preservation. During the past two years, we have successfully trained volunteers as evidenced by the fact that annual volunteer hours now exceed 18,000 (up 46%) and donations total $25,000 (up 12%). As a result, we now request funding to systematically develop a formal training model, complete with a curriculum and instructional materials; since we are like other environmentally conscious volunteer organizations, a training model developed here can be replicated in many other equivalent institutions. (96 words; four sentences)

PART SIX: BUDGET

Objective: To request a specific dollar amount in the proposal.

Preparing to Write

Be certain to ask for a precise amount. Base your request on your preproposal contact information. Translate your dollar request in meaningful units, e.g., hours of instruction, numbers of students, or healthy patients; if the per unit costs are too high, spread the figures out over several years. Advise the sponsor if you plan to submit this or a similar proposal to other sponsors as well. Indicate that these funds will supplement, not supplant, ongoing programs.

Examples

Two corporate and two foundation examples follow:

1. An elementary school requesting corporate support for new computers:
   To meet our obligation of training computer-literate children, it is essential that they have access to today's technology; otherwise, we would be guilty of educating technological orphans. The cost of maintaining state-of-the-art computer technologies is quickly becoming prohibitive. Quite frankly, this project extends beyond the financial boundaries of our high school. Accordingly, we must now reach out for assistance in what surely is a vital service to our entire community. Although we are expanding our budget allocations for technology upgrades as rapidly as possible, we intend to build an endowment that will provide ongoing support for suitable technology and staff without relying on annual operating dollars—but that takes time. With the interest that you've shown in this area, we are requesting a grant in the amount of $150,000. This represents an investment of $1.25 in every student that will use these computers in the next five years, or a cost of $0.018 per hour of instruction. (158 words; seven sentences)

2. A social service agency seeking corporate funding for a conference on rural poverty:
   It is in the spirit of this beneficial synergism between business and the community it serves that I respectfully request the John Doe Tractor Corporation grant $10,000 to provide funds for a conference on rural poverty. This project would not only flow logically from your great corporate interest in supporting communities in which your employees live and work, but it would also yield fresh perspectives on the plight faced by many of your rural customers. In making such a contribution, the John Doe Tractor Corporation will join the Rural Social Service Agency and the state Bureau of Agriculture in this effort to serve our community by finding contemporary solutions to nagging problems. Corporate marketing professionals, government policy makers, and social service agencies can use the conference findings to strengthen the vitality of rural communities throughout the nation. (138 words; four sentences)

3. A local library seeking foundation funding to digitize its holdings:
   With the commitment shown by the Brush Foundation to promote literary and educational efforts, we are seeking a $25,000 grant to digitize our entire library holding of more than 100,000 volumes. Over a 10-year period, your support will touch the lives of 50,000 library patrons. Such a gift will assure not only that timely and quality services are provided, but also extend its outreach to turn every community household into a "virtual library." Clearly, this project will enrich the lives of all whom it reaches. The average library checkout entails four books; this project has the attractive investment of five cents (5¢) per person. (105 words; five sentences)

4. A small college seeking private foundation funding support for curricular development:
   With the demonstrated concern that you have shown for preparing a professional workforce to successfully address issues of aging, we request a grant of $6,000. Funds will support: curriculum development ($3,000); development of the experimental learning component ($1,000); library resources ($500); honoraria for guest speakers ($500)

and for consultation and evaluation ($1,000). Once the course is designed, the college will assume the expense of offering it in the future, including teaching and attendant costs. These funds would go for a new academic initiative and not be used for any ongoing projects. Over a three-year period, this new course will help transform the lives of nearly 100 college students. (108 words; five sentences)

PART SEVEN: CLOSING

Objective: To nudge the sponsor to a favorable funding decision.

Preparing to Write

Avoid the hackneyed "We'd be happy to talk with you further about this. Please call if you want more information." Identify a contact person that could provide more details, if requested. Have a "heavyweight" sign the letter. This closing paragraph should be the "call to action" section that nudges them toward funding you.

Examples

Three foundation and one corporate example follow:

1. Private school seeking student financial aid from a foundation:
   We hope the Marcy Foundation will be able to support these Marcy scholars as they continue their tradition of the pursuit of knowledge. In making such a contribution, Marcy—and indeed, society—will benefit by investing in the ideas of the future. Quite simply, your investment will perpetuate excellent educational opportunities for future leaders throughout the nation. Dr. Robert Wheeler, director of Student Financial Aid, can provide additional information or answer questions via telephone (414-234-5678) or e-mail (robert.wheeler@midwest.edu). (80 words; four sentences)
2. A biofeedback clinic seeking corporate support for a pain management project:
   Your support really does make a difference. The impact of your contribution will last for years to come as a key player in the management of pain in patients with advanced disease. Your support will contribute to the only business worth pursuing, as Albert Schweitzer noted, "The business of doing purposeful good." Although this proposal follows the businesslike brevity your guidelines request, Dr. Griffin Boyes can be reached at (210) 123–4567 to answer questions or give further information. (78 words; four sentences)
3. A family resource center seeking foundation support for a family values project:
   Strengthening family ties is clearly a priority in our country. This is evidenced by collaborations among myriad local agencies to achieve these goals and the increased demand for family support services in cases where unhealthy family values exist. With your investment we will be able to foster healthy relationships between parents and their children. Please contact Sarah Spencer directly to answer questions or provide additional information by phone (202) 123–4567 or e-mail Sarah.Spencer@frc.org. (73 words; four sentences)
4. A college seeking private foundation support for a capital building project:
   Winston Churchill once observed, "At first we share our buildings. Thereafter, our buildings shape us." Nowhere is this more evident than in a library. As the accompanying drawings highlight, this new library will secure its place as the academic heart and information hub of the campus. This modern library will serve as a place that houses great books and physical collections as well as an electronic portal to information from all over the world. It will, as Churchill noted, shape the lives of generations of college students.

   This new facility will build on a rich tradition of success and be an important part of our unwavering commitment to academic excellence. The generosity of your support will help attract more students of the highest caliber to campus. The library will exemplify the core values of a college education, which seeks to develop students' full potential in understanding and serving their world. I look forward to hearing from you soon. You can reach me directly by phone: (608) 987–6543 or e-mail: Kelly.Ball@college.edu. (170 words; 10 sentences)

COMPLETE LETTER PROPOSAL

Orienting Observations

An example follows (Exhibit 27) of a complete 648-word letter proposal to a private foundation that seeks support for a project to improve police-community relations. It contains all seven sections described above

Today's Date

Mr. Hubert Williams, President
Law Enforcement Foundation
1001 23rd Street, N.W., Suite 200
Washington, DC 20037

Dear Mr. Williams:

The Center for Urban Problems (CUP), as Washington's largest organization dealing with police-community relations, invites your investment in a $66,240 research project to improve community relations among minorities.

We are encouraged that the Law Enforcement Foundation supports innovative projects that improve the delivery of police services. Over 85 percent of your grant dollars during the past three years have been invested at the local community level. Clearly, your support fills a valuable niche in light of the more conservative funding offered by the federal government. The researchers and evaluation specialists at CUP share your strong commitment to unique community-based projects.

The Problem: Spiraling Tensions. Despite proactive community relations programs, an unchecked tension exists between municipal policy and minority community members. Relationships between law enforcement officers and minorities—Hispanics and African Americans—are at a critical stage. One out of every three arrests in Washington, DC, currently involves a member of a minority community; the incidence is even higher in such cities as San Antonio, Kansas City, and Los Angeles.

Many factors contribute to the growing minority community-police tensions: unemployment, inadequate housing, and the increasing complexity of urban life. Although the police did not create these nationwide social problems, they must cope with the consequences of them. This vast social dislocation spawns minority attitudes of prejudice and contempt. To counterbalance these problems, many police communities have adopted public relations programs to "sell" their departments to the minority communities without the concomitant need to work with them. As a result, there is an ever-widening split between present and potential minority community acceptance of police behavior. Long term, this spiraling gap further alienates citizens, limits cooperation, and erects barriers to community development.

The Solution: Evaluating Police/Community Relations Bureaus. The most effective approach to successful community-based mediation lies in forming citizen/government collaborations (often called "bureaus"), according to the latest community action research. However, success claims regarding the effectiveness of police/community relations bureaus remain undocumented. Police departments often adopt a new fad without understanding the key components of a police/community relations program. Some features of the bureau approach appear to work; others don't. This project has two specific objectives: By July, 2013, we will (1) identify the successful features of existing bureaus, and (2) disseminate those "best practices" to 350 police departments serving substantial numbers of minority citizens. The CUP research staff will follow standard social science research techniques as detailed in our Project Planner, Attachment A.

CUP Credentials: National Experience and Networks. CUP is uniquely suited to conduct this research project on police/community relations bureaus. As a nonpolice-linked organization we can objectively and independently assess current practices. This project represents a systematic continuation of prior CUP efforts in this area with state and municipal organizations and private police-related associations. Our staff has a cumulative 127 years of experience in evaluating the outcomes of police-related projects. Finally, location and national networking with 28 regional offices makes CUP well postured to effectively conduct this assessment.

SAMPLE LETTER PROPOSAL

EXHIBIT 27

Budget Request: $66,240. With the demonstrated concern that you've shown in the delivery of police services to minorities, we are requesting a grant of $66,240. Quite frankly, this project extends beyond the financial boundaries of CUP. Accordingly, we must now reach out to the community for assistance in what surely is a vital service to the police community. The outcome of this project will touch the operations of over 6,000 law enforcement groups nationwide, results in an $13 investment in each existing municipal and state police organization, or a cost of seven cents (7¢) per police official.

In making this investment, the Law Enforcement Foundation will be supporting a cost-effective approach to the delivery of police services for the minority communities where major problems exist. Ms. Neva Shelby, national program director for CUP, can be reached at (202) 123-4567 or Neva.Shelby@cup.org to answer questions or give further information.

Sincerely,

Solana Raelin
Executive Director

P.S. Come visit us and see for yourself how this project helps people in need.

Enclosure: Attachment A: Project Planner
Attachment B: IRS Nonprofit Certification

EXHIBIT 27 (Continued from page 68)

and makes good use of headings. Further, notice that the proposal is left margin justified instead of having both left and right margins justified. The reasons: double justification forces proportional spacing, causing little white "rivers" down the page. Also, the eye sweeping from the end of one line to the beginning of the next line is more difficult with double margin justification. Finally, the two most common attachments for a letter proposal are (1) a copy of your IRS letter certifying that you are a nonprofit organization, and (2) a time and task chart. See Chapter 9 for examples of time and task charts.

Specific Comments

The Project Planner, Attachment A, referenced in the Enclosure, is a combination of a Time and Task Chart (Chapter 9) and a Budget (Chapter 12). For the complete copy of Attachment A, cited above, see Exhibit 46 for specifics. Note further that single spacing is used within paragraphs and double spacing between paragraphs.

Chapter 5 provided a detailed discussion of the seven elements in letter proposals along with

31 examples. Obviously, the examples can be adapted to multiple grant writing situations. To facilitate the adaptation process, you will find a crosswalk among the examples (Exhibit 28). The first column in the crosswalk table indicates the general topic area of the example. The second column identifies the type of applicant who might be writing the example. The third column specifies the type of sponsor (foundation or corporation) to which the example is targeted. The fourth column cites the page number where the complete example is found.

 Clip File Action Item # 9
Letter Proposals

Start your Letter Proposals clip file by doing the following:

• Select at least two samples from each of the seven letter proposal components that can be added to your clip file.

Topic	Applicant	Sponsor	Page
Adult Literacy	University/Community Collaboration	Foundation	65
Biomedical Research	University	Corporation	60
Capital Building Project	College	Foundation	67
Community Health	Health Agency	Corporation	62
Computer Equipment	Elementary School	Corporation	66
Conference Support	Social Service Agency	Corporation	66
Counseling	Community Mental Health Agency	Foundation	63
Cultural Diversity	Public School	Foundation	60
Curriculum Development	College	Foundation	66
Curriculum Development	Medical School	Corporation	63
Digitize Holdings	Community Library	Foundation	66
Domestic Violence	Battered Women's Shelter	Foundation	64
Emotionally Disturbed	Pediatric Hospital	Foundation	65
Equipment	Research Institute	Foundation	63
Family Values	Family Resource Center	Foundation	64
Food Pantry	Faith-Based Organization	Foundation	60
Genetics	University	Corporation	61
HIV/AIDS Prevention	Welfare Agency	Foundation	60
Juvenile Justice	Police Department	Corporation	62
Missionary	Interfaith Council	Foundation	61
Neuroscience	Alzheimer's Research Center	Foundation	61
One-Stop Shopping	Elder Care Agency	Corporation	83
Pain Management	Biofeedback Clinic	Corporation	67
Parent Training	Day Care Center	Foundation	64
Scholarships	University	Foundation	62
Service Coordination	County Department of Aging	Foundation	65
Service Delivery	Medical Clinic	Corporation	60
Social Services	Child Welfare Agency	Corporation	62
Student Financial Aid	Private School	Foundation	67
Teen Smoking Prevention	Hospital	Corporation	64
Volunteer Training	Environmental Agency	Corporation	65

CROSSWALK TO LETTER PROPOSAL EXAMPLES

EXHIBIT 28

CHAPTER 6
Letter Proposal Examples

Letters are expectations packaged in an envelope.
—*Shana Alexander*

OVERVIEW

The previous chapter provided you with a seven-step template for writing a persuasive letter proposal. From a broad perspective, your letter proposals communicate the expectation, as Shana Alexander notes, that you have identified a significant problem that you propose to solve. Exhibit 27 identified the problem of spiraling tensions between the police and members of the minority community and proposed to reduce those tensions by naming researching best practices that would be disseminated nationwide. That is just one example among many showing how a letter proposal can be crafted to solicit funding for a project that solves a crucial problem. In Chapter 6, you will learn the following:

- The versatility of the letter proposal for direct solicitations.
- The adaptability of the letter proposal as a transmittal letter or a concept paper.

More specifically, we provide eight additional examples that illustrate how the letter proposal template can be applied to various grant writing situations. For each example, we provide some orienting observations about the type of grant and some specific comments about the particular request. In this chapter, you will see—firsthand—how a letter proposal can be applied to the following funding requests.

In sum, these eight examples show how a letter proposal can be used with private foundations and corporations who have no specific application guidelines, as is the case with many sponsors. Additionally, the examples highlight ways the letter proposal template can be adapted for use with private foundations and corporations who do have specific application guidelines but are deemed to be constraining. Finally, the last example demonstrates how the letter proposal template can be modified for use with federal grant guidelines through initial submission of a concept paper, a preproposal designed to ensure your idea matches

Type of Grant	Grant Topic Example	Exhibit Number
Operating Support	Health Education Center	29
Equipment/Challenge Grant	Physical Facilities Renovation	30
Capital Campaign Support	Minority Youth	31
Training Grant	Developmentally Disabled	32
Service Delivery	Elderly Health Care	33
Continuing Project Support	Youth Mentoring	34
Additional Letter Proposal Applications		
Use as Transmittal Letter	Fire Safety	35
Use as Concept Paper	Research Center	36

with sponsor priorities. The letter proposal template is a versatile grant writing approach that has generated millions of dollars for beginning and seasoned grantseekers.

HEALTH EDUCATION CENTER REQUEST FOR OPERATING SUPPORT

Orienting Observations

As we conduct grant workshops around the county, one of the most common questions we hear is "How do you write a grant to get operating support?" Because most grantmakers provide project support, not operating support, we respond by saying that the challenge is to cast your proposal so that it de facto becomes a request for project support. The grantmakers that do provide operating support are most likely to be local community or family foundations. The letter proposal in Exhibit 29 to the Dominic Michael Family Foundation is an example of how a request for operating support can be written.

Specific Comments

Content. This 1,399-word letter proposal from a Health Education Center was really seeking general

---

Today's Date

Mr. Lee K. Wallet, President
The Dominic Michael Family Foundation
802 Great One Way
Hartford, CT 62002-1799

Dear Mr. Wallet:

The Patrick Ignatius Center for Health Education, Connecticut's largest independent provider of health education for young people, invites your contribution of $10,000 to help provide high-quality outreach programs that teach children in grades 6–12 how to make better life choices.

We are encouraged that The Dominic Michael Foundation provides funding to support the operations of innovative programs that improve the health and quality of life for children. Over the past three decades, your foundation has made important investments at critical moments to ensure that community-based educational programs are responsive to local needs. This gift request is a systematic continuation of our mutual interest in serving the greater Hartford area.

The Problem: Health Risks and Chronic Illnesses

Four priority health risks and chronic illnesses have a considerable negative impact on students' development and academic performance. These behaviors, often established during childhood and early adolescence, include: (1) alcohol, tobacco, and other drug use; (2) pediatric asthma; (3) poor diets and limited physical activity; and (4) risky sexual behaviors. Left unchecked, these behaviors contribute to the leading causes of death, disability, and social problems in the United States.

Alcohol, Tobacco, and Other Drug Abuse. The most recent Youth Risk Behavior Survey reveals alarming data about the percentage of students in Connecticut who, in the past month, have: drank alcohol = 47%; episodic heavy drinking = 28%; drank alcohol on school property = 7%; smoked cigarettes = 35%; smoked cigarettes on ≥ 20 days = 18%; smoked cigarettes on school property = 19%; used marijuana = 22%; used marijuana on school property = 8%.

Asthma. Asthma is the most common chronic illnesses of childhood, affecting an estimated 100,000 of the state's children under age 18. As a result, asthma is the leading cause of health-related school absenteeism. Nationwide, children with asthma miss an average 7.2 school days per year compared to 3.4 days per year for children without asthma. More locally, research from clinics and schools suggests that asthma affects 15% of Hartford's urban school-age children.

REQUEST FOR OPERATING SUPPORT

EXHIBIT 29

Obesity. Childhood obesity is a public health problem that has reached epidemic proportions. Obesity rates in the U.S. for children have doubled since 1990. In Connecticut, 1 in 5 children is obese or overweight; girls are at a greater risk than boys. Research indicates that obesity increases the risk of cardiovascular disease and diabetes, and may contribute to asthma. Due to state budget cuts, many schools are eliminating physical fitness and health education programs.

Sexual Behaviors. Despite recent improvements, too many high school students in Connecticut are still engaging in risky sexual behaviors. The Youth Risk Behavior Survey reveals that 44% of high school students have had sexual intercourse and 33% have had sexual intercourse in the past three months. Nearly half (45%) did not use a condom during their last sexual intercourse and almost three-fourths (72%) did not use birth control pills during their last sexual intercourse.

The Solution: Quality Health Education Programs

The Patrick Ignatius Center is dedicated exclusively to ensuring access to timely health education for young people. Our mission is to motivate students to recognize that their values, reflected in their attitudes and choices, determine the course and quality of their individual lives. During the last year, the center reached 175,000 students from 150 schools across the state. Since opening in 1973, nearly five million students have benefited from center programs.

Aided by highly sophisticated and visually stimulating exhibits, center programs utilize resources that no single school or school system can duplicate. Each of the basic programs at the center has its own rationale, instructional objectives, and balance of cognitive and affective components. Nevertheless all programs share a common underlying philosophy that is centered on preventive education. Research shows that the best way to address childhood health problems is through prevention. That's why instructional programming is always focused on helping students internalize targeted messages of personal responsibility and respect for the human body.

Outreach programs allow us to take health education messages into the community and deliver customized programs to students at their schools. Our innovative programs include:

1. **"What Takes Your Breath Away?"**—educates children, parents, and teachers about controlling asthma through trigger avoidance, taking medications, and frequent monitoring.
2. **"No Weigh!"**—employs a research-based design to promote healthy lifestyles among students by encouraging participation in lifetime fitness activities and nutrition habits.
3. **"High on Friends"**—uses trained peer leaders to education other students about the dangers of alcohol and drug abuse, and offers constructive alternatives to these unhealthy behaviors.
4. **"The Birds, the Bees, and Teens"**—is designed to help parents and teens be more open, honest, and comfortable when talking to each other about sex.

Center Capabilities: Measured Success

The Patrick Ignatius Center for Health Education specializes in presenting high-quality programs that are powerful, inspirational, and motivational. The center employs 18 staff who have a cumulative 200 years of experience in teaching general health, family living/sex education, and alcohol and drug abuse prevention. Outreach programs are regularly evaluated by center staff (administrators and instructors) and participants (students, parents, and teachers) to ensure that the information provided is accurate, timely, and in the best format possible.

- Students complete pre- and posttests during the program, and follow-up questionnaires 6 months later, which measure changes in knowledge, attitudes, and behaviors.
- Teachers and parents complete a written evaluation at the conclusion of the program rating the quality of the information presented, the instructors, and the exhibits and handouts.
- Instructors are evaluated quarterly on their teaching methods and ability to relate to students.
- Center administrators and instructors review programs on an annual basis to ensure that content is up-to-date, developmentally appropriate, culturally sensitive, timely, and engaging.

REQUEST FOR OPERATING SUPPORT

EXHIBIT 29 (Continued from page 72)

Based upon these criteria, the Patrick Ignatius Center for Health Education is viewed as "very effective" by the public and private school teachers who use the outreach service, with over 75% of program requests coming from repeat customers. In addition, Midwest University recently conducted an independent evaluation of the "What Takes Your Breath Away?" program. Their final report gives the center high marks for significantly increasing student knowledge and for an instructional approach that helps them retain this information long afterward.

Budget Request: $10,000

With the demonstrated concern that the Dominic Michael Foundation has shown for improving the health and quality of life of children, we respectfully request a contribution of $10,000 to support general program needs. Your funds will help the center to offer a variety of outreach programs to children, parents, and teachers, and to acquire new teaching resources and exhibits.

Although the center charges schools a modest $3.50 per child for providing health education programs, this fee does not cover the full cost of the outreach programs. The true cost per child is $6.35. However, the current state fiscal crisis has taken away the ability to pass on increased operating costs to the schools, teachers, and parents. This price sensitivity forces us to rely heavily on the generosity of donors. Thanks to the gifts of charitable contributors, the center is able to provide programs to school districts across the state in spite of rising program costs.

The total operating budget for the center this current year is $1,109,800. Revenue from program fees is projected to cover 35%, endowment income 23%, and charitable donations 42%. Because the center is frugally managed and expenditures are carefully planned, general operating support gifts, in reality, are scholarships for students to participate in health education programs. They are also a means to ensure the center's value to area schools, teachers, parents and children.

In making this $10,000 investment, the Dominic Michael Foundation will be supporting a cost-effective approach to the delivery of quality outreach health education programs and. at the same time, enable the center to make maximum progress toward fulfilling its mission. The outcome of this project will touch the lives of more than 175,000 students from 150 schools across the state, resulting in a five cent (5¢) investment in each child, or a cost of one cent (1¢) per hour of instruction. Please contact Mr. Jonathan Christopher, Outreach Director, to answer questions or provide additional information—phone: (860) 123-4567; e-mail: JChristopher@piche.org.

Sincerely,

Jessica Kwasny
President

P.S. Please come visit us and see this important project for yourself!

Enclosures: IRS Nonprofit Certification
          Current Officers and Board Members
          Audited Financial Statement

REQUEST FOR OPERATING SUPPORT

EXHIBIT 29 (Continued from page 73)

operating support. They recognized that few sponsors provide such funding. Their persuasive writing approach equated grant support to student scholarship support. On a per capita basis, student admission fees represented slightly more than one-half of total instructional costs. The full costs included, of course, such operating costs as instructor salaries and fringe benefits, facility costs, and so forth. The foundation "scholarship support" closed the gap between full operating costs and off-setting student admission fees.

Format. From a writing perspective, note the use of indented paragraphs as opposed to block paragraphing;

the extra white space provides the reader with a visual clue that a new thought is being advanced. The short paragraphs facilitate the skim reading style that many grant reviewers use.

PERFORMING ARTS REQUEST FOR PHYSICAL FACILITIES RENOVATION

Orienting Observations

Of the many different types of grants available, Exhibit 30 is a letter proposal submitted to a private foundation seeking challenge grant funds for a college to purchase equipment for a performing arts project. The college has already received partial funding for the project and is now attempting to use that money as a magnet to attract additional support.

While this letter proposal follows the general template presented in Chapter 5, it was modified to meet the few specific proposal submission requirements requested by the sponsor. The seven-step template is a guide, not a strait jacket.

Specific Comments

Content. This 1,212-word letter proposal from Norman College seeks funding to upgrade the physical facilities in the theater. Notice the persuasive writing

---

Today's Date

Mr. Brychan William, Director
Philanthropic Program: Cultural Heritage
American Arts Foundation
1 Rockefeller Center
New York, NY 10285-4804

Dear Mr. William:

Norman College, Vermont's only college to receive national recognition for character development in students, invites your investment of $50,000 in a special project to enrich performing arts experiences for the Northeastern Vermont community.

The American Arts Foundation has been an inspiration because of your long-standing commitment to art and culture. Indeed, in *Arts & Economic Prosperity*, Mary Beth Salerno, foundation president, said it best: "the arts are central to the economic growth and vitality of communities around the world. . . investing in the arts is good policy and good business." This request is a systematic extension of our mutual interest toward enriching the wider community.

Organization Information.	Norman College 100 Grant Street Witt, VT 05005
Contact Person.	Aidan Tyler, Director of Theatre Facilities Phone: 802-403-3124—Fax: 802-403-4081 E-mail: Aidan.Tyler@nc.edu
Funds Requested.	$50,000

Geographic Area Served. Norman College is a private liberal arts school that provides a superior education that is personally, intellectually, and spiritually challenging. Located in Witt, Vermont, 125 miles north of Boston, we enroll over 2,000 undergraduates in 33 majors and 100 graduate students in three master's programs. Over 70% of our students are from Vermont. Also of note, for 2013, we are ranked #4 among the top 10 best comprehensive colleges in the Northeast in *U.S. News & World Report's* guide to "America's Best Colleges."

REQUEST FOR PHYSICAL FACILITIES RENOVATION

EXHIBIT 30°

The College's Madison Theatre and Monroe Theatre host over 680 musicals, plays, concerts, practices, speeches, and rehearsals a year for the campus and Witt community. Last year, over 32,200 individuals attended ticketed events in these theatres. Nearly 45% of these patrons attended performances put on in collaboration with community partners such as the National Arts Program, Evergreen Productions, and the Dance Company. Compared to 10 major communities across the state, Witt ranks #2 in total nonprofit arts industry spending at $45.5 million in 2010. Only arts organizations and audiences in Dover spent more.

Project Description. The arts are essential and integral part of everyday life. They help us to better understand and interpret the world around us. They offer us the opportunity to communicate our most profound thoughts and deepest feelings. Or in the words of Robert L. Lynch, president and CEO, Americans for the Arts, the fundamental value of the arts is that "they foster beauty, creativity, originality, and vitality. The arts inspire us, sooth us, provoke us, involve us, and connect us . . . but they also create jobs and contribute to the economy."

Goals and Objectives. The **goal** of this project is to enhance performing arts experiences for the greater Witt community. Specific project objectives are:

Objective #1: To create a theatre environment that captivates community arts patrons.
Objective #2: To provide budding student performers and theatre technicians with quality training experiences using the latest tools and technology of their trade.

Beneficiaries. Direct beneficiaries include over 32,000 theatre patrons annually from Northeastern Vermont who attend performances in the Monroe and Madison Theaters. Indirect beneficiaries include the local businesses such as hotels, restaurants, and retail stores who profit from event-related spending by arts audiences. The *Arts & Economic Prosperity* report (2012) indicates that nationally arts attendees spend an average of $22.87 above the cost of admission.

Our Theatre Department is an important source for promoting the performing arts profession. Dozens of students are intimately involved in all aspects of producing shows: the acting, technical production, and community relations. Further, budding theatre technicians studying at the college learn their trade through experience with the latest tools and technology. These students work on scenery, props, lighting, and sound for the various productions, as well as work lights and sound for touring companies, nationally known speakers, and other events that occur in the two theatres. This lighting project will give students first-hand practice with the latest theater technologies, and teach them the skills necessary to visually enhance theater experiences.

Implementation Plan. To achieve the project goal and objectives, we will replace 180 antiquated 1,000-watt lighting fixtures with state-of-the-art 575-watt fixtures. Some of the existing fixtures are as old as the building—46 years. New fixtures are designed to be more effective and energy efficient, saving an estimated 176,342 kilowatts a year. Lighting systems will be installed in time for the Summer 2014 productions in the college's Madison and Monroe Theatres. These fixtures will provide the maximum viewing pleasure for spectators and superior light setting experiences for student performers and theatre technicians.

Expected Outcomes. Evaluation is essential for documenting project success. Aidan Tyler, director of Theatre Facilities, will monitor project activity and submit a progress report to the American Arts Foundation following its completion. We anticipate two key outcomes: (1) an increase in the total numbers of community patrons who attend theatre performances, and (2) an increase in student satisfaction with theatre training experiences.

Timeline. Project funding is necessary by June 1, 2014. Fixtures will be ordered from the Lighthouse, a Boston theatrical and stage lighting equipment wholesaler. Mr. Tyler will ensure that light fixtures will be installed within 10 days of delivery. The college anticipates the implementation of the project for its June 2014 musical comedy production of *I Do! I Do!* by Tom Jones and Harvey Schmidt and its July 2014 production of *Children of Eden* by score composer Stephen Schwartz. Your gift will enhance the visual appreciation of performing arts productions for over 32,000 theatre goers per year.

Project Budget. With the demonstrated concern your company has shown for enriching community arts experiences, we request a grant of $50,000. Funds will be used to purchase energy-efficient light fixtures that will enhance theatre

REQUEST FOR PHYSICAL FACILITIES RENOVATION

EXHIBIT 30 (Continued from page 75)

productions. This project represents a portion of a larger challenge grant from the Vermont Focus on Energy, which has already pledged $40,000 toward the total project cost of $150,000. To make up the remaining difference, we have targeted specific requests to other sponsors who support arts and culture projects. The specific budget request is as follows:

1. ETS Source 4 Ellispoidal Reflector Spotlights (152@296 each) = $45,4000
2. ETC Source 4 Panels (16 @ $178 each) = $ 2,900
3. ETC Source 4 PARS (12 @ $178 each) = $ 2,100

Total Requested $50,000

Evaluating Results. Norman College has established systems to track and measure project results. For example, from 2006 to 2011, the number of tickets sold for community-sponsored events increased from 9,900 to 14,500. At the conclusion of theater courses, students complete a standardized survey that evaluates the instructor, course content, and the learning experience. In addition, the "Norman College Graduating Student Follow-Up Survey" was recently enhanced to collect information about the value of internship experiences in preparing students for their first job out of school. Mr. Tyler will use information from these and other sources when reporting project progress and results to the American Arts Foundation.

Thank you for your consideration of our proposal. Your support for this one-time project will help to enhance performing arts experiences for hundreds of theater performers and student technicians, and thousands of community patrons in the greater Witt area. Please contact Aidan Tyler to answer questions or provide additional information.

Sincerely,

Mikael M. Victoria, PhD
President

P.S. Please come visit us and see—firsthand—how your support will make a difference!

REQUEST FOR PHYSICAL FACILITIES RENOVATION

EXHIBIT 30 (Continued from page 76)

approach that they took. They stressed the value of the performing arts—fostering beauty, creativity, and originality—and emphasized that theater patrons benefit from attractive performing environments. Norman College recognized a fundamental principle of grantseeking: people fund people, they don't fund things. Norman College wisely stressed the people benefits of their proposal and downplayed the benefits of improved physical facilities, which were only a means to the end of improved performances that patrons will appreciate. The fact that partial funding has already been secured also serves to enhance the credibility of the project.

Format. Finally, from a writing perspective, note the use of a serif font for the narrative (e.g., Times Roman, Garamond, Courier) and a sans serif typeface for headings (e.g., Arial, Gothic, Universal). Serif fonts are more readable than sans serif fonts. The use of a different font style for headings provides the reviewers with

another visual signal that they will be entering a new proposal section.

MINORITY YOUTH REQUEST FOR CAPITAL CAMPAIGN SUPPORT

Orienting Observations

Grant funding for operating support is difficult—but not impossible—to obtain. The same is true of capital campaign support. Usually capital campaigns for "bricks and mortar" are approached through such fundraising mechanisms as major gifts or planned giving. Nevertheless, occasions do arise where grants can help support the construction of new buildings, especially in those instances where a strong relationship exists between the sponsor and the applicant. Exhibit 31 contains an example of how one letter proposal was crafted to seek support for a new building that would provide services to inner-city minority youth and their families.

Current Date

Mr. John Calder, President
The Berger Corporation
P. O. Box 13390
Los Angeles, CA 92255–3390

Dear Mr. Calder:

Since 1996, Central City Mission (CCM) has provided educational activities and human services to the San Bernardino inner city. Over 55,000 children, youth, and adults of Latino, African American, Hispanic, and Caucasian cultures are the recipients of these services. Because of our shared values, CCM invites your investment in a $100,000 capital campaign project, the Empowerment Through Education (ETE) Center, that will reduce cultural barriers and increase cooperation, thereby empowering neighbors to become self-sustaining and melding into a community of hope.

We are encouraged that the Berger Corporation supports unique challenges in education, health, and culture. Your past support of teens (Haven House), Big Brothers and Sisters, pediatric AIDS, and Women's Work illustrate your concern for a broad spectrum of people and their needs. Equally important, your support sets a high standard of corporate social responsibility for the Greater Los Angeles area that we both serve. Our project presents a unique opportunity to corporations such as yours who have the vision and creativity to see the social benefits and value of building cultural diversity into a productive and contributing community. Education and training are the keys to the success of this project as CCM has already demonstrated. Wouldn't it be rewarding to know that the Berger Corporation has played a key role in this long-term effort to close a spiraling gap between need and resources?

The elements of the challenges and goals for this project follow.

The Problem: Mounting Educational Needs vs. Dwindling Resources

Education is the key to community empowerment. Our inner-city educational baseline falls significantly short of minimum acceptable standards. To illustrate:

- 90% of children are from families on some form of public assistance
- 70% of students suspended or expelled from San Bernardino schools live in this area
- 67% of students entering ninth grade fail to graduate from high school
- 73% of the high school graduates don't meet California university admission standards
- 36% of youth in CCM programs have been homeless at least once
- 24% of students are learning English for the first time but rely primarily on their native language

Clearly, the children and families in the CCM catchment area are the poorest, hardest to serve, and most underserved in San Bernardino, the eighth largest city in California. Few minority children, regardless of academic standing, are encouraged to apply for college admission by school counselors; most are pushed toward jobs and trade schools.

Two major consequences result from this lack of an empowered education community. First, it presents insurmountable barriers to attracting the resources essential for community development, especially service providers with a multicultural staff. Second, the community does not and cannot meet its serious responsibility to train individuals who will contribute to this ever-changing multicultural society. Bottom line: this lag in inner city educational support services pinpoints a critical and increasing problem that needs to be addressed creatively and immediately.

The Solution: Empowerment Through Education

Education constructively changes the course of marginalization and its destructive impact while empowering youth and their families to take control of their community. Education means positive growth that multiplies geometrically over time, resulting in family and community stability.

REQUEST FOR CAPITAL CAMPAIGN SUPPORT

EXHIBIT 31

Precisely, CCM's Empowerment Through Education (ETE) Center will promote literacy at all levels—child, youth, and adult—and provide life-changing opportunities through the following programs that are currently operational from early morning to mid-evening.

After School Program: Working with the San Bernardino Unified School District, neighborhood children and youth study and play on weekdays after school, tutoring, homework assistance, cultural interaction, and enrichment activities are heavily emphasized. As a result, tracking data show that 90% of children in this program advance in grade in the regular schools. Students receive much individual attention, especially those with special learning needs related to witnessing violence at an early age. Posttraumatic stress syndrome is increasingly evident. Addressing these problems head-on results in improved educational performance. At present, 100 children are enrolled.

- **Project Objective:** To increase enrollment by 100% in the next five years.
- **Project Outcome:** Significantly more children will experience school success, overcome the stresses of poverty and violence, and achieve at higher academic levels.

Power Teen Program: Teenagers from 13–15 years of age "learn and earn" by working with mentors while receiving a modest stipend. They support the Mission staff and Peer Educators in After School, Adolescent Health Care, and other programs. Experience shows that "peer learning" is often more effective than adult-based learning. This program targets neighborhood youth because they are most susceptible to enrollment in gangs. Our program provides significant time during alternative hours when schools are closed and parents are working. At present 27 Power Teens are actively involved in programs or in training.

- **Project Objective:** To increase the number of teen participants by 100% in the next five years.
- **Project Outcome:** The presence of Power Teens, as role models in the neighborhood, attracts other youth who are school delinquent or involved in gang activities. Additional Power Teens will expand this attraction effect and provide additional support to all programming.

Peer Educators Program: Young adults aged 16–21 are trained to assume leadership positions and direct programs with assistance from Power Teens. They earn a modest stipend. This program develops job readiness skills, encourages school completion, and provides role models for Power Teens. Active involvement in this program has shown that our youth have a lower interaction with the juvenile justice system, lower rates for STDs and teen pregnancy, and a higher level of school retention. At present there are 54 Peer Educators.

- **Project Objective:** To increase the number of Peer Educators by 100% in the next five years.
- **Project Outcome:** Peer Educators foster ambition and desire to grow among Power Teens as they work together in various programs. Additional Peer Educators will support the expanding education, health and intercultural programs that are currently in place and will develop in the ETE Center.

English as a Second Language: Nonnative English-speaking children, youth, and adults learn to function in an English language environment. The Mexican government, in an innovative initiative, provides satellite-based instruction to approximately 58 adults, many of whom have low literacy skills in their Spanish native language while dealing with the challenges of mastering English as a second language. Our English as a Second Language (ESL) teaching techniques focus on survival skills necessary to negotiate the education, health care, and work site systems.

- **Project Objective:** To expand the number of participants by 100% in the next five years.
- **Project Outcome:** Children and youth with improved English language skills will perform better in school. Adults with functional English language literacy will be more productive in the workforce, improve their ability to communicate with other social groups, and expand their leadership potential.

Capabilities

CCM's track record uniquely qualifies it to conduct and complete this project for two reasons. First, its trained staff represents over 150 years of cumulative experience in working with at-risk youth and families. Second, through its documented record of success, CCM has garnered the trust, respect, and confidence of community residents and local government officials. It has received national recognition from such philanthropic groups as the Robert Wood

Johnson Foundation. Its Board of Trustees fully endorses and actively participates in the projects in support of the executive director, his staff, and the youth and adults who have dedicated themselves to the success of the Mission and the control of their personal and family lives.

Budget Request: $100,000 Towards Building Construction Costs
The Berger Corporation has repeatedly recognized the importance of and has demonstrated its support for higher education. CCM's programs remind us that higher education rests on a foundation of accessible education at the preschool, elementary, and secondary levels. Significant numbers are deprived of these basic education opportunities because of social and environmental barriers they cannot control.

To close this gap, CCM is requesting $100,000 towards the construction of a 3,240 square foot building that costs $500,000 in total. The requested funds represent the cost of one 25 by 25 square foot room in the new Empowerment Through Education Center. Quite frankly, this budget extends well beyond the financial boundaries of CCM. Accordingly, we must reach out to the philanthropic community for this vital service: building a community of hope through education. While the requested funds will be pooled (but not co-mingled) with others being raised to construct the ETE Center, the physical facility embodies a means to the end of educationally empowering community residents.

This letter describes a set of needs and problems that have current and long-term solutions that contain the unanimous and unqualified endorsement of our Board of Directors. We are prepared to discuss further details, including the overall fundraising strategy, architectural drawings, and full documentation of the educational services to be provided. In making this investment, you will be supporting the ideas, dreams, and hopes for the future to perpetuate educational opportunities where many think none could exist.

Sincerely,

Rev. Calvin Key
Pastor/Executive Director

P.S. Come visit us and see for yourself the needs of the people we serve.

REQUEST FOR CAPITAL CAMPAIGN SUPPORT

EXHIBIT 31 (Continued from page 79)

Specific Comments

Content. Obviously, this 1,514-word letter proposal targets a corporation as opposed to a private foundation. The same seven-step template works for both types of private sponsors. With corporations, you must appeal to features that are profitable for them. This particular corporation placed great emphasis on "corporate social responsibility," a phrase that was repeated throughout their Web site. Corporations subscribe to the concept of "profitable philanthropy." What do you have to offer them in your next proposal? Happier employees? Healthier employees? An improved transportation or communication system? Better training for their future employees? A safer community? Your prospect research (Chapter 3) and preproposal contact information (Chapter 4) should indicate their business priorities, which you can reflect in your proposal. Finally, note that most of the sentences are written in the active voice, which is more persuasive than the passive voice (See Chapter 16).

Format. From a proposal writing perspective, set all of your margins (left, right, top, bottom) to one inch. The white space border helps frame your proposal much the same way amat border accentuates a framed oil painting.

DEVELOPMENTALLY DISABLED REQUEST FOR VOCATIONAL TRAINING SUPPORT

Orienting Observations

Many social service, welfare, and educational grant requests center on seeking support to provide training for target audiences. The following proposal(Exhibit 32) targets providing horticultural training for developmentally disabled adults to increase their employability. Because reviewers are apt to question whether this proposal will succeed, including a statement regarding a successful 12-month pilot project is particularly persuasive.

Today's Date

Mr. Cameron Nicholaus, President
Vocational Rehabilitation Foundation
123 Main Street
Denver, CO 80010

Dear Mr. Nicholaus:

Adult Rehabilitation Center (ARC), the only rehabilitation center for adults with developmental disabilities in Denver, invites your investment in a $10,000 vocational education project.

The Vocational Rehabilitation Foundation invests more than one-third of its contributions in social service projects for people with disabilities. Because of your unprecedented concern for the welfare of the developmentally disabled, we turn to Vocational Rehabilitation Foundation for its support to expand vocational training services for a special needs population.

The Problem: The Gap between Competence and Performance. One of people's great needs is the ability to achieve, and through achievement, experience psychological and financial growth. Developmentally disabled adults have limited aspirations and lost choices. Right now, only 15 percent of those capable of holding gainful employment have paying jobs. In specific terms, this means that the Greater Denver Area has over 1,200 unemployed developmentally disabled adults. The challenge for this special needs population is to identify important work environments where they can develop and nourish job skills.

People with disabilities can work independently in only a handful of job settings. As a result, they can seldom put their restricted talents to full use and rarely experience job satisfaction commensurate with their abilities. Since the number of developmentally disabled people is growing faster than the general population, the need for job training is escalating as more of them experience this competence-performance gap.

The Solution: Job Training in Plant Care. This project will close the competence-performance gap by training developmentally disabled adults in the care of plants and flowers. Two major factors justify this horticultural project. First, the results of our needs assessment document that over 75 greenhouse owners are willing to hire such people if they can work reliably. Second, a 12-month pilot project with six developmentally disabled adults demonstrated that with proper training, these individuals can and do achieve functional independence.

ARC has a greenhouse and a three-person groundskeeper crew to maintain the appearance of our 20-acre facility. The botanical expertise already resides at the center where the staff has a collective 79 years of greenhouse experience in such things as soil analysis, seeds, germination conditions, watering, fertilization, planting, and pruning.

Credential: Botany Expertise and Job Networks. This project naturally grows out of our philosophy of maximizing existing resources. The current greenhouse also represents a botanical learning laboratory, where special people can be trained in a nonthreatening environment. The staff has developed specific learning objectives for each

---

botany area. Administrators have secured agreements for tentative job placement sites as Attachment One shows. Accordingly, this project represents a systematic approach of ARC's prior efforts in "mainstreaming," by which we have transformed vision into success since 1904.

Budget Request: $10,000. With the demonstrated concern that the Vocational Rehabilitation Foundation has shown in this area, we are requesting a grant of $10,000. This represents an investment of $0.04 per hour in the 350 developmentally disabled adults over the next five years who will graduate from our three-month training program. The funds will be used to expand our worksites from five to 20 stations where our staff can provide essential job readiness skills. In making this investment the foundation will be supporting a cost-effective approach to the delivery of vocational training for the developmentally disabled. Such a grant will ensure the quality and regularity of the botany training program; more importantly, it will enrich many lives and, indirectly, create taxpayers, not tax takers.

Your support will make a critical difference, one that will last for years as job training services expand. Most of all, you will be investing in the ideas that will help exceptional people for decades. Please contact Mrs. Abby Scott, director of Development, at 915-555-1212 or Abby.Scott@arc.org to answer questions or provide additional information.

Sincerely,

Grace Hill
President

P.S. Come visit us and let Randy tell you about his flower garden.

Enclosures
Attachment One: Tentative Job Placement Sites
Attachment Two: Letters of Commitment from Potential Employers
Attachment Three: IRS Tax Exempt Certification

REQUEST FOR VOCATIONAL TRAINING SUPPORT

EXHIBIT 32 (Continued from page 81)

Specific Comments

Content. These 675 words present a succinct but persuasive appeal for project support. Note the use of Attachments One and Two to strengthen proposal credibility by showing that the marketplace is ready to hire trained, developmentally disabled adults.

Format. From a writing perspective, use 12-point type size; it is easily readable, and increasingly sponsors stipulate 12-point text as a minimum requirement.

SENIOR CITIZEN REQUEST FOR COORDINATION OF SERVICE DELIVERY

Orienting Observations

While many proposals seek money to provide education or training, as noted in Exhibit 33, a number of proposals concentrate on service delivery. These service delivery proposals may entail providing new services for existing markets, offering new services for new markets, entering new markets with existing services, increasing current market penetration, providing excess capacity to others, entering coalitions, using personnel more efficiently, or coordinating the delivery of multiple services, which is the topic of the following letter proposal.

Specific Comments

Content. This 937-word letter proposal is organized, contains essential information, and is highly readable. Note the judicious use of statistics in the problem statement to document the need for this project.

Format. Note in particular the use of headings and the boldface sentences at the end of key paragraphs. The use of bolding for text emphasis is more readable than other comparable techniques such as the use of

Today's Date

Mr. Gray American, President
Senior Foundation
123 Any Street
Memphis, TN 40239

Dear Mr. American:

The Roxbury Elder Institute, the largest hospital-based senior service system in Memphis, invites your investment in a $250,000 special project to centralize 50 elderly services.

We are encouraged that the Senior Foundation supports innovative projects that improve the delivery of elderly services. Over 69 percent of your grant dollars the past three years have been invested at the local community level. Clearly, your support fills a valuable niche in light of the more conservative and traditional federal government funding. This strong commitment to unique projects is shared by our 35 professional staff members at Roxbury who have a cumulative 348 years of service to the elderly.

The Problem: Fragmented Services and Multiple Vendors. In five years, a population tsunami of "Baby Boomers" will enter the ranks of the elderly. The latest statistics available indicate the older population—persons age 65 or older—numbered 36.3 million in 2010 (Administration on Aging, 2010). In 2000, people ages 65+ represented 12.4% (about one in every eight Americans) of the population but are expected to grow to be 20% of the population by 2030, where there will be about 71.5 million older persons, more than twice their number in 2000. Further, the Census Bureau data projects a notable increase in the "oldest old" population, persons 85 and older. Specifically, this population will double between 2000 and 2030; it will quadruple between 2000 and 2050. (U.S. Census Bureau, 2010) Over one-half of those aged 85 and older are impaired and require long-term care (American Association of Homes and Services for the Aging, 2011). **More people are living longer, require more intensive care, and consume major health care resources.**

According to the National Center for Health Statistics, 40 percent of the elderly currently use one or more community health services. The most commonly used services were those provided outside the home rather than in the home. The most widely used service was senior center, then congregate meals, followed by special transportation. **While many elderly patients now see several health care providers, their numbers will increase, especially among women, those with limited education, and minorities.**

Beyond visits to family practice physicians, internists, cardiologists, and oncologists, the elderly experience a growing need for information and referral, legal assistance, counseling, housing and employment services, outpatient rehabilitation and physical therapy, case management, and social and recreational activities. **Gaining access to these specialists involves many trips to different locations.**

The Solution: One-Stop Shopping and a Few Vendors. Current research verifies that the elderly prefer "one-stop shopping" and dealing with only a few vendors. Specifically, about two-thirds prefer purchasing additional products or services from the same vendor rather than dealing with different ones. The goal of this project is to consolidate a broad range of deliverables designed to meet the needs of older adults and their caregivers. The specific objective is to centralize 75% of the elderly healthcare and related services in Memphis under one source within the next three years.

With the full endorsement of the three major area hospitals and the Shelby County Medical Society, one centralized call center will be established and a uniform electronic records system will be implemented that links participating providers. This health information technology approach will improve the coordination of service delivery, as the Institute of Medicine has noted (2010). The delivery of these services will be characterized by consistency of quality, accessibility, and single-source reliability. The composition and utilization of these services will be determined by the needs of the individual. The consumer is advised on the best utilization of the services as a result of an intake

REQUEST FOR COORDINATION OF SERVICE DELIVERY

EXHIBIT 33

evaluation and needs assessment. The program offers flexibility to select from a menu of services. **By establishing a centralized referral system that takes full advantage of available health information technologies, Shelby County will be prepared to cope with the coming Population Explosion among persons age 65 and older.**

Roxbury Elder Institute Credentials: Senior Service Experiences. The Roxbury Elder Institute is uniquely positioned to develop an integrated system of medical and nonhealth services. The institute was established six years ago with its goal to provide quality health, education, and research services. As a result, it has established a full range of services in response to the seniors' needs. During this time, positive working relationships have been established with all sectors in the Shelby County health care community. These working relations will provide entrees to develop the nonmedical component. **This project represents a systematic continuation of prior efforts to establish a diversified continuum of services and the vision to reallocate existing resources to meet the needs of the elderly.**

Budget Request: $250,000 payable over three years. With the demonstrated concern that you have shown in the delivery of senior services, I am requesting a grant in the amount of $250,000, payable in thirds over three years. Quite frankly, this project extends beyond the financial boundaries of the Roxbury Elder Institute. Accordingly, we must now reach out to the community for assistance in what surely is a vital service to seniors. In making this investment, the Senior Foundation will be supporting a cost-effective, client-sensitive service that will address major access problems. More precisely, our 50,000 senior citizens average 10 health-related visits per year; **your support represents an investment of 5¢ per patient visit.**

Ms. Beatrice J. Hiccock, administrative director of the Roxbury Elder Institute, can be reached at 615-456-7890 to answer questions or give further information.

Sincerely,

Shandel Lear
President

P.S. I can't stress enough how much your support will improve the quality of life for our senior citizens.

REQUEST FOR COORDINATION OF SERVICE DELIVERY

EXHIBIT 33 (Continued from page 83)

underlining, italics, or all capital letters. These persuasive writing techniques facilitate skim reading on the part of the reviewers. From a writing perspective, don't try to write perfect copy initially. Remember the grant writing maxim: the first draft is for getting down, not getting good. You get the proposal "good" through subsequent editing: Chapter 16.

YOUTH MENTORING REQUEST FOR CONTINUING PROJECT SUPPORT

Orienting Observations

The following letter proposal seeks funding support to continue a youth mentoring project. The sponsor who funded the pilot year of the initiative made it clear that funding was for one year only. As a result, this request approaches a new sponsor. The narrative strikes a delicate balance, leveraging the credibility of having received funding from the previous sponsor and emphasizing the need for additional funding to realize project benefits with a new cohort of youth.

Specific Comments

Content. This 982-word letter proposal makes appeals to the private foundation through logic and emotion. Logically, the statistics show that the applicant knows its target audiences of college students and youth; the specific activities and identified student leaders demonstrate that a workable plan is in place; and prior funding from a recognized sponsor highlights institutional credibility. Emotionally, the project title appeals to the passion of sports; the problem statement tugs at the heartstrings—the unjustness of at-risk kids having no one to go home to after school and the quotable quote from the student coordinator cement the humanistic results of the project. Preproposal contact

Today's Date

Alex Zimmerman
Youth Development Foundation
500 Farnham Street
Bozeman, MT 59715

Dear Mr. Zimmerman:

Foxtrot College (FC), Montana's most selective public institution of higher education, invites your investment of $6,250 to provide positive role models to disadvantaged youth.

Using sports training as a springboard for building life skills, "Love of Learning & Sports" will enable college student-athletes to reach out to underserved and minority children at the Boys and Girls Club of Helena. Foxtrot College's "Love of Learning & Sports" program received acclaim from the National Athletics Foundation in September 2012 when it was selected as one of 23 pilot projects to be funded in a national competition.

Children in need served by college student role models

The Boys and Girls Club of Helena and Foxtrot College initiated the "Love of Learning & Sports" partnership in 2010. After considering a number of schools and child services agencies with a high percentage of minorities, FC partnered with the Boys and Girls Club because of their superior organization and strong ties to the local public school district. During the "Love of Learning & Sports" program 250 different children from the Boys and Girls Club will interact with 125 FC male and female college student-athletes from eight different FC sports teams.

Problems addressed and results achieved

Problems: Every day, hundreds of area children arrive home from school to an empty house; every week hundreds of parents make decisions to leave children home alone while they go to work, run errands, or attend social engagements. These young boys and girls are too often left to find their own recreation and companionship in the streets. It is during this unsupervised time when youth can get into trouble: alcohol and drug use, gang involvement, and other delinquent behavior. Children need positive role models who will help them to make responsible choices and develop life skills.

Many of the youth at the Boys and Girls Club of Helena are considered to be at-risk. The Boys and Girls Club serves over 1,000 children ages 9 to 14 years from six elementary and middle schools in Helena. More than 58% of the children are minorities. Nearly 68% of the children in the After School Adventure Program are eligible for free or reduced price lunches. Of all children registered at the Boys and Girls Club, 65% are from single parent households; few of the children have family members who can demonstrate the advantages of a college degree.

Results: "These kids are in need of a role model, a leader or just someone to listen to them."

—Bobby Hall, student co-coordinator of 2012 Love of Learning & Sports program

Sports are an inroad to introducing children to caring and understanding young adults. A national survey recently confirmed that middle and high school students look to athletes to get their messages on life. It is no wonder that athletes make ideal role models; they symbolize that dedication, confidence, hard work, and teamwork can bring success.

Love of Learning & Sports is a long-term commitment strategically scheduled over the course of the entire school year. College student-athletes participate in a variety of interactive activities with the boys and girls, including:

- Teaching the skills of their respective sports
- Organizing and participating in sporting tournaments with the children

REQUEST FOR CONTINUATION OF PROJECT SUPPORT

EXHIBIT 34

- Providing a listening ear as a "big brother" or "big sister"
- Hosting the children at four intercollegiate sporting events during the school year

For this project, 125 Foxtrot College student-athletes will engage 250 different children from the Boys and Girls Club. During the academic year, student-athletes from eight different FC teams will visit the club for sports skills training and conversation. Members of each team (e.g., football, baseball, basketball, volleyball, gymnastics, hockey, track, and cross country) will visit with the children for 12 straight weeks each semester. Boys and Girls Club program director Luisa Oliver notes that student-athletes offer "star power" that other volunteers simply cannot provide. These athletes are stars because of their commitment to service *and* the tournament appearances and championships that they have achieved.

The relationship between the boys and girls and the student-athletes also addresses the need for at-risk youth to learn that they too can succeed in school and life. Discipline, teamwork, respect, and self-confidence are skills that apply equally to social, athletic, and academic pursuits. College students are powerful role models to children from first-generation college families. Through this program, children realize that a quality college education is within their reach.

Administrative responsibility

Foxtrot College helps instill the value of community service and student leadership among its students. Surveys indicate that more than 83% of the student body are involved in some form of community service during their academic careers. Love of Learning & Sports will be administered following a successful model from its pilot year. In particular, student coordinators will be responsible for recruiting current student-athletes to volunteer at the Boys and Girls Club, arranging the Love of Learning & Sports schedule and activities, and evaluating the program.

In 2013–14, Love of Learning & Sports will be led by student coordinators Liam Curdy and Gillian Way. Mr. Curdy will coordinate in the fall semester and Ms. Way will coordinate in the spring semester. Mr. Curdy is a FC junior majoring in economics. He is a catcher on the baseball team and lettered in his first two years. Ms. Way is a FC junior majoring in Spanish and star on the volleyball team and in two honor societies. Both student-athletes have extensive experience leading student service projects.

Thank you for your consideration. I am also enclosing a letter of support for Love of Learning & Sports from Luisa Oliver, program director of Boys and Girls Club of Helena. Please contact me directly with questions: 212-363-4994; Ramsey.Griffith@fc.edu.

We look forward to working with you to serve the needs of at-risk children in Helena.

Sincerely,

Ramsey Griffith III
Executive Director

REQUEST FOR CONTINUATION OF PROJECT SUPPORT

EXHIBIT 34 (Continued from page 85)

with the program officer revealed that this dual appeal of logic and emotion in the narrative would be key to funding success.

Format. To call extra attention to the student quote, it was presented on a line by itself. A one-line quote, when surrounded by four- to six-sentence paragraphs, stands out immediately.

LETTER PROPOSAL USE WITH EXISTING SPONSOR GUIDELINES

So far, this chapter has focused on how to write a letter proposal to private foundations and corporations who **do not** have particular guidelines to follow. And that is the case for most—but not all—of them. This chapter now concludes with strategies for writing proposals to sponsors when they **do** have submission guidelines to be followed.

A growing number of foundations use what is called a "common application form," a phrase that can be used in your favorite search engine to find current examples used in larger cities (e.g., the Association of Baltimore Area Grantmakers—www.abagrantmakers.org), states (e.g., the Minnesota Council on Foundations—www.mcf.org), and regions (e.g., Philanthropy Northwest—www.philanthropynw.org). The common application form typically includes a cover letter, participating funders list, cover sheet, narrative instructions, attachments list, and budget page.

Whether the sponsor requires use of a common application form or has a unique one, you can adapt the letter proposal format described above to serve as a transmittal letter. Sometimes, a sponsor's guidelines may be constraining, not letting you present all of the information you think reviewers need to know. Accordingly, the transmittal letter approach enables you to supplement the sponsor's guidelines with additional important information.

Orienting Observations

Exhibit 35 is an example of a letter proposal adapted for use as a transmittal letter. In this situation, the applicant, a local fire department, was seeking funding to improve their services to the frail minority elderly in their community. The grant development team at the fire station found the application form somewhat limiting, not letting them tell their full "story." They decided to adapt the letter proposal template and use it as a transmittal letter, enabling them to highlight key proposal content and actually include a few summary statements that were not requested in the constraining application guidelines.

Today's Date

Federal Emergency Management Agency
USFA Grant Program Technical Assistance Center
16825 South Seton Avenue
Emmitsburg, MD 21727-8898

RE: FIRE Grant Proposal
Northshore (WI) Fire District

Dear Colleague:

Northshore Fire District, Milwaukee's suburban community with the greatest population density, invites your investment of $50,000 in a fire prevention project for the frail minority elderly that will save lives—and lifetimes.

Enclosed you will find the required original and two copies of our proposal, entitled PROJECT FIRE. As you review specific details in the accompanying proposal, you will note in particular the following:

- The frail minority elderly represents the most rapidly growing—and most at-risk—segment of our community population.
- The existing firefight staff had had limited experience in interacting with the target population and their special needs.
- A growing need exists for a culturally sensitive fire prevention program that will decrease exposure of the minority elderly to fire hazards while, at the same time, increase their fire safety.

Accordingly, this proposal offers dual benefits to: (1) firefighters, through customized training and access to essential resources; and, (2) citizens, through installing and training in fire detection devices.

The proposed program is decidedly cost beneficial to firefighters and the community alike. All direct firefighters will participate in PROJECT FIRE at a nominal opportunity cost, while 1,000 citizens will benefit at a nominal cost, amortized over a five-year product life.

LETTER PROPOSAL ADAPTED AS TRANSMITTAL LETTER

EXHIBIT 35

NFD is uniquely postured to conduct this project, which is similar to an early project targeting at-risk youth, a project recognized by the governor of Wisconsin as a "model youth fire safety project." However, given the population size at risk among the frail minority elder, this proposed project simply extends beyond the financial boundaries of the community. For this reason, we reach out to FEMA in providing essential services to a worthy, deserving, and needy population.

Sincerely,

Matt Hazard,
NFD Fire Chief

LETTER PROPOSAL ADAPTED AS TRANSMITTAL LETTER

EXHIBIT 35 (Continued from page 87)

Specific Comments

Content. Experienced grant writers consider application guidelines as merely guides, not as limitations. While you want to respond to all of the requested information, include additional information you feel essential, even if it is not requested. Frankly, some grant guidelines are not well conceived.

Format. A writing challenge arises when you have to put 10 pounds of information in a one-pound package. The solution to squeezing a lot of information in a limited space? Rely on priorities learned from your pre-proposal contacts and apply your best editorial writing skills, as evidenced in this 313-word version.

LETTER PROPOSAL AS A CONCEPT PAPER FOR FEDERAL GOVERNMENT GRANTS

Orienting Observations

Our final application of the letter proposal template concerns its use with federal government grants. Most government proposals are lengthy and require substantial time and effort in their development. Exhibit 36 shows how the letter proposal template can be modified and used as a concept paper to seek preliminary proposal feedback before developing a full-length proposal.

Specific Comments

Content. Exhibit 36 uses the 639 words in this letter proposal template as an economical trial balloon to see whether your idea merits the substantial energies required to write a full-length federal government proposal.

Format. The persuasive writing challenge is to present enough information so the program officer can see whether your idea has merit, but avoid getting bogged down in lengthy details. The solution is to concentrate on the statement of the need, the rationale for conducting this project. If program officers think you have identified a significant problem, then they are apt to encourage submission of a full-length proposal, recognizing that methodological details will be forthcoming in the expanded version. On the other hand, if your proposal idea does not match with program priorities, you have saved valuable time by seeking a different sponsor to support your project. Experience shows that most program officers are willing to review a concept paper—also called a "White Paper" in some mission-oriented agencies—when given sufficient lead time, say, two months before the proposal deadline.

 ### Clip File Action Item # 10
Letter Proposals

Start your Letter Proposals clip file by doing the following.

- Select two letter proposals from this chapter and create electronic copies as models.
- Add an electronic copy of a letter proposal used as a transmittal letter (Exhibit 35).
- Reexamine all of the letter proposal examples and notice that each one contains a different P.S. statement. Psychologically, many people read the salutation, signature, and P.S. statement in a letter before reading its body. The P.S. helps establish a positive mindset as the reader studies your letter. Make a list of P.S. statements to include in your clip file. Use these as a starting point.

RERC Concept Paper

Today's Date

Dr. Melissa Moyer, Program Officer
Rehabilitation Engineering Research Centers
Rehabilitations Services Administration
U.S. Department of Education
400 Maryland, SW
Washington, DC 20202

Dear Dr. Moyer:

This brief letter presents our current concept of an interinstitution, interdisciplinary proposal to create a Rehabilitation Engineering Research Center for Low Vision and Blindness and invites your candid feedback.

Overview: The National Association of Rehabilitation Engineers (NARE), the world's largest organization of engineers serving persons who are blind or visually impaired, seeks $4,950,000 over five year years to launch a Consumer-Based Rehabilitation Engineering Research Center for Low Vision and Blindness. A virtual center binds eight academic collaborators from Massachusetts Institute of Technology, University of Virginia, Florida State University, University of Wisconsin–Eau Claire, Oklahoma State University, Michigan State University, University of Iowa, City College of Los Angeles; two commercial firms: Sensory Technologies, Inc. and Vision Enhancement Systems, Inc.; and our nonprofit organization: NARE.

Need: Persons who are blind or visually impaired face substantial barriers when accessing information or moving about the environment. More precisely, they encounter major barriers when attempting to identify and evaluate the following:

    Visual Displays. The exploding array of consumer electronics exacerbates the challenges the blind face to fully participate in all aspects of society. New technologies can erect information access barriers. At present, technology and marketplace considerations limit options for the blind.

    Graphical User Interfaces. Attempts to master graphic information result in early frustration for young blind learners and limited career aspirations for blind adults seeking gainful employment. Assistive technology developers must follow universal design standards and conventions for interoperability. Many constraining factors impede graphical user interfaces for the blind.

    Signage. Currently three major technologies have been used to reduce access barriers to signage information: infrared technology, radio frequency identification technology, and global positioning satellite technology. Infrared technology applications are limited and only work best in controlled environmental settings. RFID tags have multiple advantages, although human applications remain underdeveloped. GPS systems need further refinement to be of value as blind persons move about metropolitan areas. These barriers must be reduced from the perspective of the consumers who represent the litmus test of user satisfaction.

Hypotheses/Questions: Eight specific research and development projects cluster into three thematic areas: visual displays, graphical user interface systems, and signage. Each project has specific research hypotheses or questions as well as outcomes indicating what will be different at the end of the project period.

Methods: To address the three primary project areas, eight different research/development teams will concentrate on the following topics: developing accessible environmental systems; a nanobiotechnology approach to a dynamic tactile tablet; Web annotation software; alternative graphical display, RFID tags, sign location and recognition technology; low vision enhancement solutions; and multimodal I/O systems.

Training/Dissemination: Multiple training and dissemination strategies include an Online Campus linked to the NARE network, poster sessions, Web sites, conferences, demonstrations, site visits, Web casts, teleconferences,

LETTER PROPOSAL ADAPTED AS CONCEPT PAPER

EXHIBIT 36

consumer summaries, journal articles, press releases, and conference papers—targeted to consumers, vocational rehabilitation professionals, university professors and students, and clinicians.

Evaluation: Throughout the project period, formative and summative evaluations will be conducted by internal and external evaluators. The project director and eight project PIs will conduct internal evaluations using their measurable objectives and timelines as benchmarks. Additionally, two external evaluator consultants will independently assess (1) the R&D projects, and (2) the training activities and the overall center functioning.

Outcomes: The project outcomes go beyond reducing barriers in the three priority areas. More importantly, they expedite the transfer of technology from the research laboratory to the marketplace, technologies that are driven by broad-based consumer demands.

Dr. Moyer, thanks for taking the time to see if this concept paper matches with your program priorities. I'll call you in 10 days to learn your feedback.

Sincerely,

Otto Jaskolski, PhD
Executive Director

P.S. We share your continued commitment to serving people with special needs.

LETTER PROPOSAL ADAPTED AS CONCEPT PAPER

EXHIBIT 36 (Continued From Page 89)

PART III
Writing Government Proposals

OVERVIEW OF PART III

A complete government proposal usually requires substantial detail; most include nine basic proposal elements shown in the table below. The elements are listed twice: once in the sequence that proposal reviewers typically read them and once in the sequence that proposal writers usually write them; in other words, the sequence that one follows to write a proposal is not the same as the order reviewers follow when reading a proposal.

The reviewer column shows the way in which most proposals are assembled for mailing and reviewed by specialists; the writer column shows the progression followed when authoring a government proposal. For example, to begin writing your proposal, start with the need section first.

In contrast to proposals to private sponsors, which typically involve two to five pages, a complete government proposal to a local, state, or federal agency may range from 10 double-spaced pages to 100+ single-spaced pages. Some government agencies and programs use a two-tier application process; that is, they initially require a letter of intent (Chapter 5) or short proposal before accepting a full proposal. Sponsors may request a letter of intent when they want to know in advance how many full proposals to expect. Or, sponsors may use short proposals as a screening device: only a select number of applicants with projects of the greatest interest are invited to submit a longer and more detailed proposal. This is the case for some programs in the Directorate for Biological Sciences at the National Science Foundation: a required four-page preliminary proposal is used to identify a limited pool of applicants who will be encouraged to submit a 15-page full proposal.

Part III discusses each proposal element, and its following components:

- Purpose of the proposal section
- Key questions to answer about your proposal narrative
- Examples from successful grant proposals
- Writing tips to consider as you begin writing
- Rejection reasons from actual proposals that were declined
- Grant gaffes: annotated examples of proposal sections that invited reviewer rejection
- Starter sentences to stimulate your writing

Some public proposals do not require all nine elements, so you should follow your grant guidelines. Finally, successful grant writers sometimes include valuable information, even if it was not requested. For example, if no dissemination discussion is requested, include it in your methods section. If no needs statement is required, include it when you introduce your agency's mission. If no sustainability plan is called for, include it in your budget narrative.

Proposal Reviewer Sequence	Proposal Writer Sequence
Abstract	Problem Statement (Chapter 7)
Problem Statement	Goals, Objectives, Outcomes (Chapter 8)
Goals, Objectives, Outcomes	Methods (Chapter 9)
Methods	Evaluation (Chapter 10)
Evaluation	Dissemination (Chapter 11)
Dissemination	Budget (Chapter 12)
Budget	Sustainability (Chapter 13)
Sustainability	Appendixes (Chapter 14)
Appendixes	Abstract (Chapter 15)

CHAPTER 7
Problem Statement

A problem is a chance for you to do your best.
—*Duke Ellington*

PURPOSE OF THE PROBLEM STATEMENT

To Duke Ellington, a problem was music to his ears. For grantmakers, a problem statement answers one primary question: "Why do this project?" The emphasis is on the "why." To answer this question, grant writers must (1) define the problem and (2) document its existence. In Chapter 7, you will learn the following:

- Importance of the needs section.
- Framing the need in terms of sponsor values.
- Strategies to quantify the need in education, training, equipment, outreach, and service delivery grants.
- Techniques for justifying the need for conducting basic science research projects.
- Sources for accessing scholarly literature and needs data.

Effective grants produce change. Your problem statement describes precisely and persuasively why change is necessary.

DEFINING THE PROBLEM

Beginning grant writers typically make three mistakes in defining their grant problems. They may define it from their perspectives, not the sponsors'; they may—in reality—end up describing opportunities and not needs; or they may define their project using circular logic. Each grant writing error is discussed below.

When we ask beginning grantseekers why they want a grant, typical answers include the following:

- "We lack sufficient resources to serve our frail elderly population."

- "Our agency needs sufficient operating support to meet our growing client demands."
- "We want a new roof for our building."

Unfortunately, these problem statements all share one common difficulty: they are written from the perspective of the applicant, not the sponsor.

Experienced grant writers avoid the self-focus and instead concentrate on the sponsor's needs when writing this proposal section. Why? Because seasoned grant writers recognize that sponsors won't fund you because you have a need; rather, sponsors will fund you because you can be a change agent to solve a problem they consider important. Grantmakers award grants when you enable them to do something about a major problem or issue that makes a positive difference. **Sponsors fund their needs, not yours.**

Let's take a closer look at the difference between your needs and the sponsors. In Exhibit 37, the first column lists a few of the reasons why applicants write grants. The second column lists major reasons why grants fulfill sponsor needs. The two columns are quite different. Proposal writers who base their problem statement on the first column items severely limit their likelihood of getting funded. A more successful approach would be to frame your problem statement from the perspective of the sponsor. When sponsors see you share their "values glasses," you increase your likelihood of getting funded.

A second mistake of beginning grant writers is to describe an opportunity instead of a need. They reason, "Our organization doesn't really have a need. We see grants as an opportunity to expand our outreach into the community, to do more and better things." Such a perspective fails to recognize that sponsors focus on their concerns, not yours. To sponsors, your wants and

Applicant Needs	Sponsor Needs
• Ensure operating support	• Solve a societal need
• Expand services	• Fulfill existing mission
• Acquire new training materials	• Acquire new knowledge
• Make capital improvements	• Apply existing knowledge
• Purchase new technology	• Improve the community
• Obtain endowment funding	• Benefit from tax write-offs
• Support existing programs	• Increase name recognition
• Meet payroll costs	• Ensure a big bang for the buck
• Market services	• Help people
• Acquire new physical space	• Fill a gap in community services
• Run a conference	• Improve public image
• Conduct research	• Avoid loss
• Sustain operations	• Develop new products, systems

COMPARISON OF APPLICANT AND SPONSOR NEEDS

EXHIBIT 37

needs are opportunities; sponsors award funds to solve the societal needs that they see. Sponsors fund you when they believe that your project will help them solve their need to close gaps in society. Funding you helps them fulfill their mission. Said differently, there are no solutions to opportunities. When you write your next proposal, be sure you present the sponsor with a problem, not an opportunity. **Sponsors fund needs, not opportunities.**

As a third writing pitfall, grantseekers often use circular proposal logic. To illustrate, grant proposals may seek support for new equipment, e.g., computers or highly technical research instruments. The proposal logic often argues as follows:

> The problem is that our institution lacks (and therefore needs) some new computer equipment. The objective of our proposal is to acquire the computer equipment. Our implementation strategy is to plan to acquire the equipment and put it to good use. Our evaluation plan will be to find out if we acquired and used the equipment.

This example used circular logic to form its problem statement; no real need was established first, the starting point for proposals. A much stronger approach would have been as follows:

> The problem is that our students' failure rate is too high in five key courses. Our objective is to decrease the failure rate from 40 percent to 30 percent in

the next three years. Our implementation strategy, chosen from among many, is to acquire some new computer equipment. Our evaluation plan will focus on our implementation plan execution to see whether the failure rate decreases.

The lack of something does not justify acquisition: that's circular logic. Note the revised example quantifies a problem, thereby creating a need that can be addressed in other proposal sections.

In sum, your problem statement should quickly summarize the problem from the vantage point of the sponsor as revealed through your preproposal contacts (Chapter 4), document its frequency and severity, show your familiarity with prior research or work on the problem, reinforce your credibility for investigating the problem, and justify why this problem should be investigated. Do not assume that everyone sees the problem as clearly as you do. Even if the problem is obvious, your reviewers want to know how clearly you can state it.

DOCUMENTING THE PROBLEM

By definition, a problem is a gap, a discrepancy between the way things are and the way things ought to be. To persuade proposal reviewers that you have identified a significant problem, you must present two data points or lines that are separated by a gap. Suppose, for example, that you are a high school principal who wants to increase the number of students who are prepared to succeed in postsecondary education. What, then, are your two data points?

- **Data Line A**: The increasing number of students who score at minimal and basic levels on state proficiency tests from 8th to 10th to 12th grade in mathematics and reading.

  As educators, you recognize that students must have a solid foundation of academic knowledge in reading, writing, and arithmetic to enter postsecondary education programs and to prosper in a global economy.

- **Data Line B**: The limited use of technological tools in classrooms to engage learners and differentiate instruction.

  Interactive white boards, student response systems, and mobile devices hold the potential to significantly transform student learning. Teachers, however, must have regular access to technology, training in its use, and protected time for integrating it effectively into updated lesson plans designed to achieve student learning outcomes.

Your proposal narrative could document the following:

- The frequency of the problem: what is the number and percentage of students who are scoring at minimal and basic levels on state proficiency tests? Have an increasing number and percentage of students been underperforming over time? To what extent are students from low-income and minority backgrounds even more disadvantaged? Are teacher complaints of lack of access to and training on technology growing? Is teacher use of technology in the classroom on the decline because it is not supported or it is in disrepair?

- The severity of the problem: have the gaps in mathematics and reading scores from 8th to 10th to 12th grade been growing larger over time? Have mathematics and reading scores been in decline when compared to neighboring districts? Have mathematics and reading scores been diverging in a negative direction from state average scores? Have teachers given up on using technology because of limited time and support for curricular redesigns? Has instructional time been adversely affected due to ineffective use of technology?

- The consequences of not addressing the problem: Is a culture of lost hopes and limited aspirations becoming the norm for students? Are parents becoming disenchanted with the quality of instruction provided at the school? Have the top performing teachers been leaving the school to find employment in other districts with greater access to resources? Is the school on the path to being labeled as a persistently low-achieving school? Are employers in the community unable to fill entry-level job vacancies due to lack of qualified applicants?

Visually, you could graph your statement of the problem to show how the gap is widening over time, as Exhibit 38 indicates.

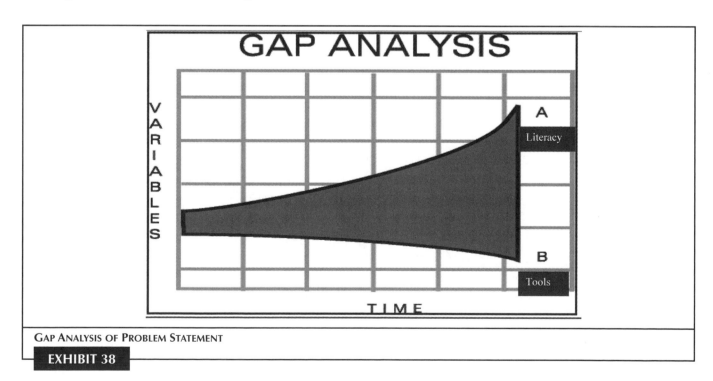

GAP ANALYSIS OF PROBLEM STATEMENT

EXHIBIT 38

Your gap analysis tells your sponsor that the number of low test scores is on the rise while the use of technological tools to engage students has been declining over time.

As you write your next proposal, conduct your gap analysis. What is your A Line and your B Line? Consider the following brief problem statements that could be graphed as shown in Exhibit 39.

The A/B gaps may exist for multiple reasons. Possibly stakeholders are unaware that the problem exists, that it doesn't appear on the "radar" screen of many people. Perhaps stakeholders are aware of the problem but unable to do anything about it because they lack the human, fiscal, or physical resources necessary to solve it. Perhaps stakeholders know about the problem and are able to solve it but are unwilling to do so because of attitudes or beliefs that they hold. Your gap discussions can address the reasons why you think they exist.

As you write your need section, what are your A and B lines? If you don't have well-defined answers, then you need more conceptual clarity before you start writing. Reviewing the preproposal contact questions in Chapter 4 may help you defuzzify your problem statement.

Finally, you should regard the problem statement as *the* single most important section of your proposal that influences funding success. It tells reviewers that the applicant organization has done its homework, establishes the thesis, and presents credible, current, and appropriate evidence to support both the need and the organization's proposed solution. It's a "teaching tool" for reviewers that prefaces everything else in the proposal.

The statement of the problem is so important in proposals that it should be stressed regardless of the point value assigned to it in the reviewer's evaluation form. That is, the need section may or may not receive the highest point total, based on the reviewer's evaluation form. Nevertheless, *you* should consider it as the most important proposal section, since it will weigh most heavily in the minds of reviewers.

Problem Statements for Scholarly Research

The problem statement, as discussed so far, addresses immediate humanistic needs. However, not all grant proposals address pressing people problems. Some scholarly research, for instance, aims to contribute to the stockpile of knowledge with no known immediate

Problem Statement	A Line	B Line
Inadequate health care services exist in Eastern Tennessee, despite the fact that access to basic health care is a fundamental right.	Multiple indices show a growth in health problems and a decrease in the quality of life.	The number of health care providers has remained constant.
Youth suicide is a significant public health issue in Wyoming.	State vital records show suicide is the second leading cause of death among teenagers and is growing each year.	The number of schools with suicide prevention programs remains low and has remained constant over time.
Sedentary lifestyles and poor eating habits contribute to the dramatic rise in childhood obesity.	The incidence of childhood obesity has more than tripled in the past three decades.	Elementary schools have limited time and expertise to teach students about dietary and physical activity behaviors.
New Common Core State Standards require high school instructors to teach current and new topics in new ways.	A district survey of high school teachers revealed that 77% lack balance between procedural and conceptual understanding.	High school teachers lack guidance and support to transform their instruction and assess student proficiency.
The Golden River Valley is being contaminated by rural nonpoint source pollution.	Fertilizer and pesticide runoff from agricultural areas has increased 26% in eight years.	The DNR's capacity to enforce existing nutrient management plans is insufficient.

EXAMPLES OF A/B GAPS

EXHIBIT 39

application. Researchers in the following disciplines might investigate in various ways the age-old question: "How much wood could a woodchuck chuck, if a woodchuck could chuck wood?" A cognitive neuroscientist might study the brain of the woodchuck using multiple technologies. A mathematician might deduce a generalizable theorem for expressing "chucked-ness." A political scientist might assess the relationship between the chucking behavior and prevailing local and state laws and systems. A psychologist might analyze the woodchuck's desire to chuck the wood. A historian might develop a timeline of activity from the first instance of wood chucking to the present event of a woodchuck chucking wood. A philosopher might explore "What is it like to be a woodchuck?" Each scholar makes a contribution to understanding, but there is no clear end in mind for their research.

How, then, do you justify the need for scholarly research when writing a proposal? Five basic reasons for conducting scholarly research include the following:

- **To test hypotheses:** Hypothesis testing is a predominant domain of much of scholarship. Researchers formulate "best guesses" (hypotheses) about the nature of some phenomenon and then conduct experiments to see whether their hunches were right. Hypothesis testing underlies much of scientific inquiry and is a legitimate reason to explore a problem, whether or not it will contribute immediately to something that is better, cheaper, faster, broader, more comprehensive, more economical, more efficient, or healthier.

- **To indulge curiosity:** Curiosity is just human nature. The average three year-old child asks more than 100 "Why, mommy?" questions each day. Everyday curiosity often stops when the curiosity has been satisfied. Scholarly curiosity goes beyond and seeks out the methods by which the answers to its questions are obtained. Suppose a child asks, "Why are all those bees in the garden?" and the father replies, "They are gathering pollen from the roses so that they can make some honey from it." The run-of-the-mill child stops here because his curiosity is satisfied. The future researcher will wonder if bees are attracted by certain colors. Perhaps the shape of the petals is important. Perhaps the pollen that sticks to the bees' legs is only incidental to their search for some substance that makes them attractive to potential mates. These possibilities can be resolved only by controlled observation and experimentation. Everyday curiosity is easily settled with a few answers. Scholarly curiosity means continually asking questions, even without knowing the outcomes, and is an essential part of the discovery process.

- **To try out a new method or technique:** Sometimes a new technique is developed because the desired information could not be produced by standard means. Sometimes a new technique is advanced because a new instrument has come into existence. Sometimes a new technique is employed simply to see what kind of data it will yield. Researchers recognize the desirability of technical advances, which may include improvements in measuring instruments, advanced methods of recording data, sophisticated data analysis, design of a specialized instrument to do a particular job or extend old techniques into new areas. Any of these outcomes could result from doing scholarly research to try out a new method or technique.

- **To establish the existence of a phenomenon:** Prior experiments may demonstrate previously unobserved, unmeasured, or uncontrolled phenomena. In such cases, it is perfectly justifiable to conduct an experiment to demonstrate a particular effect. Knowledge proceeds by manipulating variables in a systematic fashion and unifying the results with a conceptual framework. The demonstration of a particular phenomenon is a prelude to theory building.

- **To explore the conditions under which a phenomenon occurs:** Any new experimental finding or promising theory remains in an intellectual silo, unrelated other findings and theories, until the conditions under which the phenomenon occurs are discovered, the first step in theory integration. Scholarly theories are built on a foundation of small findings, none of them necessarily world-shaking by themselves, without which the final step could never have been taken. Often data are important only as they establish or refute the soundness of other data or of some conceptualization of natural phenomena. They serve to strengthen the internal consistency of knowledge.

Compared to basic research, it is relatively easy to define and document the problem to be addressed in applied research projects, as well as in education, training, equipment, outreach, and service delivery initiatives. While it may be more difficult to frame a problem statement when doing scholarly research, the solution often lies in one or more of the five justifications above.

When asked why he engaged in basic research, a prominent psychology professor from an East Coast university responded:

> When I conduct basic research, it is because basic research has the potential to impact the largest variety of practical problems. This is a subtle point and one that is often missed when contrasting basic with applied research: basic science is also applied, but the application is farther down the road and harder to see. For example, discovering the laws of physics was a basic science endeavor, but the practical consequences are enormous. Curing alcoholism solves one important problem, but understanding addiction impacts many important problems.

In short, while there are many differences between basic and applied research, three key distinctions are: the intent of the research (i.e., whether an application is directly in mind during the conduct of the research), the immediacy of the application, and the variety of problems affected.

KEY QUESTIONS TO ANSWER

As you write your problem statement, answer these questions. Does your proposal:

1. Specify the conditions you wish to change?
2. Define the gaps in existing programs, services, or knowledge?
3. Include appropriate statistical data about the frequency and severity of the problem?
4. Clarify what will happen if nothing is done about this problem?
5. State the problem in terms of human needs, not your opportunities?
6. Cite pertinent theoretical literature, research findings, or ongoing studies?
7. Convey the focus of your project early in the narrative?
8. Establish the importance and significance of the problem from the sponsor's perspective?
9. Point out the relationship of your project to a larger set of problems or issues?
10. Supply an appropriate and compelling introduction to the rest of the application?

Use this list both as a guide to develop your need section and as a checklist to critique your draft, making sure you have included all essential elements.

EXAMPLES OF PROBLEM STATEMENTS

As you read the following examples, note the repeated emphasis on two points:

1. The frequency and severity of the current problem or need.
2. The failure of the status quo to address the need.

Example 1

This grant proposal from a social service agency is seeking foundation funding to expand its outreach to underserved people:

> Although the Family Crisis Center is currently operating at near capacity, the center intends to reach more fully those families who are underserved. This group includes minority citizens, senior citizens, and individuals with disabilities. While approximately 5 percent of the general population in our catchment area uses the services of the center, minorities and others do not traditionally use our services. In addition, the newly appointed coordinator for Community Outreach Services has identified for the first time the community's population with disabilities—a potential new target group for specialized services.

The gap? The center's disparity between its heavy service demands and its need to serve other clients. This problem statement is unpersuasive because it focuses on the needs of the center: to add more staffing so it can do a better job of serving underserved families. A more persuasive approach would concentrate on the needs of the underserved, as the following rewritten example indicates:

> Inner city, urban living—what some would call ghetto survival—is stressful. As evidence, all social service agencies report heavy demands for social services, and many have lengthy waiting lists. The primary users of social services are families with more than high school educations and above average socioeconomic status.
>
> Unfortunately, three major community groups are notably underrepresented among social service agencies: minorities, seniors, and the handicapped. Each group faces special stressors that are further exacerbated by their urban environment. Most social service agencies have a monocultural staff, yet serve a multicultural clientele. Seniors face transportation barriers in traveling through what they perceive to be

risky neighborhoods to receive various medical services. Minorities often distrust welfare agencies. The handicapped face substantial architectural barriers in moving through urban neighborhoods.

Since the Faith and Justice Foundation and the Family Crisis Center share the same mission of serving the needs of all community residents, we invite your investment in the following project.

This revised need statement refocuses the gap on the inconsistency between the service needs of special populations (A Line) and their ability to obtain those services (B Line).

Example 2

This example is taken from an application for a research proposal submitted to a social and rehabilitation service agency to evaluate the comparative effectiveness of different types of service and income maintenance programs. This short excerpt is included to show you an approach for tying the need at the local level to an interest of the funding agency itself:

> The national investment in social welfare demonstration projects continues to expand, yet the local consequences of these projects on client and family functioning have been only partially evaluated. Without careful assessment, the relative merits of any given project will be lost or incorrectly estimated while errors may be repeated if the project serves as a prototype.
>
> A favorable set of conditions has arisen that warrants a careful assessment of a demonstration project jointly sponsored by the Bureau of Health and Family Services and the Department of Public Welfare. The State Department of Public Welfare has created four groups of AFDC clients who will receive various combinations of increased services assistance.

What is the gap in this example? The information void between national activities being provided (A Line) and their impact at the local level (B Line).

Example 3

This research proposal suggests a new way to produce a substance thought to cure certain types of cancer:

> Convincing evidence exists that interferon is a powerful antiviral and antitumor substance. Wide medical application of interferon therapy

will depend upon production of large quantities at a price the public can afford. It is doubtful whether the current technology of cell culture will be economical enough to allow mass production of this material. Other alternatives include organic syntheses or productive insertion of the interferon gene into microorganisms. The proposed research offers a lead to both procedures, thereby opening the door to application of interferon therapy beyond a few clinical trials. Success in any one of the steps outlined in this proposal would be a major breakthrough in achieving progress toward eventual use of interferon in the treatment of human disease.

> Human interferon has only recently been obtained in preparations approaching homogeneity. The amounts of such highly purified preparations, available only in the laboratories where they have been produced, are exceedingly small. Partially purified preparations of human interferon, on the other hand, are commercially available.

The gap? The growing need for crucial medications (A Line) continually outstrips the capacity of current technologies to produce sufficient quantities (B Line). This proposal need section went on to delimit the specific topic and show its possible contribution. The sentences are short and use simple syntactic structures, making it easy for a reviewer to follow a technical topic.

Example 4

In an application to a federal agency, a private university states the need for endowment funding to better fulfill its educational mission:

> The fundamental issues in the philosophy of human nature have remained relatively constant over the centuries. However, new discoveries generate new approaches, bringing new questions, new hypotheses, and new challenges. Across the country, few philosophy departments encourage the kind of interdisciplinary research and teaching that is essential to human nature. An Endowed Chair in the Philosophy of Human Nature will enable us to attract exceptional teacher/scholars to enhance and complement the expertise of our philosophy faculty. A $3,000,000 endowment will yield approximately $150,000 annually, which will be used to support salary, fringe benefits, professional development, and collaborative research activities. Students will benefit from expanded

opportunities to explore current issues in human nature—in a preliminary way in the required PHIL 1000 course, in greater breadth via subsequent philosophy electives, and in greater depth through faculty-student collaborative research projects. Further, faculty in all disciplines who intentionally and systematically infuse a human nature focus into core curriculum courses can build on a shared academic foundation to further develop students' content knowledge and skills in critical thinking and effective communication.

What is the gap in this example? The growing number of thoughtful questions, hypotheses, and challenges (A Line) and the current capacity of the institution to attract scholars with interdisciplinary interest and expertise to actively investigate them (B Line).

Example 5

A hospital-based bioethics proposal submitted to a federal health care agency. Note the use of subheadings to help organize the various dimensions of the overall needs statement:

Overview of Need for Bioethical Sensitivity. While the relevance and rectitude of ethics in medicine are indisputable, their extent and form produce far less agreement. Ethics often has a second-class status in medical school training and subsequent patient management; both situations add to the ethical insensitivity prevalent in the contemporary world. Moreover, the complexities of the human condition require specialized and applied knowledge. The following paragraphs elaborate on the multiple dimensions of the need for this project.

Growing Insensitivity to Ethical Issues. The world has been described as becoming increasingly amoral. The prevalence of major ethical problems in the popular press, such as gambling among athletes, swindles in the ministry, or political sex scandals, underscore a lack of ethical sensitivity. While the mass media has made the public well aware of the ethical problems, the scope of the problems in bioethics is less popularized but more prevalent and includes such issues as the following:

- Use of artificial heart as a bridge to transplant
- Economic dilemmas in ethical decision making
- Involuntary medical detention
- Withdrawal of tube feeding
- Forgoing CPR in elderly patients

In reality, many clinicians encounter these ethical decisions, and others, on a daily basis. Relegating ethics to a second-class status in medical training programs and practice contributes to our society's lack of ethical awareness. Certainly, colleges and universities need a more salient and explicit focus on the legitimacy of ethics to nurture the moral sensitivity of its students and of its local community.

Conflicting Trends in Biomedical Ethics. The study of ethics has become increasingly compartmentalized and applied, with specialists in such areas as nursing ethics, physician ethics, and patient ethics. These targeted emphases are notably deficient in the study of the theoretical principles of ethical decision making. Ironically, the "technologizing" of ethics education has developed at the same time as a renewed national emphasis on holistic medicine.

In an analysis of trends in ethics, Marcus Singer noted, "The first thing to be said about ethics in this day and place is that it is different—different from what it was and has been and in the process of becoming what it is going to be." Philosophers automatically think of ethics as identical with moral philosophy. But there is a sense of ethics gaining currency in which it is not a branch of philosophy, in which ethics is regarded as a new, independent (yet interdisciplinary) subject, exercising the skills of physicians, psychologists, lawyers, economists, sociologists, scientists, and others who would not normally think of themselves as doing philosophy.

Distortion of Ethics Studies by Specialization. Ethics has a sweeping interdisciplinary nature with a multifaceted relevance to theoretical, characterological, professional, and theological domains. Consequently, the clinical application of ethical principles cannot be limited to a single discipline without producing a restricted and distorted sense of ethics. This constrained focus divorces ethics from its true richness as a central facet of the human experience and from the history of human intellectual and spiritual achievement. As one ethicist recently argued, "Is there one unitary discipline, ethics, somehow involved in these otherwise apparently diverse areas of environment, ecology, science, medicine, biology, engineering, technology, law, government, and business? This is not a question that can be answered merely *a priori* and in advance; it must wait for reasonable settlement until each of these areas has been explored further and until a better grasp than we have now is achieved of the underlying structure of ethical or moral problems in each of these areas of human endeavors."

Prevalence of Ethics Training in Medical Schools. According to the American Medical School Association (2007), all medical schools recognize the importance of ethics training and include it in their curricula. A closer look, however, reveals a number of training gaps. First, only 18 percent of the 127 medical schools in the United States offer a specific ethics course. Most medical schools include it as a teaching unit in clinical courses. Typically, one to two hours of ethics training is included in courses taken in each specialization area, e.g., family practice, internal medicine, or radiology. As a consequence, the average medical student receives 20–30 hours of ethics-related training, which is usually taught by a physician with little or no training in philosophy or bioethics. As a result, there is an ever-widening gap between the need for bioethics expertise and the training provided in medical schools, which has plateaued for years.

The gap? The growing demand for bioethics expertise resulting from advances in medicine and technology (A line) and the steady-state training provided by medical schools (B line).

WRITING TIPS FOR THE PROBLEM STATEMENT

1. Describe the problem, its causes, and consequences if left alone.
2. Describe the need in human terms. For example, if you want to buy a van for your health clinic, talk about the transportation barriers that patients encounter when getting access to the health care to which they are entitled.
3. Review the preproposal contact questions in Chapter 4. They were all focused toward pinpointing the problem. They followed a logical progress from analyzing the baseline position, existing rationale, future expectations, and priorities that lead to the needs.
4. In addition to visiting your local library and searching university institutional repositories for scholarly literature to document your problem statement, you can explore online tools such as Education Resources Information Center (www.eric.ed.gov), Google Scholar (scholar.google.com),

HighWire (highwire.stanford.edu), PubMed (www.ncbi.nlm.nih.gov/pubmed), and Scirus (www.scirus.com).

5. In your literature review, check on currently funded (but unpublished) research in progress. Contact the National Technical Information Service. They serve as a clearinghouse for recently initiated projects and can provide you with information at a nominal charge that indicates who might be doing something similar to what you propose. Their Web site address is www.ntis.gov.
6. Beyond discussing the importance of the project's topic, you should also demonstrate the need for your methodology; that is, the reviewers should be able to anticipate your solution based upon your analysis of the problem. The ability to foreshadow a solution from the problem statement represents a very logical, fluent writing technique.
7. Don't say "little is known about …," "there is a lack of information about …," or "no research dealt with. …" Arguing for something that isn't is a weak need statement; it's circular logic. Go one step further. Explain the consequences of the information void. So you don't know something about this problem. So what?
8. GIS (Geographical Information Systems) can provide new ways of conducting a gap analysis for a strong problem statement on your next grant. Some local counties have qualified staff and software in their planning departments to help you analyze U.S. Census information and other local geographical data. For example, one county grant writer tapped her local Planning and Zoning experts for information on the percentage of the county that required off-road access for emergency response. The GIS experts "lifted" the roads and streets from the county map along with a margin of access along those roads and determined the percentage of the county that required off-road access in case of emergencies. She used this data to build a winning national grant. On a different public transportation grant, she asked her GIS colleagues to calculate the percentage of the land coverage in her county that did not have access to the established public transit bus routes. The possibilities are endless for GIS applications and uses of GIS maps that can be generated from the software.
9. Your needs section is the "sad" section of the proposal. Use appropriate "sad" words: almost, barrier, below, bleak, bottom, decreased, deficit, dependent, depressed, desperate, destitute, disadvantaged,

Agency	Web Address
U.S. Census Bureau—general	census.gov
U.S. Census Bureau—data sets	factfinder2.census.gov
Bureau of Justice Statistics	bjs.ojp.usdoj.gov
Bureau of Labor Statistics	stats.bls.gov
Centers for Disease Control and Prevention	cdc.gov/healthyyouth
Data.gov	data.gov
National Center for Education Statistics	nces.ed.gov
National Center for Health Statistics	cdc.gov/nchs

FEDERAL DATA COLLECTION AGENCIES

EXHIBIT 40

discouraged, disheartened, disregarded, disruption, distressed, failed, gloomy, grim, harsh, highest, high-risk, hopeless, hurdle, ignore, impaired, inadequate, increased, infested, lacking, less than, lowest, minimum, miserable, needy, neglect, obstacle, outbreak, overlooked, pathetic, pitiful, plagued, poorest, poverty, severe, sparse, substandard, trapped, unacceptable, violent, widespread, worst.

10. Investigate sources of national, state, and county health and education-related data online, including Children's Defense Fund (www.childrensdefense.org), County Health Rankings (www.countyhealthrankings.org), Health Reform Source (healthreform.kff.org), KIDS COUNT (www.kidscount.org), and State Health Facts (www.statehealthfacts.org).

11. Six major federal agencies collect, analyze, and disseminate data on virtually all aspects of society and its individuals. Web addresses are provided in Exhibit 40.

The national "fact-finders" in Exhibit 40 are rich with data useful in most proposals. Beyond these federal agencies, consider approaching local and regional health planning councils; city, county, or regional planning departments; vocational rehabilitation agencies; crisis centers in your field; law enforcement and judicial departments; chambers of commerce; universities (libraries, academic departments, computer centers, research offices); national associations; other grantees; United Way (community resource file); and development departments in state and local governments. Don't overlook your state and federal legislators. They survive in large part by providing constituency services. They can help you find government reports on your project topics.

REJECTION REASONS

Reviewers have rejected some proposals for the following reasons, which are clustered into two categories of shortcomings: Problem Conceptualization and Problem Documentation.

Problem Conceptualization

1. The problems to be investigated are more complex than the applicants realize.
2. The applicants need to acquire greater familiarity with the pertinent literature.
3. It is doubtful that new or useful information will result from the project.
4. The basic hypothesis is unsound.
5. The project director appears to lack knowledge of published relevant work in this area.
6. The project codirectors fail to present an acceptable scientific rationale for conducting this project.
7. Although the proposal targets expansion in year 2 to address mental health services and transportation issues, there is no discussion of the quantifiable need for such services.
8. There is no evidence of nurse buy-in: the narrative should state the extent to which nurses, not just physicians, were involved in the selection of the problem and the formulation of the solution.
9. Given that student test scores are higher in all subject areas than state averages, it is unclear whether the proposed project will have a true impact on student achievement.
10. The application calls attention to the disparities in academic achievement for students with disabilities and students who are economically

disadvantaged but does not present approaches or strategies that cater specifically to these students.

11. The narrative would benefit from a richer description of the system's changes that could be affected by the alliance and would most likely contribute to improvements in the environment. It appears that the implementation plan includes lobbying, which is an unallowable grant expense.

12. It is unclear that the proposed project will contribute to a reduction of infant deaths, particularly since some of the leading causes (e.g., complications of prematurity and congenital abnormalities) are based more in genetic makeup than lifestyle choice.

Problem Documentation

1. The proposed research is scientifically premature; the supporting knowledge is inadequate.

2. The relationship of rationale to regional needs is not clearly delineated.

3. Some significant efforts in the state are not mentioned in the rationale.

4. The rationale is heavily based on local needs rather than regional impact.

5. The demographic analysis is not developed; implications are not explored.

6. Overall rationale is inadequate. Evidence to support training and specific patient care needs is lacking.

7. The proposal relies heavily on state-level data to justify local needs. The narrative is silent as to whether the local needs mirror those of the state as a whole.

8. The "Problem Statement" should be twofold: identify and quantify the health care needs of the community, and discuss the inadequacies of the current system to address these needs.

9. This proposal offers no evidence of a formal needs assessment to identify and prioritize community needs. What sources were used to determine and prioritize the most important needs?

10. The proposal does not quantify or support its claim, "The need for mental health services is great within the community."

11. This project doesn't explain why the needs of this subpopulation are greater than the needs of other community residents.

12. The applicants have great theories unsubstantiated by data.

In each case, the reviewers have serious reservations about the credibility of the investigators and/or the chosen topic area. After you write your problem statement in your next proposal, reread these rejection reasons and see whether any of them cause you to say "ouch."

GRANT GAFFES

Exhibit 41 presents an annotated sample of a common grant gaffe in the problem statement, namely, switching too soon from describing the project need to detailing a proposed solution. This example is taken from an application for a curriculum development project to a federal agency.

STARTER SENTENCES

To help you get started in writing your need section, we offer few phrases and sentences you might begin with:

1. A spiraling gap exists between A and B. . .

2. A growing body of evidence suggests three major problems exist. . .

3. Despite the increase in technology, we continue to lag behind. . .

4. XXX is a formidable obstacle to solving major needs in the area of. . .

5. We are in dire need of innovations to combat several increasingly prevalent problems that voraciously devour our social and economic resources.

6. A current limit to solving this problem regards. . .

7. Nationally, the frequency of the problem is xxx. Statewide, it is even worse at xxx. But, locally the incidence is an overwhelming xxx.

8. Our understanding of this problem is currently hindered by a lack of a clear relationship between xxx and yyy.

9. To overcome this barrier, new insights into xxx and yyy are essential.

10. Our preliminary studies have highlighted the need to address this urgent problem.

Clip File Action Item # 11
Problem Statement

Fill your clip file with data documenting the frequency and severity of the problem you propose to solve in ways that meet your sponsor's needs, not yours. Follow these tips:

- Sources of data include surveys, statistical analyses, key informants, community forums, case studies, legislative bureaus and officials, universities, community agencies, professional associations, crisis centers, chambers of commerce, planning commissions, and clearinghouses.

The literature is full of examples indicating the benefits to student learning when faculty transition from teacher-centered classes to student-centered classes, from passive lecturing to active hands-on doing, from sage-on-the-stage to guide-on-the-side. And yet, our department has yet to face this issue in any concerted way. Part of that is the normal inertia of academia, where neither accreditation committees nor the faculty are willing to allow massive reworking of the curriculum every few years. Further complicating this picture is the fact that it is unclear what, if any, approaches will be viable in the next 3 to 4 years' time.

Fully addressing these points will require a significant, broad-based, multi-institutional effort. This proposal aims to form an initial set of reference materials from which such an effort could be constituted. We focus here on the tools, curriculum, and evaluation components. Our work is grounded in the preliminary work we have been doing recently in our department, but we also leverage ongoing interactions with a number of academic and industry partners to both enrich the proposed work and to form the seed of a larger community that we can feed back into.

> The first two sentences of the paragraph start out on the right track: they acknowledge as a problem the gap between best practices in the field and the current practices of the department.

> The final two sentences of the paragraph begin to go off track: they portray the problem as insurmountable—change is impossible because faculty are resistant to change and the future is uncertain. This creates a mindset for grant reviewers of "Okay, then why bother doing the project?"—a question that remains unanswered. This paragraph should describe the frequency and severity of the problem, quantifying the percent of time that faculty spend lecturing in the classroom, which impacts a specific number of students per year.

> The narrative transitions too early from the "problem" to the "solution." The information in this paragraph is solid, establishing the credibility of the project through an identified overarching aim, the credibility of the project director through preliminary work already completed, and the credibility of the organization through leveraged relationships with academic and industry partners; however, it should appear later in the proposal. Grant reviewers have not yet been convinced a significant problem exists that must be addressed now. This paragraph should instead elaborate on the consequences of perpetuating the status quo, such as the inadequate development of students' critical thinking and problem solving skills.

GRANT GAFFES

EXHIBIT 41

CHAPTER 8
Goals, Objectives, and Outcomes

*Those who cannot tell what they desire or expect, still sigh
and struggle with indefinite thoughts and vast wishes.*
—Ralph Waldo Emerson

PURPOSE OF GOALS

Three interrelated grant concepts that are not well understood by many grantwriters and grantmakers alike include goals, objectives, and outcomes. These terms are similar in the sense that they all focus on the grant deliverables. They are different in their perspective, level of detail, and timing. As Emerson points out, those who discern among the concepts can manage expectations while those who do not are bound to struggle. In Chapter 8, you will learn the following:

- Differentiate between "big picture" vision, measurable actions, and humanistic changes.
- Exploit powerful action verbs and avoid imprecise generic verbs.
- Establish the context for evaluation success.

Your project goals represent the idealized dream of what you hope to accomplish. They are usually presented in terms of hopes, wishes, or desires. Goals project the "big picture" vision of what you wish to accomplish. They communicate global purposes. Typical goal-oriented words include advocate, analyze, appreciate, extend, illustrate, improve, integrate, participate, promote, recommend, or understand. Goals are not observable or quantifiable. For instance, a recent health education proposal included four goal statements:

- To analyze the special needs of underserved populations and to develop new programs to meet those needs.
- To extend services to underserved target populations.

- To improve the quality of services while experiencing an increased demand for those services.
- To integrate new educational materials for special focus programs.

While these are valuable goals, they cannot stand by themselves. They need to be followed by concrete, measurable objectives that represent observable behaviors.

PURPOSE OF OBJECTIVES

Your objectives specify the end products of your project. When sponsors fund your project, they are literally "buying" your objectives. That's why it is extremely important to state your objectives in clear and measurable terms.

In essence, the objectives answer one fundamental question: "What will this project change?" The emphasis is on the "what."

When you write your objectives, follow the acronymic advice: "Keep them S-I-M-P-L-E." Your objectives should be:

- *Specific*: Show precisely what you intend to change through your project. What will be different when your project is finished? What will people know, feel, or be able to do once the project is completed that they couldn't do before?
- *Immediate*: Indicate the time frame during which a current problem will be addressed. Why should the project be acted on right now? How long will it take to achieve your goals and objectives?

- *Measurable*: Specify what you would accept as proof of project success. What qualitative and quantitative data will you gather? What tools will you use to measure project success?
- *Practical*: Point out how each objective is a real solution to a real problem. Are your objectives realistic and feasible? Does your organization have the skill, experience, qualifications, resources, and personnel to carry out each objective?
- *Logical*: Describe how each objective systematically contributes to achieving your overall goal(s). Are you really doing what you think you're doing? Do your objectives relate to your goal and the sponsor's priorities? Does it make sense to do this?
- *Evaluable*: Define how much change has to occur for the project to be effective. What are your criteria for success? What impact will your project make? What is the value of your project?

Although these categories are not mutually exclusive, each of your objectives should meet several of these criteria. For instance, given the goal of "improving the quality of life for homeless individuals in our city," a proposal objective might be stated as follows:

Midwest Home Shelter Agency will increase the number of homeless people who transition into dependent and independent housing [Specific] [Practical] [Logical] during the next 24 months [Immediate] by 15 percent [Evaluable] as noted in the Department of Social Welfare Homeless Survey Report [Measurable].

The following example of a goal and its objectives is taken from a demonstration project submitted to the U.S. Department of Education. The objective has several parts that meet each of the six criteria, with some overlap:

Goal. This program is designed to prepare parents to function independently and effectively in helping their children develop to their own potentials.

Objectives. During the next 18 months [Immediate] the parents who participate in the program will demonstrate the following behaviors [Specific]:

- identify the education content in the events that occur in the home [Logical]
- structure sequential and cumulative instructional tasks in the home for the child [Logical]
- observe the child and use checklists to monitor progress [Measurable]

- use available equipment and processes in the home to teach children specific skills [Evaluable]
- use packaged materials prepared by the project or other agencies in teaching specific skills [Practical]

Your objectives represent the yardstick to evaluate your proposal results; that is, if you write your objectives in precise, measurable terms, it is easy to write your proposal evaluation section because you know exactly what will be evaluated.

PURPOSE OF OUTCOMES

Outcomes are the benefits, changes, or effects that occur to the target population due to participation in your project. Outcomes express project results in humanistic terms; they are the desired changes in peoples' knowledge, skills, attitudes, or behaviors. Identifying outcomes means going beyond outlining how the project will operate to describing how participants will be able to think, do, act, or behave differently by the conclusion of your project.

In the increasingly competitive world of grant-seeking, accountability is key. Sponsors want to know that their funds are being spent wisely and that your project is really making a difference in the lives of people; hence, outcomes. Your proposal must balance process and outcome objectives. Process statements answer "What?" What are you going to do? Outcome statements answer the question "So what?" What are the benefits of this project to the target population?

Consider the following pairs of statements—the first describes a process, and the second describes an outcome:

Process: Provide firefighters with new communications and personal protective equipment.
Outcome: Firefighters will increase coordinated service delivery to the community and decrease average response times.
Process: Conduct 10 cultural sensitivity training courses.
Outcome: Employees will respect and value diversity.
Process: Enroll 6,000 at-risk youth in summer school classes.
Outcome: Students' academic performance will improve.
Process: Meet with students in the ELL (English Language Learner) Program for one hour per day twice a week for 30 weeks.

Outcome: Students of the ELL Program will be able to translate a paragraph of text from Mandarin Chinese to English.

Process: Provide 10,000 free meals to low-income senior citizens.

Outcome: Senior citizens are able to remain in independent living.

Process: Have 60 undergraduate university students contribute a total of 3,600 hours to service learning projects at the Hispanic Community Center.

Outcome #1: Students will make real world connections to the local community through service, educational outreach, and employment.

Outcome #2: Continuing education adults at the Hispanic Community Center will earn their General Educational Development (GED) diplomas.

Process: Distribute 25,000 "So You're Having A Baby" educational packets to pediatric physicians' offices.

Outcome #1: Teen mothers immunize their newborns by age 2.

Outcome #2: Teen mothers understand the value of breastfeeding their babies during the first year of life.

Outcome #3: Teen mothers do not have a repeat pregnancy until after age 18.

The final two examples illustrate that even when projects appear on the surface to be similar, they may in fact target very different outcomes. That's why prior to developing intervention strategies, you must identify outcomes that will be meaningful to your project. Outcomes borrowed from or imposed by individuals external to your organization are unlikely to be valuable to your efforts. Chapter 10 takes a closer look at evaluation and outcomes, including outcome indicators—specific characteristics selected for measurement to demonstrate success in achieving project outcomes.

ESTIMATING CHANGE

Objectives and outcomes produce change. But how much change is reasonable to expect as the result of a grant project? In a stack of grant applications, your proposal may stand out from the competition if you can define for reviewers not only what changes your project aims to effect but also the degree of change. Six strategies you can use to identify and justify that a specific amount of change is realistic include the following:

- *Ask the Program Officer*: During your preproposal contacts with program officers, you might ask a broad question, such as, "What is the desired impact you'd like to see on these problems, balancing project breadth, depth, and financial resources available?" or ask a more pointed question, such as, "What outcomes do you expect of grantees?"

- *Review the Literature*: After examining major works published in books and scholarly articles, you may be able to situate your anticipated outcomes in this larger context: "Research from Larry, Moe, and Curly (2007) and Shemp (2012) confirm that a 12–17 percent reduction can be expected from this type of primary prevention program."

- *Examine Other Models*: When your approach is so new or original that no baselines for comparison exist, you might argue by analogy: "The purpose of this pilot project is to test the efficacy of *Stop the Aggression*. Given our innovative approach, we anticipate outcomes that exceed established models such as *Good Behavior Game* and *Fast Track*."

- *Solicit Expert Testimony*: Congress regularly solicits expert testimony from individuals and organizations to provide authoritative perspectives on significant issues and you can too: "According to Dr. Ray Linn, the state's leading expert on perinatal health topics, first-time mothers will experience a 50 percent improvement within 6 weeks of participation."

- *Invoke Professional Opinion*: Even if you don't consider yourself to be an expert, it may be that you are in the best position to make a well-informed prediction: "Based on thirty years of experience working directly with more than 19,000 children and families in these rural counties, it is conceivable that an 8 percent increase is achievable in the first year."

- *Conduct Statistical Analyses*: In some instances, rather than quantifying an amount of change, statistical analyses might demonstrate that the change from baseline will be statistically significant: "Given the large size of the sample population, the independent evaluator will have the power to determine statistical significance at $p=.0001$."

These strategies presume that a benchmark exists or will be established against which to measure. More broadly, this depth of thinking goes a long way to persuade reviewers that your objectives and outcomes are meaningful as well as measurable.

KEY QUESTIONS TO ANSWER

Answer these key questions as you write your proposal goals, objectives, and outcomes. Does your proposal do the following:

1. Clearly describe your project's objectives, hypotheses, and/or research questions?
2. Identify observable behaviors that can be measured?
3. Signal project goals and objectives without burying them in a morass of narrative?
4. Demonstrate that your objectives are important, significant, and timely?
5. Directly address the chosen problem?
6. Demonstrate why your project outcomes are appropriate and important to the sponsor?
7. Reflect the need for the project and show clearly its purpose and direction?
8. Include one or more objectives for each need discussed in the problem statement?
9. State objectives in terms of outcomes and not methods or activities?
10. State the time by which the objectives will be accomplished?

EXAMPLES OF GOALS, OBJECTIVES, AND OUTCOMES

Example 1

A child safety proposal from a community-based organization to a local corporation. Notice that because objectives are expressed in terms of process activities, a subsequent paragraph is included that defines humanistic outcomes for parents participating in the project:

Misuse of child safety seats is widespread. Although 95 percent of parents believe they install their child seat correctly, 80 percent of children are improperly restrained. The goal of this project is to enhance existing collaborative partnerships to prevent injuries to motor vehicle occupants. By December 31, 2016, we will accomplish the following objectives:

Objective #1: Offer car seat education to 500 parents attending birthing/prenatal classes at County Community Hospital.

Objective #2: Train 50 staff members at 10 pediatric offices in our county on the importance of using car seats properly and motor vehicle safety resources available within our county.

Objective #3: Create 10,000 educational packets to be distributed at birthing/prenatal classes and pediatric offices, promoting car seat safety checks and other community resources.

We will measure the intended effects that this program is trying to produce on parents' knowledge, attitudes, and behaviors. Specifically, the outcomes of this project will enable parents to

better identify, access, and use community resources that will help prevent unintentional childhood injuries. Increasing parents' knowledge of community resources will motivate them to participate in car seat checks at local fitting stations, i.e., police stations, fire departments, and hospitals. Education provided at fitting stations, in turn, will prompt behavior changes so parents continue to install and use car seats correctly.

Example 2

This example is taken from a Blood Center seeking private foundation funding for a hemophilia proposal:

Goal: To provide modern care for all persons affected by hemophilia, related bleeding disorders, and complications of those disorders or their treatment, including HIV infection. By the target date of July 1, 2015, four objectives will be met:

Objective 1: 90 percent of the identified persons with hemophilia at risk of HIV infection enrolled in comprehensive care programs will be tested for HIV status with appropriate pre- and posttest counseling, with maximum consideration to confidentiality.

Objective 2: 80 percent of persons with hemophilia, all their identified sexual partners, and their families will be provided with comprehensive risk-reduction information and psychosocial counseling and support.

Objective 3: 100 percent of the hemophilia treatment centers will offer hemophilia and HIV-related medical and psychosocial care to sexual partners and offspring of persons with hemophilia, with consideration for their independent needs.

Objective 4: 90 percent of persons identified with severe hemophilia will have access to medically supervised home therapy.

Example 3

A recent wastewater management RFP (Request for Proposals) from the Environmental Protection Agency asked for a distinction between primary and secondary objectives. Further, it wanted objectives to be classified by type. A local community-based organization submitted a proposal for a decentralized wastewater demonstration project. Their proposal presented the objectives in a table format as indicated in Exhibit 42.

Work Plan Objectives	
Primary Objectives	
Type	**Objective**
Needs Assessment and Analysis	By January 2013, identify and prioritize wastewater management needs responsive to local deficiencies
Planning	By February 2013, develop a local model for addressing rural wastewater management needs
Financing	By March 2013, secure project financing
Community Capacity Development	By April 2013, develop local capacity to effectively administer rural wastewater management systems
Project Management and Coordination	By May 2013, maximize project administration through shared local governance
Construction	By June 2013, implement designs resulting from local needs assessment
Education and Outreach	By July 2013, report local project accomplishments and management model to state and national audiences
Evaluation (Outcome)	By August 2013, assess the benefits and changes to local public health and environment as the project ends
Secondary Objectives	
Type	**Objective**
Financing	By September 2013, identify and assess public and private financing options
Community Capacity Development	By October 2013, develop local capacity to design, construct, operate, inspect, maintain, and repair rural wastewater treatment systems
Project Management and Coordination	By November 2013, develop and maintain a process to manage and coordinate the project with maximum local community involvement
Construction	By November 2013, develop design alternatives and create a local construction plan
Education and Outreach	By December 2013, create an education and outreach plan for local residents to encourage further installations
Evaluation (Process)	By December 2013, monitor local progress in evaluating repairs and installations of wastewater treatment

SAMPLE WORKPLAN OBJECTIVES

EXHIBIT 42

Example 4

The following example from a proposal to the USAID (U.S. Agency for International Development) presents a goal statement and eight measurable objectives for an international health project targeting individuals (called internally displaced persons) living near camps in Northern Uganda:

Project Goal

Our project goal presents the "big picture" vision of what we wish to accomplish. It communicates our desired long-term outcomes.

This project goal matches isomorphically with the purpose of the Request for Application, namely. . .

To increase the delivery of HIV/AIDS and infectious disease services (tuberculosis and malaria) with a focus on Internally Displaced People (IDP) living beyond the municipalities in the insecure Acholi and Lango subregions in Uganda.

Specific Measurable Objectives

The project objectives specify the end products of this project. They show what will change in concrete terms over the course of the next five years. The objectives cluster into three categories: training, service delivery, and systemic capacity building, which are listed below for Year One only. Subsequent years will follow the same objectives, although the numbers will likely increase by at least 15 percent, since out-years will not have the project start-up responsibilities found in the first two months of this project:

1. To prevent HIV infection in 750,000 individuals
2. To prevent HIV mother-to-child transmission in 4,500 individuals
3. To provide HIV and TB counseling and testing to 15,000 individuals
4. To provide palliative care to 15,570 individuals, excluding those with TB
5. To provide palliative care to 1,250 individuals with TB
6. To provide antiretroviral therapy (ART) drug services to 1,769 individuals
7. To provide infrastructure support to 15 laboratories
8. To support five local organizations with systemic capacity building

The action items supporting each of these eight objectives are described in detail in the Project Implementation Plan, which is a separate document accompanying this proposal and incorporated herein by reference. The collective outcome of these objectives is that new structures, systems, and roles will be defined, thereby providing staff with a new infrastructure to increase their skills to deliver improved HIV/AIDS, malaria, and tuberculosis services to persons in Northern Uganda.

This was a large-scale, interdisciplinary, intercontinental proposal involving approximately 50 health providers. Since this proposal was going to be read by health specialists in several countries, the proposal writer thought it wise to present an operational definition of "goal" and "objectives" since these terms may not carry the same meaning across cultures.

Example 5

An asthma management project from a community health coalition to a national private foundation:

The **goal** of this project is to develop a sustainable strategy for asthma management in the community. By October 31, 2017, we will accomplish the following key **objectives:**

- Significantly improve asthma-related qualify of life among children participating in coalition intervention activities.
- Reduce missed school and childcare days by 25 percent among children participating in coalition intervention activities.
- Reduce the number of children admitted for acute asthma at the Midwest Pediatric Hospital by 15 percent.
- Reduce the number of children making emergency visits for asthma to five area hospitals by 15 percent.
- Institutionalize the coalition and develop a financially sustainable strategy for childhood asthma control.

We recognize that measuring outcomes for some objectives will be more challenging than others, for example, asthma-related qualify of life among children under age five. Thus, survey tools selected will balance statistical reliability, validity, and responsiveness; cultural relevance and sensitivity; and be minimally burdensome for community members. Collectively, these objectives contribute to achieving our ultimate outcome goal: to control asthma in the county's high-risk pediatric population.

Example 6

A chemistry research proposal to NIH (National Institutes of Health). The application form uses the language "Specific Aims," which means the same as "Objectives":

Specific Aims: Considerable attention has recently been focused on the use of phospholipid bilayer vesicles as a means for encapsulating and delivering antitumor agents to neoplastic cells. Although there have been some encouraging signs, the ultimate therapeutic value of this technique remains unclear. The basic premise underlying this proposal is that carriers of the type currently being examined have limited potential and that new ones need to be developed that are more stable and offer better control over drug delivery. Our immediate chemical objective is to synthesize and characterize four new classes of phospholipid carriers within the next two years. One carrier is based on vesicles whose lipids contain two polar head groups, each of which is covalently attached to the terminal positions of a rigid hydrocarbon chain. Based on close analogy with surfactant analogs recently described in the literature, these molecules should yield monolayer phospholipid vesicles. A second type of carrier is based on vesicles comprised of phospholipid dimers covalently coupled at the polar head group. The third and fourth classes of carriers we propose are polymerized forms of micelles and vesicles, and they are termed ultrastable micelles and ultrastable vesicles. Each of the above has been specifically designed to equip the drug delivery vehicle with (1) greater intrinsic stability, (2) slower and more controllable time-release action, (3) preferred endocytotic and adsorption modes of interaction with cells, and (4) greater targeting potential.

NIH uses two terms relevant to this chapter: "Broad, long-term objectives" and "Specific Aims." As the terms are defined and commonly used in many grant sectors, the phrase "Broad, long-term objectives" is equivalent to "goals" and "Specific Aims" is interchangeable with "specific, measurable objectives." NIH recommends allocating one page to a discussion of Specific Aims. In practical terms, successful NIH grantseekers begin this section with a short paragraph describing the context for the Specific Aims. A fuller discussion of the application background is provided in another NIH proposal section. The Specific Aims describe what the research is intended to accomplish. The discussion should include the hypothesis to be tested and usually avoids methodological details, again a topic discussed in another proposal section.

Example 7

A chemistry research proposal to NSF (National Science Foundation). This writing approach uses questions as a technique for stating proposal objectives:

The chemistry of molecular oxygen compounds has been studied extensively. Yet a number of basic questions remain unanswered. This reality is particularly true for the electronic and vibrational spectra of these compounds. The questions we propose to address are:

1. What is the range of v(02) and its relationship with the M-02 (M:a metal) bond strength?
2. Does v(02) reflect the effect of the axial and equatorial legends?
3. Where are the M-02 CT bonds responsible for the embracement of v(02) and v(MO) in resonance Raman spectroscopy?
4. Is it possible to prepare novel symmetrical, side-on adducts with large legends such as metalloporphyins?

The objectives of our systematic spectroscopic study are to examine the effects of molecular oxygen adducts on a number of CO(11) chelates. The techniques employed include UV-visible, enforced, resonance Raman, and C-13 NMR spectroscopy.

The use of questions is an alternative way of indicating project objectives, an approach commonly found in some science research proposals. Beyond the use of questions, note the last two sentences serve as a transitional bridge to the methodology section. This approach provides continuity in a proposal that flows smoothly between sections.

The NSF application guidelines indicate "The Project Description should provide a clear statement of the work to be undertaken and must include: objectives for the period of the proposed work and expected significance; [and] relation to longer-term goals of the PI's project." The NSF definitions of "goals" and "objectives" are consonant with those used throughout this chapter.

Example 8

The NEA (National Endowment for the Arts) defines outcomes they expect of grantees. The following example of a music project comes from a university-community partnership. Note that the opening paragraph identifies one primary and one secondary outcome and the subsequent paragraph details the performance measurements to be used as evidence of outcome achievement:

This project directly addresses the NEA outcome of "engagement": engaging the public with diverse and excellent art. A secondary outcome of "learning" is addressed as well: enabling participants to acquire knowledge in the arts. By design, the domestic touring will reach new audiences from underserved areas, such as Springfield, Greenville, Ashland, Milford, Kingston, and Centerville. By presenting new works of music based on modern social themes at a combination of university and community settings, this project aims to: (a) cultivate an interest in new audiences for modern music, (b) stimulate a passion in high school music students for the creative process, and (c) showcase solo piano as a universal stage for budding and seasoned musicians to share their art. Particularly for the music students, the outcomes of engagement and learning are inextricably intertwined.

Consistent with the expectations of the required NEA Final Descriptive Report, evidence will be gathered to document project activity, individuals benefitted, population descriptions, organizational partners, and geographic locations of project activity. For instance, in addition to tracking measures such as attendance and downloads of music performed at the recitals, audiences will be encouraged to provide feedback on their experience through a short survey administered via smart phone and tablet technologies. High school music students will complete a pre- and postworkshop assessment to measure changes in knowledge of and attitudes toward modern solo piano.

Example 9

Because writing objectives can be a bedeviling experience for some people, in an attempt to level the playing field, the U.S. Department of Education is experimenting with a new approach: fill-in-the-blank objectives. As the following example illustrates, the language of the objectives is prescriptive and cannot be altered; applicants simply write in number percentages. Subsequently, however, they need to justify why the percentages are simultaneously "ambitious" and "attainable":

_____% of participants will complete research and scholarly activities that directly impact their educational progression each academic year.
_____% of new participants served in each academic year will attain a baccalaureate degree within three years.
_____% of bachelor's degree recipients will enroll in a postbaccalaureate program by the fall term of the academic year immediately following completion of that degree.

This standardized approach to writing objectives offers an additional benefit to the U.S. Department of Education: normalized outcomes can be reported to Congress as part of an effort to justify continued (or perhaps increased) federal support for the program.

WRITING TIPS FOR GOALS, OBJECTIVES, AND OUTCOMES

1. Be sure to differentiate sufficiently between writing broad goal statements and specific, measurable objectives. An early alert to potential difficulties is as simple as skimming over the number of objectives associated with each goal statement. When there is one objective for each goal, it's probable that not enough differentiation exists. Conversely, when there are too many objectives for each goal, it's likely that some of the "objectives" are actually activities.

2. List each specific objective in no more than one or two sentences, each in approximate order of importance.

3. List your specific objectives in expected chronological order of achievement if you are submitting a phased proposal.

4. Avoid confusing your objectives (ends) with your methods (means). A good objective emphasizes what will be done and when it will be done, whereas a method will explain how it will be done.

5. Include goal (ultimate) and objectives (immediate) statements.

6. Limit this proposal section to less than one page.

7. Avoid verbs that are fuzzy: appreciate, assist, become aware of, become familiar with, believe, consider, contemplate, contribute to, discourage, encourage, envision, explore, foster, help, imagine, inspire, look for, promote, reflect, support, think about, understand.

8. Use action verbs. The following list provides a few action verbs to get you started. Usually, the action verbs are written in the infinitive verb form, e.g., to advocate, to analyze, to anticipate.

• Anticipate	• Discriminate
• Arrange	• Display
• Assemble	• Distinguish
• Assess	• Establish
• Build	• Estimate
• Categorize	• Evaluate
• Classify	• Explain
• Compare	• Illustrate
• Conduct	• Increase
• Construct	• Investigate
• Contrast	• Measure
• Coordinate	• Motivate
• Decrease	• Organize
• Demonstrate	• Quantify
• Describe	• Solve
• Design	• Stimulate
• Detect	• Summarize
• Discover	• Translate

9. Use with caution verbs that tend to describe "activities" rather than "objectives": acquire, buy, charter, check with, consult with, contract with, discuss, employ, file, hire, lease, obtain, pay, pick up, procure, purchase, reserve, save, sort, staff.

10. As an alternative to using the infinitive verb form, some proposal writers prefer to start out using the word "By" followed by some date, e.g., "By January, 2020, such and such will happen."

11. Sometimes grant awards will be announced later than originally cited in an RFP (Request for Proposal). This can disrupt your project timetable. Unfortunately, there have been instances where grantmakers hold successful applicants to timeframes even when those awards were announced late. That is, if you indicated you would accomplish certain activities during the first year of your project and the award announcement arrived six months late, a few grantmakers expect you to do 12 months of work in six months. To avoid this grant compression through no fault of your own, one option is to not specify exact calendar dates (e.g., "By January 1, 2013") but instead cite objectives in terms of project months or years (e.g., "By project month three"). Using this approach matches your project timeframe to the award announcement cycle of the grantmaker.

REJECTION REASONS

These common rejection reasons were noted in actual reviewers' critiques of rejected proposals:

1. The objectives are more like global purposes than specific, measurable, achievable activities.
2. The realism of some objectives is questionable.
3. Some of the objectives are confusing, nonspecific, not measurable, and clearly not appropriate to the purpose of the grant.
4. Objectives are general and stated as "activities"—thus nonmeasurable. It is unclear how activities will relate to the professions involved.
5. The project objectives are more comprehensive than covered by the methods.
6. Project objectives are vague, nonspecific, and difficult to measure. No targets set in terms of faculty reached, trainees enrolled, disciplines involved.
7. The project outcomes are of limited significance.

8. The project outcomes are nebulous, diffuse, or unclear.
9. The research hypothesis is not testable.
10. The narrative would benefit from greater clarity and differentiation between project goals and objectives. For instance, the stated goal and one objective of the project are identical: "to increase student learning."
11. It is unclear exactly what will be done to achieve the three overarching goals.
12. The description of the relationship between the project goal, objectives, and outcome measures should be clearer: Exactly who will be asking the key research questions that will be answered by the dataset? Which types of interventions will be developed as a result of that data? To what extent will interventions have a net effect on targeted outcome measures such as monthly homicide and other violent crime rates?
13. There is a significant focus on teacher professional development in the proposal, including extended literature citations and as evidence of systemic change, but there is not a corresponding objective related to it. The proposal even identifies targeted activities relevant to teacher training in technology, but it does not include a measurable objective for teacher professional development.
14. Additional justification should be included for the targeted amount of change from baseline. The reasonableness of the increase in the percent of students passing the state high school exit exam from 55 percent to 85 percent by the end of year 5 is questionable.
15. The applicant does not address how this project will result in wide-scale system change or improvement.

GRANT GAFFES

As illustrated in Exhibit 43, a common grant gaffe occurs when there is insufficient differentiation between goals, objectives, activities, and outcomes. This example comes from an application submitted to a private foundation for establishing a transitional employment infrastructure network.

STARTER SENTENCES

To help you get started in writing your goals, objectives, and outcomes, we offer a few phrases and sentences with which you might begin.

Our ultimate goal is to advance poverty-reducing, employment-generating policies and thereby improve health and reduce health disparities. Its primary policy change goal is to make transitional jobs broadly available to California's unemployed and underemployed adults through sustainable, state-level policy changes.

> On the plus side, the opening paragraph uses the word "goal" and attempts to connect with the sponsor's stated interest in reducing health disparities and effecting sustainable change. On the negative side, the narrative seems to take the approach of "throw it out there and see what sticks." It is unclear, for example, whether there is one "ultimate" goal and a separate "primary" goal or whether the terms are meant as synonyms. There is confusion about whether the goal is to change policy, reduce poverty, or generate employment.

Specifically, the project's objective is the enactment of state-authorizing legislation and follow-up budget appropriations that create and fund a network of highly qualified transitional jobs "employers of record" across California that would: (1) reach out to the state's unemployed and underemployed adults ages 18–64 who have been unsuccessful for at least four weeks in finding regular full-time employment and offer them the opportunity to work in a wage-paying transitional job; (2) identify employment "host sites," both nonprofit and for-profit organizations, at which transitional jobs workers can do productive work for up to 40 hours per week and up to six months per year (with the possibility of an extension); (3) pay transitional jobs workers minimum wage for each hour of work performed (as certified by the "host sites"); (4) pay the required federal payroll taxes; and (5) manage the transitional jobs program.

> On the plus side, the second paragraph attempts to operationalize the goal by defining five underlying objectives. On the minus side, the items listed represent a mixture of nonmeasurable "objectives" and "activities." For instance, establishment of the network could be recast in quantifiable terms with respect to the number of individuals and host sites that will be engaged, e.g., "A network of 200 employers who hire 100 temporary workers in the next six months." The final lists three items—paying workers, paying taxes, and managing the program—which are activities that belong in the methods section, not in the goals, objectives, and outcomes section.

GRANT GAFFES

EXHIBIT 43

Goals

1. The **goal** of this proposed project is to . . .
2. Based on our preliminary data, our project goal is to. . .
3. We will pursue four measurable objectives, detailed below, to achieve our goal of . . .
4. Our project goal—(to do something)—represents our "big picture" vision of what we wish to accomplish.
5. To achieve this goal, our broad vision of what we hope to accomplish of (doing something), we will pursue three specific, measurable objectives. . .

Objectives

6. Our three specific aims (objectives) are . . .
7. In this proposal, we will test the hypothesis that. . .
8. This proposal presents two major goals with three specific objectives for each goal. . .
9. To assess the extent to which the proposed project solves the problems noted above, the project's effectiveness will be measured using the following project objectives: . . .
10. By October 31, 2016, we will accomplish the following measurable **objectives**. . .

Outcomes

11. We will advance fundamentally our understanding of . . .
12. Specifically, the **outcomes** of this project will enable us to better identify. . .
13. Achieving our goals and objectives will result in three major benefits. First. . .
14. At the end of the project period, three significant changes will occur. First. . .
15. Here's what will be different upon project completion:. . . .

Clip File Action Item # 12
Goals, Objectives, and Outcomes

These suggestions will get you started on building your Goals, Objectives, and Outcomes clip file:

- Collect lists of well-written statements from other proposals, whether or not they are in your interest area. Often, clear statements of goals, objectives, and outcomes can be adapted to other proposal circumstances.
- Beyond successful proposals, many program announcements have carefully worded goal, objective, and outcomes statements that can be added to your clip file.

CHAPTER 9
Methods

Vision without action is merely a dream. Action without vision just passes the time. Vision with action can change the world.

—*Joel Arthur Barker*

PURPOSE OF METHODS

In the methods section, reviewers discover whether the approach is novel, the project is well designed, the resources are adequate, and the results will be interpreted correctly. Further, other proposal sections are weighted against the methods: grant reviewers consider the extent to which the methods are appropriate for achieving the objectives, can be implemented by the identified project personnel, and are realistic within budget parameters. In Chapter 9, you will learn the following:

- Three categories of project personnel.
- Techniques for justifying methodological selection.
- Importance of detailing project activities and management plans.
- Options for illustrating project timelines.
- Sources for information on data collection instruments.

Your methods represent your action plan to reach your project goals, objectives, and outcomes. It explains how your project activities will accomplish your objectives, including your project sequence, flow, and interrelationships. Methods answer one key question: "How will I do this project?" In essence, this section of your proposal—sometimes called "methods," "methodology," "plan," "statement of work," "approach," or "procedures"—tells **who** is going to do **what** and **when** it will be done, and **how** it will be managed. Each of these four components is discussed below, followed by examples, tips, common rejection reasons, and starter sentences.

KEY QUESTIONS TO ANSWER

Does your proposal do the following:

1. Explain why one methodological approach was selected and not another?
2. Include preliminary data to show the feasibility of the project?
3. Describe the major activities for reaching each objective?
4. Specify the frequency of activities and interventions?
5. Detail strategies for identifying, recruiting, and retaining project participants?
6. Indicate the key project personnel who will carry out each activity?
7. Show the interrelationship among project activities?
8. Identify the project data that will be collected for use in evaluating proposal outcomes?
9. Stipulate which tools will be used to collect data on project activities?
10. Link closely with the budget and budget narrative?

The Who: Key Personnel

There are three categories of key personnel in most projects:

- The **staff** who will be conducting the project.
- The **subjects** participating in the project.
- The **collaborators** who will join you in conducting the project.

Each should be described in sufficient detail to establish credibility.

Project Staff. Name all key project staff, including consultants and subcontractors in your proposal. If all people are not known, include job descriptions for the people you propose to hire. At a minimum, describe the major roles each will play whether they are already onboard or proposed to hire, e.g., responsible for overall project management, liaison with project collaborators, office manager, project fiscal officer, recruiter of project participants, volunteer coordinator, evaluation specialist, and so forth. Your appendixes should contain brief résumés (or job descriptions) that stress prior relevant training and experience that will transfer to the proposed project. (See Chapter 14, Appendixes, for preparing résumés.) To enhance credibility, add the number of years your project staff has worked in this year and mention the total in your proposal:

> Our project staff of six has a cumulative 119 years of experience in dealing with this nagging problem.

Consider this project staff section as a credibility statement about you and your other key project personnel. While your résumé documents your expertise, particularly in governmental proposals, it may not communicate the fact that you work in an environment conducive to your project. Weave this point into your introduction.

> Our Detroit United Way Agency has extensive facilities, equipment, and personnel resources to support this project. They include, but are not limited to, computer support that delivers exceptional technology capabilities, business office services to ensure accurate tracking and reporting of the work effort, and evaluation specialists who are experienced with a broad range of qualitative and quantitative measurement tools.

Further, tell reviewers about your track record in similar projects. If you don't have a strong track record in your proposed project area, borrow credibility from other field experts through the use of project consultants, letters of endorsement, and supporting statistics.

Exhibit 44 is from a for-profit corporation seeking funding from a Small Business Innovation Research (SBIR) grant to develop new technologies for use with persons who have low vision or blindness. It provides a fuller description of the project director, followed by briefer descriptions of two key project personnel and a consultant. Résumés for all key project personnel are presented as appendix material.

Project Subjects. Most—but not all—grant projects involve interaction with some target audience, usually called "subjects," "clients," "patients," or "participants," who are your ultimate focal point. Often these projects involve some research, training, or service delivery that interfaces with people. Your methods section should answer these basic questions, as suggested in the examples that follow:

1. How will you identify, recruit, and retain your subjects?
   - All patients between the ages of 6 and 16 seen in the emergency room during the past 12 months will be contacted to solicit their participation in this project.
   - All children with Iowa Reading Test Scores one standard deviation below their grade level will constitute the initial project subject pool.
   - Each project collaborator will refer 10 subjects for participation in this study.
   - To select the participants for this project, 25 volunteers will be sought from local community welfare agencies. Additionally, a newspaper advertisement will invite interested participants to call our office, where screening questions will determine subject eligibility.

2. What are their basic geographic and socioeconomic characteristics?
   - All subjects must live within the four-county area and have access to transportation, to be compensated by the project.
   - All participants must have an income level of at least 150 percent below the federal poverty level.
   - To be eligible for participation in this study, the children must have received a grade of D or below in eighth grade algebra within the past 12 months and parental approval for participation in our "Math Rules and You're the Ruler Project."
   - All volunteers must be members of a community Senior Citizens Center and hold a valid driver's license.

3. How long will they be involved in the project?
   - The subjects will participate in three two-hour focus group sessions.
   - The patients will participate in a 30-minute checkup once a month for 12 months in the Emergency Room at no cost to them.
   - To measure attitudes, the clients will take a 45-minute pencil and paper test asking questions about their opinions regarding spirituality: The Grace Hope Scale.

This proposal section summarizes the key project personnel and the project responsibilities. Collectively, they have the professional training and R&D experience necessary to successfully complete this project on time and budget. They have a track record spanning over 100 years in dealing with wayfinding technologies.

Michele Major, project director, has been a pioneer in new product and business development for 24 years. Her current adaptive technology company is Wayfinding, Inc., founded in January 1990 to make location information accessible to the blind. Ms. Major is principal investigator on a five-year $2.25 million NIDRR funded grant (award number J248A023943) for the research and development of accessible wayfinding technology for blind and visually impaired individuals. The NIDRR Wayfinding grant focuses on navigation for blind people and is distinctly different from this SBIR proposal that focuses on people identification and information transfer.

Ms. Major is directly responsible for the development, implementation, monitoring, and day-to-day supervision of this project. Further, her broad-based networks enable her to stay informed about telecommunication industry trends and for creating products and distributing them to blind users. Based on extensive networks and linkages, she works directly with and can rely on support from the various universities involved in the wayfinding field, namely, University of California–Santa Barbara, Western Michigan University, University of Minnesota, Smith Kettlewell Institute, Carnegie Mellon University, and the Department of Veterans Affairs R&D division.

Charles Dakota, project engineer, Wayfinding's chief technology officer and lead software engineer, holds a patent for the first commercially available accessible Global Positioning System for blind and visually impaired individuals. He is an electrical engineer with an MSEE degree from Midwest University whose work has involved the integration of GPS and dead-reckoning technology. He has been a software engineer for four adaptive technology companies, VisuAide, Arkenstone, Benetech, and Wayfinding, Inc. He and Michele Major have a successful track record in obtaining the cooperation of software and hardware manufacturers in order to leverage the development of products for the blind. For example, Wayfinding, Inc., has negotiated low-cost and no-cost map licenses worth hundreds of thousands of dollars. We anticipate continued cooperation with industry on issues such as these, and we recognize that cooperation with industry and government is essential to accomplishing our specific aims. His primary project responsibility is to create a working technology prototype of the wayfinding device to be developed.

Casey Malek, technology transfer specialist, is Wayfinding's training coordinator and marketing manager. She has more than 12 years of experience working with accessible GPS systems. Her expertise spans from testing and development to end user training. Ms. Malek also possesses the ability to market using various media—World Wide Web, HTML programming, video, print, and audio presentations. She has a demonstrated track record of leading product from the research bench to the marketplace.

Dr. Paul Vargas, project consultant, Department of Blind Rehabilitation at Western California University, will bring his expertise in consumer needs assessment, rehabilitation outcomes, program evaluation, focus groups, and development of technological devices to the project. He has worked with the key project personnel on other similar projects.

SAMPLE PERSONNEL DESCRIPTION

EXHIBIT 44

- Both the experimental and control groups will participate in pre- and posttests of motor coordination. In addition, the experimental group will receive six one-hour sessions in eye-hand coordination training.

4. To what extent do special client issues need to be addressed, e.g., compromised health status, transportation barriers, restrictive home environments, unsafe neighborhoods, unfavorable publicity, controversial policies, limited educational opportunities?

- To ensure the clients' physical health status is not compromised during the period of intense physical exertion, an emergency room physician will oversee all stress testing.
- Since the After-School Project ends after sunset, our mobile vans will transport the students directly to their homes, rather than risk them walking home in unsafe neighborhoods.
- Our physical facilities comply wholly with the American Disabilities Act; accordingly, our

wheelchair clients will face no physical barriers entering the building or negotiating its interior.

- Since our HIV clients could risk unfavorable publicity if they were identified by name, all records will use fictitious first names only, and only the project director will have the master list of record identifier numbers in order to ensure confidentiality and respect individual privacy.

Project Collaborators. Increasingly, sponsors encourage—and indeed expect—collaboration. Collaborations show a large "buy-in" to projects and increase the likelihood of sustainability beyond the granting period as project components are institutionalized. (See Chapter 13, Sustainability.)

A collaboration is defined as an interaction between two or more persons or organizations directed toward a common goal that is mutually beneficial. Because of their respective commitments to a shared cause, collaborators may agree to engage in a mutual exchange in order to reap larger benefits. In practical terms, this means that collaborators (1) must communicate through preferred formal and information means at agreed-upon intervals and (2) share human, physical, and financial resources such as equipment, instrumentation, databases, personnel, target populations, business office service, intellectual property, and cash and in-kind contributions. In a successful collaboration, the whole is greater than the sum of the individual parts. All collaborators must identify what resources they will bring to the table and their preferred channels of communication.

Collaborations range from casual to formal relationships, such as informational collaborations, consortia, interdisciplinary teams, and centers or institutes. Four common types of collaborations include coexistence, coordination, cooperation, and coalition, which vary in their degrees of goal sharing and interaction. Good business practices suggest committing the understanding and agreements to writing (see Chapter 14 for sample consortium agreements and memoranda of understanding). Picking collaborators is like picking a mate: you want to do it carefully, for it has long-term relationship and financial consequences. In essence, project collaborations are valuable for informing people, solving problems, and creating support.

Successful collaborations often entail many hours of meetings. Experienced grantseekers have learned through trial and error these tips for conducting effective grant collaborations:

- Limit the meetings to no more than 1.5 hours.
- Invite no more than nine people.
- Include the key players in meetings; if they can't attend, reschedule.
- Provide a two-week advance notice of the meeting.
- Distribute a detailed written agenda one week in advance of the meeting.
- Take thorough minutes.

The What: Project Activities

Justification of Methods. Each project will have its own unique set of methods, activities, and tasks to accomplish the stated objectives. Whatever methods you deem appropriate for your project, justify their selection. You had choices, and reviewers will want to know why you chose this approach and not some other alternative. A few sentences of methodological justification prior to describing specific project activities will anticipate and answer an important question in the minds of the reviewers: "Of the universe of possible methodologies, why did you pick this one?"

- The method of choice is to use a double blind study; it is the only experimental design available that can isolate the effects of the independent variable on the project outcomes.
- This project is using the Grace Hope Scale to measure spirituality since it is, according to Buros's *Yearbook of Mental Measurements*, the only instrument with acceptable reliability, validity, and normative data for our target population.
- Because no psychometric instrument exists to measure teenage attitudes toward learning a foreign language, according to Buros's *Yearbook of Mental Measurements*, it is necessary for us to develop our own measurement instrument; Dr. Don Sprengel from the Department of Research Methodology at the local university has agreed to serve as a project consultant in this regard and has the requisite expertise in psychometric methodology.
- Since it is imperative we have the broadest possible community input in the most cost-effective manner, our approach relies on the time-proven benefits of using focus groups, a survey procedure that the project director has used successfully in similar past situations.
- Research over the past 15 years documents that mentoring is the most cost-effective approach to integrating individuals with severe physical

disabilities into the workplace; accordingly, it is our preferred method to solve the existing needs.

Larger projects are sometimes difficult to understand, especially when reviewers might only skim read your proposal. One way to bring clarity to large-scale projects is to "chunk" it up into phases.

> Our campaign to build stronger STEM learning environments for undergraduate research as a high-impact practice consists of six phases. In this proposal, we are seeking funding for Phase V, while appreciating the fact that reviewers might like to see the scope of our entire initiative:
>
> Phase I: Audit of physical conditions of our science facility (2010).
>
> Phase II: Campus master plan that includes renovating the science facility (2011).
>
> Phase III: Academic master plan that includes integrating undergraduate research experiences into the curriculum (2012).
>
> Phase IV: Assessment of proposed curricular improvements for STEM majors and nonmajors (2013).
>
> Phase V: Schematics for the science facility renovation, with one floor below grade and three above (2014).
>
> Phase VI: Renovation of the science facility, adding 90,000 square feet of collaborative research space and 60,000 square feet of learning space (2015).

This example illustrates project phasing within the context of a large-scale, multiyear STEM (Science, Technology, Engineering, and Mathematics) initiative. This phasing concept can also be used within a single project. For instance, a regional conference could be presented as consisting of three phases: (1) disseminate best practices to constituents,

(2) integrate best practices among constituents, and (3) evaluate the adoption of best practices. The notion of proposal phasing is useful any time many activities will occur in a proposal and there is need to clarify and organize project tasks.

Data Collection. You will probably need to collect some data as a part of your project. Common types and sources of data collection include those listed in Exhibit 45.

You can either construct your own data-gathering instruments or use existing ones. To find out whether an appropriate instrument already exists (and avoid reinventing the wheel), consider looking through reference books such as Buros's *Mental Measurements Yearbook* and Jones's *Handbook of Tests and Measurements for Black Populations*, which list available tests in many different fields. Buros's yearbook, for instance, reviews the various attitude, behavior, and motor tests that are commercially available. Each review contains a description by the test author(s) and critiques by several experts in the field. The descriptions include the purpose, statistical characteristics, and, when available, the test norms. For example, if you are studying the relationship between spirituality and wellness, you could look in Buros's to see if any attitudinal measures of spirituality exist. Buros's yearbook and Jones's handbook can be found in the reference section of most larger libraries.

Relationship of Objectives and Methods. Your objectives tell your reviewers **what** you propose to do. Your methods tell your reviewers **how** you will accomplish each objective. Put differently, you should include one or more methods for each objective. Use transitional language in your proposal to signal to the reviewers the relationship between your objectives and your methods, as the following example shows.

• Achievement tests	• Government records	• Referral forms
• Archival information	• Historical program records	• Reviews of literature
• Attendance records	• Interviews	• Role-playing exercises
• Case histories	• Personal diaries or logs	• Searches of news media
• Clinical examinations	• Physical tests	• Surveys
• Controlled observations	• Psychological tests	• Telephone logs
• Daily program records	• Questionnaires	• Tracking slips
• Focus groups	• Ratings by program staff	• University research offices

COMMON DATA COLLECTION TOOLS

EXHIBIT 45

To address the first objective, developing an Internet-based geriatric dentistry program, the following action items will occur:

- An Internet service provider will be selected, one with prior experience in mounting distance learning programs.
- The instructional modules will be storyboarded to flush out content.
- The instructional designer will take our content and develop visually literate formats.
- The first draft will be checked for content accuracy and user-friendliness.
- The revised draft will be field-tested with 10 geriatric dentists around the country.
- Appropriate revisions will be made.
- The service provider will market the resulting distance learning program.

The next example is from a proposal targeted to a private foundation seeking funding to develop a geriatric education curriculum for use in a medical school. Note the approach taken in this persuasive writing segment. The specific measurable objective is restated to remind the reader, followed by the specific activities, their purposes, and the processes to be followed.

Activities for Objective 1

Objective 1: By June 30, 2012, develop three geriatric eLearning curriculum modules for the evaluation and management of frail and minority elderly patients to age in place.

Activity 1.1: Develop Module One: Approaches to Frailty

Purpose of 1.1: This module presents the fundamental techniques for the prevention, screening, assessment, and management of frail health.

Process Tasks for 1.1: Review literature, survey practitioners, survey healthy elders, determine learning objectives, develop pre- and postevaluation measures, finalize content (Curriculum Development Team led by Dr. Simon), finalize instructional levels (Curriculum Delivery Team led by Dr. Schuster), technologize module, critique by Oversight Committee and Geriatric Advisory Board, revise and resubmit as appropriate.

Outcome Tasks for 1.1: By June 30, 2013, this module will be developed as a case-based, small group activity in Clinical Medicine 1 and will be supplemented with a Web-based assignment. It will introduce the concept of frailty along with the concept of healthy aging.

Activity 1.2: Develop Module Two: Aging Successfully in Place

Purpose of 1.2: This module describes the concept of aging successfully in place and its role in home health care services.

Outcome Tasks for 1.2: By December 30, 2013, this module will include a Web-based assignment that describes the stages of aging successfully in place.

Activity 1.3: Develop Module Three: Continuum of Care for the Elderly

Purpose of 1.3: This module broadens the concept of elder care and identifies paramedical services that enhance the quality of life and its longevity.

Process Tasks for 1.3: Same as Tasks for 1.1.

Outcome Tasks for 1.3: By March 31, 2014, this module will cover the continuity and continuum of care throughout the elderly years, including the role and identification of essential support services.

In sum, the Curriculum Development Team and the Curriculum Delivery Team will work in parallel to ensure that the content and technology meet the highest standards for each of the nine modules. The specific team members are listed in Attachment Five.

The When: Project Timelines

Time and Task Charts. The use of a time and task chart represents one common and successful means of clearly communicating the methods section in your proposal. This visual device segments your total project into manageable steps and lets your reviewers know exactly who will be doing what and when. It tells reviewers that you are organized and have thought out the major steps of your project. This way, your reviewers know you have done significant planning and are not just proposing a wild whim. With a time and task chart, they can look at a road map of the territory you plan to cover. Finally, the time and task chart represents a clear, one-page, visual summary of the entire methodology section. It would, for example, be a logical addition to the end of the bioethics methodology section described in example 2 below.

Many different types of time and task charts can be used. Which type you use is not as important as the fact you do include one that the reviewers can easily grasp. Some grant writers prefer to include it at the beginning of the methods section to provide the reviewers with an orientation to the narrative that follows. Others like to put it at the end of the methods section as a visual summary of the preceding verbal narrative. The choice is yours. Successful grantseekers often include their favorite time and task chart—whether or not it is requested in the application guidelines.

As you study the time and task chart shown in Exhibit 46, notice that it presents goals, objectives with pertinent activities, including beginning and ending dates as well as the responsible individual. In essence, it is a comprehensive work plan seeking funding for a preschool curriculum development project. Mechanically, it is merely a four-column table generated from your favorite word processing program.

The second example of a time and task chart, Exhibit 47, is sometimes called a project planner. Also prepared in a four-column table format using word processing software, it outlines the major activities of the project and the key individuals responsible for conducting the activities. In addition, it lists the duration of each activity; rather than name specific calendar months, it identifies project months. The final column contains a budget for each activity. While it requires extra effort to determine costs for each activity, this information is useful in those instances when agencies ask you to reduce your budget. If you must reduce your budget by, say, $10,000, which project activities will you eliminate? The program survey? The final publication? Neither makes sense for this project, which is the Project Planner for Exhibit 27 in Chapter Five, Letter Proposal Template. Once sponsors realize how thoroughly you have planned your project, they may show more flexibility in funding your full budget request.

Work Plan for June 1, 2013, through December 31, 2015			
Goal: To enable 200 children between the ages of six weeks and four years the opportunity to maximize their cognitive, social, and emotional potential through participation in a state-of-the-art early childhood learning experience.			
Activity	**Begin Date**	**End Date**	**Responsibility**
Objective # 1: Train 200 children on Houston's northwest side in a culturally competent early childhood program.	Jun 2013	Dec 2015	Executive Director
• **Activity 1.1.** Develop and field test a modular early childhood enrichment curriculum based on early brain development research.	Jun 2013	Nov 2013	Curriculum Consultant, Health Education Center
• **Activity 1.2.** Train 10 trainers in the curriculum modules.	Aug 2013	Aug 2014	Curriculum Consultant
• **Activity 1.3.** Establish formal collaborations between White's Child Development Center, Multicultural Family Services, Silver Lake Neighborhood Center, and affiliate family care.	Jul 2013	Dec 2015	Project Manager
Objective # 2: Coordinate education, training, and supportive services for parents of at least 200 young children.	Dec 2013	Dec 2015	Executive Director
• **Activity 2.1.** Explain curriculum to 50 parents.	Aug 2014	Dec 2015	HEC Project Manager
• **Activity 2.2.** Show 25 parents 1/2-hour training video.	Sep 2013	Dec 2015	Project Manager
• **Activity 2.3.** Train 10 parents of special needs infants and toddlers, and link them with support services.	Dec 2014	Dec 2015	Curriculum Consultant
• **Activity 2.4.** Stimulate parental involvement in education sessions, parent-teacher meetings, and class volunteers.	Jan 2014	Dec 2015	HEC Project Manager

TIME AND TASK CHART

EXHIBIT 46

Activities	Responsibility	Duration	Budget
• Identify Target Urban Areas	• Jane O'Connor, Project Director	• Month One	• $3,345
• Design Evaluation Tools	• J. O'Connor	• Month One	• 2,845
• Survey Program Practices	• Audra Hill, Assistant Director	• Months One and Two	• 8,976
• Analyze Survey Data	• J. O'Connor, A. Hill	• Months Three and Four	• 5,190
• Draft Preliminary Report	• Tera Maki, Technical Writer	• Months Five and Six	• 4,690
• Publish Preliminary Report	• Wise Publishing Company	• Months Seven and Eight	• 7,345
• Disseminate Report	• T. Maki	• Month Nine	• 3,238
• Seek Report Feedback	• J. O'Connor	• Months Nine and Ten	• 4,345
• Revise Preliminary Report	• T. Maki	• Months Eleven and Twelve	• 5,805
• Publish Final Report	• Wise Publishing Company	• Months Thirteen and Fourteen	• 11,690
• Distribute Final Report	• T. Maki	• Month Fifteen	• 3,476
Total Direct Cost			• $57,600
+Administrative Cost			• 11,520
=Total Project Cost			• $69,120
-Cost Sharing			• 2,888
=Amount Requested			• $66,240

PROJECT PLANNER

EXHIBIT 47

Another approach to developing time and task charts involves the use of computer software specifically designed for such purposes, such as Microsoft Project (www.microsoft.com/project) and 2-Plan (www.2-plan.com). The following example from Microsoft Project includes specific project tasks, start and end dates, and personnel responsible for each task; additionally a bar graph indicates the duration of various activities. The example in Exhibit 48 deals with the process to develop a training module to prevent the mother-to-child transmission of HIV, a problem that accounts for roughly 20 percent of all HIV cases in sub-Saharan Africa. This software also contains a number of other features, including resource allocations, activity costs, and adjustments for time slippages, that are not reflected in this example.

The How: Project Management

Your project management approach represents a disciplined way of organizing, allocating, communicating, and managing your human, physical, and financial resources so that your project successfully meets its objectives on time and within budget. More specifically, your resources include money, people, materials, energy, space, supplies, equipment, quality control, and risk management. Your project management plan in your proposal describes how you will administer your grant.

The following example comes from a proposal that seeks to empower inner city, low income women with young children by providing them training in securing housing, finding jobs, and gaining an education. Note, in particular, the organizational chart of the project management team and their communication plans, an essential component of project management:

Our Project Management Team (PMT) represents the governance body that provides project leadership and oversight. The PMT bears the ultimate responsibility for ensuring successful project completion. The PMT includes the

Task Name	Start	Finish	June	July	August	September	October	November	December
0 Kenya Technical Assistance Model	Mon 7/2/07	Fri 12/28/07							
1 Basic Initiatives	Mon 7/2/07	Fri 12/28/07							
2 1.1 Train The Trainers on Standardized Curricula	Mon 7/2/07	Fri 7/20/07							
3 1.2 Module One: Prevent Mother To Child Transmission	Mon 7/9/07	Fri 12/28/07							
4 1.2.1 Training	Mon 7/9/07	Fri 8/17/07							
5 1.2.1.1 Intro to HIV/AIDS	Mon 7/9/07	Fri 7/13/07		Dr. Jones					
6 1.2.1.2 Interventions to Prevent MTCT	Mon 7/16/07	Fri 7/20/07		Dr. Smith					
7 1.2.1.3 Counseling, Testing, Supportive Care	Mon 7/23/07	Fri 7/27/07		Dr. Chan					
8 1.2.1.4 Infant Feeding	Mon 7/30/07	Fri 8/3/07			Dr. Griffith				
9 1.2.1.5 Advanced PMTCT	Mon 8/6/07	Fri 8/10/07			Dr. Jackson				
10 1.2.1.6 Program Implementation Overview	Mon 8/13/07	Fri 8/17/07			Dr. Barker				
11 1.2.2 Implementation	Mon 8/20/07	Fri 12/28/07							

MICROSOFT PROJECT AS TIME AND TASK CHART

EXHIBIT 48

project director (Mike Johnson) and team leaders in our three program areas: housing, jobs, and education. Collectively, this four-person PMT will be responsible for successfully integrating the services that empower inner city single mothers and their families. All teams must rely on collaboration with community partners and the various resources they offer to our target population, as the following PMT organizational chart indicates.

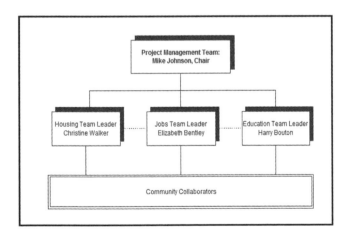

The PMT will meet biweekly to monitor project progress and ensure the technical objectives are met on time and budget. Communication is a core value for the PMT as they connect with various external audiences (e.g., community partners and project participants) and internal audiences (e.g., field managers and evaluation personnel). At a minimum, the PMT will address the major project issues and communicate outcomes, including the following:

1. Appropriate deployment and use of resources
2. Project progress and status reports: administrative, programmatic, and fiscal
3. Interim and final process and outcome evaluations
4. Project deliverables
5. Accountability for project human resources
6. Changes in project processes, procedures, and policies
7. Critical incidents
8. Major milestones

The intended results of the PMT's communication efforts are to affect the knowledge, attitudes, and behaviors of key internal and external project stakeholders. Among the timing for the various messages to be disseminated are the following:

- Monthly written status reports that summarize accomplishments, timelines, budget, and risk management
- Ongoing face-to-face communications
- Biweekly teleconference PMT meetings
- Quarterly written quality assurance status reports
- Quarterly teleconference best practices meetings
- Biweekly project management coordination meetings
- Personal on-site orientation, as needed
- Semiannual site visits by PMT

- Press releases by PMT to mass media, as appropriate
- Journal articles and convention papers by key project personnel, as appropriate
- Monthly electronic project newsletter
- Written minutes of all meetings
- Evaluation reports of training sessions by provider and consumers

The PMT has over 12 years of experience in working together on similar past projects and is familiar with the management style of each person. Collectively, the PMT has spent more than 50 years working on empowerment projects for young women.

Getting Started

Begin with your objectives. Describe the precise steps you will follow to carry out each objective, including what will be done, who will do it, and when it will be done. If you have trouble writing this section, assume the sponsor's check just arrived in the mail. What is the first thing you would do? Hire additional staff? Order equipment? What would you do next? Keep asking and answering the "What's next?" question and you will lead yourself through the methodology section.

EXAMPLES OF METHODS

Example 1

Exhibit 49 contains the key methodological section in a proposal from a nonprofit organization submitted to a federal agency seeking support to hold a statewide conference alerting healthcare providers to the problem of perinatal depression. The applicant placed this proposal in a larger context of its long-term initiatives; specifically, this request for conference support represented phase four of a five-phased initiative. The methodology section of this proposal concluded with a time and task chart that identified the specific people who would carry out the four different activity areas for its two objectives and their targeted timeframes.

Example 2

An example from a hospital seeking federal funding to establish a bioethics center.

Bioethics Center Approach and Methods.
Overview. For each of the three major center goals described above, this proposal section details precisely what will be accomplished, methods of choice, task sequences, responsible individuals, time frames, and expected outcomes.

Organization. From the objectives, it is apparent that the center has a tripartite focus: clinical, educational, and administrative. The center organization chart (see table 1, following page) reflects this service aim. The center project director, Dr. David Schwartz, is a full-time staff member at the Jones Memorial Hospital. Additionally, associate directors in each service area will be appointed: Dr. Marvin Todd, associate director for Clinical Affairs, Jones Memorial Hospital; Dr. William Ashmore, associate director for Administrative Affairs, Medical University; and Dr. Robert Starr, associate director for Educational Affairs, Midwest University. Brief personnel descriptions are provided in the institutional overview statements beginning on page 13. Complete curriculum vitae are appended.

Mechanisms of Commitment and Cooperation. The three core institutions will sign the Consortium Agreement specified in Appendix 1. The agreement describes the programmatic, fiscal, and administrative protocols that form the foundation of the center. Additionally, the center will want to quickly expand its affiliation with other medical centers and universities who share a mutual interest and concern in clinical ethics. Those institutions will be actively encouraged to quickly sign the Affiliation Agreement listed in appendix 2. This formal affiliation will give them early access to the center and quickly build a national base of operation. Finally, some institutions may not be prepared to make a full affiliation commitment, but they may want to be formally identified with and participate in center activities. Those institutions will be urged to sign the Participant Institution Agreement listed in Appendix 3.

The lengthy methodology section in this proposal went on to restate each specific objective and describe what specific actions would be taken to carry out each objective. Since the central focus of this proposal was to establish an ethics education program for health and allied health professionals, the methodology section then concluded with the following discussion of a Clinical Ethics Education Program:

Clinical Ethics Education Program. To promote ethics education programs, the center proposes to establish a program in Clinical Ethics

Request for Regional Conference Support

This proposal identifies two major goals and subsequent measurable objectives, along with appropriate *dissemination* and *integration* activities.

Goal #1: To disseminate best practices to constituents

Objective 1.1: By March 2009, develop an information architecture for disseminating best practices.

Activities for Objective 1.1

In order to disseminate best practices, an information architecture must exist to provide the key intellectual content and delivery systems for transferring research knowledge to practitioners. Information architecture, in this case, represents the knowledge base generated from the Symposium Proceedings (Phase II) and the Blueprint for Action (Phase III). In essence, the approach of choice establishes the communication infrastructure for disseminating knowledge. To accomplish this, the knowledge base for the information architecture will come from Phase II, the Best Practices Conference and Phase III, the Blueprint for Action. Electronic (Web-based) proceedings will be hosted on the Perinatal Care Web site. The deliverable for this objective is to collate, print, and bind the Blueprint for Action that will be distributed to an estimated 300 symposium attendees in advance of the regional conferences.

Objective 1.2: By June 2009, disseminate select prenatal and postpartum depression information throughout seven regions in the state.

Activities for Objective 1.2

Once the information architecture is built, the host information will be widely disseminated to targeted consumers and prenatal and postpartum practitioners throughout the state using two different approaches. First, the Phase I mailing campaign identified 15,000 prenatal and postpartum health care providers who will be notified by a third postcard (earlier ones sent on November 2007 and January 2008) about access to an electronic version of Symposium Proceedings/Blueprint for Action (15,000 distribution). Second, beyond the symposium participants, electronic (Web-based) and bound printed Symposium Proceedings and a Blueprint for Action will be distributed to an estimated 350 conference professionals who will participate in the regional conferences, described below.

Goal #2: To integrate best practices among constituents

Objective 2.1 By August 2009, conduct seven regional conferences: Integrating Best Practices.

Activities for Objective 2.1

Seven regional constituent-based conferences will be convened to encourage and support the exchange of effective implementation strategies; Appendix Six contains a map of regions and probable site locations. The regional conferences will identify culturally sensitive topics, define best practice models relevant to each region, present an overview of Symposium Proceedings and a Blueprint for Action, define cultural and/or systemic barriers that hinder integration into clinical practice, identify criteria for regional customization, and generate customized regional integration strategies.

Objective 2.2: By August 2009, promote partnerships that will stimulate the integration of best practices.

Activities for Objective 2.2

The following actions will promote the development of new strategic partnerships. (1) Expert clinicians, as conference presenters, will establish communications with regional leaders at the seven regional conferences. (2) Practitioners at the local level will identify clinical and systems opportunities of mutual interest as a result of networking. (3) Strategic partners will identify interventions and topics for multiregional clinical research through networking.

SAMPLE PROPOSAL METHODOLOGY

EXHIBIT 49

Education (CEE). The CEE program assumes that (1) ethics is appropriate for all health care providers and (2) instruction in clinical ethics demands a novel curricular implementation. Central to the program are two clinical institutes that will provide the groundwork for developing a strengthened interdisciplinary, hospital-wide curriculum in clinical ethics education and for training health care professionals to teach clinical ethics within the hospital. The CEE program also will include ethics seminars, speaker programs, and guest lecturing clinicians and ethicists.

The guiding vision of the CEE program will be to focus the attention of health care professionals upon the principles of ethical theory and their practical application to a broad range of health care matters in other disciplines. Each participating hospital will gain newly energized clinicians, an increase in ethical sensitivity, and relevantly revised training programs in clinical ethics. Moreover, health care providers will gain a new interdisciplinary perspective on ethics and will receive varied supports for collegiate collaboration.

In essence, the major center outcome will be to provide this cadre of health professionals with focused training in ethics theory and crosswalks that foster interdisciplinary communication. This focus will allow the center to more fully centralize its clinical ethics curriculum around fundamental philosophical and theological ethical models. Clinicians who are versed in the basic principles of the theoretical study of ethics are better able to see how these principles converge with applied practices.

Rather than allowing ethics to be learned in isolated fragments from different disciplines, the CEE program would coordinate the resources of different disciplines under one umbrella to provide clinicians with a more organized and integrated exploration of ethics. Ethics will achieve a first-class status within the participating hospital as a result of the CEE program. All clinicians will benefit from the increased excellence in the study of ethics.

CEE Program Administration. The associate director for Educational Affairs will administer the CEE program with extensive consultation from the Advisory Board of the Center for Ethics Studies at Midwest University, and a broad network of hospital affiliates. Specifically, Professor Starr, of Midwest's theology department, will serve as program coordinator. Professor Johnson, of the philosophy department, will function as associate coordinator. As shown in Appendix 5, both the

program coordinator and associate coordinator have strong professional records in the field of ethics and are oriented to interdisciplinary ethics education. In general, the program administrators will be responsible for directing the functions of the program and for assessing the success of these activities.

CEE Program Functions. The CEE program will include the following three major functions:

- A *Series of Two Summer Clinical Institutes*
  These institutes will bring together clinicians from different specialties interested in ethics (a) to provide an organized seminar in basic ethical theory, (b) to explore the application of this theoretical framework to the various specialties, (c) to plan curricular changes in medical education at each affiliated hospital, and (d) to provide training for implementing the revised curriculum. Specifically, the first summer institute will concentrate upon the key elements of the theory of ethics. The following summer institute will explore curricular changes that incorporate the theory into practical situations.

- *Development of the Interdisciplinary Curriculum in Ethics*
  As previously described, the ultimate objective of the CEE program is to develop an explicitly highlighted interdisciplinary curriculum in clinical ethics. In light of the natural enrichment generated by interaction of ethicists and clinicians in diverse health care disciplines, proposals will be developed and implemented for incorporating clinical ethics components throughout the hospital system.

- A *Series of Sponsored Programmed Meetings*
  Interested clinicians and medical students will attend a regularly scheduled forum on clinical ethics to share their respective insights and efforts in the study of ethics. These seminars, administered jointly by the associate director for Clinical Affairs and the associate director for Educational Affairs, will address issues in ethical theory and the application of that theory to problems in the applied fields.

Example 3

A health education center seeking funding from a local private foundation to develop a video on early brain development for childcare providers:

This program will be made available to communities throughout the center's current service area, which includes 13 counties in southeastern Wyoming and two in northern Arizona. The intended audience for this program would be the parents, grandparents, guardians, public health nurses, parish nurses, home visitors, and child care providers. It is anticipated that approximately 30 people will participate in each session of the program. Twelve presentations will be made during the project period, thereby directly targeting 360 people.

The content of the program will address the healthy growth and development of a child socially, physically, emotionally, and cognitively. A variety of learning formats will be employed, including lecture, small-group discussions, role playing, interactive videos and models, and group participation. Among these training techniques, the research literature shows that interactive videos are particularly effective in producing long-term behavioral changes. This program will provide participants with the ability to model healthy adult-child interactions for each other. Most important, adults will learn skills that promote healthy brain development and relations building from 0–3 years of age.

Example 4

An institution of higher education seeking funding from a government program to increase recruitment and retention of underrepresented groups in STEM (Science, Technology, Engineering, and Mathematics) disciplines:

> The STEM (Science, Technology, Engineering, and Mathematics) Summer Plus Program will provide first-generation, low-income, and multicultural undergraduates with an opportunity to participate in an intensive faculty-student research collaboration for 10 weeks full-time in the summer *plus* 30 weeks part-time during the following academic year. It is essential that the students are fully engaged in all aspects of research: they will set up experiments, experience methods such as electron microscopy and nanoindentation, use state-of-the art instrumentation to acquire data, analyze data, and present results. Research is integral to understanding the process of science and a way to apply what they learned in class to new questions.
>
> Of the six students participating in the program, four will be between their freshman and sophomore years and two will be between their junior and senior years. This will provide an opportunity for already established students to provide peer mentoring to the students with less experience. The peer mentors' primary role is not shepherding the individual projects but rather providing insight on difficulties that can be encountered during the research process. The PI will mentor one cohort of students and the co-PI will mentor the other cohort. The entire group will meet once a week to discuss the research progress, science issues, responsible research, and employment opportunities after graduation.
>
> Several avenues will be used to identify eligible students. The PI and co-PI will solicit recommendations from the Multicultural Affairs Office, Admissions Office, faculty teaching the introductory STEM courses, and instructors for MATH 120, PHYS 210, CHEM 105–106, and BIOL 210. Broad announcements will also be posted on the university Web page and department Facebook site, two key means for delivering mass messages to students. The primary selection criteria will be potential for success in a research setting: problem-solving skills and lab skills are often a better indicator of student research potential than GPA.

WRITING TIPS FOR THE METHODS SECTION

1. Justify your selection of methods.
2. Describe what is unique about your approach. Have others used your procedures? Is there solid reason to believe they will work? If you use experimental methods, indicate why you chose them over others.
3. Pay attention to project scope. If you find it difficult to include everything that you want to address, the scope may be too broad. If you find there is only one objective—to buy a piece of equipment—and the methods section focuses on the instrument as an end in itself rather than as a means to a larger end, the scope may be too narrow.
4. Segment your methodological approach into activity areas; this organization makes the project design easier to understand. Note the use of subheadings in Example 2.
5. Discuss the risks with your methods and why your success is probable.
6. Include a time and task chart. Listing the names or titles of personnel who will carry out each activity

foreshadows for reviewers the role each person plays in your project budget.

7. Establish the credibility of key personnel to perform the planned work: identify academic degrees, relevant education, experience, training, awards, and recognition received.
8. Restate or summarize your objectives at the beginning of each major activity area.
9. If you are generating data, explain how you will collect, analyze, and interpret it. Describe the survey tools that you will use, including reliability and validity characteristics.
10. Explain how information collected will be used to monitor program progress and indicate when final reports and outcomes will be available.

REJECTION REASONS

The following 15 statements from rejected proposals represent methodological shortcomings in three categories: Project Personnel, Project Methods, and Project Timelines.

Project Personnel

1. The project appears to incorporate little personnel expertise in the disciplines involved.
2. This proposal seems premature. Not until an interdisciplinary group is in place can this project be expected to operate effectively.
3. Project staff is not specified in the narrative, i.e., job descriptions are not included and prior relevant work experience is not explained.
4. The project director lacks experience in the essential methodology.
5. The applicant does not provide any indication of the number of clients to be served.

Project Methods

1. There is insufficient experimental detail to approve the project.
2. The methodology is diffuse, superficial, and unfocused.
3. The proposal narrative does not describe why the target population of the homeless was selected over other needy populations. Are the homeless disproportionately represented compared to other

groups, e.g., frail elderly, battered women, or drug abusers?

4. There is a gap between the "problem" identified in the opening section of the proposal and the "solution" presented here. The "problem" focuses on the needs of uninsured patients. The "solution" focuses on meeting the needs of the providers.
5. It would have been helpful if the applicant had delineated the existing activities versus the proposed program activities as directed in the application instructions.

Project Timelines

1. Greater care in planning is needed. It is highly unlikely that the methods can be accomplished within the specified timeframe.
2. No timelines are provided for the major tasks; this represents a serious planning gap on the part of the applicants.
3. While major time frames are provided for each milestone, the applicants do not indicate who is responsible for carrying out each activity.
4. The timelines are extraordinarily ambitious.
5. The sequence of project activities needs to be reexamined. It does not appear that the requisite resources will always be in place to complete the individual activities.

GRANT GAFFES

The annotated example in Exhibit 50 of a methods grant gaffe represents a social science research project on climate change submitted to a private foundation. To overcome the ill-defined nature of the methodological approach, the principal investigator relies heavily on previous successful work to say to reviewers, in essence, "Don't mind the lack of details. Trust me. I'll figure it out."

STARTER SENTENCES

These 10 sentences may help you start writing your methods section. Use them as springboards to generate your first draft.

1. Our methodological approach will produce a paradigm shift in. . .

My current climate change research was initiated with the help of faculty at major public universities in four states (California, New York, Pennsylvania, and Texas) and Chinese universities in four provinces (Beijing, Hunan, Shaanxi, and Zhejiang). We conducted two online surveys in Fall 2010 to investigate college student perceptions of climate change. Our results reveal significant differences between U.S. and Chinese college student opinions: U.S. students are less likely to admit the existence of climate change and are less likely to attribute climate change as being caused by human activities. Chinese students rank the economy and environment essentially equal as the most important issue for their government to address, whereas U.S. students rank the economy nearly four times more important than the environment.

My past and proposed climate change research relies heavily on faculty connections at a variety of universities in China and the United States to obtain convenience samples to conduct our surveys. Because samples are not randomized, our research may not indisputably generalize to all populations in both countries. However, we have and will continue to carefully identify and select our samples so that respondents are reasonably representative of the populations we are surveying.

Our plan for data collection in China is reasonably well defined: student leaders will be trained in the specifics of face-to-face survey methodology and then will go out in public to conduct the interviews. Although the details still need to be worked out, in the United States we will likely use postcard mailings with a link to an online survey in combination with conducting face-to-face surveys in public places. Our goal is to obtain about 1,000 completed surveys split evenly between 500 Chinese and 500 U.S. respondents. As our planning evolves, we may determine this process is too time consuming and inefficient, in which case we will consider contracting with a firm that specializes in survey research for data collection purposes. The final questionnaire is still being developed, but the goal is to have the survey take less than 10 minutes to complete. We will perform statistical analyses comparing survey responses across countries and age groups as well as other characteristics using regression analysis, crosstab and chi-squared tests.

GRANT GAFFES

EXHIBIT 50

While the information in this paragraph is valuable and goes a long way to establish the credibility of the PI, it might have a greater impact elsewhere in the proposal, such as in the problem statement to justify the need for additional research. By itself, this paragraph does not provide reviewers with any insights to the methods that will be used with the proposed project—the theoretical approach, new questions to be explored, core activities for reaching project objectives, target audiences to be surveyed, or data collection tools to be used.

In an unusual rhetorical move, the narrative calls extra attention to the limitations of convenience sampling, namely, the potential for bias because subjects may not be representative of the entire population. This is counterbalanced in the final sentence with an attempt to reassure reviewers that care will be taken during the participant selection process. More broadly, however, two paragraphs into the methods section, very little has been said about who is going to do what activities and when, and how they will be managed.

"Wiggle words" dominate two-thirds of this paragraph. Note phrases such as "plan . . . is reasonably well defined," "details still need to be worked out," "we will likely use," "as our planning evolves," "we will consider," and "is still being developed." These syntactic constructions suggest that the project is not yet on solid footing. Only two sentences in this paragraph are stated with conviction: the number of survey respondents from each country and the statistical analyses to be performed. The take-home message in this paragraph to grant reviewers from the PI is "Trust me. I'll figure it out." Reviewers do not require iron-clad guarantees, but they do expect the methods plan to be well thought-out.

2. Viewed broadly, this project will provide an innovative approach to the study of. . .
3. Recent advances in XXX approaches justify. . .
4. We will validate the most promising. . .
5. Our approach combines the power of XXX to investigate YYY.
6. This innovative and ambitious project will integrate. . .
7. If successful, our method would represent a novel therapeutic approach to. . .
8. The innovative approaches of this proposal capitalize on our unique expertise in. . .
9. Our approach offers a cost-effective solution to the problem of . . .
10. Three distinguishing features characterize our approach. First. . .

Clip File Action Item # 13
Methods

The following action items will help build your Methods clip file:

- Gather examples of time and task charts from other proposals.
- Collect details on data collection instruments of interest in Buros's *Mental Measurements Yearbook* and Jones's *Handbook of Tests and Measurements for Black Populations*.
- List your resources that might support upcoming projects: computers, equipment, and instruments; laboratory, clinical, and animal facilities; clerical, technological, financial, fundraising, and office personnel.

CHAPTER 10
Evaluation

True genius resides in the capacity for evaluation of uncertain, hazardous, and conflicting information.
—*Winston Churchill*

PURPOSE OF EVALUATION

Evaluations pinpoint what is really happening in your project so you can improve its efficiency, effectiveness, and equity. That is, you can ensure that project funds are being spent wisely, the project is making a difference, and project benefits are being distributed across the target population or community. In Chapter 10, you will learn the following:

- Importance of conducting evaluations.
- Three types of evaluation: process, outcome, and impact.
- Five types of outcome indicators: functional status, humanistic, academic productivity, employment, and economic.
- How to choose and use evaluators effectively.
- Value of logic models to portray project evaluations.

Based on evaluation information, you can better allocate resources, improve your services, and strengthen your overall project performance. Beyond these immediate benefits, a good project evaluation can discover needs to be served in your next proposal as well as make it easier to get and sustain funding. As Churchill notes, grantseekers conduct their evaluation to resolve uncertain or conflicting information.

In essence, evaluations are conducted for a combination of internal and external reasons. Externally, sponsors may require it to make sure that their project funds are having the desired impact, or as a prerequisite for renewed funding. Conceivably, sponsors may use evaluation information to deal with radical funding cutbacks; applicants without a strong evaluation component are particularly vulnerable to funding cuts.

Especially in the public arena, federal sponsors may use project evaluation results to justify to Congress the effectiveness of the grant program as a whole, lest the program funding itself be zeroed out.

Beyond these external reasons, many internal reasons exist for conducting an evaluation. You may not have a firm grasp of your project strengths and weaknesses or socioeconomic implications. You may wonder if you need to improve your project effectiveness or to eliminate some duplication of effort. Perhaps, your project is getting little publicity or, worse yet, negative publicity. Maybe your staff feels ineffectual, frustrated, or in need of guidance. A comprehensive evaluation can provide answers to these important project questions.

If you want to include an evaluation component in your proposal but know nothing about the subject, consider borrowing ideas from the evaluation plans developed for other similar programs or ask a colleague or consultant to review your proposal and develop an appropriate evaluation strategy. Too frequently, proposal writers don't explain how they will evaluate their projects. At best, they may mention some vague process such as conducting a group discussion or assigning the evaluation to an expert, with no specifics on how the evaluation will be conducted or what will be learned from it.

TYPES OF EVALUATION

You may engage in different types of evaluations to assess the effectiveness of your proposed project during, at the conclusion of, and beyond the granting period. Three types of evaluations include process, outcome,

During the grant period	Conclusion of grant period	Beyond the grant period
Process	Outcome	Impact
• Structure	• Outputs	
• Process	• Outcomes	
Formative	Summative	Impact
Immediate Outcomes	Short-term Outcomes	Long-term Outcomes
Initial Outcomes	Intermediate Outcomes	End Outcomes

EVALUATION TERMINOLOGY AT DIFFERENT GRANT TIME PERIODS

EXHIBIT 51

and impact. Public and private sponsors sometimes use different terms to describe the same types of evaluations. For instance, the U.S. Department of Education uses the terms *formative* and *summative evaluations*, whereas the W. K. Kellogg Foundation uses the terms *process* and *outcome evaluations*; they are synonyms.

A few sponsors have refined distinctions in the types of evaluations they expect. For example, one program in the Health Resources and Services Administration requires you to distinguish between outputs (products) and outcomes (humanistic benefits) that will accrue by the conclusion of the grant period. Pre-proposal contacts (Chapter 4) will help you to identify the types, levels, and degrees of evaluation strategies you will need to include in your proposal. The sponsor may well require different types of evaluations during different time periods in the grant. Exhibit 51 lists some of the common evaluation terms used during different grant periods.

Note that some evaluation terms overlap; that is, one term can have more than one meaning. For instance, "process" is the umbrella name given to evaluations conducted during a grant; it is also the name of one facet of that evaluation, along with "structure." The semantics of evaluation terminology are not consistent among grantmakers; the following discussion attempts to defuzzify the different evaluation terms.

Process Evaluation

Process evaluations generate information that will improve the effectiveness of the project *during* the granting period. They systematically examine internal and external characteristics associated with the delivery and receipt of services. This may include evaluating structure, the environment and settings in which services occur. Understanding the strengths and weaknesses of the structure of your organization,

the target population and their community environment, and the procedures your organization is using to interact with the community will provide immediate feedback to help you meet project objectives. When writing a process evaluation, you'll need to consider the following types of questions.

Your Organization. Are sufficient numbers of key personnel adequately trained to carry out the project? Do staff members reflect the ethnic, cultural, and linguistic make-up of the community? Are suitable facilities and equipment available? Do current services respond to the needs of the target population and community? What is your relation to other organizations who provide similar types of services?

Target Population and Community Environment. Have individual and community needs been identified through a formal needs assessment or an informal survey of perceived needs? Has the community's knowledge, attitude, and behavior toward the problem been assessed? What is the prevalence and distribution of physical, social, and economic risks in the community? Does the community face any geographic, cultural, or linguistic barriers to overcoming the problem? Does the target population have access to additional personal, family, or community resources that will help your project succeed?

Organization and Community Interaction. What types of services are being provided to whom and how often? Who from your organization is collecting what type of evidence to document the quality and quantity of interactions? Is the target population satisfied with services? Are your staff members satisfied with their experiences? What barriers still need to be overcome in order to improve participant satisfaction?

Evaluation indicators are specific characteristics that you will track and measure to gauge project success. Process-level indicators may examine features such as the intensity of the intervention, quality of service provided, and cultural competence of the intervention. Structure-level indicators may assess elements such as who provided the intervention, what type of intervention was used, where the intervention occurred, when and how long the intervention took place, and length of participant involvement.

Outcome Evaluation

Outcome evaluations examine the end result of an intervention. The goal here is to document the extent to which the project did what it was designed to do and the strength of the effect. Outcomes are the benefits, changes, or effects that occur to the target population due to participation in your project. Outcomes are generally expressed in humanistic terms, e.g., improved health status, increased knowledge of parenting skills, decreased youth violence. Some sponsors may also ask you to identify outputs, products generated as a result of program activities, e.g., a curriculum to teach oral health to middle school students, the number of conflict resolution classes taught, the number of volunteers recruited. Keep in mind that "ideal" outcomes can vary with perspective: your organization, the target population, and potential sponsors may value different outcomes. Your project might need to evaluate several types of outcomes simultaneously.

The core of outcome evaluations is measurement: collect data to document the extent to which project objectives were accomplished. Outcome indicators—specific characteristics selected for measurement—must best describe an associated end result. For instance, a program whose desired outcome is to improve asthma-related quality of life could measure "improvement" through participants having a written asthma action plan; using anti-inflammatory inhalers, spacers, and peak flow meters; reducing the amount of sleep, exercise, school days lost due to asthma; and reducing the number of hospital admissions and emergency room visits for asthma. Participants who demonstrate these behaviors are the indicators of the project's success in achieving this outcome.

As another example, a project whose desired outcome is to improve academic mastery of key science concepts by undergraduate students could use indicators such as results from Web-based polls administered during class; midterm and final exam results compared against classes taught in previous years and against course sessions taught in traditional formats by other instructors; performance on standardized exams

(e.g., major field tests) compared against other course sections and against national norms; and electronic portfolios that track performance from freshman to senior year.

Five common types of outcome indicators include: functional status, humanistic, academic productivity, employment, and economic. Collecting data to evaluate all aspects of each type of outcome indicator would be extremely difficult and prohibitively expensive. Instead, do like successful grantseekers do: identify a few outcome indicators that will demonstrate meaningful end results to your organization, target population, and the sponsor.

Functional Status. Performance measures such as physical, mental, social, and spiritual well-being can be used to demonstrate individuals' functional status. Examples include suffering pain when performing everyday activities, experiencing sudden onset of fatigue, noticing diminished strength, feeling blue and depressed, having a lot of energy, sensing a clarity of thinking when solving complex problems, connecting with family and friends, and feeling calm and peaceful. Performance measures are generally evaluated at set intervals, such as prior to intervention, and six and twelve months postintervention. Functional status indicators demonstrate that, as a result of the intervention, the client's quality of life improved in a meaningful way.

Humanistic. Humanistic indicators tell you how clients feel about the intervention and reflect how well the project is working. Measures tend to be subjective in nature, for instance: awareness of program services, access to services, convenience of services, quality of services, satisfaction with services, and individual perceptions of well-being. Client satisfaction, which is usually measured by administering an appropriate attitude scale, is a key outcomes measure because those who are satisfied with their experiences are more likely to continue participating in an intervention.

Academic Productivity. Measures of academic productivity highlight the value of investments in education. Indicators may relate to student achievement as well as faculty teaching, scholarship, and service. Examples include the following: student achievement—grade point averages, standardized placement exams, employer feedback, and rates of retention, graduation, graduate school acceptance, and job placement; teaching—new course creations, existing course redesigns, and students supervised in research, clinicals, practica, internships, study abroad, living learning communities, and service-learning experiences; scholarship—publications, citations, scholarly presentations, commissioned performances, creative readings, competitive exhibitions, grants, patents, honors, and awards; service—committee appointments, supervision of theses and dissertations, community outreach, and leadership positions in professional organizations. These types of indicators appeal directly to calls for academic quality, accountability, and transparency.

Employment. Good jobs, and the income and financial security they produce, allow individuals greater flexibility in making decisions about where to live, learn, work, worship, eat, and play. Quantifiable measures include new business start-ups, wages and salaries, payroll taxes paid, FTEs, vendor FTEs, average weekly hours, retention rates, unemployment records, job training programs, transitional jobs, minimum wage figures, average placement wage, workforce legislation, job placement programs, wage progression, average family income, job placement costs, and legislative authorizations and appropriations. Employment indicators can often be tied to outcomes relating to health, education, safety, environmental conditions, civic engagement, and family and social support.

Economic. Five measures typically used to calculate the costs and consequences of project interventions include cost-benefit analysis, cost-effectiveness analysis, cost-minimization analysis, cost-utility analysis, and return on investment analysis. Each type of analysis values costs in dollars but differs in the outcome measures used. Sponsors value project outcomes that demonstrate the greatest benefit at the lowest cost.

- *Cost-benefit analyses* identify the most favorable cost-to-benefit ratio of two or more alternatives that have similar or different outcomes for the target population; that is, given finite resources, which project intervention gives the best return for the dollars invested?
- *Cost-effectiveness analyses* compare two or more approaches to a specified outcome, assuming that members of the target population value the outcome equally and that adequate financial resources are available to pursue the most beneficial strategy.
- *Cost-minimization analyses* identify the least expensive of two or more alternatives that have identical outcomes for the target population.
- *Cost-utility analyses* compare the costs of two or more approaches to an outcome, adjusting for preferences of the target population. That is, a child with mild asthma may not value an additional year

of life as much as an adult with an advanced stage of the AIDS virus.
- *Return on investment analyses* look at projected benefits or revenue generated by the intervention over a period of time compared to the initial investment and operating costs.

In the public arena, the fundamental method for formal economic assessment is cost-benefit analysis. Cost-benefit analyses attempt to identify the most economically efficient way of meeting a public objective, particularly when measurable benefits or costs extend three or more years into the future. You can find federal guidance for this analysis in U.S. Office of Management and Budget: "Circular A-94 Guidelines and Discount Rates for Benefit Cost Analysis of Federal Programs" at www.whitehouse.gov/omb/circulars/a094/a094.html.

Impact Evaluation

Impact evaluations generate information to measure the overall worth and utility of the project beyond the granting period. An impact evaluation goes further than assessing whether goals and objectives were achieved and focuses on the project's larger value—long-term, fundamental changes in participants' knowledge, attitudes, or behaviors. That is, improving outcomes at the program level may impact change over time at the community level. By their nature, many outcomes are delayed, occurring beyond the granting period. Impact evaluations attempt to attribute outcomes exclusively to an intervention, although data may be difficult to obtain over the long term.

You can demonstrate impact at several levels: the target population, the community at large, and beyond. Lasting changes in the target population demonstrate the project's overall value. Inclusive participation by the community may contribute to long-term project sustainability. Regional and national buy-in for targeted interventions and outcomes can promote large-scale project replication. Consider the following types of questions when writing an impact evaluation:

Overall Value. What enduring changes will occur in participants' knowledge, attitudes, or behaviors as a result of this project? Over the long term, will you be able to demonstrate that the project's impact extended beyond the target population to the entire community, area, or region? Will this project serve as a catalyst for other related community actions, services, and programs?

Sustainability. Will project activities continue beyond the granting period? Will you be able to mobilize continued support for the project internally and/or externally? Will your organization institutionalize strategies deemed effective? Will key champions for the project be able to increase levels of community involvement and fiscal support? Will your project influence changes at provider, policy, or system levels?

Replicability. Will key findings be disseminated to local, regional, national, and international stakeholders so that the project can be replicated? Does the project's design have flexibility to be adapted to other populations, topics, or conditions? Could your organization serve as a national clearinghouse to educate and train other communities about implementing your program? Does your project have the potential to serve as a public policy model?

Collectively, conducting process, outcome, and impact evaluations is a strategy to achieve a competitive grantseeking advantage by increasing project accountability. These assessments also provide essential information about the direction that the project should take in the future and if additional public and private funding will be needed. As evaluation data are generated, be sure to disseminate relevant findings to key constituents.

CHOOSING AN EVALUATOR

Evaluations can be done using someone within or outside of your organization. An individual from within your organization conducting an internal evaluation has great intuitive knowledge of your program and is less likely to be seen as an intruder. Evaluation costs are usually less expensive when the evaluations are conducted in-house. The ability to communicate useful information is high. On the other hand, the internal evaluation may be biased because of involvement with certain program aspects. Evaluation findings may be ignored or not seen as professional enough; that is, the evaluation may not be taken seriously. The skill set that your internal evaluator should have includes knowledge of and experience in research design and statistical analysis, data collection tools and techniques, psychometric methodology (when measuring attitudes), research ethics, and pertinent regulatory agency requirements.

Using external evaluators offers considerable objectivity. They often have a fresh perspective and can see things not noticed before. They have a high autonomy and freedom, and specialized training. Outside evaluators usually have high professional and scholarly competence. They can mediate and facilitate activities with staff and management while ensuring public confidence in evaluation results. On the other hand, they may be perceived as a threat by the staff and may require extra time to understand the program rationale. Outside evaluation costs may be high. The findings may be ignored because the evaluator doesn't really know the program and can miss essential issues or because the staff perceives this to be the case. Evaluation energies may distract from program activities.

Using Evaluators Effectively

Whether you use an internal or an external evaluator—or both—be sure to include an evaluation section in your proposal. A common proposal-writing mistake is to budget an amount for evaluation costs and worry later about the evaluation procedure. Instead, involve the evaluators in the proposal writing. Be sure to give them a copy of your project objectives. Recall that pointed objectives will simplify the evaluation process.

Evaluators should provide you with important information to strengthen your proposal. Specifically, ask your evaluators to identify precisely the following:

- What will be evaluated?
- What information they will need to conduct the evaluation?
- Where that information will be obtained?
- What data collection instruments will be used to get that information?
- With what frequency will data be collected?
- What evaluation design will be used?
- What analyses will be completed?
- What questions you will be able to answer as a result of the evaluation?

If you are looking for a good evaluation consultant, contact the grants office at a nearby university. That office is familiar with its faculty expertise and often finds an appropriate evaluator for area organizations and agencies. Alternatively, professional societies, such as the American Evaluation Association (www.eval.org), may provide lists of their members who possess the types of evaluation expertise you seek.

KEY QUESTIONS TO ANSWER

As you write this section of the proposal, ask yourself if it does the following:

1. Provide a general organizational plan or model for your evaluation?
2. Identify the type and purpose of your evaluation and the audiences to be served by its results?

3. Demonstrate that an appropriate evaluation procedure is included for every project objective?

4. Demonstrate that the scope of the evaluation is appropriate to the project? To what extent is the project practical, relevant, and generalizable?

5. Describe the information that will be needed to complete the evaluation, the potential sources for this information, and the instruments that will be used for its collection?

6. Define standards that will be used in judging the results of the evaluation?

7. Summarize any reports to be provided to the funding source based on the evaluation, and generally describe their content and timing?

8. Discuss who will be responsible for the evaluation?

9. Establish the credentials of your evaluator, including pertinent prior experience and academic background?

10. Describe mechanisms to disseminate the results of your evaluation?

EXAMPLES OF EVALUATIONS

Example 1

This example presents one type of model that can be used for a project evaluation. It was a portion of a university-based proposal to a federal agency seeking funding to train vocational rehabilitation personnel how to work effectively with hearing-impaired youth who are job hunting. Exhibit 52 illustrates process and outcome evaluation questions, outcome criteria, and information collection and reporting plans for one project objective. The remainder of this proposal section went on to list the evaluation approach for other objectives, using this same model format.

Example 2

A geriatrics education proposal submitted to a federal agency that trains health care personnel:

Process. Evaluation is a multifaceted term. In a general sense, the term "evaluation" means to gather information to judge the effectiveness of the project. However, more precise types of evaluation are warranted for this proposal. Specifically, we envision the following evaluation categories:

Formative Evaluation: Generating information to improve the educational effectiveness of the center during the grant period. This evaluation will help determine whether the processes and procedures are working, whether the participants are satisfied with their instruction. This approach represents a good management tool for making "mid-course corrections," providing the center director and governance council with immediate feedback to make constructive revisions in the training, resource development, and technology transfer activities of the center.

Summative Evaluation: Collecting data necessary to judge the ultimate success of the completed project. The goal is to document the extent to which the project objectives were achieved; that is, to what extent did the proposal do what it was designed to do? Evaluation feedback will be used for formulating or modifying the sponsor's policy and organization structure, which will improve the likelihood of successfully accomplishing program goals.

The Midwest Geriatric Education Center is not only a structure developed to provide multidisciplinary training, resources, and technology for staffing and service delivery objectives, but it is also a structure that serves as an administrative mechanism to achieve such objectives in the Urban Corridor, which is its geographical focus. This administrative mechanism is designed to be a catalyst and facilitator for change among the educational institutions, the elements of the service delivery system, and the organized professions that also serve the geographic region of the Urban Corridor. Therefore, particular attention will be paid in the evaluation plan to the effectiveness of the center as an administrative mechanism for achieving professional and institutional change.

To achieve the evaluation goals of this project, the assistant directors of Geriatric Education Services will collaborate on the development of data-gathering instruments. This collaboration will express itself in the creation of an Evaluation Steering Committee that the assistant directors will chair. To this committee, the MGEC program director will name seven additional individuals representing the affiliate institutions, agencies, and professions.

The Evaluation Steering Committee shall be charged to agree upon specific measures and data-gathering strategies for each of the variables in the program evaluation protocol. The Evaluation Steering Committee will also review and recommend approval to the program director for requests to use data, programs, and products of the Midwest Geriatric Education Center for research, and it will assure that the evaluation of the center is not compromised or contaminated. Finally, the Evaluation Steering

Project Evaluation Protocol. To ensure the appropriateness and comprehensiveness of evaluation methods and the use of objective performance measures to produce quantitative and qualitative data, this project follows an evaluation model (Brinkerhoff, et al., 1983). This evaluation model makes certain that specific questions are posed for the evaluation, that objectives and outcome criteria are clearly stated, that an information plan is in place and there are plans for data analyses, interpretation, and reporting of results. The following table depicts the relationships of the major elements in this evaluation model for all project objectives, which arise from the one major project goal, namely, to increase the number of qualified personnel trained to provide rehabilitation services to transitional youth who are hearing impaired.

Objective 1: By June 2006, develop an O&M curriculum for transition-age youth *(Baseline: No comparable curriculum exists)*

Process Evaluation Questions	Outcome Evaluation Questions
Has pertinent literature been reviewed? Has adequate input been sought from training program directors, vocational rehabilitation professionals, and transitional youth who have recently entered the workforce? Have interviews been held with a convenience sample of youth who failed to gain employment?	Has a curriculum manual been written that includes objectives, materials, procedures, and evaluation for each educational activity? Has the curriculum manual been critiqued by three senior educators and three rehabilitation professionals? Have at least 125 students been successfully trained using this curriculum?

Outcome Criteria Associated with Specific Strategies

1. The resulting curriculum will be developed and independently evaluated.
2. The resulting curriculum will be integrated with the existing curriculum on Individuals with Disabilities Education Act (IDEA) legislation.
3. The "Consumer-Based Model" principles will be applied to "School-to-Work" initiatives.
4. The existing child development course will be modified to include increased emphasis of adolescent behavior and development.

Information Collection Plan	Interpretation and Reporting Plan
Methods and Instruments Literature review of existing curricula. Focus groups with training program directors, Vocational Rehabilitation professionals, and recent youth entering workforce. Interviews with youth who failed to secure jobs. *Types of Data* Curriculum manual. Focus group reports. Interview reports. Curricular evaluations.	The resulting data will be critically reviewed internally and appropriate revisions will be made before reporting outcomes to the appropriate educational and rehabilitation communities through the use of a Web site, www.midwest.edu/transtionalyouth, conference presentations, journal articles, and white papers to all directors of training programs and state agencies serving the hearing impaired.

EVALUATION MODEL

EXHIBIT 52

Committee will review evaluation activities in progress to identify suggestions that should be made to the program director concerning program, structure, or policy that seem warranted on the basis of interim or final results obtained in either the process or outcome evaluation activities. Members of the Evaluation Steering Committee must be appointed in such a way that they are representative of the affiliates and target constituencies, but external to the operations of the MGEC. Thus, the Evaluation Steering Committee will assure objectivity to the evaluation, while permitting maximum feedback to the center's operations.

Each of the four MGEC goals and the associated objectives are expressed in measurable terms. While the Evaluation Steering Committee bears the responsibility for specific evaluation methodology, their approach will seek, as a minimum, answers to the following questions for each MGEC goal:

1. *To increase the number of highly trained geriatrics educators*
   Determine the number of health professional training institutions in the Urban Corridor. What percentage are consortium members? What are the characteristics of the decision makers within the institutions that joined the consortium? What reasons are given for not joining the consortium? How many geriatrics health care providers exist in the Urban Corridor? How many have links with the consortium academic faculty?

2. *To practice a multidisciplinary approach to geriatric health care*
   To what extent was each faculty lecturer able to make an effective and pedagogically sound presentation as evidenced by trainee evaluations? To what extent will trainees be able to utilize multidisciplinary approaches to identify the need for effective patient training packages?

3. *To develop geriatrics education materials*
   To what extent will trainees be able to effectively evaluate educational materials in concurrence with peer evaluations? To what extent will the faculty be able to produce and evaluate effective educational packages?

4. *To establish a geriatrics education resource center*
   During the grant period, how many requests were received for information, technical assistance, instructional materials, and consultations?

Example 3

A proposal to a federal science agency seeking support for minority students:

> The program evaluation process serves two purposes: (1) to provide feedback during program operation, and (2) to provide quantifiable data regarding the short- and long-term effectiveness of the program.
>
> Near the end of the first and second semesters of each program year, each minority fellow and faculty mentor will complete a questionnaire, ending with a section of free commentary. The questionnaires will be prepared and evaluated by the Evaluation Advisory Committee and the project director, who will use the feedback obtained from student and faculty participants to "fine-tune" and improve the operation of the program.
>
> In addition, upon completion of the program, each faculty mentor will complete a

student evaluation survey. Additionally, the student fellows will agree in writing to maintain current addresses on file with the department for six years following completion of the Minority Fellowship Program, and to complete an existing evaluation survey upon receipt of their doctorates, a three-year follow-up survey, and a six-year follow-up survey. The data obtained from these surveys will be compiled and analyzed to evaluate the effectiveness of the program in meeting the primary objective of increasing the number of minority individuals entering university teaching and research in electrical and computer engineering.

> Observations of the participants would be valuable to the Science Agency in establishing similar programs in the future. Further, comparing national and departmental data can help assess the program. The success of the program will be determined based on the grade point averages of the minority fellows, the quality of their dissertation research, the number and quality of their publications, the percentage of minority fellows completing the program, the number of minority fellows actually beginning university teaching careers, the starting salaries of the minority fellows, the quality of the institutions they join, and, finally, the progress of their careers after three and six years in the profession. The results of these studies will be reported in the literature after completion of the program, and again after three and six additional years.

Example 4

A child care development proposal submitted to a private foundation.

> **Evaluation.** An outcomes-directed evaluation plan means collecting data to document the extent to which objectives and activities were achieved. Evaluation feedback will be used to modify childcare programming, trainings, and technical assistance to improve the likelihood of accomplishing project goals. To ensure that the evaluation is objective, meets rigorous standards of research, and is sensitive to ethnic and cultural differences, we will subcontract with external evaluation consultants, Dilworth & Associates, Inc. Methodologically, they will set up appropriate systems to collect, analyze, and report progress on:

1. **Structural measures:** the environment and settings in which services occur, e.g., licensing, accreditation, group size, adult-child ratio, and staff experience and turnover.

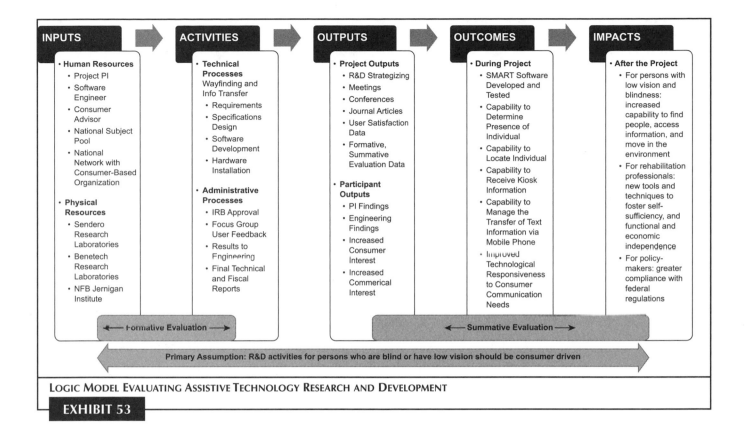

INPUTS

- **Human Resources**
  - Project PI
  - Software Engineer
  - Consumer Advisor
  - National Subject Pool
  - National Network with Consumer-Based Organization
- **Physical Resources**
  - Sendero Research Laboratories
  - Benetech Research Laboratories
  - NFB Jernigan Institute

ACTIVITIES

- **Technical Processes** Wayfinding and Info Transfer
  - Requirements
  - Specifications Design
  - Software Development
  - Hardware Installation
- **Administrative Processes**
  - IRB Approval
  - Focus Group User Feedback
  - Results to Engineering
  - Final Technical and Fiscal Reports

OUTPUTS

- **Project Outputs**
  - R&D Strategizing
  - Meetings
  - Conferences
  - Journal Articles
  - User Satisfaction Data
  - Formative, Summative Evaluation Data
- **Participant Outputs**
  - PI Findings
  - Engineering Findings
  - Increased Consumer Interest
  - Increased Commerical Interest

OUTCOMES

- **During Project**
  - SMART Software Developed and Tested
  - Capability to Determine Presence of Individual
  - Capability to Locate Individual
  - Capability to Receive Kiosk Information
  - Capability to Manage the Transfer of Text Information via Mobile Phone
  - Improved Technological Responsiveness to Consumer Communication Needs

IMPACTS

- **After the Project**
  - For persons with low vision and blindness: increased capability to find people, access information, and move in the environment
  - For rehabilitation professionals: new tools and techniques to foster self-sufficiency, and functional and economic independence
  - For policy-makers: greater compliance with federal regulations

← Formative Evaluation →

← Summative Evaluation →

Primary Assumption: R&D activities for persons who are blind or have low vision should be consumer driven

LOGIC MODEL EVALUATING ASSISTIVE TECHNOLOGY RESEARCH AND DEVELOPMENT

EXHIBIT 53

2. **Process measures:** the type, intensity, and frequency of services provided, e.g., nurturing caregiving, length and quality of teacher-student interactions, responsiveness to children's needs, and cultural- and age-appropriate materials and activities.

3. **Outcome measures:** the effectiveness in achieving goals and end results, e.g., cognitive, social, emotional, physical, and language development improvements in children.

Dr. Katrina H. Davidson, director of Outcomes Evaluation, will assess the program for usability, satisfaction, and efficacy, including a sophisticated return-on-investment analysis for the community at large and individual participants. Evaluation measures will be practical, efficient, consistent with NAEYC Accreditation Standards, and mirror the Healthy Children Foundation's national evaluation of "Excellent Childcare Centers."

Dissemination is essential to project success because education has a multiplier effect. Consistent monitoring and reporting of evaluation measures will improve children's development, help shape program direction, ensure sustainability, and promote program replication. The intended outcomes of dissemination effort are to affect the knowledge, attitude, and behavior of parents and providers relative to child care principles and practices.

Example 5

Exhibit 53 shows use of the logic model technique for portraying project evaluations. The specific example deals with a government proposal to develop some wayfinding technologies for persons with low vision and blindness. In succinct form, it shows the major project components: work planned, intended results, primary assumption, and formative and summative evaluation domains. The missing information pieces, of course, are the who and when, which presumably are indicated on a time and task chart (See Chapter 9).

Example 6

The logic model in Exhibit 54 uses a simple yet effective presentation. To facilitate skim reading, the goal of the project is restated in one sentence and three bulleted points establish the baseline against which long-term outcomes will be measured. The six-column table illustrates the relationship of inputs, activities, outputs, short-term outcomes, intermediate outcomes, and long-term outcomes for an initiative to reduce risky and problem alcohol use and behavior.

Alcohol Use Logic Model

Project Goal: To reduce risky and problem alcohol use and behavior among high school students.

Baseline Problems:

- 73% of 12th graders had at least one drink of alcohol during the past 30 days (77% males; 69% females);
- 55% of 12th graders had five or more drinks of alcohol at a time in the past 30 days (59% males; 51% females);
- 22% of 12th graders drank alcohol before last sexual intercourse (23% male; 22% female).

Inputs	Activities	Outputs	Short-Term Outcomes (Learning)	Intermediate Outcomes (Actions)	Long-Term Outcomes (Conditions)
Staff Money Strategic plan Training materials Physical space Partners	Media campaigns and counteradvertising Responsible beverage service training Enhanced enforcement of laws prohibiting sales to minors Host alcohol-free activities for youth	# media spots Categories of media messages # beverage service trainings # beverage service training attendees # purchase attempts by underage decoys # sales to underage decoys # hosted activities # activity attendees	Increase community awareness of teen alcohol social norms Increase teen exposure to positive normative messages Increase awareness of legal consequences for underage drinking Increase awareness of legal consequences for serving minors Increase teen opportunities for positive community involvement	Decrease alcohol availability to minors Increase local compliance with alcohol laws Increase in informed decision making by teens Increase in use of community supports by teens	Significantly reduce underage drinking Significantly reduce binge drinking Significantly reduce risky alcohol behavior

LOGIC MODEL FOR REDUCING RISKY AND PROBLEM ALCOHOL USE AND BEHAVIOR

EXHIBIT 54

Example 7

To stem the tide of the growing percentage of adults and children who are overweight and obese, a proposal to a government agency aims to improve eating habits of residents in rural counties. The logic model in Exhibit 55 includes considerable levels of detail in succinct format. For instance, the planned work specifies by type the groups that are contributing project inputs and by type the groups that are participating in grant-funded activities. Further, data sources for both the process and outcome evaluation are clearly delineated. The situation statement provides the baseline data against which ultimate project success will be measured for the target of reducing overweight and obese residents by 10 percent.

Example 8

The logic model in Exhibit 56 is from a proposal seeking government support for increasing the number of underrepresented minorities with baccalaureate degrees in STEM (Science, Technology, Engineering, and Mathematics) disciplines. The logic model contains many of the same elements as in previous examples; however, note that the layout is vertical rather

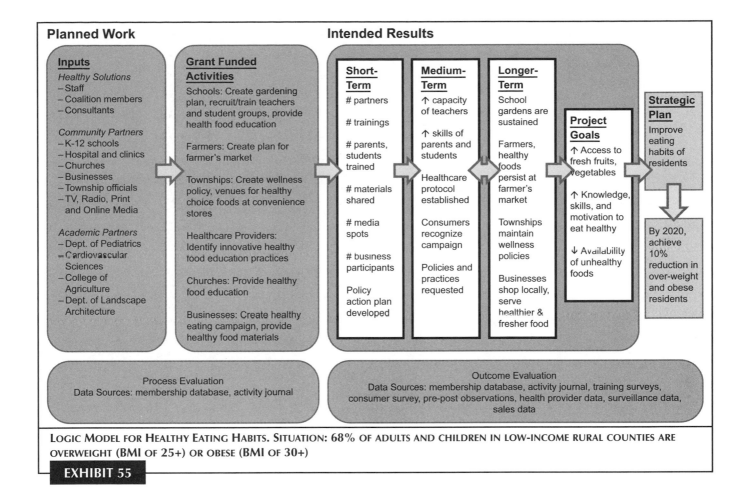

Planned Work **Intended Results**

Inputs

Healthy Solutions
– Staff
– Coalition members
– Consultants

Community Partners
– K-12 schools
– Hospital and clinics
– Churches
– Businesses
– Township officials
– TV, Radio, Print and Online Media

Academic Partners
– Dept. of Pediatrics
– Cardiovascular Sciences
– College of Agriculture
– Dept. of Landscape Architecture

Grant Funded Activities

Schools: Create gardening plan, recruit/train teachers and student groups, provide health food education

Farmers: Create plan for farmer's market

Townships: Create wellness policy, venues for healthy choice foods at convenience stores

Healthcare Providers: Identify innovative healthy food education practices

Churches: Provide healthy food education

Businesses: Create healthy eating campaign, provide healthy food materials

Short-Term

partners

trainings

parents, students trained

materials shared

media spots

business participants

Policy action plan developed

Medium-Term

↑ capacity of teachers

↑ skills of parents and students

Healthcare protocol established

Consumers recognize campaign

Policies and practices requested

Longer-Term

School gardens are sustained

Farmers, healthy foods persist at farmer's market

Townships maintain wellness policies

Businesses shop locally, serve healthier & fresher food

Project Goals

↑ Access to fresh fruits, vegetables

↑ Knowledge, skills, and motivation to eat healthy

↓ Availability of unhealthy foods

Strategic Plan

Improve eating habits of residents

By 2020, achieve 10% reduction in over-weight and obese residents

Process Evaluation
Data Sources: membership database, activity journal

Outcome Evaluation
Data Sources: membership database, activity journal, training surveys, consumer survey, pre-post observations, health provider data, surveillance data, sales data

LOGIC MODEL FOR HEALTHY EATING HABITS. SITUATION: 68% OF ADULTS AND CHILDREN IN LOW-INCOME RURAL COUNTIES ARE OVERWEIGHT (BMI OF 25+) OR OBESE (BMI OF 30+)

EXHIBIT 55

than horizontal. This presentation style was a deliberate effort by the project director to highlight the grassroots nature of the proposed initiative: the inputs, activities, and outputs grow organically from a deep-seated passion and commitment faculty have made to supporting undergraduate research as a high-impact learning practice, which will yield initial, intermediate, and long-term outcomes for students. The formative evaluation will examine the inputs, activities, and outputs while the summative evaluation will assess initial, intermediate, and long-term outcomes.

There is no perfect logic model template. The elements, level of detail, and design of your logic model will depend on factors such as your audience, purpose, and rationale (e.g., illustrating the interrelationship of activities for staff, enlisting new collaborative partners, summarizing anticipated outcomes for project participants, or satisfying sponsor requirements). Further discussions and examples of logic models are available through:

• U.S. Department of Housing and Urban Development portal.hud.gov/hudportal/documents/huddoc?id=FBCIEvalStratLogicMods.pdf

• Innovation Center for Community and Youth Development www.theinnovationcenter.org/files/Reflect-and-Improve_Toolkit.pdf

• Innovation Network www.innonet.org/client_docs/File/logic_model_workbook.pdf

• W. K. Kellogg Foundation www.wkkf.org/knowledge-center/resources/2006/02/WK-Kellogg-Foundation-Logic-Model-Development-Guide.aspx

• National Science Foundation www.nsf.gov/pubs/2002/nsf02057/start.htm

• University of Wisconsin-Extension www.uwex.edu/ces/pdande/evaluation/evallogicmodel.html

You may find that it is easier to develop a logic model for a new program rather than for a currently operating program. Reason being: for existing programs, elements might not line up as well as you'd like and institutional inertia makes them difficult to change. For instance, a long-standing output measure of services rendered, collected via enrollment forms, may not be the best immediate outcome indicator of increased understanding by participants, which could be collected via satisfaction surveys. In a perfect world,

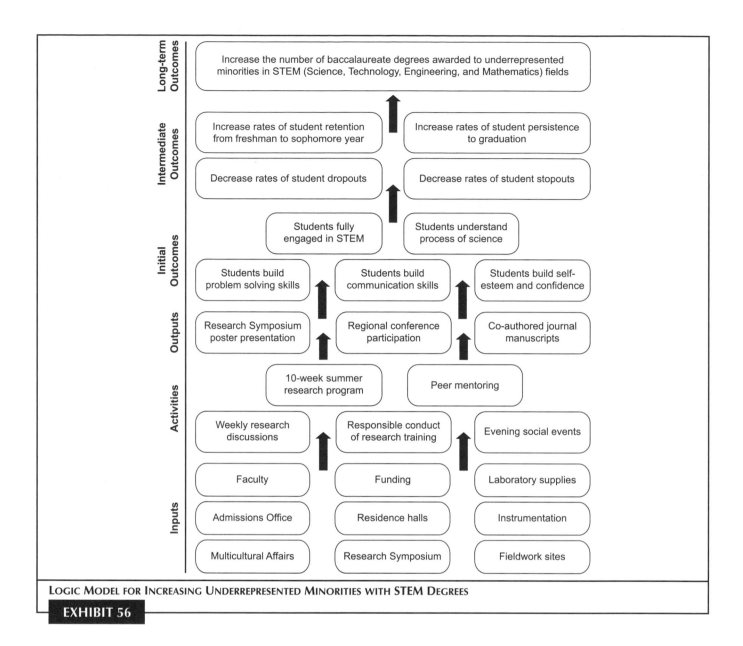

Long-term Outcomes

Increase the number of baccalaureate degrees awarded to underrepresented minorities in STEM (Science, Technology, Engineering, and Mathematics) fields

Intermediate Outcomes

Increase rates of student retention from freshman to sophomore year

Increase rates of student persistence to graduation

Decrease rates of student dropouts

Decrease rates of student stopouts

Initial Outcomes

Students fully engaged in STEM

Students understand process of science

Students build problem solving skills

Students build communication skills

Students build self-esteem and confidence

Outputs

Research Symposium poster presentation

Regional conference participation

Co-authored journal manuscripts

Activities

10-week summer research program

Peer mentoring

Weekly research discussions

Responsible conduct of research training

Evening social events

Inputs

Faculty

Funding

Laboratory supplies

Admissions Office

Residence halls

Instrumentation

Multicultural Affairs

Research Symposium

Fieldwork sites

LOGIC MODEL FOR INCREASING UNDERREPRESENTED MINORITIES WITH STEM DEGREES

EXHIBIT 56

the logic model would provide sufficient justification to add, remove, or modify historical program elements to better fit the present context. More broadly, whether your program is new or established, the logic model is a valuable tool for conceptualizing, articulating, and assessing program success.

WRITING TIPS FOR THE EVALUATION SECTION

1. Make sure that you include a separate evaluation component for each project objective. Designing an evaluation section for each objective forces you to examine the clarity of your objectives, the ease with which they can be measured, and the possibility of their being achieved. A Basic Guide to Program Evaluation (Including Outcomes Evaluation) is available online at http://managementhelp.org/evaluation/program-evaluation-guide.htm and a free User-Friendly Handbook for Mixed-Method Evaluations is available online at: http://www.nsf.gov/pubs/1997/nsf97153.

2. Include baseline data if it is available. This detail will demonstrate to grant reviewers that the first year of project activities will be used for measuring change rather than establishing an initial reference point from which to compare.

3. When surveys are used to collect data for evaluation purposes, be sure to specify whether the instruments already exist or will be developed by the project evaluator.

4. Clarify whether the evaluator will be responsible for data collection, data analysis, or both. Specify the frequency with which data will be collected, analyzed, and reported.

5. For projects that utilize both internal and external evaluators, describe the extent and frequency of communication that will occur between them. For instance, will the internal evaluator be responsible for the formative assessment and share information twice per year with the external evaluator? Who will be responsible for the summative evaluation?

6. If outside consultants are used, identify costs, credentials, and experience.

7. While evaluation costs vary depending on the scope of the project, experience suggests that evaluation costs are approximately 5–20 percent of total project costs. As opposed to process and outcome evaluations, impact evaluations are a challenge for grant writers because they usually occur after the grant funds have run out. Consequently, this proposal section is more speculative and is typically handled through best professional judgments.

8. Evaluation sections are less likely to be included in NSF and NIH basic science research grants. Therefore, to include an evaluation section in a research proposal may give you a competitive edge. Replicability is the primary evaluation criterion in most basic science research proposals.

9. Think about developing a logic model for your project regardless of whether the sponsor requests one. A logic model can be a great strategic planning tool, bringing clarity to what you propose, creating consensus on project activities, and focusing short-, medium-, and long-term evaluation considerations.

REJECTION REASONS

Reviewer comments concerning poor evaluation sections cluster into two categories—personnel and design—and include the following:

Personnel

1. Evaluation strategy is weak; much of it is yet to be developed with the help of unidentified consultants.

2. The proposal does not identify a specific expert or organization to conduct the evaluation. What are the evaluator's qualifications?

3. The application does not describe the types of data that will be collected or indicate who will be responsible for collecting the data.

4. A heavy burden is placed on an external evaluator to design and implement an evaluation system for the overall project, including providing data analysis services, without an appropriate level of effort committed to the project.

5. The evaluation plan is unclear as to whether only the applicant institution will be accountable for meeting performance measures or whether there will be a mechanism by which participants from partnering institutions in neighboring states will report data back to the project director for assessment purposes.

6. There is no description of the project director's previous experience conducting evaluations such as the one proposed.

7. Because a to-be-determined external evaluator was not involved with proposal development and will not be brought on board until almost a year into the proposed project activities, this individual will have considerable responsibilities to establish baseline data and measure progress and outcomes.

8. The narrative provides a broad statement that the project director will meet regularly with persons involved in the evaluation process but does not specify frequency or duration of meetings.

9. The application proposes to engage both an internal evaluator and an external evaluator but does not explain their respective roles, nor does it explain the relationship between them.

10. It is unclear the extent to which the "external" evaluator can be independent since he works for the same university, albeit in a different department, as the project director.

11. The timetable for evaluation activities is fuzzy. The narrative should clarify when evaluation activities will occur and which activities will be the responsibility of the internal evaluator and the external evaluator.

12. The application does not provide a description of or a CV for the external evaluator that describes his qualifications and experience in employing a variety of evaluation methods.

Design

1. The evaluation section belabors obvious problems in reliability of measurement but is thin on specific procedures directly relevant to the purposes of the proposal.

2. Although evaluation is tailored to individual objectives, specific outcomes are rarely mentioned. Much of the evaluation plan is philosophical, rather than describing methodology.

3. Program evaluation funding, representing 2 percent of the total budget, is inadequately low to carry out a quality evaluation that looks at process and outcome measures across multiple collaborators, and to participate in a national evaluation.

4. The proposal does not describe methods, objectives, and instruments to measure and evaluate clinical quality. The proposal does not describe how data collection will be standardized across partner agencies so that evaluation results will be meaningful.

5. The sample size of subjects is inappropriate to produce reliable and valid results.

6. The design of this project fails to evaluate important gender, age, and racial/ethnic population differences.

7. A lack of alignment exists between goals, outcomes, and performance measures. The goal statement is consistent with the required performance measure of the percentage of faculty trained through the project activities, but the outcome of increased enrollment of students with disabilities is not.

8. The evaluation plan does not include quantifiable baseline data or benchmarks against which to measure progress and ultimate success of the proposed activities.

9. The application does not describe how feedback will be used to make program improvements.

10. Specific project evaluation forms and guidelines to evaluate the progress of students will not be developed until the first year of the project, so it is unclear whether the evaluation will produce objective and quantifiable data.

11. The evaluation plan does not describe a method for assessing mentoring relationships, such as the frequency, intensity, quality, and satisfaction of interactions from the perspective of faculty mentors and the perspective of student mentees.

Because grantmakers are increasingly insisting on an evaluation component in proposals, you need to have a strong one. Be sure you avoid problems like those cited above. If you lack evaluation expertise, call your nearest university grants office and ask them to help you select a professor with a specialty in your area.

GRANT GAFFES

The grant gaffes in Exhibit 57 are from a proposal seeking support from a federal grantmaker to create a Web-based training program for home health workers in identifying and treating depression. This annotated example highlights two evaluation gaffes: (a) using the

"magic bullet" approach—tasking an external evaluator to figure it all out once the project is funded, and (b) using the "buzzword" approach—sprinkling in enough fashionable lingo to feign that the evaluation plan has substance. Details, not positively ambiguous terms, persuade reviewers that an evaluation plan is solid and will produce meaningful data to assess project efficiency, effectiveness, and equity.

STARTER SENTENCES

Consider these sentences to help you being writing your evaluation section:

1. Our evaluation protocol uses a strategic mix of qualitative and quantitative methods.

2. We will conduct a process evaluation to make any necessary "mid-course" corrections and an outcome evaluation to ensure that we achieve our final project results.

3. To ensure full project accountability, we will conduct internal and external evaluations.

4. To ensure the appropriateness and comprehensiveness of evaluation methods and the use of objective performance measures to produce quantitative and qualitative data, this project follows an evaluation model.

5. Our evaluation model poses specific questions, states outcome criteria clearly, adopts an information plan, analyzes data, interprets results, and disseminates outcomes.

6. We will conduct formative evaluations to assess the effectiveness of the project during the grant period as well as summative evaluations to judge the ultimate success of the completed project.

7. To achieve our project evaluation goals, we will appoint an Evaluation Steering Committee, consisting of the project director and seven additional individuals representing the affiliate institutions, agencies, and professions.

8. Our evaluation protocol serves two purposes: (1) to provide feedback during program operation, and (2) to provide quantifiable data regarding the short- and long-term effectiveness of the program.

9. Our outcomes evaluation plan involves collecting data to document the extent to which objectives and activities were achieved.

10. We will conduct a rigorous evaluation in order to gain feedback that will be used to modify child care programming, trainings, and technical assistance to improve the likelihood of accomplishing project goals.

An outside evaluator will be used to provide an independent assessment of the overall success of the project. The evaluator will develop specific questions to be answered in the formative and summative evaluations. The impact of the project will be evaluated using a mix of qualitative and quantitative data. Working in tandem with the external evaluator, the project director will administer pre- and posttests (true/false questions) to the home health workers taking the two-hour online training. The evaluator will be responsible for developing the tests as well as analyzing the data and reporting key findings.

A within groups repeated measures design will be used for both educational knowledge and enactment variables. Variables will be categorical and thus Chi Square analyses will be used to find significance. Effect sizes will be calculated.

The first paragraph reflects a mixed bag of ideas: the first sentence identifies that an "outside evaluator" will be used, which this federal grantmaker would generally consider a proposal strength, but the fourth sentence refers to an "external evaluator" and it is not clear whether or not this is the same individual. The second sentence is an explicit admission that the project director does not understand the purpose of or how to conduct an evaluation; it drops the buzzwords of "formative" and "summative" and, simultaneously, invokes the magic bullet of the outside evaluator to determine what is really important. The third sentence uses more buzzwords—"qualitative and quantitative data"—but the fourth sentence specifies only quantitative data collection via true/false questions on pre- and posttests.

In comparison to the glittering generalizations of first paragraph, the details of the second paragraph are so specific that it appears to be written by a different voice and inserted at the last minute as a way to "beef up" the evaluation description. This second paragraph also begs the question, "If the evaluator has not yet developed the formative and summative questions, how do you know these tools and analyses will be appropriate?" Of greater concern is the discrepancy that exists between the assessment data, which focuses on changes in home health workers' knowledge, and the project's objectives, which focused on home health workers' behaviors toward treating depression. The evaluation plan should line up directly with the objectives.

GRANT GAFFES

EXHIBIT 57

Clip File Action Item # 14
Evaluation

These suggestions will help launch your Evaluation clip file:

- Secure copies of successful evaluation strategies used in other, similar proposals.
- Collect names and résumés of potential project evaluators.
- Retrieve examples from projects you have successfully evaluated in the past.

- Explore the evaluation and logic model Web sites cited above.

- Review the STAR METRICS (Science and Technology in America's Reinvestment—Measuring the EffecT of Research on Innovation, Competitiveness and Science) Web site, which represents the best of a federal and university partnership to measure the outcomes of science investments and demonstrate the benefits of scientific investments to the public: http://sites.nationalacademies.org/PGA/fdp/PGA_057189.

CHAPTER 11
Dissemination

A crank is someone with a new idea—until it catches on.
—Mark Twain

PURPOSE OF DISSEMINATION

Dissemination is the means by which you tell others about your project: its purpose, methods, and results. It's also a way for sponsors to get "more bang for their buck." Some grantmaker application forms may treat the dissemination portion as part of the methodology section while others may require it in a separate proposal section. Whether separate or a part of the methods, give serious consideration to dissemination if you want to construct a highly competitive proposal. In Chapter 11, you will learn the following:

- The benefits of discussing project dissemination strategies.
- The difference between active and passive dissemination strategies.
- 26 different dissemination strategies.
- A template for summarizing dissemination strategies in your proposal.

Project dissemination offers many benefits, including increasing public awareness of your program or project, soliciting additional support, locating more clients, alerting others in your field to new ideas, and adding to the stockpile of knowledge. You may need to use different dissemination techniques for different audiences. Remember to justify the budgeted costs of dissemination to the sponsor.

KEY QUESTIONS TO ANSWER

As you write the dissemination section, answer these key questions. Does your proposal do the following:

1. Clearly identify the intended results of the dissemination effort?
2. Include a feasible and appropriate plan for dissemination?
3. Succinctly describe any products to result from the dissemination effort?
4. Demonstrate that you understand dissemination principles and practices?
5. Provide sufficient detail to justify your dissemination budget request?
6. Include imaginative and practical dissemination?
7. Specify precisely who will be responsible for dissemination and why they are capable?
8. Discuss internal as well as external project dissemination?
9. Evaluate the effectiveness of the dissemination efforts and products?
10. Indicate how and when the target audiences will receive the timely and useful information?

DISSEMINATION STRATEGIES FOR GRANT PROPOSALS

Your specific project dissemination strategies can be active or passive. The active/passive distinction refers to your target audiences and the role they play in processing the information you present. To illustrate, if you write up a report on your project results, your reader will respond passively, since reading is a passive process. On the other hand, if you involve your target audience in a hands-on demonstration of a project's result, your strategy is active, since your participants are doing things with their hands. While the active/

passive distinction is not wholly discrete, Exhibit 58 illustrates how the more common dissemination strategies might be classified.

As a proposal writer, you should write "generic" versions of each dissemination strategy, about two paragraphs long, and store them in your clip file (see Chapter 1), ready for final editing in your next proposal. A "generic" two-paragraph example follows for each of the 26 dissemination strategies in Exhibit 57. Each example can be adapted to your specific situation. The examples arise from the same theme and assume a proposal is being submitted to develop some training materials in bioethics that would be used to train members of institutional review boards, committees that approve the use of human subjects in research experiments. Obviously, not all examples would be used in any one proposal. No "right" number exists for inclusion in proposals. Review the options and select those that make sense in your situation. Many proposals only discuss this topic lightly, using one or two strategies. If you use more than two, you may be establishing an edge over your competing proposal

We begin our example with an orienting paragraph:

> Dissemination of project activities is essential because education has a multiplier effect. The intended results of the project's dissemination

effort are to affect the knowledge, attitude, and behavior of health care providers within the hospital system relative to ethical principles and practices. Accordingly, the project will use the following strategic mix of active and passive dissemination strategies.

Active Dissemination Strategies

1. Commercial Distributors may agree to produce or market project results. Do you anticipate using a commercial vendor to produce and distribute your project products?

> All resulting tangible products—training manual, demonstration video, and training video—will be produced and distributed by Woodgrain Publishers, who has a 25-year history of successful marketing of biomedical training materials. A preliminary draft of a marketing and licensing agreement has been approved in principle by all parties and now awaits formal completion of the training manual.
>
> One key feature of the marketing agreement sets minimum sales thresholds. Should Woodgrain fail to meet those minimums for whatever reason, we have the option to cancel our agreement and change distributors.

Classification of Common Dissemination Strategies	
Active Dissemination Strategies	**Passive Dissemination Strategies**
1. Commercial Distributors	14. Books & Manuals
2. Conferences & Workshops	15. CD-ROMs & Flash Drives
3. Courses & Seminars	16. Conference Papers
4. Demonstrations	17. Executive Summaries
5. Displays/Poster Sessions	18. Interim Working Papers
6. Instructional Materials	19. Journal Articles
7. Site Visits	20. Live Streaming, Video on Demand, & Podcasts
8. Social Media	21. National Information Sources
9. Teleconferences	22. Newsletters & Listservs
10. Video Calls & Video Conferences	23. Pamphlets
11. Web Casts & Chat Rooms	24. Press Releases
12. Web Sites & Blogs	25. Staff Presentations
13. Webinars & Instant Messaging	26. Text Messaging

COMMON DISSEMINATION STRATEGIES
EXHIBIT 58

While this seems unlikely in actual practice, it is an important contract mechanism to ensure widespread distribution of the intended project results.

2. Conferences and Workshops are hosted for individuals or groups that might be interested in the project results. What regular forums exist that would be attracted to your project findings?

During the final quarter of the project period, we will sponsor a Midwest Regional Conference on Bioethics, tentatively titled "Managing Change with Fewer Resources: How to Do More with Less—Ethically." Dr. Roberta Griff from the Kennedy Bioethics Institute, a nationally recognized expert in bioethics, has tentatively agreed to present a keynote speech titled "Application of Ethical Principles to Bioethical Decision-Making." Concurrent breakout sessions will use the case study approach to apply ethical principles in specific patient situations.

Conference invitations will be sent to all central hospital administrators, all department heads, and institutional review board members in a five-state area, representing approximately 2,500 health professionals; a minimum audience of 250 is anticipated. No registration fees will be charged, although participants will be asked to pay $25.00 for two luncheon meals during the two-day conference, which will be held at the Wingspread Conference Center. Dr. Howard Thornberg will serve as conference observer and write a conference evaluation report, a role that he has repeatedly fulfilled over the past decade. Résumés for Drs. Griff and Thornberg are included in the proposal appendix.

3. Courses and Seminars show how the information resulting from the project can be explained to others in a formal instructional setting. Does the nature of your project warrant creation of a special course?

The instructional materials that result from this project form the basis of a continuing education course that could be presented either in person or via the Internet. If presented as a course or workshop, the project director would, working in conjunction with the hospital director of Continuing Education, arrange for Continuing Medical Education credits (CMEs) to be awarded, thereby counting toward certification requirements. An all-day (eight-hour) seminar would permit sufficient coverage of the topic. The hospital administers approximately 75 CME programs per year and brings a prior history of success in coordinating similar seminars.

If the seminar proves successful after several presentations, then it would be converted to a Web-based format and be available online, on-demand, so that health professionals could view the training program over the Internet at their convenience. The Office of Continuing Education has instructional designers and Web technology experts who can adapt the content of the training materials to this electronic format that allows for self-paced learning.

4. Demonstrations illustrate techniques and materials developed by the projects. Will you develop instructional materials requiring demonstrations?

To increase distribution of the *IRB Bioethics Training Manual*, a 10-minute video demonstration DVD will be prepared to highlight its contents and applications. More specifically, typical clinical scenarios will be presented to show the complexity and impact of bioethical decision making. Appealing to adult learning styles, the demonstration video will emphasize the practical applications of ethical theory. In essence, the demonstration video becomes a marketing tool for Woodgrain Publishers to stimulate sales; Woodgrain will underwrite all costs associated with preparation of the video.

The video will be shot in standard DVD format and be of commercial broadcast quality. Woodgrain will use its production studio to shoot and edit the video, once the script storyboard has been prepared. Woodgrain has used this marketing approach with 10 other products in the past two years and found it very successful. The sponsor's role in funding the entire project will be, of course, properly acknowledged.

5. Displays and Poster Sessions can be held at appropriate meetings and conferences. Which meetings? Where and when? How many individuals typically attend?

Besides presenting a paper at the National Bioethics Society Convention on July 1, 2015, we will also conduct a poster display of our major project results. The poster display will be titled, "Avoiding the Horns of Ethical Dilemmas: A Case Study at the Midwest Agency." More precisely, a case study will trace key bioethical issues and their effective resolution. Poster sessions offer the advantage of one-on-one interaction with interested convention participants.

Beyond disseminating information about the project results, the poster display represents an opportunity to build our newsletter mailing list and identify new collaborators who share our project values. The convention regularly draws 500 attendees from across the country. In particular, we will be seeking other organizations in different geographic locations who might like to replicate our project results, thereby increasing its generalizability.

6. Instructional Materials include such things as films, slide shows, filmstrips, videotapes, CDs, DVDs, PowerPoint presentations, or television programs. Will audiovisual materials be produced internally or commercially?

Beyond the demonstration video for marketing purposes, Woodgrain will prepare and distribute a video companion to the *IRB Bioethics Training Manual*. The video will supplement, not supplant, the text. More specifically, it will show typical IRB case studies and invite viewer comments based on pertinent bioethical principles prior to showing the actual IRB result.

The final DVD will be approximately 45 minutes long and of commercial broadcast quality. To ensure the appropriateness of the content, two separate focus groups will view the draft cuts and offer suggestions for final editing. The training manual and the video will be marketed as one companion unit and not sold separately. The resulting royalties will be used to continue the project beyond the grant period.

7. Site Visits are arranged for representatives of key professional associations or organizations. Could you host a site visit, a special briefing that allows key representatives to capture your enthusiasm and results first hand?

During the final project year, a series of four *Bioethics in Action* site visits will be held for key officials, including central hospital administrators, IRB chairs, health care advocates, and governmental officials. Our objective of the site visits—frankly—is to have the administrators and policy makers see the personal and practical consequences of bioethical decision making. This information, in turn, should have a positive impact on future ethical policies upon which these decision-makers must act.

Each site visit will include the following activities during its day-long schedule: overview of policies and implementation strategies, brief case history reviews, a grand rounds tour of pertinent patients, observation of an IRB meeting,

interviews of select patients and families, and a question and answer session. Preparatory materials will be sent to the site visitors one month in advance of their arrival at our facility.

8. Social Media include a variety of platforms where people can interact virtually, sharing thoughts, opinions, ideas, interests, and positions in written, pictorial, audio, and video formats. To what extent can you use social media—such as Facebook, Twitter, LinkedIn, YouTube, Flickr, Instagram, Tumblr, and Pinterest—to reach audiences large and small?

The Midwest Regional Conference on Bioethics will serve as a springboard for launching our social media platform. In particular, speakers have agreed to be interviewed at the conference and to share their insights on hot topics that emerge during the concurrent sessions. Responses to hot topic questions will be recorded individually, thus generating an initial pool of 100 video clips, each 2–4 minutes in length, which will be posted on YouTube one per week immediately following the conference. Participants will receive an e-mail blast notification with the link to the new video when it is posted online.

In addition to YouTube, participants will have the option to link to us via Facebook. Here they will be able to remain connected to the knowledge and networks they developed at the conference as well as invite new colleagues into the discussion. Our Facebook page (www.facebook.com/midwestbioethics) includes a calendar of upcoming meetings, an events page of bioethics activities occurring throughout the Midwest, links to recent articles related to the protection of human subjects, and a comments box that supports moderated discussion. Collectively, these social media strategies will open up content to an audience even wider than central hospital administrators, department heads, and institutional review board members in our five-state area.

9. Teleconferences are group telephone conference calls. Should you hold a group conference call about your project results?

Teleconferences are one of the most cost-effective and time-efficient dissemination strategies available. Live, real time interactive audio communications occur no matter where the key participants are located, whether they are participating on their smart phone or in a large group on speaker phone.

One objective of this project is to disseminate the results to policy makers. The strategy is to hold a teleconference call with the staff members in each congressional office that handles health and aging issues. A one-page Results Fact Sheet will be e-mailed to the participants one week in advance of the teleconference. At the agreed-upon conference hour, participants will dial in to the central number and be connected so all parties can hear each other. The project director will present a 10-minute summary of the major project results that have significant policy implications. Next, a 30-minute question and answer period follows. Finally, a 20-minute list of potential legislative policy action items will be generated and subsequently shared with all federal legislators in the state through their key staff members.

10. Video Calls and Video Conferences are televised versions of telephone conference calls. They are particularly useful in those instances when participant visual feedback is important to disseminating information. Will video calls with a few people at a time and video conferences with large groups of people at a time expand the reach of your project?

Video conferencing joins people from across town, across country, and across the globe in live interaction. Its applications range from live video lecturing to large audiences, to a point-to-point, individual-to-individual desktop PC chat. In essence, it integrates the best of distance and convention information exchanges as participants get together on a "virtual" basis.

One of the target audiences for the project results is health professionals and bioethicists in the 147 Veterans Administration medical centers (VAMCs) located throughout the nation. Accordingly, a two-hour teleconference, titled, "Bioethics: Nice Solutions to Nagging Problems," will be held for this audience. Two-way audio and video will connect all VAMC locations; each has the necessary polycom send and receive technology and has been involved in video conferencing for the past six years. The video conference will focus on three main topics: major project finds, clinical applications, and two case studies, including a question and answer period, all coordinated by the project director.

11. Web Casts are similar to TV broadcasts over the Internet and are often accompanied by a live **Chat Room.** Could you broadcast and discuss your project results over the Internet?

The widespread use of the Internet offers new dissemination strategies. One novel technique

growing in popularity is Web casting. With this approach, one literally broadcasts a program over the Internet much like a television show is broadcast. The technological requirements are minimal. At the broadcast end, a camera is attached to a personal computer, which, in turn, is logged on to the Internet. At the receiver end, one only needs a free software program to receive the broadcast, e.g., RealPlayer.

Our broadcast, *Bioethics 101,* will be available to anyone worldwide who can access the Internet. Simple instructions for accessing the broadcast will be posted on our Web site two weeks in advance of the broadcast. Participants can download handouts in advance of the presentation. An e-mail address will be used for participants to send in questions and receive answers during the broadcast. A chat room will be created so participants can continue their electronic discussions in real time after the Web cast.

12. Web Sites are international electronic libraries with collections of pages, images, audio recordings, and videos; Web site visitors can chronicle their thoughts, opinions, and reactions as part of a **Blog.** Can your project results be filed in the world's electronic library—the Internet?

It is axiomatic that the project results will be filed on our Web site (www.bioethics.org). This offers multiple advantages. It is not appreciably constrained by length. It can easily be updated. It represents a familiar technology trend in information dissemination. It is also a friendly communication tool for the end users.

Hosting the report on our Web site is a necessary but not a sufficient condition of information dissemination. Equally important, the report must be structured to attract the major search engines, e.g., Google, Yahoo, and Bing. This is done by registering the site with the major search engines and using targeted strategies that will facilitate search engine optimization. Without belaboring details, we have the technological expertise to attract top search engine hits.

13. A Webinar is an interactive multimedia presentation that is transmitted over the Web. Participants view PowerPoint (or Word, Access, or Excel) presentations through their Web browser and listen to the instructor through their computer's speakers or a teleconference call. When participants have questions, they can ask directly on the phone or via **Instant Messaging** on the Web. Does your project warrant a presentation to a disparate audience of professionals?

Webinars are a cost-effective and efficient way of using technology to disseminate information on a nationwide scale. Two 90-minute webinars will be offered during the course of the year to 2,500 nationwide members of the Bioethicists of America. The first webinar, "A Primer on Bioethics," will target professionals new to the field; the second webinar, "Bioethics: Turning Theory into Practice," aims to reach seasoned veterans who are ready to take their programs to a new level.

Not only will participants be able to view the PowerPoint presentation from the comfort of their own offices (and thus save their limited travel dollars), but they will be able to participate in instant polls and ask questions via instant messaging. Web-based polling allows information to be processed immediately and provides instructors with a simple way to gauge participant learning and, in response, incorporate results into the presentation. Both instant polls and instant messages can be set up to ensure a level of anonymity and, as a result, help to create a positive environment where there are no "dumb questions."

Passive Dissemination Strategies

14. Books and Manuals are either issued by your organization, the sponsor, or commercial publishers. Do you anticipate textual material to be published for public consumption?

The primary result of this project is to produce a training manual for use with institutional review boards as they consider complex bioethical issues. The leading publisher in the field is Woodgrain Publishers, who has expressed strong conceptual interest in publishing our *IRB Bioethics Training Manual* after review of two initial chapters and the table of contents. Because of their national reputation as a publisher of biomedical books, they have the marketing distribution channels and networks necessary to ensure a reasonable market penetration.

A 200-page training manual is envisioned and will consist of three parts: Ethical Principles, Biomedical Applications, and Case Studies. We will provide appropriate text and references, while Woodgrain will handle graphics and illustrations in addition to marketing. In the event Woodgrain decides against publication, three other publishers in the bioethics field will be contacted. A text delivery date of November 2014 is anticipated.

15. CD-ROMs and Flash Drives can be used to disseminate project reports instead of the more traditional printed reports. Could you prepare an electronic report that could be produced inexpensively and shared with other computer users?

We propose taking a cost-effective approach to the dissemination of our final project report. Rather than spend valuable project dollars printing a more traditional, four-color report with fancy graphics, we propose to prepare our report on a CD that can be widely disseminated at low cost. The final report consumers are extensive computer users and will find great convenience in being able to read and search the report for items of special interest to themselves.

Project staff are experienced in producing high-quality reports in-house with desktop publishing applications, such as Publisher, and then converting the reports to PDF (Portable Document Format) files for distribution. While most desktop and laptop computers are preloaded with software for viewing PDF documents, instructions will be provided so recipients needing software can download the latest version of Adobe Reader for free. The final project report cost will be approximately 20 cents per disk.

16. Conference Papers are delivered at regional or national conferences, conventions, trade shows, or professional society gatherings. Which conferences? Where and when? How many individuals typically attend?

The project results will be presented at the National Bioethics Society Convention to be held in San Diego on July 1, 2014. The convention has an average attendance of 1,500 bioethics professionals from throughout the United States. The tentative working title of the conference paper is "Avoiding the Horns of Ethical Dilemmas: The Midwest Agency Experience."

The main thrust of the paper is to disseminate project results to the leading national bioethicists. Through the case study method, we will explain how the rather abstract principles of ethical decision making apply in some very concrete ways to people with seriously impaired health status. Copies of our paper will also be placed on our Web site at www.bioethics.org for those individuals wishing copies; our Web site home page receives approximately 1,300 hits per month. Web site analytics will provide information on the number of visitors, page views, and duration of stay on the conference paper page; we will include this information in our final project report to the sponsor.

17. Executive Summaries of project results can be e-mailed to appropriate persons. Are there significant professionals who would appreciate a brief but very timely abstract of your project results?

E-mail is a ubiquitous communication tool to disseminate executive summaries of project results. Timely project summaries will be distributed to top hospital administrators, IRB chairs, and policy makers. Taking advantage of skim reading techniques—bulleted lists, bolded headers, and short sentences—the executive summaries are intended to keep the project and its results foremost on the minds of executives.

To meet this goal of high visibility, the content emphasis has to focus on how the project results impact the daily lives of executives, e.g., selection of members to local IRBs, ethical treatment of patients, mediation of ethical disputes, and new regulatory agency requirements. The overarching principle is to add value to the executives' understanding of bioethics.

18. Interim Working Papers can be used to describe those portions of project findings of most immediate interest to other audiences. Do you have significant provisional findings to share with various publics?

Because our project work progresses in distinct phases, we plan to issue interim progress reports. These white papers will briefly summarize project results to date and concentrate on the findings from each ethical principle and its application; that is to say, since the project involves six different ethical principles, six different white papers will be issued, each within 30 days after the completion of each project phase.

Each white paper will follow the same general format. Following introductory remarks, a basic principle of ethics will be described from its philosophical roots, followed by a discussion of some practical applications of the principle. An annotated bibliography will conclude each white paper, which is projected to be about 10 pages long. All white papers will, of course, also be posted on our Web site in addition to being distributed to key policy makers.

19. Journal Articles can be submitted to scholarly, professional, or trade journals. Which publications? What tentative article titles?

Bioethics professionals read two major journals: the *National Journal of Bioethics* and the *Bioethics Society Journal*. Each has a circulation in excess of 1,000 subscribers, consisting of theoreticians and practitioners alike. Our first submission will be to the *National Journal of Bioethics* no later than August 1, 2014. Since this journal encourages a more theoretical perspective, our tentative working title is "Theoretical Perspectives on Bioethics: The Midwest Project." In our 1,500-word article, we shall trace the ethical roots of the major decision-making principles that confront bioethicists. If accepted for publication without revision, Summer 2015 would be a reasonable publication date.

The article for the *Bioethics Society Journal* requires a slightly different approach. Since its readers are primarily practitioners and clinicians, our tentative working title is "Practical Applications of Ethical Principles: the Midwest Project." In this 1,200-word article to be submitted by October 1, 2014, we will emphasize how this project has taken basic ethical principles and applied them to complex biomedical problems. Barring major changes, a Fall 2015 publication date is expected.

20. Live Streaming, Video on Demand, and Podcasts are ways that live and prerecorded audio and video can be sent over the Internet for viewing on mobile devices, such as smart phones, tablets, and computers. Will your project generate more interest when people have the opportunity to watch it live?

The Midwest Regional Conference on Bioethics is a cornerstone of our dissemination strategy. A minimum audience of 250 attendees is anticipated; however, this represents only a small fraction, roughly 10 percent, of the number of central hospital administrators, department heads, and institutional review board members in the five-state area that would benefit from participating in the conference. In an effort to reach out to the 90 percent who are unable to attend in person, Dr. Roberta Griff, executive director of the Kennedy Bioethics Institute, has expressed a willingness to live stream her keynote address. Given her status as a nationally recognized expert in bioethics, we anticipate that this free live stream will attract an additional 250 viewers.

Without belaboring the details, YouTube live stream is the platform that will support the broadcast of the keynote address to audiences watching on their smart phones, tablets, and computers. To generate maximum viewership, text messages will be sent to individuals on our mailing list who are not registered for the conference, reminding them of the date and time of this free event. In essence, live streaming represents an effective strategy for building affinity with our target audience and for piquing their interest in purchasing the *IRB Bioethics Training Manual,* thus extending the project's impact.

21. National Information Sources like the National Technical Information Service can be used as a repository for reports and raw data. Can you make your data and major reports available to a nationwide information service?

Our primary source data and major project reports will be filed with the National Technical Information Service (NTIS), a branch of the U.S. Department of Commerce. This information warehouse makes federal grant data available to interested individuals. More precisely, other professionals concerned with bioethics will be able to learn the project title, project director, information about our organization, and a detailed description of the project along with the resulting data.

We anticipate filing the NTIS documents no later than August 1, 2014. Our entry will then be included in their electronic catalog within two weeks, thereby making the project results instantly available, as opposed to waiting a year or more for an article to be published in a professional journal. Our newsletters and poster displays will direct interested professionals to NTIS for more project details. NTIS averages over 400,000 information requests annually.

22. Newsletters and Listservs can be circulated to selected organizations and individuals in the field. Who are the influential decision makers that share your concern for this project?

To disseminate the results of this project, we will publish a monthly electronic newsletter entitled "Bioethics Briefings," with the tagline "Tips, Ideas, and Techniques to Promote Bioethics among Health Professionals." The target audience includes central hospital administrators, all department heads and institutional review board members from all participating hospitals. Feature columns include From the Editor's Desk, Practically Speaking, Ethically Speaking, Clinician's Calendar, Field Focus, and Medicolegal News. Since health professionals are very busy, it will be written for newsletter skimmers: short copy, highly practical, bolded

text for emphasis, white space, and bulleted lists. Readers can skim, skip, surf, and flip through the text quickly.

The newsletter will emphasize four features under the direction of Robert Hopkins, director of Staff Communications:

1. It will tell people who we are, where they can find us, and what we can do for them.
2. It will draw people into the newsletter by showing that we can provide what the readers need and that we have expertise in the area.
3. It will give specific features and reasons why readers should follow the principles of ethical behavior.
4. It will tell the readers what action to take—attending a seminar, joining a study group, participating in a focus group, or discussing cases with colleagues.

23. Pamphlets describe available project products and their potential use. Do you anticipate a tangible, marketable product?

One major result of this project is the development of training materials in bioethics that are specifically targeted to institutional review board members. Since IRB training is now federally mandated, an identifiable need and market exists. The budget requests $5,500 to publish and distribute a brochure that would announce the availability of the training materials.

Since our organization lacks the capacity to publish attractive but reasonably priced pamphlets and brochures, this production item will be outsourced to the Midwest Brochure Publishing Company. For a cost of 75 cents per pamphlet, they can produce and mail a three-fold, four-color document. In total, 3,000 pamphlets will be distributed nationwide. The resulting income from product sales will be used to continue the project beyond the grant period.

24. Press Releases can be issued to the mass media. Do you have the necessary resources to issue quality press releases?

The project staff have 84 years of cumulative experience in issuing successful press releases. Over time, the following rules of writing press releases have become clear. Press releases attract attention when they emphasize the relevant. Include all of the who-what-when-where-why-how facts. Write in simple sentences. Don't jam too much into a sentence. Make the lead paragraph strong. Include a humanistic flair.

Writing strong press releases is only part of the job; the other part is distributing it to the right targets. The first rule of trash-can avoidance is: don't send trash. Take the time to do a good job but don't bury the recipients in a paper blizzard. The case study applications of bioethics have strong human interest appeal and will be the focus of mass media press releases. The press releases will be distributed through PRLog, a free press release distribution service.

25. Staff Presentations might be made at local, state, and national meetings. Can you and your staff proactively reach out to various professional forums?

Dissemination of project results is a project priority. Among the multiple dissemination strategies used in this project, key staff members will use their existing networks to make presentations at local and regional meetings. To ensure quality and uniformity of presentations, the project director will oversee the development of a PowerPoint presentation, approximately 30 minutes in length, that can easily be adapted for different audiences. A minimum of one presentation per month is planned.

The content of the presentation will mirror the *IRB Bioethics Training Manual* and video, namely, ethical principles, bioethical practices, and case studies. While all key staff members are experienced in making public presentations, the chairman of the Speech Department at Midwest University will present a short in-service workshop to ensure quality field presentations.

26. Text Messages are a quick, easy, and quiet way to send and receive brief information. Will your target audience be responsive to this means of mass communication?

Smart phones offer an easy and affordable way to keep in contact with workshop participants: group text messaging. At the conclusion of the workshop, participants will have the opportunity to sign up for personalized text alerts to be sent to them monthly. Alerts will serve as a reminder to visit our Web site for announcements about upcoming workshops, recently published white papers, and new video-on-demand offerings. A private group chat can also be established for particular topics of interest.

Sending group text messages is quite simple: messages of up to 160 characters are typed in using the touchscreen and then sent to smart phones or e-mail addresses. Many workshop participants can be reached with a single text message. What's more, regular messages prevent this topic from becoming "out of sight, out of mind."

WRITING TIPS FOR DISSEMINATION

1. Identify the specific information you wish to disseminate, e.g., interim findings, project results, project outcomes, project impacts. Your evaluation data will help pinpoint significant findings.
2. Determine your dissemination target audiences, e.g., staff members, parents, politicians, educators, clinical providers, environmental groups, policy makers, community leaders, grantmakers, media representatives, business officials.
3. Select the appropriate dissemination strategies from among the options listed in Exhibit 58.
4. Include an appropriate level of detail. If you are going to present at a professional association, name the conference, location, and likely session title. If you are going to publish an article, identify the journal, submission date, and tentative title. If you are going to offer a course, identify the location, duration, and anticipated number of attendees.
5. If you have experience with the particular dissemination strategy, be sure to let reviewers know (e.g., you've published or presented at the venue one or more times in the past).
6. Where possible, be sure to identify the number of people who will be reached by each dissemination strategy.
7. Your time and task chart (Chapter 9) may specify the timing of various dissemination activities.
8. Don't forget to evaluate the effectiveness of your dissemination strategies.
9. Remember to include dissemination costs in your project budget.
10. Consider introducing your dissemination strategies to your reviewers by use of a table, as illustrated in Exhibit 59.

Exhibit 59 presents the beginnings of a table summarizing how you might write up your dissemination strategies. You would, of course, begin with an introductory paragraph. After the table, you would include the two-paragraph descriptions of each dissemination strategy, adding perhaps a sentence or two about the specific target audiences. If space is limited, perhaps some of the fuller descriptions of dissemination strategies could be included as an appendix item.

Project Dissemination Strategies		
Specific Information	**Target Audience**	**Dissemination Strategy**
Project Policy Implications	17 Local, County Politicians	Executive Summary
Final Project Report	55+ Professional Colleagues Program Officer	Journal Article Conference Presentation
Practical Health Implications	275+ Community Citizens	Press Release Media Presentation

TABLE DEPICTING PROJECT DISSEMINATION STRATEGIES

EXHIBIT 59

REJECTION REASONS

Some reviewer comments from rejected proposals include the following:

1. The project is unique but lacks an effective strategy for disseminating some potentially significant results.
2. This proposal contains no plans for translating the results into a highly readable form, drawing practical implications, and getting this information into a dissemination network.
3. Unfortunately, the proposal advances no mechanism to share the project results with influential policy makers.
4. While the proposal offers some novel dissemination strategies, the costs of dissemination are not addressed in the budget.
5. The application does not provide a sufficient justification for international travel as part of the dissemination plan.
6. The résumé of the project director is silent on his technical capabilities to handle video conferencing

as a dissemination strategy. Before funding can be recommended, the project director should either document his technology expertise, especially as regards bandwidth, or agree to hire a consultant in this area.

7. The narrative would benefit from a stronger dissemination plan. It is unclear what exactly is meant by participants will be "encouraged" to share content knowledge and methodology with students, colleagues, and the public. It appears as if the project director is not engaging personally in specific strategies to actively disseminate project processes and results.

GRANT GAFFES

Here's an all-too-common example of what you don't want to do. The dissemination grant gaffe in Exhibit 60 was taken from an application submitted to a national private foundation for a research project.

This one-sentence dissemination plan lacks specific details. In this instance, grant reviewers will be other scientists in the field; they expect, as part of standard practice, key results to be published in journals and presented at conferences. At a minimum, subsequent sentences in the dissemination plan should identify: targeted journals, with submission deadlines and tentative titles; expected conferences, including location and anticipated number of attendees; and the Web site address, along with baseline analytics.

To share our project findings with the scientific community, we will publish two papers, present at two conventions, and post our papers on our Web site.

GRANT GAFFES

EXHIBIT 60

STARTER SENTENCES

Select one of these sentences to help you begin writing your dissemination section:

1. Our project uses a strategic mix of active and passive dissemination strategies to communicate our results to all stakeholders.

2. Since our target audience of teenagers relies heavily on social media as a communication tool, we will disseminate our health education program to them in short segments via Facebook and Twitter.

3. Traditionally, academics rely on publications in journal articles and presentations at large conventions to disseminate their research findings. In this project, we will go beyond the standard strategies and host a Webinar, issue press releases, and make our data instantly available through the National Technical Information Service.

4. Since our primary project purpose is to advocate for a new temporary jobs policy, we will issue interim working papers to state legislators and invite them for a site visit to see firsthand the employability and work productivity of persons formerly incarcerated.

5. Through the dissemination of study results in peer-reviewed publications, the project will inform and strengthen the education of Occupational Therapy students and other practitioners working with older adult patients.

6. Because dissemination has such a positive multiplier effect, we have formed a Dissemination Steering Committee consisting of the project director, the head of our Department of Media Communications, and a news reporter from our local ABC-TV affiliate to ensure widespread distribution of project results through the mass media.

7. Our strategic dissemination plan targets both internal and external audiences. Our internal staff will monitor project progress through weekly staff meetings and ad hoc e-mails. Our primary external audience of elementary school teachers and parents will be kept abreast of project progress through Web site postings and an annual open house. More specifically, we will…

8. The distinctive feature of our dissemination plan is its cultural sensitivity. Since our video will disseminate infant nutrition information to new Hispanic mothers, we will first ensure that our script will be translated into "street level" Spanish, and we will hire actors and actresses who are native speakers. The video will be made available free to the maternity wards in all three local hospitals for playing on their in-house closed circuit TV system on-demand.

9. Since our key project collaborators are geographically spread over 1,000 miles, we will disseminate interim project status reports by use of a group Web conferencing system such as Webex or GoToMeeting. They have the capacity to handle large numbers of participants. For smaller group discussions, we will use Skype.

10. To effectively disseminate our project results, we have created an information architecture that will provide the key intellectual content and delivery systems for transferring our research findings to practitioners. Our information architecture represents the knowledge base generated from our three-phase project.

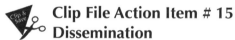

Clip File Action Item # 15
Dissemination

To build your Dissemination clip file, follow these suggestions:

- Each day, pick one of the dissemination strategies cited above and write a "generic version" for your organization: proper names, project titles, and dates can be inserted later. In one month, you will have a smorgasbord of dissemination strategies that can be called upon when needed.
- Garner examples of successful dissemination strategies used in other proposals.

CHAPTER 12
Budgets

There are no price objections, only value questions.
—Helen Feden

PURPOSE OF BUDGETS

A project budget is more than a statement of proposed expenditures. It is an alternate way to express your project, establish its credibility, and judge your project's value. Reviewers will scrutinize your budget to see how well it fits your proposed objectives and activities. In fact, some reviewers see the budget as a do-or-die section. If there are math errors or unrealistic numbers, the ability of the organization to successfully deliver on the grant is immediately called into question. Incomplete budgets are examples of sloppy preparation. Inflated budgets are signals of waste. Low budgets cast doubt on your planning ability. In essence, your budget is as much a credibility statement as your project narrative. In Chapter 12, you will learn the following:

- The major categories of direct costs.
- Tips for requesting indirect costs from government, foundation, and corporate sponsors.
- Forms of cost sharing: mandatory/voluntary, cash/in-kind, internal/external.
- Strategies for determining appropriate budget size and including allowable budget items.
- Importance of coordinating budgets and proposal narratives.

In addition to the size of your budget, your distribution of expenditures gives important clues about your organization's commitment to the project. For instance, with training or service grants, don't ask for all the money up front with a vague promise that you will share the costs in subsequent years. Instead, when preparing multiyear budgets, show you will pick up an increasing amount of the costs each year. In doing this, you communicate your intent to continue the project after the sponsor's funds are gone (See also Chapter 13, Sustainability). Further, you are developing your capacity to fund the program. In this way, you demonstrate that you will be a good steward of the sponsor's funds. Future funding is not apt to be an issue in most research grants, which may have limited time spans.

Preparing proposal budgets can be a bedeviling experience for beginning writers. The starting point is to understand the different types of costs included in budget building. Some key budget terms are discussed below, namely, direct costs, indirect costs, and cost sharing. In mathematical terms, the amount of money you request from the sponsor is the sum of your direct and indirect costs minus any cost sharing. All three budget factors are discussed below.

DIRECT COSTS

Direct costs are explicit project expenditures listed as line items in the budget. Direct costs are usually categorized into personnel (people) and nonpersonnel (things) components. Personnel costs include such items as salaries, wages, fringe benefits, consultant fees, participant support costs, and contractor/subcontractor charges. Nonpersonnel costs include such items as equipment, materials and supplies, travel, lodging, subsistence, and publication charges. Usually, direct cost figures are easy to pinpoint. For example, grant-funded salaries are calculated as a percentage of the time and effort devoted to the project relative to one's annual salary. Salary calculations follow this mathematical formula.

Grant Salary = base salary × percent effort × duration

To illustrate, if a key project person had an annual base salary of $60,000 and was going to spend 25 percent effort on a grant for one year, the formula says:

Grant Salary = $60,000 × 25% × 1 year = $15,000.

If the grant were to be for 18 months, the formula says:

Grant Salary = ($60,000 × 25% × 1 year) + ($62,400 × 25% × 0.5 year) = $22,800

This latest calculation assumes in the last six project months (duration = 0.5), the key project person received a 4 percent cost of living adjustment (base salary = $62,400).

As another illustration, travel costs can be computed on the basis of reimbursement costs per mile or round trip airfare, as appropriate. If your organization does not have a standard mileage reimbursement rate, consider using the current IRS rate, which can be found at www.irs.gov—enter "mileage rate" in the search box. Fringe benefits are typically expressed as a percentage of salaries and often include such elements as social security, health insurance, dental and vision insurance, retirement, unemployment compensation, and disability insurance. Consultant costs may be expressed on an hourly, daily, or project basis. Contractors and subcontractors should provide you with a written quotation of their costs. Space and utilities may be reflected either as direct costs or included as a part of your indirect cost rate, which is described next.

INDIRECT COSTS

Indirect costs are perhaps the most perplexing cost component to include in grant budgets. It is perplexing for grantseekers because (1) it is not always clear which cost components should be included in such calculations, and (2) indirect cost policies vary among grantmakers—that is, no one strategy works in all circumstances. To help clarify matters, we introduce this topic with a conceptual map of indirect costs (Exhibit 61), followed by in-depth discussions.

Indirect costs represent other project costs not itemized as direct costs. Typically, grant budgets don't list *all* of the costs associated with a project because

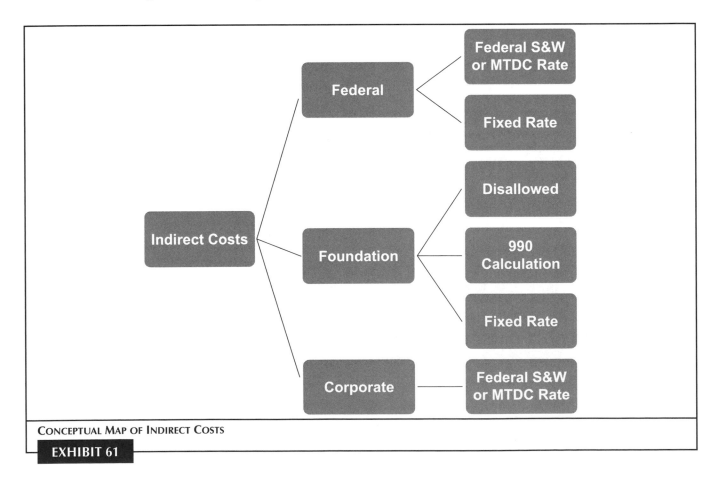

CONCEPTUAL MAP OF INDIRECT COSTS

EXHIBIT 61

some costs are hard to pin down, e.g., payroll and accounting, library usage, space and equipment, and general project administration. Do you include in your proposal budget the costs associated with preparing payroll or the time your boss spends talking with you about your project? While you could cost out those factors, and others, with some effort, they are more difficult to quantify. At the same time, they are real project costs, e.g., someone has to write your payroll checks. Rather than calculating a strict cost accounting of these nebulous factors, many sponsors allow you to compute them as a percentage of your direct costs and add it to your budget request as an indirect cost item.

Federal Indirect Costs

Semantically, most federal agencies now use the term *facilities and administration costs* (F&A) instead of indirect costs to refer to these additional project operating costs. These F&A grant costs are usually calculated on a percentage figure assigned to you by the federal government as a result of an indirect cost audit. The percentage figure may be based on either the modified total direct costs (MTDC) or a percentage of the total project salaries and wages (S&W). To illustrate, assume the federal government assigned you an indirect cost of 45 percent of modified total direct costs. (The "modified" means certain costs components are excluded from the calculation base such as equipment and student stipends). This means that for every dollar you receive in federal direct costs, the government would give you an additional 45 cents to administer that dollar expenditure. The government recognizes that it costs something to do business.

To make their dollars stretch further, a few federal agency grant programs fix the percentage of F&A costs that can be requested. For example, capacity building grants awarded through the U.S. Department of Agriculture may limit F&A costs to a maximum of 30 percent of federal funds awarded; training grants awarded through the U.S. Department of Education may limit F&A costs to a maximum of 8 percent of MTDC; and, social service pilot grants awarded through the U.S. Department of Labor limit administrative costs, which could be direct or indirect costs, to no more than 10 percent of the total request. Federal grant programs typically clarify in the application guidelines whether full or restricted F&A rates may be requested. In some instances the application guidelines also stipulate that the difference between an institution's full F&A rate and the restricted amount included in the grant request may be shown as in-kind cost sharing.

Organizations regularly receiving federal grants have an approved federal F&A rate that is included in the budgets of federal proposals; it consists of two major component categories: facilities and administration. *Facilities* is defined as depreciation and use allowances on buildings; equipment and capital improvements; interest on debt associated with certain building, equipment, and capital improvements; and operations and maintenance expenses. *Administration* is defined as general administration and general expenses such as the director's office, accounting, personnel, library expenses, and all other types of expenditures not listed specifically under one of the subcategories of "*Facilities*." Whether your F&A rate is based on S&W or MTDC typically depends on the dollar volume of your current federal grant portfolio: if less than $3 million, it's often S&W; if more than $3 million, it's often MTDC.

If you plan to periodically submit federal proposals and do not have a federal indirect cost rate, your federal program officer can refer you to the appropriate federal agency to find out how you negotiate a federal indirect cost rate for your organization. Currently, you must have a federal grant before you can apply for an F&A rate, unless you seek a minimal provisional rate. This means, for example, if you receive a three-year federal grant, you can apply for an F&A rate during your first award year that might be added to the funds you receive for years two and three. To learn more about F&A rates, visit the Office of Management and Budget Web site www.whitehouse.gov/omb/grants/attach.html#cost.

Foundation Indirect Costs

Foundations often use the term *administrative costs* rather than indirect costs or F&A costs when referring to additional project operating expenses, although the terms are interchangeable. Foundations vary considerably in their practices regarding administrative costs. Some will pay fixed administrative costs on grants, and their application guidelines specify the allowable percentage of total direct costs. For instance, one health-related foundation has a fixed administrative cost rate of 20 percent; to submit a budget, you add up all of the direct costs and add an additional 20 percent to the total to cover your operating expenses.

Other foundations will say explicitly in their application materials that they disallow or do not fund administrative costs. In those instances, you have two options: (1) absorb those operating costs within your organization's budget, or (2) itemize those operating costs as direct costs within your proposal budget and recover those costs as direct line item costs.

To illustrate, if you think you will need 5 percent of your boss's time to provide updates on your project progress, include that 5 percent time as a direct proposal cost. If you choose the first option of absorbing those costs, at least show it as a cost-sharing component to your project, as discussed below. If you choose the second option of direct cost itemization, you are, in reality, taking your administrative (or indirect cost) rate apart and budgeting it as a direct cost item. Many nonprofit organizations fail to realize they can recover these operating costs if only they would ask for them. Administering a grant should not cost your organization any money.

While some private foundations have fixed administrative cost rates and others disallow administrative costs, the majority of the foundations remain silent on this budget issue; that is, sponsors' application materials do not specify their policy on funding administrative costs. And yet, they have administrative costs themselves. Somebody has to pay their utilities, payroll, insurance, and other operating costs. In such instances, the preferred approach is to request of private foundations the same indirect cost rate that they are paying themselves. To do that, look at a foundation's tax returns, annual reports, or description in the Foundation Directory (See Chapter 3) and identify two figures: (1) the total amount of grants awarded and (2) the total expenditures for the year.

For instance, the 2011 tax records (990s) for the Helen Bader Foundation reveal that they spent (line 26) $10,643,444, including $8,947,947 in grants (line 25). What happened to the other $1,695,497? That amount (16 percent) represented their operating costs. Accordingly, when submitting a budget to the Helen Bader Foundation, you might include this language:

> In addition to the direct costs of $10,000, we are requesting 16 percent or ($1,600) in administrative costs, the same rate that the Helen Bader Foundation incurred in your fiscal year 2011, according to your tax records. Our total project investment is $11,600.

You could use this same strategy for any foundation that does not specify its administrative cost policy, using, of course, information from the latest available fiscal year.

Corporate Indirect Costs

In contrast to governments and foundations, corporations use the term *overhead* to mean the same thing as administrative, indirect, or F&A costs. As business professionals, they are accustomed to the concept of overhead and are apt to have a high overhead rate themselves.

In most instances, corporate application materials do not specify a policy regarding the payment of overhead. Unlike foundations, you do not have access to their tax records to request a comparable corporate rate for your project, but you do have another option for determining a reasonable overhead rate to include in your proposal.

Assuming the corporate overhead rate is not available in their latest annual report (if a publicly held company) and you lack a corporate connection who can give you inside information, you can use your federally negotiated indirect cost rate since it is an audited figure. Knowing that it is a federally audited rate will be acceptable to most corporate sponsors. If this is not acceptable, your fallback position is to list everything as direct cost items.

COST SHARING

The costs that your organization will contribute to the total project costs are called "shared costs" or "matching costs." You may contribute partial personnel costs, space, volunteer time, or other costs toward the total project expenses. Your cost sharing may be in the form of a "hard" dollar match or one of in-kind contributions—costs not requiring a cash outlay to your organization, although they would represent real dollars if you had to pay for services rendered, e.g., the value of time contributed by volunteers. Use a fair market value to calculate in-kind contributions; simply determine what it would cost you if you had to buy those volunteered services or goods outright. For example, if teens are helping you stuff envelopes as a part of a direct mail campaign, you might use a minimum wage figure to show cost sharing. On the other hand, if you have a volunteer attorney giving you pro bono services to evaluate a new rental contract, you would use that person's hourly billing rate multiplied by the number of donated hours as a cost sharing budget item.

Because expectations about cost sharing vary considerably, check with your program officer to determine their preferences. In fact, preproposal contact (Chapter 4) is essential to determine the value cost sharing carries in evaluating budgets. Many sponsors still look upon cost sharing as evidence that your organization is committed to your proposed project to the extent that you are willing to absorb some of its expenses. Some sponsors and grant programs will require a minimum amount of cost sharing, as indicated in their proposal guidelines. For instance, equipment grant proposals to the National Science Foundation may require a 30 percent cost sharing effort on the organization's part. On the other hand, some sponsors and grant programs don't place a high value on cost sharing, even to the extent of insisting that the cost sharing be dropped from the proposed budget as a condition of awarding a grant. For example, most research grant proposals to the National Science Foundation are prohibited from including quantifiable cost sharing in the budget. Since sponsor attitudes toward cost sharing vary widely, ask your program officer.

Mandatory Versus Voluntary Cost Sharing

Cost sharing may be mandatory or voluntary. Mandatory cost sharing is often referred to as "matching funds"; it is required whereas voluntary cost sharing is optional. Your promise of cost sharing in a proposal budget may be a key factor in a sponsor's funding decision.

Mandatory As one of the eligibility requirements of the grant, the sponsor requires you to share a certain percent of the total project costs. For example, "Local organizations are required to provide a local match totaling 75 percent of the requested grant funds." In this case, if a sponsor provides $20,000, you must provide an additional $15,000 toward the total project cost of $35,000.

Voluntary You offer cost sharing in your proposal as an incentive to get the grant award. For instance, a sponsor may indicate, "Consideration will be given to organizations with in-kind contributions." In response, you may offer 20 percent cost sharing of personnel time toward the total project cost of $150,000. In dollar amounts, this means the sponsor would contribute $125,000 and you would provide $25,000 of the total project costs. However, you can cost share too much: for some sponsors, higher levels of cost sharing require more administrative monitoring on their part, something program officers may wish to avoid. Accordingly, check with your project officers to see if they have a "preferred level" of voluntary cost sharing.

Cash Versus In-Kind Cost Sharing

Cost sharing may be in the form of a cash match (hard dollars) or an in-kind contribution (soft dollars).

Cash Your organization contributes so-called hard dollars toward your proposed project. Perhaps you were planning to purchase some equipment with your regular internal budget. Those dollars can be allocated toward your project. Usually, you had already planned to spend the money; now, in a tactical budget building mode, you link those planned expenditures to your proposal.

In-kind These "soft dollars" do not require a cash outlay by your organization, yet represent real dollars you would have to pay if the costs were not absorbed elsewhere. Personnel effort is perhaps the most common form of cost sharing, since it can include salaries, fringe benefits, and associated indirect costs. To illustrate, Ms. Ida Know, project director, may allocate 50 percent of her time (salary and fringe benefits) to a project grant, yet request sponsor funding for only 10 percent effort. Ms. Know's institution could cost share the remaining 40 percent of her salary and fringe benefits. As a further example, you can also cost share indirect costs. So, if your organization has a 26 percent indirect cost rate and your sponsor only allows a maximum reimbursement of 20 percent on direct costs, you can show the 6 percent difference as cost sharing.

Internal Versus External Cost Sharing

Assuming you've decided to cost share on your proposed budget, the funds may come either from internal or external sources—or both.

Internal You may allocate a portion of your direct or indirect costs to your proposed project. These shared costs may take on the form of cash or in-kind contributions. Consider this internal cost sharing example: assume you decide to cost share 20 percent of the project director's salary toward your proposed project. This means that instead of your project director receiving 100 percent of her salary from your agency personnel budget, she will now receive 80 percent from that source and the remaining 20 percent from the cost sharing account on the grant; you merely reallocate a portion of her salary; her income remains the same; the source(s) of income are changed on the bookkeeping records.

External You may allocate extramural dollars from other sources to the project, as indicated in the following three examples:

- You have a matching grant from another sponsor.
- A wealthy philanthropist has given you unrestricted dollars that can be earmarked to this project.

Item	Amount Requested	Cost Sharing	Total Amount
Project Director ($30,000/ yr × 1 yr × 20% effort	$3,000	$3000	$6,000
Fringe Benefits (28% of salary)	$840	$840	$1,680
Indirect Costs (30% of salary)	$900	$900	$1,800
Total $	$4,740	$4,740	$9,480

SAMPLE COST SHARING

EXHIBIT 62

- Revenue is generated from another fund-raising activity, e.g., golf outing income can be directed to this project.

In each case, you can redirect dollars from those sources to help support the total costs of your proposed project, thereby showing your sponsor you are financially committed to supporting your proposal.

Cost Sharing Example

If your sponsor requires or strongly encourages cost sharing, then you obviously should do this. But where do you find the cost sharing dollars, particularly if your organization has a modest budget? Cost sharing is often done through a portion of salary, fringe benefits, and indirect costs. For instance, assume that a project director will spend 20 percent of her time on the project, but is only requesting the sponsor to fund 10 percent of that effort. The other 10 percent of the project director's salary can be shown as cost sharing. In addition to the cost sharing on salary dollars, additional cost sharing can be shown on the fringe benefits and indirect costs associated with the salary dollars, as Exhibit 62 shows.

In essence, this cost sharing portion of the overall budget tells your sponsor that your organization is willing to absorb one-half of the personnel costs, provided the sponsor will pay the other half. Once funded, your organization uses the grant-funded salary dollars ($3,000 in this example) to pay the project director. In turn, your organization can use the deobligated salary dollars ($3,000 in agency dollars) to hire someone else part-time to do those tasks that the project director is surrendering during the course

of the funded project. The project director will still receive the same salary. Instead of 100 percent of the salary coming from the organization, now 90 percent will come from the organization and 10 percent from the grant.

If your project personnel are not spending 100 percent of their time on the grant, you should identify how the remainder of their time will be spent. For example, the one-year budget shown in Exhibit 63 suggests that the project director will be spending 40 percent of her time on the grant. Among other things, that means she must "give up" doing 40 percent of her current activities in order to devote 40 percent of her time to the grant. In turn, 40 percent of her agency salary is now "deobligated" and can be used to temporarily hire someone else part-time to pick up those duties that were relinquished by the project director in order to administer the grant.

BUDGET NARRATIVES

In addition to preparing a budget, you should develop a budget narrative. The budget narrative serves as a bridge between the proposal and the budget. It should include an explanation for every budget line item that describes: (1) the specific item, (2) the item's relevance to the project, and (3) the basis of cost calculation for the item. Reviewers are subject to eliminating or supporting only a percentage of line items that are not well justified. Include a budget narrative with your proposal immediately following your budget to explain or justify any unusual expenditure items, even if it is not specifically requested in the sponsor's application guidelines.

Budget Item	Requested from Sponsor	Cost Shared by Applicant	Total
Personnel			
➤**Salaries**			
Jane Doe, Project Director $30,000/yr × 1yr × 40% effort	$6,000	$6,000	$12,000
Carol Wooden, Survey Coordinator $20,000/yr × 6 mo × 50% effort	$5,000	$0	$5,000
Emily Johns, Secretary $15,000/yr × 1 yr × 25% effort	$3,750	$0	$3,750
10 Volunteers @ 100 hours each $8/hr × 100 hr × 10 volunteers	$0	$8,000	$8,000
➤**Fringe Benefits**			
Jane Doe, Project Director 30% of salary	$1,800	$1,800	$3,600
Carol Wooden, Survey Coordinator 25% of salary	$1,250	$0	$1,250
Emily Johns, Secretary 20% of salary	$750	$0	$750
10 Volunteers 20 % of salary (entry level)	$0	$1,600	$1,600
➤**Consultants**			
James Ball, Project Evaluator $300/day × 5 days	$1,500	$0	$1,500
➤**Personnel Subtotal**	$20,050	$17,400	$37,450
Nonpersonnel			
➤**Physical Facilities**			
Space Rental $700/month × 12 months	$4,200	$4,200	$8,400
Utilities (Gas, electric) $125/month × 12 months	$1,500	$0	$1,500
➤**Equipment**			
WG-99 Recorder with JK-17 Monitor	$7,000	$0	$7,000
Annual Maintenance Contract	$0	$700	$700
➤**Supplies**			
Basic Office Supplies $300/person × 3 people	$900	$0	$900
Survey Printing and Mailing $1.27/survey × 1,500 surveys	$1,905	$0	$1,905
Long distance phone + fax charges $50/month × 12 month	$600	$0	$600
➤**Travel**			
Local mileage: Smith (1,000 miles) + Wooden (500 miles) @ 33.5¢/mile	$502	$0	$502
Volunteers 300 miles × 10 volunteers × 33.5¢/mile	$0	$1,005	$1,005
Smith R/T Airfare ($400) + Per Diem ($125/day × 3 days)	$775	$0	$775
➤**Subtotal Nonpersonnel**	$17,382	$5,905	$23,287
Total Direct Costs (Personnel + Nonpersonnel Subtotals)	$37,432	$23,305	$60,737
Indirect Costs (30%)	$11,230	$6,692	$18,222
Total Project Costs	$48,662	$30,297	$78,959

SAMPLE ONE-YEAR BUDGET WITH COST SHARING: FEDERAL HEALTH EDUCATION PROJECT

EXHIBIT 63

Budget Narrative for "Rich" Nonprofits

Larger nonprofit organizations with big annual budgets sometimes worry that they can't get a grant because foundations would think they are "too rich," especially when so many nonprofits are seen as "so poor," at least for now.

The response strategy is to first concentrate on documenting your project need, its frequency and severity, and the consequences of not addressing it. With your problem statement clearly established, you can address the "too rich" issue head on in your budget narrative by saying something like this:

> This project requests $xx,xxx in funds. Our total organizational budget is $xx,xxx,xxx. On first impression, it would appear that our proposal project could be absorbed within our annual operating budget. However, a fuller audit of our annual funds reveals that seven major projects are receiving support to provide a broad array of services to over x,xxx worthy, deserving, and needy persons. That is to say, the existing operating budget is dedicated to on-going project support and no unobligated funds exist for new start-up projects, despite the compelling need as noted above. Accordingly, we must reach out for assistance to implement the proposed project.

Using this strategy, institutions of higher education with operating budgets in the hundreds of millions of dollars have received grants as small as a few hundred dollars. You can do it too. Use the budget narrative to inform and persuade reviewers that the funding is not an end in itself but rather a means to a larger end, namely, the achieving of the purposeful good described in the project.

KEY BUDGET QUESTIONS TO ANSWER

Use these key questions to prepare your next grant budget. Does your proposal do the following:

1. Adhere to all pertinent guidelines governing your project's budget?
2. Provide sufficient resources to carry out your project?
3. Include a budget narrative that justifies major budget categories?
4. Present the budget in the format desired by the sponsor?
5. Show sufficient detail so reviewers know how all budget items were calculated?
6. Separate direct costs from indirect costs and describe their components?
7. Relate budget items to project objectives?
8. Specify the type and amount of any cost sharing?
9. Include any attachments or special appendixes to justify unusual requests?
10. Identify evaluation and dissemination costs?

EXAMPLES OF BUDGETS

Example 1

A one-year complete budget for a federally funded health education project is presented in Exhibit 63. The sponsor allows full F&A rates to be charged to the grant, and a copy of the federally negotiated indirect cost rate agreement must be included in the attachments. The grant program encourages a significant level of cost sharing, which is highlighted in the third column.

Example 2

Exhibit 64 represents a budget request submitted to a private foundation to fund an intensive reading group and discussion with diversity students. The sponsor limited indirect costs to 5 percent of the total project request. The application was submitted electronically, and the sponsor's fillable forms did not allow for a budget narrative to be included.

Example 3

The budget in Exhibit 65 is a request to a federal agency for a project aiming to preserve rare historical books and periodicals. The grant program specified that funds may not be used for the recovery of indirect costs. The budget narrative includes details to note that a discounted rate has already been negotiated with consultants and to confirm that vendor quotes include shipping and handling charges.

Example 4

A multiyear budget request to a federal science agency is presented in Exhibit 66. The budget table includes enough information so that reviewers understand the basis of calculations. The budget narrative explains why the principal investigator is receiving funding only for work in the summer while the undergraduate researchers will receive funding for work both during the summer and the academic year; the sponsor allows in-kind contributions to be acknowledged but not quantified. The budget narrative cites its federally negotiated indirect cost rate to justify inclusion of full F&A costs at 42.6 percent of salaries and wages and fringe benefits.

Example 5

Most grant budgets require precision in their calculations. However, as illustrated in Exhibit 67, the National Institutes of Health (NIH) approaches budget construction differently. For grant budgets less than $250,000 annually, no detailed budget or budget justification is required. Budget requests are

Items	Year 1 Costs
Salary and Wages: Senior Personnel Guillermo Sainz Rocio Witt	$2,000 $2,000
Salary and Wages: Other Personnel Student participants (stipend, $8/hr, 42 hr, 40 students)	$13,440
Employee Benefits Standard rate for faculty: 45.5% Standard rate for students: 2.5%	$1,820 $336
Materials and Supplies Books ($14.25/book, 40 books, $14 shipping) Meeting refreshments ($5 person/meeting, 7 meeting, 42 people) Capstone·dinner ($50/person, 42 people)	$584 $1,470 $2,100
Indirect Costs (5%)	$1,250
TOTAL REQUEST	$25,000

SAMPLE ONE-YEAR BUDGET WITHOUT A BUDGET NARRATIVE: FOUNDATION EDUCATION PROJECT

EXHIBIT 64

Budget Categories	Cost
Consultant Fees:	
Horton W. Hoo ($225/day × 4 day)	$900
Samuel I. Yamm ($225/day × 4 day)	$900
Travel:	
From There to Here (125 mi)	
2 people, 4 total travel days, $65/day subsistence, $250 transportation	$770
Materials and Supplies:	
1 climate control monitor @ $350 each	$350
1 climate notebook software @ $500 each	$500
1 data transport device @ $100	$100
1 flash drive @ $25 each	$25
1 foot-candle-LUX meter @ $200 each	$200
1 UV light meter @ $1,996 each	$1,996
1 water leak sensor alarm @ $35 each	$35
4 water leak sensors @ $6 each	$24
4 environmental management books @ $50 each	$200
Indirect Costs: (Not Applicable)	$0
TOTAL REQUEST:	$6,000

BUDGET NARRATIVE: The project director has secured commitments from the consultants to provide four days of specialized professional development training, two days in the fall and two days in the spring, at a discounted rate of $225/day each. Horton W. Hoo and Samuel I. Yamm are well-respected experts on preservation and have direct experience with the climate control monitors that will be installed in special collections. They will travel from There to Here, which is approximately 125 miles one way: (2 Trips @ 250 mi RT × $.50/mi = $250). Per diem is calculated at prevailing state rates of $65/day: ($65/day × 4 day × 2 people = $520). Vendor quotes for the supplies are included as attachments; all quotes include shipping and handling.

SAMPLE ONE-YEAR BUDGET WITH RESTRICTED F&A RATE: FEDERAL PRESERVATION PROJECT

EXHIBIT 65

Budget Categories	Year 1	Year 2	Year 3	Total
Salaries and Wages: Senior Personnel–Phoebe Ross (one month summer salary; 4% COLA)	$8,255	$8,585	$8,929	$25,769
Salaries and Wages: Other Personnel-Undergraduate students (2 students; $9/hr, 5hr/wk, 30 wk Academic Year; $9/hr, 40hr/wk, 10 wk Summer)	$9,900	$9,900	$9,900	$29,700
Fringe Benefits Standard university rates: 38% Faculty 7.65% Students	$3,137 $757	$3,262 $757	$3,393 $757	$9,792 $2,271
Travel: National conference for dissemination [$625 airfare + ($150/night*3 night) hotel + $40 per diem * 3 day) + $305 registration = $1500]	$1,500	$1,500	$1,500	$4,500
Equipment: High-resolution atomic scanning probe	$27,750	$0	$0	$27,750
Materials and Supplies: Reagents	$5,000	$5,000	$5,000	$15,000
Total Direct Costs:	$56,299	$29,004	$29,479	$114,782
Federal F&A Rate: (42.6% of Salaries and Fringes)	$9,393	$9,587	$9,789	$28,769
TOTAL REQUEST:	$65,692	$38,591	$39,268	$143,551

SAMPLE MULTIYEAR BUDGET WITH FULL F&A RATE: FEDERAL RESEARCH PROJECT

EXHIBIT 66

BUDGET NARRATIVE

Senior Personnel: Salary is requested for the principal investigator Dr. Phoebe Ross to oversee all programmatic and research activities as specific in the proposal narrative for 1 summer month each year of the three-year project (base salary: $74,295). Salary calculations include a projected 4% cost of living adjustment for each year. The time Dr. Ross spends on this project during the academic year will be contributed in-kind as part of her scholarship commitment.

Other Personnel: Two undergraduate students will participate in the research activities for an anticipated 5 hours per week during the 30-week academic year and for 40 hours per week during the 10 weeks of summer.

Fringe Benefits: Standard university rates for faculty are 38% of salaries and wages, and include health, life, disability, retirement, and FICA. Standard university rates for students are 7.65% and include FICA only.

Travel: The principal investigator will travel to one national conference per year to disseminate research results. She has a history of presenting at leading conferences and venues such as Science Association of America (Orlando, FL), Equipment Applications International (Chicago, IL), and Council for Research (San Diego, CA).

Equipment: A vendor quote for the high-resolution atomic scanning probe is included in the attachments. Beyond the initial equipment purchase, the PI's department will assume responsibility for maintenance until such time when it is deemed necessary to retire the equipment. There is sufficient space, power supply, and security for the equipment in the PI's lab.

Materials and Supplies: A variety of consumable chemical reagents will be necessary for the research and are estimated at $5,000 per year.

Total Direct Costs: $65,692 in year 1, $38,591 in year 2, and $39,268 in year 3 for a total of $143,551. The year 1 budget is higher than subsequent years due to the one-time start-up cost of the high-resolution atomic scanning probe.

F&A Costs: The university's federally negotiated F&A rate of 42.6% of salaries and fringes is effective 07/01/2013–06/30/2016. F&A costs are $9,393 in year 1, $9,587 in year 2, $9,789 in year 3 for a total of $28,769.

TOTAL REQUEST: $65,692 in year 1, $38,591 in year 2, $39,268 in year 3 for a total of $143,551.

SAMPLE MULTIYEAR BUDGET WITH FULL F&A RATE: FEDERAL RESEARCH PROJECT

EXHIBIT 66 (Continued from page 170)

recorded in units of $25,000. In this particular example of a biomedical research initiative, $150,000 is requested in direct costs and an additional 40 percent of Salaries & Wages is requested in indirect costs, for a total of $176,300.

Modular budgets save reviewers' time, keeping their attention focused on the science being proposed rather than on nitpicking budget elements such as "Could you buy that $2,000 laptop for $1,500?" The NIH offers an additional example of a modular budget on their Web site at http://grants.nih.gov/grants/funding/424/SF424R-R_PHS398_ModularBudget_Sample.pdf.

WRITING TIPS FOR BUDGETS

These tips will help you plan and write your next budget:

1. Show the basis for your calculations: Fuzzy: Travel = $534. Specific: Local mileage for project director, 100mi/mo @ $0.445/mi × 12 mo = $534; if attending conventions, indicate name, location, and date.
2. Desktop supplies (pens, pencils, paper clips, and so forth) average $350 year/key person. It is not necessary to itemize these costs; just indicate that this is an estimate.
3. Tell sponsors the components of your fringe benefit rate. Indicate if it includes FICA; health, life,

Budget Period: 1	Start Date: 07/01/2014	End Date: 06/03/2016

A. Direct Costs

	Funds Requested ($)
Direct Cost Less Consortium F&A	$150,000
Consortium F&A	$0
Total Direct Costs	$150,000

B. Indirect Costs

Indirect Cost Type	Indirect Cost Rate	Indirect Cost Base	Funds Requested ($)
	(%)	($)	
S&W	40%	$65,750	$26,300
Cognizant Agency: DHHS		Indirect Cost Rate Agreement Date: 07/01/2012	

C. Total Direct and Indirect Costs (A+B)

	Funds Requested ($)
	$176,300

PERSONNEL JUSTIFICATION:
The Principal Investigator and two upper-class undergraduate students will dedicate three years to achieving the project activities described in the proposal narrative. The PI is budgeted for two months summer salary each year. Students will work approximately 5–10 hours per week during the academic year and approximately 40 hours per week during the summer.

EQUIPMENT JUSTIFICATION:
To conduct the analyses described in sections D:1.2.2 and D:3.1.4 of the narrative, it is essential to purchase a nano-character system with i-beam scope. This state-of-the-art imager will measure reactions in the unparalleled range of 8600 NSMs.

SAMPLE MULTIYEAR MODULAR BUDGET: NIH RESEARCH PROJECT

EXHIBIT 67

retirement, vision, dental, and disability insurance; and other benefits.

4. In university-originated proposals, separate graduate student stipends from tuition.

5. In multiyear budgets, allow for yearly increases; indicate annual percentage increases. Ask your program officer what percentage cost of living adjustments are currently being approved in multiyear budgets.

6. Some grant application guidelines do not specifically request a budget narrative. Nevertheless, you should include one immediately following your budget figures to explain or justify any unusual expenditure items.

7. Include your organization's overall budget, if requested, showing how the grant budget request fits into your general operating budget.

8. If you have applied for or received other funding, say so. It will enhance your credibility, for they recognize your commitment to supporting your project.

9. Check agency regulations for indirect costs and your approved rate, if applicable.

10. Some grant budgets require cost sharing; that is, the sponsor and you must co-pay for the project. If so, distinguish between your cost sharing and the sponsor's share.

11. Itemize the budget and justify each item, such as travel, equipment, personnel, and other major expenses. Don't lump costs together. You can either round numbers to the nearest ten dollars or show exact numbers.

12. If the project is to occur in phases, identify the costs associated with each phase.

13. Don't overlook budget support for such items as service or maintenance contracts, insurance, shipping, installation, power sources, security,

background checks, campus visits, and moving expenses. If you anticipate training costs associated with the purchase of new equipment, include those costs in your budget as well. Your budget clip file should contain basic financial information needed in preparing proposal budgets, such as fringe benefit components, and indirect cost rates. Use your computer spreadsheet to draft various versions of your budget.

14. All costs must be incurred during the proposed project period. You cannot prepay someone for follow-up work that will be performed before or after the grant. All costs must be auditable.

15. Budgets should be close approximations of what you plan to spend. You do have some flexibility in the expenditure of funds and often it is possible to reallocate dollars between certain cost categories. For example, one federal agency will allow up to a 25 percent cost transfer between supplies and equipment. If you need to shift more than 25 percent of your supply budget to equipment, prior written approval is required. Your award notice will indicate the flexibility you have in rebudgeting your grant dollars. If you are uncertain about budget flexibility, ask your program officer for a copy of their grant administration guidelines *before* you submit a proposal.

BUDGET SIZE

"How much should I ask for?" is a common question asked when preparing a grant budget. Your prospect research will reveal typical sponsor award amounts and represent one important clue in establishing your target budget, but use it only as a guide. Study the list of grant awards from government agencies or the tax records of private foundations to learn past giving amounts. If your organization is new to the sponsor or lacks an established track record, you may want to request something less than their average grant size. On the other hand, if your needs are well documented and you have strong credibility, you may wish to exceed the average amount awarded by the sponsor. Remember, nobody gets an "average" grant. "Average" is a mathematical concept and organizations continually receive grant awards above or below the "average."

If you need bigger dollars than your sponsor typically awards for a grant, you may wish to take your larger project and divide or "chunk" it up into smaller but logical segments, thereby inviting the sponsor to fund a phase of your overall effort. If phase-one fund-

ing for them proves to be successful, they are reasonable candidates for phase-two funding. As another alternative, you can approach multiple sponsors, requesting each to partially fund your project. While this can be done, frankly, it is difficult to do because it requires an extensive amount of marketing and intersponsor coordination on your part. Experienced grant-getting organizations seek partial funding from multiple sponsors only as a last resort; their preferred alternative is to target a different sponsor, one who is capable of giving the entire amount.

SUPPLEMENT OR SUPPLANT FUNDS

Most grantmakers want to be sure that you use their money to *supplement*, not *supplant*, existing funds. In other words, they don't want to have their money used to replace—supplant—existing dollars. Said differently, they generally don't want to provide money for regular operating support. Instead, they want their money to supplement or expand projects, programs, or services. They want their money to be used as an "add-on" instead of a substitute for existing dollars. In essence, they want their funds to be used for project support, not operating support.

The supplant provision simply means that the grant funds will be used to augment regular, ongoing activities and not be used to substitute for funds or services that would otherwise be provided during the time period in question. The bottom line question on supplanting is: For the time period at issue, what would have occurred in the absence of grant funds? Accordingly, you may wish to include a sentence like the following in your budget narrative: "The requested funds will be used to supplement not replace existing internal budgets."

ALLOWABLE BUDGET ITEMS

What can you include in your budget? Answer: usually every reasonable expense associated with the project. Unless sponsor regulations indicate otherwise, you can include such personnel, nonpersonnel, and indirect cost components as indicated in Exhibit 68.

Occasionally, a sponsor's guidelines will prohibit a specific budget item, e.g., alcoholic beverages, computers, contingency funds, equipment, or lobbying activity. In such cases, show them as cost sharing items. Program officers can provide useful reactions to draft budgets.

Accounting	Indirect costs	Renovation
Advertising	Instruments	Rent
Audiovisual instruction	Insurance	Repairs
Auditing	Legal services	Research participant incentives
Binding	Maintenance	Salaries and wages
Books	Per diem	Security
Computers	Periodicals	Space
Construction	Postage	Subcontracts
Consultants	Publications	Supplies
Curriculum materials	Recruitment	Telecommunications
Dues	Refreshments	Travel
Equipment	Registration fees	Tuition
Fringe benefits	Relocation	Utilities

ALLOWABLE BUDGET ITEMS

EXHIBIT 68

The budget exhibit and narrative are meant to persuade the reviewer that sufficient funds are requested to achieve the project goals and objectives in a cost-effective manner. The budget in Exhibit 63 is for one year only. If it were requesting multiyear funding, it would look the same, except that three additional columns per year would be added on the right side of the ledger, namely, amount requested, cost sharing, and total. First-year funding is usually higher because of inevitable start-up costs, while subsequent funding levels decrease over time.

USING SPREADSHEET PROGRAMS

Spreadsheet programs, such as Excel, enable you to manipulate numbers and automatically recalculate whenever you change a budget figure. As a result, they are particularly helpful in preparing grant budgets. With a spreadsheet program, you could extend the budget over multiple years, showing what would happen as salaries rise and year-one start-up costs drop. Multiyear budgets are easy to calculate. If you plan to submit a three-year budget request, you need to prepare four budgets: one for each year separately and the fourth for a cumulative total. Similarly, consortium budgets can detail figures for each strategic partner as well as a collective budget total.

Spreadsheet numbers can be sorted, extracted, or merged with other spreadsheets. You can display your values as pie charts or graphs. Consider attaching a bar graph to your proposal budget that shows the requested and cost-shared amounts each year over a multiyear grant; many sponsors will respond favorably if you can systematically increase your cost sharing portion over time.

There are many variations in assembling meaningful grant budgets. Public and private sponsors vary within and among themselves regarding the cost categories they use on budgets. Some require more detail than others. One size does not fit all. Occasionally, a sponsor may request a list of other sponsored support or a copy of your most recent independently audited financial statement. Looking at past winning proposals and talking with your program officer will help clarify expectations. The following Web addresses will suggest other budget models that may be adapted to your situation:

- A university-based sample budget page www.indstate.edu/osp
- Grants.gov sample SF 424 R&R (Research & Related) forms apply.grants.gov/apply/FormsMenu
- National Endowment for the Humanities sample budget form www.neh.gov/grants/manage/organizations
- National Institutes of Health sample modular budget forms grants2.nih.gov/grants/funding/424
- U.S. Department of Education sample budget narrative www.ed.gv/admins/grants/apply/techassist/resource_pg8.html

- A common application form used by multiple private foundations in Rochester, NY www.grantmakers .org/application/GFNYLogin.asp
- A common application form used by many private foundations in Milwaukee, WI www.marquette.edu/ fic/commonapp2006.doc
- A copy of the budget template used by the Scan Foundation www.thescanfoundation.org/grants-rfps/ templates-samples

To locate other budget models, use the phrase "grant budget forms" in your favorite search engine.

When reviewing grant funding histories, many sponsors report their average grant size. That "average" may be misleading for organizations like yours. Consider entering funding histories from a targeted sponsor onto a spreadsheet, sorting out the organizations that are like yours, and computing averages and ranges on this narrower information. It may give you an entirely different picture of how much to request in your proposal.

COORDINATING BUDGETS AND PROPOSAL NARRATIVES

One of the biggest "mistakes" in grant budgets is not that too much money has been requested; rather, it's that too little funding has been identified to implement all of the activities described in the narrative. Big ticket items are easy to identify: personnel salaries, equipment purchases, and travel costs. It's the associated costs that more frequently get forgotten—fringe benefits, shipping and instillation costs, and per diems. These costs are real and necessary to carry out the project.

Another common budget problem is when smaller ticket items are expressed in the narrative but not accounted for in the budget request. For instance, have funds been budgeted for refreshments at the quarterly meetings with community members? Does the request include support for the child care coverage provided while parents are attending the evening meetings? Do mailing costs take into consideration postage paid return envelopes to increase survey response rates? Will participant incentives be funded by the organization or by the grant budget?

Reviewers watch for disconnects between the budget and narrative sections of the proposal. Sometimes, proposals include budgets assembled by finance people and a project narrative drafted by program people with very little connection between the two. This becomes an easy reason to decline a proposal or to reduce a budget request.

To prevent budget oversights from occurring, use this simple tip: after the first complete draft of the grant application is developed, read through the proposal narrative and put a "$" in the margin next to anything that might cost money. Then try to match those items to the budget. Notable cost items identified in the proposal narrative should be addressed in the budget; items may be offered as in-kind contributions or requested from the sponsor, but they should be explained. Incidentally, the reverse holds true as well: major cost items listed in the budget should be described in the proposal narrative. For instance, if funding is included in the budget for an independent evaluator, then the narrative should describe that individual's roles, responsibilities, and levels of effort as related to the project's objectives and activities.

REJECTION REASONS

Reviewers have rejected some proposals for the following reasons, which are clustered into two categories of budget shortcomings: Conceptualization and Documentation.

Conceptualization

1. The budget is too high for the expected results. Approximately $1,225,000 is requested to redesign 24 courses, which translates into an investment of $51,000 per course, or an investment of $37,000 in each of the 33 participating faculty members, or an investment of $6,300 in each of the 195 students who will participate in the courses over the next three years.
2. The principal investigator is asking the sponsor to carry costs normally borne in his institutional operating budget.
3. While full funding of this project cannot be recommended, given its highly innovative nature, pilot support should be provided.
4. The budget does not seem to reflect costs associated with the marketing of the newly proposed services.
5. Is it realistic for the project director to dedicate 50 percent effort in year one and only 20 percent effort in years two and three, especially when year two proposed to expand into new and larger communities?
6. The narrative and budget narrative need to provide greater detail about the roles and responsibilities

of the project consultant to justify budgeted costs of $10,000 per year.

7. The budget request for project evaluation seems inadequate given the magnitude of the evaluation plan. The equivalent of four days per year is simply too modest for the level of work involved.

8. The proposal doesn't identify who will be doing the project evaluation or indicate what will be evaluated, so how do they know that the evaluation will cost 5 percent of the budget?

9. The travel budget for year three dissemination activities is excessive. It is overly ambitious to budget for eight conference presentations in year three.

10. Inconsistencies exist between the proposal narrative and the budget narrative about the levels of effort the training specialist will commit to the project (40 percent versus 35 percent) and the education coordinator will commit to the project (40 percent versus 50 percent).

Documentation

1. The budget request is unusually excessive, not justified, and not linked to specific project objectives.

2. The budget does not identify personnel full-time equivalents.

3. The budget does not identify sources or amounts of in-kind contributions.

4. Insufficient information is provided to determine the reasonableness of costs in relation to achieving project objectives. The budget narrative does not include a breakdown of salary information, so it is unclear as to which two personnel are being supported by the grant and which are contributed as in-kind.

5. The budget does not appear to include a line item for project evaluation, nor does the budget narrative identify an evaluator. Who is doing the evaluation and how much will it cost?

6. The budget does not identify the fringe benefit rate or its components.

7. If you have a federally negotiated indirect cost rate, you should say so in the narrative and include a copy of it in the appendix.

8. It is unclear why very modest line items for telephone/fax and copying/duplication are included as direct cost items rather than elements of the indirect cost rate.

9. Since the budget requests funds for substitute teachers, according to the application guidelines, the budget narrative is required to include the approving school administrator's name and contact information. These details are missing.

10. Without adequate justification, the proposal appears to request support for resources already in place.

GRANT GAFFES

Exhibit 69 illustrates a familiar budget grant gaffe: failing to justify project expenses. It was taken from an application submitted to a government agency for a health outreach project. The budget may pass an initial quick scan—it stays under the maximum request amount; it's reasonable for approximately two-thirds of the request to support personnel costs and one-third to support nonpersonnel costs; and the indirect cost rate is specified. However, the budget does not hold up to more intense reviewer scrutiny as they try to understand the basis of calculations and relationship to the project activities.

STARTER SENTENCES

1. The following itemized budget requests $xx,xxx in direct costs (xx%) and $y,yyy (yy%) in indirect costs for a project total of $zz,zzz.

2. With the demonstrated concern that you have shown in the delivery of quality services, we are requesting a grant of $x,xxx, which represents a cost of y¢ per individual served over the next three years.

3. To close the spiraling gap, we are requesting $xx,xxx toward the construction of a new building that costs $500,000 in total. The requested funds represent the cost of one 25 × 25 square foot room in the new building.

4. Since this current project extends beyond our financial boundaries, we must reach out to the community for a grant of $xx,xxx to support this vital service.

5. Although we are expanding our budget allocations to this project as rapidly as possible, it is our intent to build an endowment that will provide ongoing, long-term support. To that goal, we are request your support of $xx,xxx.

6. In the first year of operation, this may look like an investment of $xx,xxx, but over a five-year period, we will train yyy students who will use this equipment, resulting in a per student cost of $zz.

The budget raises more questions than it answers. For instance, personnel salaries are usually calculated as a percentage of time devoted to a project relative to an annual salary, but this budget does not indicate the level of effort various staff will be contributing to the project. Even if reviewers make the assumption that the project coordinator and Webmaster are full time positions, the budget does not justify funding for both a program director and an executive director. The fringe benefits are also suspect: it is unusual for interns, who are likely to be students, to receive the same rate as other program staff.

The nonpersonnel items in the budget request raise a number of red flags. For example, there should be a basis of calculation provided for the consultants, such as (3 people × $500/day × 10 days each). Greater detail should be provided for the travel expenses, helping to clarify the number of people traveling, the purpose of the travel, and the means of transportation. Reviewers may perceive the allowability, allocability, and reasonableness of the proposed travel very differently depending on whether the funding is for the program director to fly to two international conferences or for the project coordinator to drive 590 miles per month for 12 months at standard IRS mileage rates. Entertainment costs are unallowable expenses, according to the Office of Management and Budget, and should not be listed. It would be helpful for reviewers to know whether the federally approved indirect cost rate is based on salaries and wages or modified total direct costs.

Item	Cost
PERSONNEL: Executive Director	6,000
Program Director	10,000
Project Coordinator	45,000
Communications Interns (2)	4,000
Webmaster	45,000
BENEFITS (@ 23%):	25,300
EXPENSES: Consultants	15,000
Advertising	2,000
Conference	4,000
Technology	8,000
Travel	4,000
Meals & Entertainment	1,000
TOTAL PROGRAM COSTS	169,300
INDIRECT COSTS (@ 18%)	30,474
TOTAL EXPENSES	199,774

GRANT GAFFES

EXHIBIT 69

7. Over a 10-year period, your equipment gift of $xx,xxx will touch the lives of yyy handicapped persons. Such a gift will assure the quality and regularity of the programs to be provided and will enrich the lives of all whom those programs reach.

8. In the spirit of beneficial synergism between business and the nonprofit community, I respectfully request the foundation to grant $xxx,xxx, payable over three years to provide funds for. . .

9. Mindful of your great interest in incorporating state-of-the-art technology into the learning experiences of students, we are requesting a grant of $xx,xxx for. . .

10. Maintaining adequate facilities is quickly becoming prohibitive for our 50-year-old building. Quite frankly, the costs extend beyond our financial boundaries. Accordingly, we must reach out for assistance of $xx,xxx in what surely is a vital service to our entire community.

 ### Clip File Action Item # 16 Budgets

Consider these action items to build your Budgets clip file:

- List all of the items included in your fringe benefit package.
- Get a copy of your current indirect cost rate.
- Include a copy of your overall organizational operating budget.
- Add a copy of your most recent audited financial statements.
- Use Exhibit 68 as a checklist of items for possible inclusion in your next budget.

CHAPTER 13
Sustainability

The strategist who is unconcerned about sustainability is akin to architects who care not whether their building stands or falls.

—James Mackenzie

PURPOSE OF SUSTAINABILITY

"How will your project be sustained beyond the granting period?"

This is one of the most dreaded questions among grant writers. Among novice grantseekers, it may produce initial gut responses that range from wildly positive, "Our project idea is brilliant! Tons of people will want to support us," to cautiously optimistic, "We'll figure something out—we always do," to downright cynical, "Why worry about sustaining the project when we don't yet know whether or not it will work?" At the same time, it's perfectly understandable that before making a significant financial investment, grantmakers want to know what will happen after the grant funds run out. In Chapter 13, you will learn the following:

- Two core questions you must answer in designing your sustainability plan.
- Five different types of sustainability: financial, structural, social, technological, environmental.
- Project goals, population needs, and grant type can influence sustainability duration.
- Seven "secrets of success" from grantees who have sustained projects over extended durations.

As competition increases for grant dollars, evidence of a sustainability plan can differentiate good projects from excellent projects. The fact that you've given thought to a project's sustainability demonstrates to a sponsor that you are committed to its success and are not merely chasing grant dollars because they are available. Sponsors find it reassuring that you've identified a combination of internal and external sources for continuing support rather than relying on them for funding year-after-year in perpetuity.

Sustainability plans also highlight for the sponsor the added benefits they may experience by funding your project now. For instance, there may be focused attention by project partners and diverse constituents on a problem of mutual interest. Local, regional, national, and international publicity that goes along with dissemination and replication may increase. The sponsor may receive wide-ranging recognition and respect as a leader in the field. Other grantmakers and individual donors may make additional philanthropic investments in the project. Systemic changes may have long-term positive impacts for the target populations.

EXAMPLES OF GRANTMAKER REQUIREMENTS FOR SUSTAINABILITY

As the following examples illustrate, grantmakers have varying expectations about sustainability. In some instances, sponsors require a special section of the proposal dedicated to describing your sustainability plan. In other instances, application guidelines include sustainability as part of the methods, evaluation, or budget narrative. Most grantmakers allow you to decide individually how much narrative space to devote to sustainability within the overall framework and page limits of the proposal; currently, only a few electronic submission systems limit responses about plans for sustainability to a certain number of words or characters.

Some sets of grant guidelines define sustainability incredibly narrowly, asking you to commit to institutionalizing the project beyond the granting period, while other sets of guidelines consider sustainability quite broadly, allowing you great flexibility to present a comprehensive plan with multiple strategies. Regardless, you should keep in mind that grant reviewers do not necessarily expect a gilt-edged guarantee of project sustainability; rather, they expect you to have a feasible and well-reasoned action plan.

Public Sponsors

U.S. Department of Justice. The U.S. Department of Justice, Office on Violence Against Women, issues the following guidance for grant applications to Reduce Sexual Assault, Domestic Violence, Dating Violence, and Stalking on Campus.

Sustainability Plan: Applicants are required to include a plan describing how they would sustain project activities if federal funding through the campus program were no longer available.

- Applicants must describe at least one locally, privately, state, or federally funded project that the applicant has sustained in the past.
- For continuation applicants only, applicants must submit a signed letter (i.e., by the president/chancellor/provost of the institution) outlining a commitment to the project by describing what portions of the current project have been institutionalized, what steps remain, and the timeline for completion of institutionalization of project activities.
- Consortium partners must submit a signed letter from the president/chancellor/provost of each participating institution.

U.S. Department of Education. Instructions for writing to the Center for International Business Education Program at the U.S. Department of Education include the following:

Quality of Project Design: Describe the extent to which the proposed activities include a coherent, sustained program of research and development in the field.

U.S. Department of Labor. Applications for Green Capacity Building Grants through the U.S. Department of Labor must address the point below in the narrative.

Application Guidelines: Applicants should provide a complete description of their strategy

to sustain the core training and placement activities in their project after grant funds are expended.

Private Sponsors

Robert Wood Johnson Foundation. Applicants to the Robert Wood Johnson Foundation's program for Healthy Eating Research: Building Evidence to Prevent Childhood Obesity are advised that reviewers will use several criteria to assess proposals, including the following:

Selection Criteria: degree to which the strategies are widely applicable, feasible, and sustainable.

Retirement Research Foundation. The Retirement Research Foundation indicates that proposals for funds should include, as appropriate, a description of plans for continued support.

Plans for Continued Support: if the project is expected to operate beyond the period for which grant funds are requested, describe plans for continued support.

Eau Claire Community Foundation. The program grant guidelines for the Eau Claire Community Foundation request that applicants answer the following question in a maximum of 1,200 characters:

Program Description: How will the program be sustained without future funding from the Eau Claire Community Foundation?

TYPES OF SUSTAINABILITY

Viewed narrowly, project sustainability is about finances, identifying the sources of internal and external funding that could be used to continue project activities. Internally, you may be able to reallocate existing dollars from other areas, liquidate assets no longer being used, or make greater use of volunteers. Externally, you may be able to secure additional grants, gifts, or revenue from investments, intellectual property, and fee-for-service.

This narrow view of sustainability typically assumes that the same amount of money will be needed in the subsequent year as in the granting year, i.e., if you receive a $50,000 grant for year one of a project, then you will also require $50,000 to sustain the project in its second year. In reality, the validity of this assumption may depend on the type of grant project being proposed. For instance, an education, training, scholarship/fellowship, or service delivery project might indeed require a consistent level of funding year-to-year as new cohorts enter the program.

On the other hand, a conference, curriculum development, equipment, or research project might require only modest amounts of funding in subsequent years. The conference may be a one-time event based on unique circumstances, and future funding is not necessary at all. Once the curriculum is developed, costs to implement the project might be covered by participant fees. After a major piece of equipment is purchased, it may last for many years without needing replacement, so continued expenses might be limited to periodic maintenance. A research project may run its course during the granting period, and the next phase of research would merit a new proposal.

A broader view of sustainability means considering the two core questions below. Most grant writers tend to focus only on the first question, which deals most directly with financial sustainability. As a result, your project may stand out to reviewers as being distinctively different if your proposal addresses both questions:

- *Exactly what needs to be sustained?*
  Recognize the difference between means and ends—between sustaining project funding and program processes; between supporting staff positions and participant engagement; between continuing project activities and program outcomes. As the project unfolds, you may discover process efficiencies (means) that allow you to achieve results (ends) in a more effective and equitable manner.
- *Exactly what will live on beyond the grant?*
  Identify the program elements that will continue to exist regardless of whether any future external or internal monies are available to support them, such as an evidence-based model, products and services, infrastructure, knowledge, policies and practices, networks, and results and impacts. Pinpointing these types of outputs and outcomes reinforces the long-term significance of the project.

This broader view allows you to address different types of sustainability. In addition to financial, other types of sustainability include structural, social, technological, and environmental. For instance, perhaps you will develop training manuals and processes that will be used by staff in the future. These policies and practices could contribute to structural sustainability. Maybe your outreach activities will encourage young adults to vote in an election. A percentage of these young adults will embrace their civic responsibility and, without further prompting, vote in future elections, which reflects a social sustainability. Imaginably, your school district will purchase interactive whiteboards to help engage students in learning mathematics and science. With an average lifespan of 5–7 years, the initial purchase has technological sustainability to serve multiple cohorts of students annually. Or possibly, your project will install engineered log jams in several forest preserves to enhance the natural function of streams. The large woody debris of the log jams will remain in place at the conclusion of the project, expanding the quality and diversity of the ecosystem and contributing to environmental sustainability. These are all ways that your project can "live on" beyond the grant. The five types of sustainability are explored in more detail next.

Financial Sustainability

The concept of financial sustainability is obvious: you need financial fuel to keep the engine running. You may need money to keep certain project aspects going, such as travel to service sites, medical supplies for patients, training materials for attendees, and incentives for research participants. Multiple financial sustainability options exist and include, but are not limited to, special events, fee-for-service, membership fees, grants, direct mail, planned giving, investment income, and phone-a-thons. Each is discussed below.

Special Events. Special events fundraisers encompass a broad variety of options ranging from the ubiquitous golf outing to the novel cow chip bingo. Other examples of special events include: antique shows, auctions, balloon races, beach parties, bingo, book signings, business openings, car shows, casino nights, celebrity appearances, chili cookoffs, concerts, cooking demonstrations, costume parties, dances, dine-arounds, home tours, pancake breakfasts, races, radiothons, raffles, runs/walks, sidewalk sales, telethons, and tournaments.

Regardless of the option, special fundraising events should follow these basic principles:

- Be restricted to ones that your organization can effectively carry out.
- Bring in significant revenue for the efforts of paid and volunteer staff.
- Attract new volunteers and new money.
- Provide positive community relations.
- Be followed up for future volunteer/donor support.
- Be evaluated each year to determine your future involvement.

The following example presents some future funding grant language, using a celebrity dinner as the special event:

To sustain this project after the initial grant period, we plan to initiate an annual fundraising event called Dinner with the Docs. The dinner will feature local prominent physicians who support our project outcomes, or other individuals who are well known in the community. The main purpose of this special event is to raise funds and heighten attention to volunteer service opportunities. Briefly, one high-profile physician will be selected as head waiter who will assist in recruiting other physician/waiters. Each waiter will personally invite their own guests to fill a 10-person table or provide a list of colleagues and friends to which invitations could be sent. Additionally, they will choose a theme to decorate their table and be in a costume to match the theme. Finally they will entertain their guests as they wait on their tables, competing during the evening for tips. A four-course gourmet meal will be served at a leisurely pace, allowing ample time for waiters to dream up new ways to work for their tips, e.g., serve meals in bedpans. Finally a master of ceremonies will auction off the head waiter's apron autographed with the signatures of all CEO waiters.

While many special events can be a financial disaster, this one has the elements of success. The event is great fun, and the volunteers love to be involved with no begging. Ticket sales are generally nonexistent; most often the waiters invite their own table guests. Decoration committees are not needed, as the waiters select their own themes and decorations. The Celebrity Waiters provide most of the entertainment for their table. The event is repeatable every year. The event stimulates natural competition between visible leaders in the community. Our past experience has shown that people are more likely to donate to a cause in a competitive social event than to respond to direct, one-to-one solicitation.

Fee-for-Service. In many social service delivery projects, it is common for grants to launch a start-up phase and use a fee-for-service, sometimes based on a sliding scale, to sustain the initiative beyond the granting period. For instance, to boost family participation in addiction recovery services, an organization that specializes in substance dependency might provide onsite child care on a sliding scale, fee-for-service basis. Individuals who have the ability to pay full-price effectively offset the costs of those who pay a little less. The following grant language shows one way this might be written.

We believe it would be ethically irresponsible to initiate the important social services described in this proposal and then abruptly terminate the services at the end of the grant period. That notion flies contrary to our mission of helping people help themselves. The support requested in this proposal seeks start-up funding to establish the awareness, systems, and service delivery procedures. Once beyond the three-year implementation phase, services will be sustained on a fee-for-service basis. Even using a sliding scale, fee schedule based on patient income, our business plan analysis suggests this service can be self-funded, as evidenced by the budget and expenditure projects included in the appendix. Our patient surveys reaffirm not only the need for this service but the willingness of patients to sustain it. Their bottom line message: the nearest comparable service is more than 100 miles away.

Membership Fees. Membership fees as a sustainability mechanism are similar to the fee-for-service option. The difference lies in the fact that membership fees provide access to specialized benefits in contrast to the fee-for-service that renders direct help or personal service. The following example shows how membership fees can provide access to research information. Also note the layering of membership fees; higher layers afford more membership benefits:

Once the Biomedical Research Institute is established and fully operational within the three-year grant period, it will continue its activities by charging corporate membership fees. Within a two-hundred-mile radius of the institute, there are 247 different manufacturers of biomedical equipment. They will be offered different membership levels and benefits.

Basic Membership: $1,500/year
- Discounts for attending seminars and workshops
- Publications including the institute newsletter, seminar and workshop materials, and membership directory

Executive Sponsors: $10,000/year
- All basic membership privileges
- Opportunity to do projects with center staff
- Participate in center program activities
- Referral of qualified personnel for internships and recruitment

- Serve on institute advisory board
- Contribute to newsletter articles
- Participate in collaborative activities with other members

   Corporate Sponsors: $25,000/year
- All above privileges
- List company name prominently on institute letterhead, the banner in the center newsletter, and all press releases
- Serve as speakers in program activities
- Unlimited access to institute-initiated project reports
- Staff presentations to sponsor clients or prospects once at no charge

Grants. Grants are, of course, another way to seek financial sustainability. Returning to the initial grantmaker for continuation support is one option, especially if you have done a good job of stewardship with the grantmaker during your first grant. You must also recognize that a program or project cannot be sustained indefinitely through grants. Nevertheless, additional grant funding from public and private sponsors is always possible, particularly if you segment your project into distinct phases and your request is in support of a new project phase. Some introductory language follows:

> For years, grants have been the lifeblood of our organization. As a result, we have established long-term relationships with major grantmakers. More than two-thirds of our annual budget over the past decade has come from grant-funded support. While one cannot run a program on grants forever, our grantmakers recognize us as a responsible steward of their funds. Once the funding for the demonstration phase of this proposed project ends, other grantmakers will be approached for implementation funding. In that sense, the demonstration funding requested in this proposal will become a magnet to attract follow-up support. Preliminary conversations with two local foundations have been encouraging; more precisely, the Bayside Bluff Community Foundation and Mills Family Foundation both reacted favorably to our preliminary proposal and have expressed interest in jointly funding the next project phase.

Direct Mail. "Direct mail" is often synonymous with "junk mail," or so it seems as our mailboxes become flooded with requests for support from alumni offices, hospitals, and a broad range of community-based organizations. Yet this fundraising strategy persists with no sign of it disappearing. To the contrary, with online donation a reality, the direct mail may come in the form of an e-mail. To enhance credibility in your proposal, if your organization has had prior experience with direct mail, the outcomes should be summarized; if your organization does not have an established history with direct mailing, the contracted PR firm should cite their track record of success with organizations similar to yours. Sample direct mail grant language follows:

> Direct mail campaigns usually have four main goals:
>
> - To acquire new donors
> - To encourage prior donors to increase their giving size
> - To renew lapsed donors
> - To bolster public relations
>
> Acquiring new donors is an especially important goal since direct mail experience shows that 50–80 percent will donate again.
>
> An effective direct mail campaign involves multiple mailings. For purposes of sustaining the project after the grant funds lapse, we plan to initiate quarterly mailings during the final project year. The most crucial element in a direct mail campaign is the quality of the mailing list. Beyond mailing to prior donors, new donors will be identified by consulting with a mailing list vendor to target people who live in upper-income geographic areas, meet minimum income levels, and subscribe to magazines compatible with our overall mission. A preliminary check of individuals living in the 532XX zip code range with family income levels exceeding $75,000 and subscribing to the *Strengthening Family Values* magazine identified 938 mailing targets. The project director will oversee the direct mail campaign, which will be crafted with the help of board member Joyce Kunkel, who is director of advertising for Zigfried and Associates, a leading advertising and public relations firm with more than 200 cumulative years of experience in direct mail advertising.

Planned Giving. Planned giving takes a long-range view of ensuring financial sustainability. If you need near-term funding, this is not the approach to take. With planned giving, rather than receiving a gift of cash at your organization now, gifts are deferred until a future date; individual donors pledge to contribute some of their assets either within a certain number of years or upon their death. In more practical terms, a combination of shorter- and longer-term strategies represents a nice balance of sustained revenue. Some sample grant language follows:

> Planned giving integrates personal, financial, and estate planning with the individual donor's plans for lifetime giving. Through bequests or other planned gifts, donors have the capacity of funding a charitable gift annuity with relatively small investment. Planned giving is an intricate, long-term fundraising strategy that requires special training in financial planning and tax laws. Although no staff members have this type of training or expertise, we are fortunate that attorney Terrence Case, trust officer at the Wells Fargo Bank, is an active member of our board and has volunteered to lead a planning giving campaign on behalf of our organization. His interactions with potential donors will include bequests, charitable gift annuities, charitable remainder trusts, life estate contracts, life insurance policies, and revocable trusts.

Investment Income. Investment income mirrors a strategy used by many private foundations: preserve capital, spend interest. That is to say, rather than spending the dollars your organization receives as philanthropic gifts, fee-for-service, and revenue from sales, royalties, and licensing agreements, you invest them. Subsequently, following your institutional policies, you use payments from interest, dividends, and capital gains to support program operations. Similar to planned giving, investment income often takes a long-range perspective on financial sustainability. As financial planners will attest, disciplined saving and investing can produce sizable annual income. The following example defines the investment vehicle, identifies the institutionally approved payout rate, and offers samples of what might be purchased with the investment income.

> In anticipation of the challenge grant opportunity, an individual donor recently pledged the full amount of the matching gift required ($100,000) to support the enhancement of library acquisitions. These matching funds will be invested into endowment. Under our institutional spending policy, annual expendable endowment income is a maximum of 5 percent (See Appendix C). As described in Appendix D, the endowment will be administered by the Dean's Council and will follow established procedures: in the fall semester it accepts applications for library acquisitions and then awards funding in the spring according to the merits of individual proposals. Immediate uses for the new funds might include: *Humanities Full Text* journals database ($3,500 per year, online), *Essential Humanities Research* ($595), *Encyclopedia of Science & Technology* (4 vols., $425), *Journal of Mind over Matter* ($128 per year), and *Translational Science International* ($175 per year, online).

Phone-a-Thons. Telephone solicitation is a powerful fundraising strategy. While the idea of telephone solicitation does generate some negative semantic reactions—people don't like to be bothered—experience has shown that relatively few people are annoyed by telephone solicitations from well-respected charities. Universities, for example, use phone-a-thons with great success, often employing current students to connect with and solicit contributions from alumni. With the prevalence of caller ID and voicemail, it can be a challenge to reach potential donors "cold." As a result, a direct mail postcard is often sent in advance, alerting potential donors that they soon will be called. Consider the following grant language as an example:

> Using the facilities at a local telemarketing firm, we will conduct a phone-a-thon by having volunteers call people and solicit donations. This approach enables us to reach out to people who don't give on a regular basis. Additionally we can encourage regular donors to give more. Our primary target audience will be current and past donors. The key is the training of volunteers, who will undergo a six-hour program that will consist of two parts: (1) the carefully scripted opening, and (2) the follow-up question-objection-ask sequence. Because telephone solicitations are most effective when conducted by a peer of the prospect, the volunteers will come from backgrounds that match as closely as possible to those of the prospects. No paid solicitors will be used. Since the phone banks are donated for this project, no up-front money is required.

Of the financial sustainability options cited above, some will be appropriate for your organization, while others will not. Here are some questions to help identify some more viable options:

1. Can your organization absorb future funding in your general operating budget over the next few years?
2. Could you contract with a third party to subsidize your services to clients?

3. Could your future expenses be covered as a part of a nongrant fund-raising program?
4. Do you have another profitable service or activity that can be expanded to cover costs of running your new project in the future?
5. Could the financial responsibility for your project be transferred to some other organization?

Proposal reviewers are not looking for 100 percent proof positive that you can provide future project funding. Rather, they want specific evidence that you have a tentative plan in place. Such a plan also shows that you have an extensive project network of support, thereby enhancing your credibility. Some types of research grants may not need extensive funding beyond the grant; nevertheless, this proposal section may be used to lay the groundwork for future support requests.

Structural Sustainability

Structural sustainability borrows the notion from engineering that projects should be rooted in permanence. When applied to grant projects, this means that infrastructure, systems, and procedures must be in place in order for services to be delivered and received in a particular setting. In some instances, you will already have these elements in place, such as access to the target population, service sites in the community, a means for communicating regularly with stakeholders, institutional policies to guide training in research conduct, an established database, validated survey instruments, processes for collecting data, a ready supply of volunteers, and laboratory equipment. In other cases, you will need to develop, enhance, or acquire these elements so that the project can be implemented as planned. Regardless of whether the elements came into existence before or during the granting period, structural sustainability means describing the extent to which they will exist beyond the conclusion of the grant.

To get more "bang for their buck," many public and private sponsors strongly encourage, if not outright require, collaboration in grant applications. Collaboration is one way to increase the odds that the project will continue in some form even after the grant ends. Sponsors hope that partners will be so invested in the project that they will continue to commit resources to keep it going. To earn the grant award, collaborators may have made changes internal to their respective organizations so that personnel time, physical space, and financial resources could be pledged toward the project. When these elements can be continued into the foreseeable future, you have a commitment to structural sustainability. An example of grant structural sustainability language follows and calls attention to an established history of collaboration in the community.

> While many community-based organizations have high personnel turnover, our project is rooted in an organizational structure that offers long-term stability and sustainability. Accordingly, this project has the potential to substantially change systems for health care beyond the granting period. With initial government grant support, we have sustained an effective environmental lead prevention coalition. We anticipate that your generous support will have a similar impact on health care systems in our community.

Social Sustainability

Social sustainability focuses on people, examining the humanistic benefits that will continue to accrue beyond the end of the granting period. Benefits may extend to direct and indirect audiences and vary by type of grant (e.g., research, service delivery, training). For instance, longer-term benefits experienced by a direct audience of scholarship/fellowship winners may include acceptance into highly competitive graduate schools and career placements. International travel grantees may increase appreciation for other cultures and for their place as global citizens. Families in sub-Saharan Africa may gain long-lasting insecticide-treated nets for malaria prevention as part of a service delivery project.

Grants may produce enduring advantages not only for direct project participants but also for secondary, indirect audiences. For example, a conference grant may directly increase awareness among nurses of evidence-based practices for early detection and prevention of perinatal depression, which ultimately improves a child's development and the mother-infant relationship. A research grant may lead to synthesizing a new compound that improves the efficacy of medications for cancer patients who have developed a drug resistance. A capacity-building grant may train an organization's staff in marketing and communications, which, in turn, raises community responsiveness to incidents of cyberbullying among adolescents. The following example of social sustainability highlights the benefits a training program will have on the primary audience (teachers) and a secondary audience (students); this strategy allows you to show a greater human impact over a longer period of time:

> This training program will have a multiplier effect that will continue to touch the lives of

participants well beyond the yearlong grant period. Specifically, during the summer, 25 teachers will be immersed in an "Academic Boot Camp" to enhance their content and pedagogy skills. During the next school year, each teacher will apply these new skills in their respective classes, reaching about 20 students each. Over the next five years, this translates to 2,500 students who will benefit from enriched learning experiences.

Technological Sustainability

For some grant projects it may be necessary to purchase technology to implement and monitor proposed activities. Technological sustainability describes the extent to which technology—such as equipment, instrumentation, smart TVs, laptops, tablets, software, databases, and apps—will continue to be used, maintained, repaired, and replaced after the grant ends. Imaginably, once a conduct database has been purchased, it will become the institution's principal management tool for administrators and officers to use for collecting and reporting data on stalking, threats, sexual harassment, sexual assault, and physical violence. To further strengthen students' research and writing skills, perhaps use of laptops will be expanded to additional sections of 6th grade English as well as to all sections of 7th grade English. Maybe plans are in place for the confocal laser scanning microscope to be used in the future by other researchers in the chemistry department as well as disciplinary colleagues in biology, geology, and materials science, and with opportunities for interinstitutional collaboration with scientific counterparts at nearby universities.

Beyond continued technology use, sustainability includes a description of plans for maintenance, repair, and replacement. Devices may come with standard warranties that will still be in effect at the conclusion of the project period. Manufacturer extended warranties may be purchased (with grant funds!) to expand and lengthen protection coverage. Existing IT staff may have the technological know-how to service common device issues. Scheduled and unscheduled maintenance costs may be subsumed into departmental operational budgets. User fees may be reinvested to support direct repairs. One proposal to a private grantmaker included the following language about technological sustainability, which reflects an institutionalization of database use:

> In this information age, it is counterintuitive to dedicate staff time to chasing down students via e-mail and cellphone to collect health information when students will voluntarily input it on their own, if given a secure portal. Automated

scheduling and record maintenance will free up staff time to engage in higher-order tasks, such as tracking immunizations, assessing complications, conducting surveillance, and investigating disease outbreaks. Streamlined operations will help provide more time for staff to engage in data collection and analysis, and thus ensure a high quality of care.

Environmental Sustainability

Environmental sustainability considers long-term impacts to your natural surroundings, including the land, water, and air. Methodological choices during the grant period can influence the sustainability of our natural environmental in subtle and in significant ways. For instance, a construction project may install large windows to allow in plenty of natural light and install special roofing to reduce internal heating and cooling loads. A research project may use ground-penetrating radar to map archaeological features rather than physically disturbing a historical site. A service delivery project might collect gently used professional attire to redistribute to jobseekers from disadvantaged backgrounds, thus diverting tons of clothing from landfills. An outreach initiative might recruit citizen scientists to help preserve ash trees by running an emerald ash borer trapping program. As part of an educational program that promotes healthy lifestyles, children might learn to get outside, grow their own garden, and eat fresh fruits and vegetables. A training program might show farmers best management practices to reduce soil erosion. Below is an operative paragraph on environmental sustainability that was included in a K–5 education project:

> Children of today will inherit the earth of tomorrow. As elementary school teachers, we want our children to hit the ground running so they understand words like "carbon footprint" and "global warming" as easily as the name of the current pop star. As a responsible corporate citizen, funding from your grant will allow us to secure the lesson plans that span our entire elementary school grades. Our elementary science curriculum will be modified to include such lesson plans as planet science, climate change, earth day games, recycle city, and wildlife fund. These lesson plans are a necessary but not totally sufficient condition of providing our students with an "eco-education." To sustain this project we will need a broad range of consumable supplies, e.g., recycled paper, water supplies, and harmless chemicals. Fortunately, the local Parent Teacher Organization has accepted

the responsibility to conduct an annual "Eco Roundup" campaign that would encourage parents to donate common household items that can be used to continue our environmental science initiative. In sum, no additional funding is needed since volunteers will generate the required instructional resources.

KEY QUESTIONS TO ANSWER

1. What level of financial support will be required in the year after the grant ends? Two years? Three years?
2. Which elements of the project can be institutionalized?
3. Which project activities can continue with the support of collaborative partners?
4. Which elements of the project do not need to be continued in the future?
5. Will an infrastructure, systems, procedures, and networks live on beyond the grant?
6. Will your project serve as a model that can be replicated in other settings?
7. Will project participants continue to experience humanistic benefits beyond the conclusion of the granting period?
8. Will enduring advantages accrue for secondary, indirect audiences?
9. Is there a plan to continue to use, maintain, repair, and replace technology after the grant ends?
10. Do methodological choices contribute to preserving and protecting the environment?

EXAMPLES OF SUSTAINABILITY

So far, we have discussed five different types of sustainability—financial, structural, social, technological, and environmental. Examples for each type are presented below. In reality, sustainability for many projects involves more than one type. To illustrate, five additional examples are provided of grant language showing how multiple types of sustainability can be bundled together. Because sponsors typically expect sustainability to be about finances, the examples all include financial sustainability as a key feature and selectively add structural, social, technological, and environmental sustainability as well.

Example 1

In this example a university received funding from a national science agency to recruit and sustain more undergraduate students into their engineering program. The pipeline of future engineers is woefully inadequate in the United States, especially when it comes to minorities. While these minority fellowships would provide partial support toward earning a degree, additional financial funding was needed to sustain the fellows through graduation. Here's how the university proposed to close the funding gap.

Midwest University is committed to continuing this program after completion of agency funding. To help sustain the program, we have identified the following sources of future funding:

1. **Summer Employment in Industry.** The College of Engineering will use its strong partnership with industry to arrange summer employment for future participating students. Through such employment, students will gain practical experience and financial support.
2. **Consortium Membership Support.** As noted in Section V.B.1.b, the College of Engineering is part of the Midwest Engineering Consortium, which includes the membership of several local companies and three engineering colleges. (See appendix E.) Funds generated from membership fees will be targeted for future program participants.
3. **Training Grants.** The College of Engineering, working in close cooperation with the Development Office, will aggressively seek extramural funding from private sources, including corporations and private foundations, to continue the proposed Minority Fellowship Program.
4. **Engineering Fellowship Funds.** The College of Engineering will give future and continuing program participants first priority for fellowships from funds received each year from its Engineering Fellowship Fund. These funds average over $30,000 per year.
5. **Graduate Research and Teaching Assistantships.** The Department of Electrical and Computer Engineering will supplement support generated from the four sources above with research and teaching assistantships. Currently, the department has 27 university-funded assistantships.
6. **Online Fund Raising.** Since the department has thousands of graduates spread throughout the country, many in high-paying jobs, a Web site will be established to encourage online giving. Electronic

donations will be encouraged through the college's quarterly alumni newsletter.

Together, these six sources of future funding will continue the program beyond the agency grant period. Nevertheless, agency support is needed, as detailed in the budget proposal, to establish the Minority Fellowship Program.

Example 2

The following example of structural sustainability comes from a proposal for a civic engagement project submitted to a national association that administers federal funding:

> We have made great progress in developing infrastructure and partnerships that will be sustainable. For instance, partner roles and responsibilities have been clearly defined and documented on standardized worksheets. We are continuing to work with Child and Family Resources to provide more services to families. Educational and informational materials on topics ranging from diaper changing to job searching will be adapted from preexisting documents. Once these resources are in place, they can be reused for future projects. Equally significant, the project coordinator has completed a service handbook, which includes training materials that can be used to train next year's volunteer service leaders: new volunteer orientation, leadership development, organizational communication, and career counseling. A newly created intern position will be charged with updating the needs assessment and asset matches, conducting site visits, and maintaining up-to-date contact information for all partners.

Example 3

The operative paragraph below on social sustainability is from a proposal to a private foundation:

> This initiative is designed to enhance the quality of a liberal arts and sciences education and continue our rich tradition of providing opportunities for undergraduate research. With your support, $X will be used to fund competitive summer research fellowships. For the duration of the grant project, N students annually will receive a $Y stipend each to complete a faculty-directed independent research project ($Z

total). Students will need access to a variety of supplies ($A) and funds for travel to regional meetings to present their results ($B). Your generosity will allow us to increase by one-third the number of students who engage in student-faculty research.

Example 4

A request to a private foundation included a description of technological sustainability:

> In this knowledge economy, our responsibility as educators is to train computer literate children for this twenty-first century and start that training early. That's why we are requiring all of our third grade students to have iPads, which have replaced pencil and paper as the preferred learning tool. With it, they will be able to compose their own stories and share them with grandparents, take visually literate pictures, communicate via Skype with peers in foreign lands—and more. With the generous support from the KIDS IT Foundation, we will have sufficient funding to provide students with iPads for the next three years. That will provide sufficient time to fully integrate this technological capability into the school curriculum and build a budget for parents who are unable to afford them after the grant ends. Your support represents the catalytic agent to affect a curricular reform.

Example 5

A research proposal to a government agency used the following language to articulate the project's environmental sustainability:

> By the end of this research project, our primary outcome will be the identification of the sources and location of plastic debris in Lake Superior. We will disseminate our quantified organic pollutant information to the county health department in each affected area. This baseline information will enable them to apply for funding from the state-level Department of Natural Resources and the federal Environmental Protection Agency to clean up the plastic pollutants. Additionally, local nonprofit organizations concerned about environmental protection can use this baseline information to strongly advocate for legislative policy changes that would increase our environmental protection.

Example 6

In this example, a hospital secured federal funding to launch a telemedicine program. Sustainability boiled down to two factors: money (financial) and people (structural). Grant funds were used to purchase the initial medical equipment, and the hospital explained how it would continue remote medical monitoring after the grant ended:

> If a project is to be sustained beyond the grant period, it must be folded into the organization's ongoing programs and fundraising strategies. The long-term sustainability plan that follows is evidence of our commitment to the T3 project after the grant funds run out. In practical terms, sustainability rests on two components: money and people.
>
> **Money.** Additional money is NOT needed to sustain the Personal Health Records T3 project component; our hospital has made a long-term commitment to fund it through its own internal operating budget. That fiscal support will continue upon the end of formal T3 funding. While T3 project funding is needed to establish the personal health record interface, no future fiscal requirements exist for ongoing extramural funding; the interface is integrated into the personal health record operating system and ongoing maintenance will be provided, as needed, by hospital telecommunications personnel. Several options exist for device sustainability. Most devices have a warranty period of 90 days. Vendors will replace in-warranty device malfunctions. Some devices are covered by insurance, including Medicare, resulting in no direct patient cost for the device. In some cases, device supplies have a nominal cost component that the patients are already covering. To illustrate, glucose meters to monitor diabetes require test strips that are paid for by either insurance or the individual patient.
>
> **People.** The sustainability component also deals with the key project people. The principal investigator, Dr. Thomas Smith, has made a long-term professional commitment to the hospital and its resolve to be a national leader in telemedicine. In the unlikely event Dr. Smith should become unable to carry forward with this project, even beyond the granting period, other hospital personnel could readily become "lantern carriers," e.g., Dr. Timothy Hale, a 30-year hospital physician and director of the Center for Modern Healthcare.

Example 7

A proposal to a private foundation included this language, blending financial and structural sustainability:

> Whenever possible, we will connect with existing programs to allow for maximum sustainability beyond the first pilot project. Grant money used in the first year will allow for project development with an eye toward integrating all events into ongoing programs such as A, B, and C. We will also access existing education resources such as D, E, and F at no additional cost to the participants or the project. Throughout the year, our committee will seek additional external funding through grants and fundraising to sustain those elements of the program that do not currently exist in our community. Private foundations in our immediate geographic locale—within a 90-mile radius—hold the greatest potential for supporting our project; initial prospect research indicates there are 61 foundations who meet this criteria and have an interest in service projects such as ours.

Example 8

An equipment grant request to a federal science agency included this description of financial and technological sustainability.

> With the interest that you've shown in increasing access to shared research instrumentation, we are requesting a grant in the amount of $X. This represents an investment of $Y in every student that will use the equipment over an anticipated 10-year life span, or a cost of $Z per house of use. While the cost of purchasing these state-of-the-art technologies is beyond our financial boundaries, we have expanded our internal budget allocations to support their ongoing maintenance and repair.

Example 9

A proposal to a private foundation wove together elements of financial, structural, and social sustainability in one tight paragraph:

> In order to sustain the tutor program, we created a student intern position to coordinate the tutor program for 2014–15 and expect to retain this position for 2015–16. In December 2014, we also received a grant of $2,500 for tutor program support from a local business. We will continue

to provide ongoing tutor training and assessment through site visits and evaluations. Washington Elementary has subscribed to and will use a highly structured educational mentoring program that provides reading instruction to students who are behind grade level. This will allow us to monitor reading levels of participating students before and after education mentoring.

Example 10

This example links financial, structural, and social sustainability in its appeal for funding to a private foundation:

> With the demonstrated concern that you have shown for preparing a quality professional workforce, we request a grant of $X. Those funds will support: curriculum development ($A); development of the experiential learning component ($B); library resources ($C); student transportation to experiential learning sites ($D); and honoraria for guest speakers ($E). Once the course is designed, the institution will assume the expense of offering it in the future, including teaching and attendant costs. Over a three-year period, this course will help transform the lives of nearly N aspiring students.

To be clear: it is not necessary to include all five types of sustainability, nor any combination thereof as noted above, in your proposals. To persuade reviewers that you have a well-reasoned sustainability plan, you must present them with enough strategic information for them to conclude, "Yes, it seems reasonable they could continue this project beyond the granting period." In sum, it's a subjective judgment for which you might persuade your reviewers. Run your sustainability plan by a few of your peers and solicit their opinions as a litmus test of your strategy.

SUSTAINABILITY—FOR HOW LONG?

For how long should you expect your sustainability mechanisms to operate after the grant ends? One year? Five years? Ten years? In perpetuity? Should the sustainability period match the life of the grant period? There is, of course, no "right" answer to this question. Over the years, we've seen many different answers. We know of one successful proposal that promised to keep their sustainability plan in place for three years after the grant expiration deadline, which would allow sufficient time to build an internal budget to absorb these expenses. We know of another situation where a collaborative

effort was so successful, the partners formed their own nonprofit 501(c)(3) organization that existed for the purpose of sustaining the original grant project. Two decades later, they are still operating strong.

In some instances, the timeline of sustainability will be influenced by the goals of the project, the needs of the target population, and the type of project. Consider the March of Dimes, which was founded in 1938 by Franklin D. Roosevelt to combat polio. The vaccines developed by Jonas Salk in the 1950s helped to accomplish this goal. The organization then repurposed itself to take on an even larger aim: improving the health of babies, with a focus on fighting premature births and preventing birth defects. That is to say, while the original polio research project ran its course in a limited number of years, the organization's commitment to structural and social sustainability allowed new research projects and new education projects to continue.

It is rare for sponsors to specify in their grant application guidelines the duration of a project's sustainability. However, we did encounter a recent exception from the Federal Communication Commission. Their Request for Proposal (RFP) stated, "Sustainability plans should include a description of how a project will be sustainable for ten years." Few crystal balls have the ability to accurately anticipate rapid and unpredictable changes in needs, financing, and technology. Reviewers will be looking for evidence of a plan, not guarantees of perpetuation.

Grantees who have been able to sustain projects over an extended duration have identified the following seven secrets of success:

- *Start Early*: Begin thinking about sustainability early, preferably as the project is still being planned; waiting until the final year of grant funding is too late.
- *Communicate*: Communicate frequently with clients, staff, partners, and sponsors to establish trust, foster engagement, build confidence, and maintain momentum.
- *Collaborate*: Seek out possibilities with new partners, particularly ones who have similar visions and may agree to a mutual exchange of resources; many hands make work light.
- *Evaluate*: Collect data to measure the overall worth and utility of the project, its processes and outcomes; return on investment is one way to show project significance.
- *Disseminate*: Share information about project results widely; increasing project awareness can attract additional clients, staff, partners, and sponsors.

- *Solicit*: Apply for new grants while the current project is still funded; it gives the perception of a bandwagon that can still be boarded and prevents lapses in support.
- *Steward*: Say "thank you" often—to clients for their participation, to staff for their service, to partners for their contributions, and to sponsors for their support; display an attitude of gratitude.

The following is an example of an operative paragraph in a stewardship communication between a nonprofit organization and a private foundation. Though the funder did not require projects to be sustained beyond the grant period, the applicant was so committed to the project that additional financial support was secured from a different sponsor for the ensuing year. This informational update, a simple act of stewardship, put the applicant in a favorable position to garner future funding from the private foundation to launch a separate-but-related youth development initiative:

> You'll be pleased to know that we will be continuing the "Love of Learning & Sports" program again this year. As the enclosed article from the *Daily Gazette* reports, we were recently awarded funding from the Youth Development Foundation in order to support program activities in the upcoming academic year. The article also acknowledges the role of the National Athletics Foundation in providing pivotal support to pilot this important project. Your initial gift and long-standing commitment to enhancing the diversity and welfare of student athletes helped to make all of this possible. Thank you.

In addition to your own thinking about "How long?" there is another way to approach this question: preproposal contacts. Talk with past grant winners, past grant reviewers, and the program officer (see Chapter 4) to gain insights on the types of sustainability, extent of commitments, and duration of pledge periods included in proposals that have garnered awards. Triangulating information from these three sources may help to establish a minimum performance level when it comes to preparing your sustainability plan.

WRITING TIPS

1. Consider including multiple types of sustainability in your plan. When sustainability is required by the sponsor, reviewers typically expect to read about financial sustainability; your proposal may stand out from the competition if elements of structural, social, technological, and/or environmental sustainability can be included.

2. Using grant funds to hire new staff is often a red flag for reviewers with respect to sustainability. Regardless of whether the new positions will be sunset, supported in part, or fully institutionalized, describe what will happen to them when the grant ends.

3. Describe plans for maintaining, repairing, and replacing equipment and instruments purchased with grant dollars. Not saying anything suggests to reviewers that you have not considered technological sustainability.

4. Some grant reviewers have concerns about offering stipends to community members for meeting attendance, namely, that it is not a sustainable practice. They worry that community members will show up as long as the stipends are available and then stop participating in future meetings when the grant funds run out. Don't underestimate the attractiveness of being included at the ground floor of an initiative; the opportunity to be involved and shape the project may be enough to entice community members to attend meetings.

5. When it is determined that stipends are necessary to encourage community members to attend meetings, then modest stipends might be perceived by reviewers to be more palatable—and more sustainable—than cash outlays that would approach the level of a daily consulting rate. Justify the inclusion of the stipend and of the amount.

6. Call attention to instances where no future funding will be required from the sponsor to sustain the project, such as a curriculum development project that uses grant funds to support course creation and tuition fees to support the ongoing implementation.

7. Third-party certification may be available as further evidence of your commitment to sustainability, such as the LEED (Leadership in Energy and Environmental Design) green building rating system of environmentally friendly construction and remodeling practices.

8. Beyond the benefits that direct project participants will receive, highlight benefits that will be experienced long term by secondary, indirect audiences. Humanistic impacts may be even larger when rolled out over time. For instance, a professional development program for nurses may yield improvements in health care for patients; a single nurse will touch the lives of XXX patients over the next YYY years.

9. When the exact mechanics of your sustainability plan are still fuzzy as the time of submission approaches, you might make an inductive argument from analogy: give an example of a different grant-initiated program that has been sustained over time at your organization, point out the similarities between the past and present programs, and lead reviewers to the conclusion that a high probability exists for the present program to be sustained as well.

10. Commitments made toward sustainability by project partners may be summarized in the proposal narrative and detailed in letters of commitment included as attachments.

REJECTION REASONS

1. The applicants' claim that we will continue to look for alternative sources of support does little to inspire confidence.

2. No systematic funding plan beyond the termination date is presented.

3. The federal share of the project funding decreases over the five-year period, but there is no discussion of who is picking up the expense. Do partner agencies have the capacity to integrate project costs into their operating budgets?

4. The proposal narrative does not discuss a sustainability plan for this specific project.

5. The proposal narrative identifies potential sources of future private and federal government funding; however, no firm commitments of cash or in-kind funding dedicated to sustaining services exist yet.

6. The proposal's plan to secure sustainability funding is weak. Many agencies will not be able to absorb project costs to maintain efforts. A more comprehensive plan might include examples of private foundations and corporations to approach for support.

7. The narrative does not describe sustainability mechanisms for the new hires beyond the conclusion of the granting period.

8. The application does not provide evidence that the collaborative partners are willing to support the costs of stipends for the replication site coordinators beyond the granting period.

9. The narrative would benefit from additional details about plans for sustainability of the student scholarships. It is unclear how $100,000 per cohort will be sustained beyond the granting period. The majority of partner contributions represent in-kind effort, not cash that could be redirected to continuing student scholarship support in future years.

10. It is unclear how nearly $450,000 of iPads and apps will be sustained beyond the granting period.

GRANT GAFFES

The grant gaffe presented in Exhibit 70 comes from a proposal submitted to a government agency, though it is common to sustainability plans in proposals to private sponsors as well. In short, the sustainability plan is more hopeful than thoughtful. The glittering generalizations say virtually nothing in so many words. Reviewers struggled to award even partial credit points to this vague response.

The language in this example represents "empty calories." It says to grant reviewers, "We're hopeful we can find sustainability money, trust us." Grant reviewers will be hungry for additional details such as specific funder targets, requested amounts, solicitation target dates, and reasons for optimism. Consider how much more powerful it would be to include a sentence such as, "Last year, gifts of $99 or less from individual donors provided a total of $150,000 in support for project activities."

To sustain project activities beyond the granting period, we will seek additional grants from public and private sponsors as well as philanthropic gifts from individual donors. Our institution is fortunate to have a broad base of support that includes local, regional, and national funders.

GRANT GAFFES

EXHIBIT 70

STARTER SENTENCES

1. In order to sustain project services beyond the termination of the grant, we will. . .

2. We are committed to the long-term success of this project. The generosity of your support will allow us to hire an associate director in the first year of this initiative. Over the three years of funding, we will pick up an increasing share of the associate director's salary and fringe benefits with the aim to fully institutionalize the position in year four.

3. To ensure long-term sustainability, we will implement a Planning Giving program that integrates personal, financial, and estate planning with the individual donor's plans for lifetime giving in order to leave a legacy embracing this project.

4. During the three project years, our clients will learn the value of our services pro bono and have time to build budgets to absorb nominal fee-for-service costs commensurate with their ability to pay. Our business model assumes only a level of modest fee support to sustain this project.

5. This proposed project uses a distinctive blend of financial, structural, and technological sustainability to ensure that activities, outcomes, and impacts will continue well into the future. Specifically. . .

6. The proverb is well known: "Give a man a fish, and you feed him for a day; show him how to catch fish, and you feed him for a lifetime." This proverb effectively summarizes our sustainability approach: we teach functional life skills to youth with disabilities. We don't drive them to their jobs, we teach them to ride the bus. We don't feed them, we teach them how to grocery shop. We don't manage their money, we teach them to develop and stick to a budget.

7. In the words of President John F. Kennedy, "The supreme reality of our time is. . . the vulnerability of our planet." It is with this in mind that our sustainability plan takes an environmentally friendly approach and includes the following. . .

8. Once the instrument is set up, we anticipate that it will be used up to 16 hours per day by faculty researchers, post docs, graduate students, and undergraduate students. It will be available by online scheduling and accessible during supervised hours (6:00 a.m.–6:00 p.m.) and after hours by special permission. Annual maintenance costs run about $2,500/year and will be covered through departmental funds (a combination of indirect cost returns and alumni gifts).

9. We are fortunate to have a deep pool of volunteers who, once trained, will be able to continue outreach services beyond the initial grant year. The lead volunteer coordinator will be responsible for developing the protocol handbook to guide future community engagement activities. This combination of infrastructure and talent will allow us to serve an estimated 6,000 people over the next three years.

10. For more than a decade, project partners have worked together on a variety of education, intervention, and research initiatives in the state, including participating in two federally funded cooperative agreements. Collaborators recognize and embrace their role in affecting change at the local level. Trusting relationships and a strong sense of community ownership drive our long-term commitment to success.

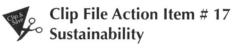

Clip File Action Item # 17
Sustainability

As you expand your Sustainability clip file, consider including items like the following:

- Collect grant application guidelines that give examples of preferred sustainability strategies (e.g., institutionalization, reallocation of resources, external funding potential, use of volunteers, extensive collaborations) to create your own menu of options.

- Write generic versions of the financial sustainability options cited above, ones that are applicable to your organization.

- Prepare brief descriptions that might be used as part of an argument from analogy of grant-initiated programs and activities that have been sustained over time at your organization.

- Retain copies of letters of commitment, memorandums of understanding, and consortium agreements as historical evidence of defined roles and responsibilities with collaborators.

CHAPTER 14
Appendixes

Great minds must be ready not only to take opportunities,
but also to make them.

—C. C. Coulton

PURPOSE OF APPENDIXES

Proposal appendixes are opportunities waiting to be finished. They contain supportive secondary information that will further strengthen your proposal narrative. In Chapter 14, you will learn the following:

- Information to include in appendixes.
- Formal and informal ways to document collaborative relationships.
- Differences between letters of support and letters of commitment.
- Types of financial and nonfinancial commitments to include in letters.
- A template for presenting résumés in uniform fashion.

As a grant writer, you may wish to include appendix items such as listed in Exhibit 71.

In essence, appendixes contain secondary supporting material for your proposal. Some grantmakers do not circulate copies of appendixes when transmitting proposals to reviewers, a practice you should clarify with your program officer. Keep essential proposal information in your project narrative. Do not attempt to use appendix material as a way to circumvent proposal narrative page limitations; all appendix items should be referenced in the proposal narrative. Each possible appendix item listed in Exhibit 71 represents a valuable addition to your clip file.

Agency awards & honors	Letters of commitment	Recent annual reports
Agency publications	Lists of board officials	References cited
Audit statements	Maps of service areas	Reprints of articles
Bibliography	Memoranda of understanding	Résumés
Blue prints	Needs assessments	Schematics
Books	Newsletters	Significant case histories
Certifications	Organizational charts	Subcontract agreements
Consortia agreements	Organizational fiscal reports	Tax exempt status
Curriculum vitaes	Past success stories	Technical specifications
Definitions of terms	Photographs	Testimonials
Diagrams	Publicity material	Vendor quotes

POSSIBLE APPENDIX DOCUMENTS

EXHIBIT 71

KEY QUESTIONS TO ANSWER

Ask yourself these key questions as you plan your appendixes:

1. Could reviewers evaluate the proposal without any appendix information?
2. Have you included strong letters of commitment and not just letters of support?
3. Are assurances of cooperation provided in instances of partnership projects?
4. Are the résumés included for all key project personnel and consultants?
5. Are all of the appendix documents required by the sponsor available, such as lists of board members, proof of nonprofit status, and audited financial statements?

WRITING TIPS FOR APPENDIXES

1. Plan ahead: it may take two weeks to secure a letter of commitment from a collaborative partner; rushing at the last minute to document relationships leads to weak letters of support.
2. Use appendixes for presentation of secondary supporting material referenced in the project narrative.
3. Resist the temptation to attach every piece of publicity material your organization has ever produced; include only the items that are critical to making your case.
4. Put long charts, graphs, tables, formulas, and other forms of visuals in the appendixes.
5. Make sure all résumés are up-to-date and reflect expertise essential to your proposed project; outdated résumés may lead reviewers to believe that an old grant application is being "repurposed" rather than tailored to the sponsor.

PUBLIC AND PRIVATE CONSORTIUM GRANT AGREEMENTS

A consortium grant is an award made to one institution (known as the lead institution) in support of a project that carries out programmatic activity in collaboration with other organizations, which are separate legal entities, administratively independent of you. Your selection of coalition partners for a consortium grant should be guided by these principles. The collaborators should be able to do the following:

1. Build on existing strengths and resources.
2. Develop and pursue concrete, attainable goals and objectives.
3. Partner on activities and evaluation.
4. Share in both processes and outcomes of the coalition.
5. Promote a learning and empowering process.
6. Disseminate findings and knowledge to all partners.
7. Foster mutual respect, understanding, and trust.

When submitting a consortium proposal to a sponsor, you should include a copy of the agreement that all agencies would sign, an agreement based on these seven principles that bind them together for a common cause. The preferred approach would be to have the agreements formally executed prior to proposal submission and to include them as an appendix item. Because that is not always possible, the fallback position is to at least include a draft of the consortium agreement in the appendix and indicate that it is the type of document all parties would sign once the grant award was made.

In consortium (or "subcontract") agreements, a separate, detailed budget for the initial and future years for each institution is submitted as well as a composite budget for all institutions. The lead institution must approve any major rebudgeting requests from collaborating institutions; additionally, the collaborators must provide the lead institution with appropriate reports (e.g., progress reports, expenditure reports, invention statements) in order to fully comply with sponsor requirements.

Following are two examples of consortium affiliation agreements often found in proposal appendixes. Exhibit 72 involves two agencies collaborating on a federal grant. In this exhibit, the lead institution, Alzheimer's Basic Care Agency, has prepared a formal subcontract agreement with its consortium partner, XYZ Agency.

In Exhibit 72, the programmatic considerations indicate how ABC and XYZ will work together to conduct a federal grant project. The fiscal considerations specify how the grant finances will be managed. The administrative considerations detail the intent to comply with existing federal regulations. With federal grants, there may be other regulatory agency requirements to be listed in the "Administrative Considerations" section. These would be indicated in your application guidelines.

Exhibit 73 involves the same two agencies collaborating on a private foundation grant, which typically does not require the same level of regulatory agency detail found in government grants.

Consortium Grant Agreement Between Alzheimer's Basic Care Agency and XYZ Agency

This Consortium Agreement is entered into this first day of May 2013, by and between Alzheimer's Basic Care Agency (henceforth ABC) and XYZ Agency (henceforth XYZ)

[Editorial note: if the lead agency has already received the federal grant, use this language]

Whereas, ABC was awarded a single grant (HRSA-09214–8421–0672) from the U.S. Department of Health and Human Services (henceforth "Sponsor") and this single grant involves multiple agencies; and

[Editorial note: if the lead agency is applying for the grant with its consortium partner, use this language instead]

Whereas, ABC, as the lead applicant, is applying for a single grant in collaboration with XYZ agency, and

Whereas, XYZ proposes to provide support for this project;

Therefore, ABC and XYZ mutually agree on the following programmatic, fiscal, and administrative considerations.

Programmatic Considerations

1. **Project Director.** Ms. Jane Smith is the project director for ABC. In the event she cannot perform in this capacity for any reason, ABC retains the right to appoint an alternative project director of its choice, subject to Sponsor approval.
2. **Project Codirector.** Mr. Jon Jones will serve as project codirector for XYZ. Any personnel change will require prior written approval from ABC and Sponsor.
3. **Scope of Work.** The scope of work to be conducted by Ms. Smith and Mr. Jones and project associates is described in the award titled "Evaluation of Service Delivery Models for the Frail Elderly," which is incorporated herein by reference referred to as the "Grant Award." Ms. Smith and Mr. Jones are responsible for directing and monitoring the grant effort as described in the Grant Award.
4. **Performance Standards.** XYZ will use reasonable efforts to accomplish work in the Grant Award following generally accepted standards of professional skill.

Fiscal Considerations

1. **Allowability of Costs.** ABC will determine the allowability of direct costs in accordance with applicable Sponsor policies and guidelines. If fiscal policies and practices at XYZ differ from those of ABC, the policies of the institution where the costs are generated will apply, provided any such policies are in compliance with those of the Sponsor.
2. **F&A Costs.** Facilities and Administrative costs for XYZ will be 8% of the total direct costs, as specified in the Grant Award.
3. **Excess Cost Reimbursement.** Any cost reimbursement to XYZ in excess of its budget award will require prior written agreement from ABC.
4. **Billing Schedule.** ABC shall pay XYZ on a monthly basis, provided invoices and vouchers are in such form and reasonable detail to verify the allowability of costs in accordance with Sponsor grant administration guidelines.
5. **Payment Schedule.** ABC shall pay XYZ no later than thirty (30) days after the receipt of each invoice or voucher, unless Sponsor delays its funding to ABC.
6. **Rebudgeting.** XYZ can rebudget up to 10% of its Grant Awards funds at its sole discretion, provided Sponsor requirements are not violated. Rebudgeting in excess of 10% for XYZ must have prior written approval of ABC.

CONSORTIUM AGREEMENT INVOLVING GOVERNMENT GRANT

EXHIBIT 72

7. **Financial Records.** XYZ agrees to provide ABC and Sponsor access to records supporting grant-related costs upon reasonable demand. Further XYZ agrees to preserve its records for five years after the expiration of the Grant Award.

Administrative Considerations

1. **Effective Date and Duration.** This Agreement becomes effective when signed by duly authorized representatives of ABC and XYZ and ends upon the project completion of May 30, 2015, unless otherwise stipulated in writing.
2. **Inter-agency Collaborations.** ABC and XYZ agree to cooperate, communicate, and collaborate in the manner and detail described in the Grant Award.
3. **Title to Equipment.** Title to all equipment purchased with funds under this Agreement resides with ABC. However, ABC may wish to make such equipment available to XYZ for an indefinite period of time, provided Sponsor guidelines allow it and XYZ agrees to furnish ABC with reasonable and appropriate inventory control information.
4. **Project Dissemination.** ABC and XYZ shall make reasonable efforts to disseminate project results through research reports and other print and electronic distribution mechanisms.
5. **Compliance.** In accepting this Agreement, XYZ agrees to comply in all applicable federal requirements, including but not limited to citations six through 12 below or their successors.
6. **Employment Authorization.** All project personnel must be authorized for employment as stipulated in the Immigration and Reform Control Act of 1986.
7. **Civil Rights and Equal Employment Opportunity.** XYZ affirms that they have filed assurance of compliance regarding the Civil Rights Act of 1964 and the Rehabilitation Act of 1973.
8. **Projection of Human Subjects.** Interactions with human subjects comply with 45 CFR Part 46, assuring individual rights are protected and no one is put to undue risk.
9. **Drug-Free Workplace.** XYZ will comply with regulations implementing the Drug-Free Workplace Act of 1988.
10. **Scientific Misconduct.** XYZ will comply with 42 CFR Part 50 governing reporting procedures dealing with possible misconduct in science.
11. **Financial Conflict of Interest.** XYZ will adhere to its own institutional policy to comply with 42 CFR Part 50 Subpart F for identifying and managing financial conflicts of interest.
12. **Patents and Inventions.** XYZ will comply with Sponsor regulations on patents and inventions. If the Sponsor declines ownership of any intellectual property arising from this Agreement, disposition of such rights will be determined by the policies of the inventor's employer.
13. **Amendments.** ABC and XYZ may amend this agreement upon written approval.
14. **Entire Agreement.** This Agreement, the Proposal, and the Grant Award constitute the entire understanding of XYZ and ABC; any oral understanding shall be without effect.

In Witness Herewith, ABC and XYZ warrant they are empowered to execute this agreement.

ABC Agency   XYZ Agency

By_____

    By_____

Adam Q. Quinkleberry   Murgatroyd Grivlovitch
President   President

CONSORTIUM AGREEMENT INVOLVING GOVERNMENT GRANT

EXHIBIT 72 (Continued from page 197)

Consortium Grant Agreement Between Alzheimer's Basic Care Agency And XYZ Agency

This Consortium Agreement is entered into this first day of May 2013, by and between Alzheimer's Basic Care Agency (henceforth ABC) and XYZ Agency (henceforth XYZ)

[Editorial note: if the grant has already been awarded, use this language.]

Whereas, ABC was awarded a single grant from the We Care Foundation (henceforth "Sponsor") and this single grant involves multiple agencies; and

[Editorial note: if the lead agency is applying for the grant with its consortium partner, use this language instead]

Whereas, ABC, as the lead applicant, is applying for a single grant in collaboration with XYZ agency, and

Whereas, XYZ proposes to provide support for this project;

Therefore, ABC and XYZ mutually agree on the following programmatic, fiscal, and administrative considerations.

Programmatic Considerations

1. **Project Director.** Ms. Jane Smith is the project director for ABC. In the event she cannot perform in this capacity for any reason, ABC retains the right to appoint an alternative project director of its choice, subject to Sponsor approval.
2. **Project Co-Director.** Mr. Jon Jones will serve as project co-director for XYZ. Any personnel change will require prior written approval from ABC and Sponsor. Mr. Jones will coordinate the institution-specific functions and activities with the overall project and serve as liaison between ABC and XYZ.
3. **Scope of Work.** The scope of work to be conducted by Ms. Smith and Mr. Jones and project associates is described in the award titled "Evaluation of Service Delivery Models for the Frail Elderly," which is incorporated herein by reference referred to as the "Grant Award." Ms. Smith and Mr. Jones are responsible for directing and monitoring the grant effort as described in the Grant Award.
4. **Performance Standards.** XYZ will use reasonable efforts to accomplish work in the Grant Award following generally accepted standards of professional skill.

Fiscal Considerations

1. **Allowability of Costs.** ABC will determine the allowability of direct costs in accordance with applicable Sponsor policies and guidelines. If fiscal policies and practices at XYZ differ from those of ABC, the policies of the institution where the costs are generated will apply, provided any such policies are in compliance with those of the Sponsor.
2. **Administrative Costs.** Administrative costs ("indirect costs") for XYZ will be 8% of the total direct costs, as specified in the Grant Award.
3. **Excess Cost Reimbursement.** Any cost reimbursement to XYZ in excess of its budget award will require prior written agreement from ABC.
4. **Billing Schedule.** ABC shall pay XYZ on a monthly basis, provided invoices and vouchers are in such form and reasonable detail to verify the allowability of costs in accordance with Sponsor grant administration guidelines.
5. **Payment Schedule.** ABC shall pay XYZ no later than thirty (30) days after the receipt of each invoice or voucher, unless Sponsor delays its funding to ABC.
6. **Rebudgeting.** XYZ can rebudget up to 10% of its Grant Awards funds at its sole discretion, provided Sponsor requirements are not violated. Rebudgeting in excess of 10% for XYZ must have prior written approval of ABC.
7. **Financial Records.** XYZ agrees to provide ABC and Sponsor access to records supporting grant-related costs upon reasonable demand. Further XYZ agrees to preserve its records for five years after the expiration of the Grant Award.

CONSORTIUM AGREEMENT INVOLVING PRIVATE FOUNDATION GRANT

EXHIBIT 73

Administrative Considerations

1. **Effective Date and Duration.** This Agreement becomes effective when signed by duly authorized representatives of ABC and XYZ and ends upon project completion on May 30, 2015, unless otherwise stipulated in writing.
2. **Inter-agency Collaborations.** ABC and XYZ agree to cooperate, communicate, and collaborate in the manner and detail described in the Grant Award and include the following: (a) participate in the Evaluation Advisory Board by designating two representatives, one of whom shall be an assistant director; (b) work with project director in organizing and offering two multidisciplinary workshops of one day during for health professionals at ABC; and (c) designate three guest lecturers to participate in the project's Speaker's Bureau.
3. **Title to Equipment.** Title to all equipment purchased with funds under this Agreement resides with ABC. However, ABC may wish to make such equipment available to XYZ for an indefinite period of time, provided Sponsor guidelines allow it and XYZ agrees to furnish ABC with reasonable and appropriate inventory control information.
4. **Project Dissemination.** ABC and XYZ shall make reasonable efforts to disseminate project results through research reports and other print and electronic distribution mechanisms.
5. **Amendments.** ABC and XYZ may amend this agreement upon written approval.
6. **Entire Agreement.** This Agreement, the Proposal, and the Grant Award constitute the entire understanding of XYZ and ABC; any oral understanding shall be without effect.

In Witness Herewith, ABC and XYZ warrant they are empowered to execute this agreement.

ABC Agency   XYZ Agency

By_____

        By_____

Adam Q. Quinkleberry   Murgatroyd Grivlovitch
President   President

CONSORTIUM AGREEMENT INVOLVING PRIVATE FOUNDATION GRANT

EXHIBIT 73 (Continued from page 199)

In essence, both exhibits 72 and 73 are examples of subcontract agreements, formal documents that stipulate how the collaborators agree to work together.

Public and private consortium grant agreements tend to be formal, contract-like documents. However, there are occasions where a less formal agreement mechanism is desired, especially when collaborative details remain to be ironed out. In such instances, a memorandum of understanding (MOU) document may suffice to assure grantmakers that a true collaboration exists. An MOU provides a conceptual framework for a future undertaking between two or more parties. Exhibit 74 shows an example of a MOU template that can be adapted to most situations.

Whether expressed in terms of a formal subcontract or an informal MOU, the key to persuading grant reviewers is to demonstrate that you have given serious thought to the nature of your consortium relationship and that it represents a real collaboration, not a phantom collaboration.

PHANTOM COLLABORATIONS

Successful grantseekers know that true collaborations must be genuine, not phantom-based. To illustrate, a local grantmaking agency recently announced its intention to fund a health-related project, but with a catch. Only one proposal would be funded per geographic area, and all interested applicants in the county should get together, join forces, and submit a collaborative proposal. The sponsor's well-intended but conceptually flawed idea was to create a grant opportunity that would automatically guarantee interagency collaboration.

Memorandum of Understanding (MOU)
Between
Party A (full and official name)
and
Party B (full and official name)

This Memorandum of Understanding (MOU) is agreed upon between Party A (hereafter called xxx) and Party B (hereafter called yyy)

I. Purpose and Scope

This MOU identifies the roles and responsibilities of each party relative to their collaboration in (proposal title), a grant application to be submitted to the (insert name of grantmaker).

II. Resources

To support the successful completion of this grant project, each party will contribute the following resources:

Party A

_____
_____
_____

Party B

_____
_____
_____

III. Activities

To support the successful completion of this project, each party will use the available project resources to do the following activities during the project period:

Party A

_____
_____
_____

Party B

_____
_____
_____

IV. Funding

Party A will distribute $_____ to Party B in payment of project services rendered.

V. Effective Date

This MOU is effective on _____ and extends to _____, unless further modified by both parties upon written agreement.

_____ _____
Party A   Date

_____ _____
Party B   Date

MEMORANDUM OF UNDERSTANDING TEMPLATE

EXHIBIT 74

Here's what happened. The lead applicant agency asked other collaborators to submit a one-page outline of what they could contribute to the proposal. On the basis of those one-page descriptions, the lead applicant crafted a proposal and sent it in without further collaborations. The other collaborators requested meetings to talk about the content and format of the proposal. Their request for collaborative meetings was denied.

To no one's surprise, the proposal didn't get funded. The lead applicant agency didn't recognize the characteristics of successful collaborative proposals. Consider these key ideas:

1. Collaborators talk about the strategic planning process used to develop the proposal.
2. Collaborators identify the contributions of each participant and how it contributes to the "big picture."
3. Collaborations usually contain an advisory board with representation from the major participants.
4. Collaborators include a draft consortium agreement showing how they will cooperate administratively, fiscally, and programmatically.
5. Collaborators schedule progress reports that involve the major players.

This proposal had none of these characteristics. As the reviewers quickly determined, this was not a "real" proposal; rather, it was a phantom proposal. Phantom collaborations don't get funded.

The elements of a successful collaboration include the following:

1. A clear statement of goals, objectives, and outcomes to which all partners subscribe.
2. Clear identification of each partner's roles and responsibilities.
3. Regular meetings to provide feedback and share or exchange information.
4. Concrete benchmarks to monitor progress and maintain focus.
5. Patience to survive periods of frustration and seeming lack of progress.
6. Open, effective channels of communication between partners.

STRATEGIC PARTNERING WITH ACADEMIA

Looking for a strategic partner? Consider partnering with a nearby college or university. They are place-bound and their futures depend on the social and economic vitality of their regions. Institutions of higher education are ecological connections to their local communities. No longer can academics expect to thrive by being aloof from the conditions, needs, and opportunities of their neighbors. Academia is shifting philosophically from the concept of the academy as a cloister to the academy as a public space directly linked to the life of society.

Bluntly, academia needs partnerships with nonprofit organizations. If you don't have a point of contact in a nearby academic institution, call the nearest one and ask to be connected to the Grants Office or the Development Office and explain your interest in collaboration. As a nonprofit organization, you can provide opportunities to enrich the educational experiences of students, focus on areas of shared concern that offer the prospect of mutual benefit, and create a "town/gown" community that values all members. Communication is the staple of any successful partnership. You'll be borrowing their credibility that will, in turn, strengthen your next proposal and increase your likelihood of getting funded.

LETTERS OF SUPPORT AND COMMITMENT

British novelist Edward Forester once said, "Letters have to pass two tests before they can be classed as good: they must express the personality both of the writer and of the recipient." This observation, nearly a century old, is relevant in the grants arena still today.

Some sponsors allow letters of support to be included as an appendix item to a grant application. These letters help establish your credibility and document that a solid base of support exists for your project. The strongest letters go beyond the customary "This is a great project" endorsement to describe the basis of past relationships and detail roles, responsibilities, and contributions collaborators will make to the proposed project. Consider the following operative paragraph:

> I am pleased to support the proposed project "Reducing the Impact of Child Abuse in Wisconsin." We have worked very closely with our colleagues throughout the 10-year lifespan of our coalition and in the three-month development of this application. We look forward to contributing our expertise on the project's executive advisory board and in-kind use of our conference rooms for bimonthly meetings. Without a doubt, this project will be an important catalyst toward achieving a unified, powerful movement in the state.

Current Date

Mr. Peter Barnett, Project Director
Organization Name
Street Address
City/State/Zip

Dear Mr. Barnett:

I enjoyed speaking with you today and am familiar with the basic goals and methods of your proposed work toward creating HealthAlert Oregon, a statewide advocacy coalition aligned to local HealthAlert Coalitions.

I am honored to be part of such a needed and forward-thinking project that will work toward expanding and extending coverage to all people in Oregon. Let me know what I can do to facilitate this important partnership endeavor.

Sincerely,

Doris Eggerding, MD
University of Oregon

EXAMPLE OF WEAK COMMITMENT LETTER

EXHIBIT 75

To get a strong commitment letter, provide the targeted letter writers with a draft copy of your proposal and a draft copy of the letter you would like them to sign. They can make whatever changes they feel warranted and have it printed on their agency letterhead.

Turning the coin over, sponsors tend to be skeptical of generic letters of support—they wonder whether the partners really know what the project is all about. Sponsors are also suspicious when letters of support from multiple partners all say word-for-word the same thing. While it may be more expeditious for grant writers to prepare one letter that various collaborators can reproduce on their own letterhead, these identical letters often lack personality and persuasiveness.

In essence, personalization moves them from being common letters of support to distinct letters of commitment. The letters convey not only a general passion for the topic at hand but also a specific agreement for working with you on this project. Equally significant, they demonstrate to the sponsor that you are well positioned for project success.

When considering letters of commitment, grant writers sometimes wonder if they should solicit endorsements from congressional officials. Often, congressional letters are one of support, and not commitment; at best, most congressional officials can "bless" you or your project as being worthy of support but are not in a position to make a firm commitment. While congressional officials will usually provide such letters when requested, use them sparingly; that is, save congressional "muscle" for big projects, not routine ones. For example, one hospital follows the "two-comma" policy for getting congressional support letters: the requested budget must have two commas in it, i.e., be greater than one million dollars. When you decide such a letter is appropriate, contact a congressional staff officer, explain your situation, and request a support letter. Offer to send background information about your organization as well as a draft of the letter you would like to receive.

A letter of commitment is usually short, less than one page. Exhibit 75 contains an example of a weak letter of commitment, the kind that you do not want to include with your proposal. It was actually included with a proposal that reviewers declined to fund.

In Exhibit 75, Dr. Eggerding only indicated that the proposed project was a good idea. She did not indicate what she would do to ensure project success. Reviewers are left wondering what specific role she might play in the project. Note the contrast provided in Exhibit 76, which does spell out her precise commitments to the project.

Current Date

Mr. Peter Barnett, Project Director
Organization Name
Street Address
City/State/Zip

Dear Mr. Barnett:

I was pleased to learn about your project to address health literacy in Oregon, an issue that many health professionals are very concerned about. I am writing this letter of commitment that the XYZ Health System will partner with you in your grant proposal, Reducing Health Disparities by Improving Health Literacy: A Model for Collaboration.

As you know, we have a network of 128 HealthAlert centers distributed throughout the state. Collectively, we have more than 300 healthcare professional that are affiliated with our umbrella organization. We have been serving communities statewide since 1964. Our tenure has afforded us opportunities to build a strong network of individuals who share the values reflected in this project. Your Health Literacy project represents a continuation of your decade-long collaboration on various health-related projects.

We are dedicated to partnering in this project by:

1. Appointing a represent to the Health Literacy Advisory Council, which would meet semiannually in Portland for three years to monitor and evaluate the progress of this project;
2. Providing opportunities for project partners to meet with our staff to obtain input into the development of this project, as needed;
3. Working with project partners to increase awareness of health literacy in Oregon hospitals by emphasizing project progress in our biweekly newsletter and including you prominently in our annual conventions; and
4. Communicating knowledge gained and relevant products developed through this project to hospitals throughout the state.

We look forward to working with all partners on this grant and believe this is a much-needed and innovative initiative.

Sincerely,

Doris Eggerding, MD
University of Oregon

EXAMPLE OF A STRONG COMMITMENT LETTER

EXHIBIT 76

The typical letter of commitment contains an opening paragraph, a statement of past relationship between the collaborating organization and the sponsor, a precise listing of what the collaborator will contribute to the project, and a closing paragraph. Some letters are taking the next step and describing commitments to project sustainability after the grant period concludes. What might your collaborator be able to contribute to a project? Your answer lies in one or more of the 24 different examples included in Exhibit 77. Put your letter of commitment on letter-head stationery and address it to the proposal project director, not the grant program officer.

RÉSUMÉS

Format

Your organization should settle on a standardized format for proposal résumés so that they all look similar. The choice of formats is not as important as the fact that all of your organizational résumés match in

Financial Funds	Human Resources	Professional Expertise
Cash support	Advisory council participation	Disseminate knowledge gained
In-kind support	Access to special populations	Fiscal accounting
Tuition	Facilitate partnership linkages	Programmatic competence
Scholarships	Loan of personnel	Testing samples
Use of credit cards	Attendance at meetings	Legal counsel
Excess equipment	Graduate students/Lab technicians	Medical advice
Postage	Marketing production	Policy and procedure guidance
Product donations	Security escorts	Technology support

EXAMPLES OF POSSIBLE TYPES OF COMMITMENT

EXHIBIT 77

order to show project cohesiveness. The format you ultimately choose should emphasize your skills that are essential to conduct your proposed project. Most grant applications call for an abbreviated résumé or biosketch, often two to four pages. Exhibit 78 shows a partially completed biosketch of an individual working at a nonprofit organization.

Exhibit 79 shows a similar biosketch format but it is focused more on university-based personnel. Both are adapted from a form currently used at the National Institutes of Health.

TRANSMITTAL LETTER

Although the transmittal letter is not an appendix item, it often emerges as a last-minute detail when the proposal narrative and appendixes are assembled. Accordingly, it is included here because of the sequence in which proposals are assembled.

Your transmittal letter should tell who you are, what your proposal is about, how much money is requested, and the grant program to which it is targeted. You want to transmit your proposal so it is reviewed by the "right" program. If you have pre-proposal contact with a program officer about this project (see Chapter 4), then mention that: "This proposal culminates the preliminary discussions I have had with Dr. Jane Wingert, program officer in Cellular Biology."

Besides the proposal copies you send to a central receiving center, send another copy under separate cover directly to your program officer. It may take weeks between the time you send it to a central receiving station and the time it is forwarded to program officers, who usually appreciate an early review opportunity so they can begin to think about the selection of appropriate reviewers.

If you are submitting a proposal to the National Institutes of Health (NIH), consider this tip. Before you submit your proposal, ask your program officer to send an internal awaiting receipt of application (ARA) notice to the Center for Scientific Review, the entry point for NIH proposal review. This will flag your proposal internally at NIH so it is forwarded to the study or review section of interest to your program officer. Further indicate such in your transmittal letter: "You should have on file an awaiting receipt of application (ARA) notice regarding this proposal from Dr. Kelby Merrick, Cellular Biology Program, National Cancer Institute."

Transmittal letters for proposals to private sponsors follow the same general approach but place greater emphasis on institutional support for the project, even to the point where a chief executive officer and/or board member should countersign the proposal. An example of a transmittal letter follows in Exhibit 80.

REJECTION REASONS

Although proposals are seldom rejected because of shortcomings in the appendixes, the reviewers nevertheless do expect to see certain information items properly presented. If their expectations are not met, then your proposal may be downgraded. These reviewer comments suggest weaknesses in proposal appendixes.

1. The proposal does not provide evidence of formal structures or relationships binding collaborators.
2. If the collaborative partners are all so committed to the project, why do their letters of support read verbatim with no customization whatsoever?

ABBREVIATED BIOGRAPHICAL SKETCH	
NAME Todd M. Randall, MBA	CURRENT POSITION TITLE Executive Director
POSITON TITLE IN PROJECT Tuberculosis Specialist: Capacity Building	PERCENT EFFORT IN PROJECT 25%

EDUCATION/TRAINING			
INSTITUTION AND LOCATION	DEGREE (if applicable)	YEAR(s)	FIELD OF STUDY
Michigan State University	BS	1990	Chemistry
University of Illinois	MBA	1992	Organizational Management

Personal Statement

The goal of the proposed project is to. . . With more than a decade's worth of experience in tropical disease management, I possess the skills necessary to lead the collaborative partners through a series of trainings to build their organizational capacity. Specifically, during the granting period, I will guide 20 nonprofit organizations through the process of readiness assessment, communication planning, data collection, feedback analysis, resistance management, and change reinforcement. This project represents a systematic extension of the work that I have done on change management (Randall et al., 1996; Crosby & Randall, 2002), applying it to organizations that serve regions targeted by the World Health Organization as "emerging risks." In short, I have the expertise and demonstrated track record to guide this project to success.

Positions and Honors

1998–2001   Assistant Director, Blood Bank, Milwaukee, WI
2001–2005   Associate Director, Blood Bank, Milwaukee, WI
2005–   Executive Director, National Health Education Center

Selected Peer-Reviewed Publications (X out of Y)

Research Support

[Editorial note: Delete any inappropriate headers, e.g., publications or research support and insert others that will best highlight relevant project credentials. Examples:]

Pertinent Project Management Experience

Special Skills

Collaborators

International Travels

Project Accomplishments

Relevant Experience

Professional Organizational Membership

Languages/Special Skills

BIOSKETCH FOR NONPROFIT PERSONNEL

EXHIBIT 78

ABBREVIATED BIOGRAPHICAL SKETCH

NAME	CURRENT POSITION TITLE
Todd M. Randall, MD	Associate Professor of Family Medicine
POSITON TITLE IN PROJECT	PERCENT EFFORT IN PROJECT
Malaria Specialist: Immunology	25%

EDUCATION/TRAINING

INSTITUTION AND LOCATION	DEGREE (if applicable)	YEAR(s)	FIELD OF STUDY
Michigan State University	BS	1990	Chemistry
University of Illinois	MS	1992	Biochemistry
University of Wisconsin	MD	1996	Medicine
Harvard University	Postdoc	1998	Infectious Diseases

Personal Statement

The goal of the proposed project is to. . . With nearly two decades' worth of experience researching infectious diseases, including a postdoctoral fellowship at Harvard, I possess the knowledge, skills, and abilities necessary to lead the work on malaria. Specifically, during the granting period, I will focus on the drug-resistant strains of parasites and insecticide-resistant strains of mosquitos. This project represents a systematic extension of the work that I have done in immunology (Randall et al., 1996; Crosby & Randall, 2002), with a targeted focus on the World Health Organization-designated "urgent risks." In short, I have the expertise and demonstrated track record to guide this project to success.

Positions and Honors

1998–2001   Assistant Professor of Chemistry, University of Pocatello, ID
2001–2005   Assistant Professor of Medicine, Northwestern University
2005–   Associate Professor of Internal Medicine, Northwestern University

Selected Peer-Reviewed Publications (X out of Y)

Research Support

BIOSKETCH FORMAT FOR ACADEMIC PERSONNEL

EXHIBIT 79

3. It is unclear why one of the letters of support is dated from five years ago. Is this a resubmitted project with a recycled letter of support?
4. The proposal does not identify or describe the qualifications of the project director to lead this collaborative venture.
5. The résumés of key project personnel do not demonstrate they have the capability and experience to administer a million-dollar grant award.
6. The applicants propose to enter an area of research for which they are not adequately trained.
7. The principal investigator intends to give actual responsibility for the direction of a complex project to an inexperienced coinvestigator.
8. The investigators will be required to devote too much time to teaching or other nonresearch duties.
9. The narrative includes citations that are not listed in the references.
10. The applicant did not provide evidence of its nonprofit status.

GRANT GAFFES

Exhibit 81 contains an example of a weak letter of commitment that was included along with a proposal to a government agency. The grant gaffe is clear: the letter does not commit to any specifics beyond naming

Today's Date

Ms. Beau Tribblehorn, President
Black Foundation
19800 18th Street, N.W.
Washington, DC 20555

Re: Proposal Title
Your Name
Your Institution

Dear Ms. Tribblehorn:

On behalf of Midwest Agency, California's most comprehensive health provider agency for the displaced Hmong population, I am transmitting the referenced proposal for your review and consideration.

The proposal requests $150,000 for a three-year project to improve the delivery of health care among the elderly Hmong, a population with limited choices, lost aspirations, and cultural/linguistic barriers.

Ms. Laura Bennett, project director, has reviewed with me in detail the proposed project plans, and I can assure you that it will receive our highest organizational priority since it is central to our institutional mission of serving worthy, deserving, and needy populations.

I invite you to contact Ms. Bennett at 619-555-1234 to answer any programmatic questions you may have. If you have any administrative questions, please call me directly at 619-555-6789.

Sincerely,

Your Name
Your Title

PROPOSAL TRANSMITTAL LETTER

EXHIBIT 80

two individuals who will participate in the project. The genesis of the gaffe can be traced back to the project director who requested the letter from the project partner but did not provide any guidance about the types of details that should be included.

STARTER SENTENCES

The following starter sentences reflect language that you can use to craft opening and closing paragraphs in letters of commitment. The intellectual heart of the letter is the specific commitment that will be made to the project.

1. I am pleased to lend official support from our agency to your project. I welcome this opportunity to blend our interests with your very real needs. I enthusiastically endorse the involvement of my agency. All will profit from this cross-pollination of ideas. I know from experience that multiple viewpoints are needed to traverse the milieu you face.

2. I have just finished reviewing your proposal. Your emphasis will certainly be of benefit to your agency and ours. Bringing together the interdisciplinary expertise you have assembled in this proposal can only augment the richness of your project. I enthusiastically endorse the involvement of our agency and will personally assure the administrative support required to reach your project objectives. We eagerly await the formal beginning of your project.

3. For more than a decade, our agencies have worked cooperatively on a variety of social service projects. In that context, I see your current proposal as a systematic continuation of our past joint efforts. The human and physical resources are in place—and have been for years—to achieve your desired project objectives.

December 12, 2012

Mr. Donald Matthews, Project Director
Organization Name
Street Address
City, State Zip

Dear Mr. Matthews:

This letter declares Title Town's intent to collaborate with the Hispanic Community Center on the project "Win Big for Your Health," which is being submitted to the U.S. Department of Health and Human Services.

Greg Neilson, nutritionist, and B. J. Finley, counselor, will be participating in the proposed activities. The total budget request for Title Town is $16,492 over the two-year project period, and includes $0 in F&A costs.

Title Town is compliant with the requirements of OMB A-122 and our latest audit did not have any findings or recommendations in the report.

Sincerely,

Erin A. Rodgers
Executive Director

> The sponsor required letters of commitment from collaborators to be included in the appendixes. This letter, however, represents a broad letter of support rather than a specific letter of commitment. While the first half of the 92-word letter confirms an intent to collaborate and identifies two individuals who will participate in the project, the letter remains silent on exactly what contributions they will make to the project—time and expertise, physical equipment and space, and/or financial resources. The remaining half of the letter acknowledges that the grant application and budget has been administratively reviewed and that the institution is compliant with federal regulations, details which do not speak at all to the nature and extent of the partnership.

GRANT GAFFES

EXHIBIT 81

4. Thank you for the opportunity to review your proposal. You have identified some very significant local problems. As you address these problems in your agency, I am particularly pleased that we can contribute our organizational strength: (specify). Our agency personnel have a demonstrated concern for and proven expertise in this area. In total, you have assembled an excellent interdisciplinary cadre of professionals to make this project quite promising. I want you to know that this project has the highest levels of support and commitment to success. We eagerly await active participation.

5. I enthusiastically support your proposal. Its interdisciplinary approach to addressing the ever-increasing challenges we face promises valuable guidance. Your leadership role provides you with unique experience and insights with which to direct this project. Your past efforts will serve as an indispensable resource to professionals and enrich the delivery of services. Your proposal has my strong support, and I will continue to allocate time for my personnel to participate in your project activities.

6. As dean and vice president of Academic Affairs at Woodland University, I am thrilled to be

a formal partner in the project titled, "Paper TIGERS: Turning Infinities and Geometries into Exceptional Results for Students." This project meets a pressing need for our students, and, as a result, it will have the highest levels of institutional support.

7. LGBTQ Foundations is deeply concerned that intimate partner violence remains a leading cause of injury and death in our state. Our participation in the Health Department's "Caring Relationships" project represents a systematic continuation of the types of educational and outreach initiatives in which we've been engaging over the past two decades aimed at curbing dating violence. Our statewide professional networks and database of 37,000 volunteers will allow us to disseminate information quickly to providers and peer mentors.

8. We are delighted to work with the Gerontological Institute on the proposed project "Decreasing Falls among the Frail Elderly." Over the course of this three-year initiative, we will train 60 coaches who, in turn, will serve an estimated 720 seniors in the community. We have partnered with the Gerontological Institute on three previous grant-funded projects and have the types of trusting relationships in place to ensure this project, too, is a success.

9. On behalf of the Anytown School District, I write this letter of support and commitment for the Tobacco Free Coalition's application to the Wellnitz Foundation. Based on my involvement on their advisory council and having participated in the community SWOT analysis, I can say without reservation that "Breathe Deep" will meet the needs of school-aged youth. There's no better way to connect with students than to use an integrated approach of meeting them where they're at—in the home, at school, and in the community.

10. For more than a decade, DoubleDown and BlackJack College have partnered together on a variety of educational initiatives. Our success is built on a foundation of shared values—quality service and relationships, mutual trust, integrity, and financial strength. That's why it is with great pride that I write this letter of support for the "Aces Project." I am committed to the success of Aces professionally and personally, including serving as a role model and mentor, answering questions, sharing knowledge, providing encouragement, and fostering growth and development.

Clip File Action Item # 18 Appendixes

To build your Appendixes clip file, return to the beginning of this chapter and begin collecting as many of the tabled items as possible. Encourage others to contribute as well. One organization, for example, requires all people attending staff meetings to come with a clip file contribution in hand.

CHAPTER 15
Abstracts

No one objects to how much you say, if you say it in a few words.

—Martha Lupton

PURPOSE OF ABSTRACTS

Successful grantseekers follow Lupton's advice: say much in a few words. The abstract is usually the first read and last written section of your proposal. It provides a cogent summary of your proposed project. It should offer a quick overview of what you propose to do and a rapid understanding of the project's significance, generalizability, and potential contribution. Project outcomes should be clearly identified. In Chapter 15, you will learn the following:

- The value of writing concise abstracts.
- The variability of grantmaker expectations for abstracts.
- The components of a persuasive abstract.
- The common mistakes made in writing abstracts.

Often, proposal reviewers must write up a summary of your project for presentation to a larger review panel. If you write a persuasive abstract, program officers may use it as a basis for their proposal review, thereby simplifying their job. If your abstract is poorly written, their job is more difficult and your funding chances diminish.

EXAMPLES OF GRANTMAKER REQUIREMENTS FOR ABSTRACTS

As the following examples illustrate, grantmakers use varying terminology to refer to abstracts. The term *abstract* has many pseudonyms among public and private sponsors, including *summary*, *executive summary*, *project summary*, and *overview*. Grantmakers also have varying expectations about the details to be included in abstracts. Some sets of grant guidelines allow you great flexibility to select the key ideas to include in the abstract while other sets of guidelines prescribe to an extraordinary degree the specific elements target audiences expect to read. Grant guidelines and online submission systems may limit abstracts in terms of character and word counts or line and page lengths.

Public Sponsors

National Endowment for the Humanities. Instructions for writing abstracts at the National Endowment for the Humanities differ by division and program. Within the Division of Education Programs, the Enduring Questions program offers the following guidance:

> Abstract—Not to exceed two hundred words or one thousand characters. The abstract should be clear, free of jargon, and accessible to nonspecialists.

National Institutes of Health. The U.S. Department of Health and Human Services issues the following guidance for submitting applications to Public Health Service agencies, such as the National Institutes of Health:

> The Project Summary is meant to serve as a succinct and accurate description of the proposed work when separated from the application. State the application's broad, long-term objectives and specific aims, making reference to the health relatedness of the project

(i.e., relevance to the mission of the agency). Describe concisely the research design and methods for achieving the stated goals. This section should be informative to other persons working in the same or related fields and insofar as possible understandable to a scientifically or technically literate reader. Avoid describing past accomplishments and the use of the first person. Finally, please make every effort to be succinct. This section must be no longer than 30 lines of text, and follow the required font and margin specifications. An abstract which exceeds this allowable length may be flagged as an error by the agency upon submission. This would require a corrective action before the application will be accepted.

National Science Foundation. The National Science Foundation's "Grant Proposal Guide" contains proposal preparation instructions, which include the following for developing a project summary:

The proposal must contain a summary of the proposed activity suitable for publication, not more than one page in length. It should not be an abstract of the proposal, but rather a self-contained description of the activity that would result if the proposal were funded. The summary should be written in the third person and include a statement of objectives and methods to be employed. It must clearly address in separate statements (within the one-page summary):

- the intellectual merit of the proposed activity; and
- the broader impacts resulting from the proposed activity.

It should be informative to other persons working in the same or related fields and, insofar as possible, understandable to a scientifically or technically literate lay reader. **Proposals that do not separately address both merit review criteria within the one-page Project Summary will be returned without review.** To that end, proposers are encouraged to include separate headings within the one-page document for both "Intellectual Merit" and "Broader Impacts."

Private Sponsors

Commonwealth Fund. The Commonwealth Fund offers two different sets of guidance: for the small grants fund (amounts less than or equal to $50,000), no abstract is requested; for board-level grants (amounts greater than $50,000), an executive summary should be included. The guidance does not specify content or length requirements.

Joyce Foundation. The Joyce Foundation indicates that formal proposals should include an executive summary or overview (1–2 pages).

W. M. Keck Foundation. The W. M. Keck Foundation employs a two-tier application process. Phase I applications must include a one-page project summary that includes the following:

Project Summary (1 page maximum)

1. **Abstract:** Provide an executive summary of this project, including overall goal, methodology, and significance, for a well-educated lay audience.
2. **Unique Aspects:** Describe unique distinctive aspects of this project.
3. **Key Personnel:** Name the key personnel and describe their credentials, expertise in the field, and role in this project.
4. **Budget:** State total cost of this project, amount requested from the W. M. Keck Foundation, and the amount of institutional support. Describe how funds requested from the W. M. Keck Foundation will be allocated among capital, personnel, and equipment.
5. **Justification for WMKF support:** Explain why support from the W. M. Keck Foundation is essential for this project.

Phase II proposals must include a 15-line project abstract and a 2-page executive summary that addresses the following:

Project Abstract (Maximum of 15 lines)
Executive Summary (Maximum of two pages, written for a well-educated lay audience)

1. Methodology/Implementation: Briefly describe the methods that will be employed, highlighting what is unique or distinctive, and summarize the timeline.
2. Personnel: Identify the principal investigators and other key personnel, and summarize their expertise and roles in the project.
3. Budget: State total cost of the project, amount requested from the W. M. Keck Foundation, and amount of institutional support. Describe how the percentage of funds requested from the W. M. Keck Foundation will be allocated among personnel, equipment, and related costs. Describe how institutional funds will be allocated.

COMPONENTS OF ABSTRACT

A thorough yet concise abstract includes the following information elements:

- **Subject**: What is the project about? What is the problem or need being addressed?
- **Purpose**: Why is the project being done? Why is the project significant?
- **Activities**: What will be done? What methods will be used?
- **Target Population**: What special group is being studied or served?
- **Location**: Where is the work being performed?
- **Outcomes**: What types of findings will result? To whom will these be useful?

Inexperienced grant writers often make four significant mistakes in writing proposal abstracts. First, they compress their information into one or two paragraphs paying little attention to readability. Second, they fail to include headings in their text, thereby making it difficult for reviewers to obtain a clear project overview. Third, they write the abstract prior to writing the narrative, which can lead to "slippage"—ideas are introduced in the abstract with no further explanation in the proposal. Fourth, they treat the abstract as page one of the narrative; consequently, from the perspective of grant reviewers, there is no project summary to read.

The proposal abstract should be the last written proposal section. The easy way to craft the abstract is to first identify the primary headings, such as those listed above, and repeat one or two key sentences from your project narrative that addresses each element. Among other things, this approach enables the readers to foreshadow the entire proposal. The length of your abstract will vary, depending on sponsor requirements. The range varies from 100 words to three pages.

KEY QUESTIONS TO ANSWER

As you write your abstract, ask yourself if it does the following:

1. Effectively summarize the project?
2. Place appropriate emphasis on the various proposal components?
3. Enumerate project outcomes?
4. Comply with the character, word, line, or page length requirements of the sponsor?
5. Introduce key concepts that are explained fully in the proposal narrative?
6. Use major headings to highlight proposal sections?
7. Meet sponsor stipulations for comprehension by specialist or generalist audiences?
8. Avoid using technical jargon, acronyms, and abbreviations?
9. Conform to sponsor expectations of voice (i.e., written in first or third person)?
10. Serve as a condensed substitute for reviewers who do not read the narrative?

EXAMPLES OF ABSTRACTS

Example 1

The following is a project abstract statement for private foundation support for a parent training center. This abstract is presented twice: first as it was originally written and second as it was rewritten prior to final submission.

> At the conclusion of extensive long-range planning, the Parent Training Center has defined its priorities for the next decade. To implement its plan, the center has undertaken a comprehensive, multiyear development program to generate funding for its highest priorities and aspirations. The New Parent Training Program is one of the special programs for which support is sought. To date, a training curriculum has been created and a parent advisory board and a lending library were begun. The program is proposing activities that include parenting classes, a parenting clinic with further agency referral, and an annual one-day parenting convention. Six sites have been chosen for training sessions for more than 100 parents between January and April 2016. A three-year budget and explanatory narrative are attached delineating the fund-raising goal for the program. Because the foundation has evidenced a strong concern for families and children and because of the need for a New Parent Training Program in the metropolitan area, the Parent Training Center is requesting a $30,000 grant, payable over three years, to assist in addressing a pervasive problem in our society.

In contrast, consider this rewritten version that uses bold headings and white space to improve the readability of this abstract:

> **Overview.** The Parent Training Center, the only nonprofit agency in the state exclusively dedicated to teaching parenting skills, is seeking

$30,000 to establish a new program to train teenage parents.

Need for Training Teenage Parents. Child abuse and neglect have grown dramatically, up 18 percent in the four county area over the past two years. While the growth occurs across all socioeconomic levels and races, the greatest rate of growth is occurring in families with teenage parents. These parents are poorly informed about child development and often favor corporal punishment as a means of managing their children.

Objectives of Teenage Parent Training Program:

- Conduct 10 parenting classes for teenage parents by January 2016.
- Establish a clinical program for serious problems by June 2016.
- Disseminate information about teenage parenting by January 2017.

Methods for Implementing Teenage Parent Training Program. A four-week series of parenting classes will be offered at sites that serve high-risk, teenage parents. Instructional techniques include discussion, videos, handouts, and parent support groups. Two clinical psychologists will conduct the Teenage Parent Training Program and, through their linkages with other appropriate agencies in the community, create a referral network. Annually, a one-day parenting convention will present informative sessions and speakers on a variety of topics, e.g., toy safety, young children's literature, health issues. Additionally, exhibits will also show relevant community resources, e.g., hospitals, day care centers, preschools.

Outcomes for Teenage Parent Training Program. The effectiveness of the program will be measured through consumer satisfaction questionnaires and pre- and posttests of parenting knowledge and skills to be developed. Pilot data suggest the culturally sensitive training materials will have a positive impact on parental behaviors. The one-day conference will heighten community sensitivity to this issue.

Notice how the use of headings enhances the readability of the proposal. The key sentences in each section are taken from key sentences in the actual proposal narrative, a persuasive writing technique also used in the following example, which is taken from a federal grant proposal to hold a series of regional conferences on the subject of perinatal depression.

Example 2

The following is a project abstract written by a nonprofit organization seeking federal funding to conduct some statewide workshops on the topic of perinatal depression:

Overview. The perinatal period, pregnancy through early life, is a developmental epoch that is critical to maternal and infant mental health. With a grant of $50,000 from the Substance Abuse and Mental Health Services Agency, the Perinatal Care Group will host seven regional conferences throughout Wisconsin to bridge the gap between knowledge and practice regarding prenatal and postpartum depression— a clinically significant diagnosis affecting more than 10,000 Wisconsin women annually, especially those representing culturally diverse backgrounds.

Problem. Depression during the prenatal and postpartum period is a major public health problem affecting 15 percent of all women and up to 30 percent of women living in poverty. Depression does not often resolve without treatment, yet many practitioners are untrained or inexperienced in identifying depression, or may lack referral sources for effective treatment. Of approximately 70,000 Wisconsin births last year, more than 10,000 mothers experienced clinically significant yet treatable depression that often remained undiagnosed. The consequences affect not only the mother-baby dyad but usually the entire family unit as well.

Solution. Prenatal and postpartum depression is identifiable and treatable. Early identification and treatment by primary care providers or mental health specialists is crucial. The goal of this proposal is to disseminate and integrate knowledge about prenatal and postpartum depression into the practice of providers throughout the state. Since research shows that best practices are more likely to be adopted when providers participate in face-to-face interactions, a series of seven regional conferences will be held. Given the ethnic and cultural diversity that exists within Wisconsin, improving cultural competence is a major thematic focus of the seven regional conferences that will reach 350 participants. The outcomes will produce nine different conference products that will be distributed verbally and visually, actively and passively to appropriate culturally diverse audiences.

Evaluation. Since the four project objectives are expressed in measurable terms, an external evaluation consultant will evaluate each one.

Culturally and linguistically appropriate evaluation tools will collect participant feedback at the end of the conferences and again 30 days later with a minimum of an 80 percent response rate among regional conference participants.

Long-Term. The Perinatal Care Group has made a long-term commitment to reducing the knowledge-practice gap regarding prenatal and postpartum depression. The proposed regional conferences represent Phase IV in a series of initiatives to achieve this goal. Earlier activities have included public awareness campaigns (Phase I), a best practices symposium (Phase II), and a blueprint for action initiative (Phase III). The proposed Phase IV regional conferences represent a systematic continuation of prior events on this topic of prenatal and postpartum depression, which has enormous human and economic consequences for women, their families, and the health care system.

Again, notice the use of headings to highlight proposal content. The primary federal reviewer for this proposal was charged with the responsibility to write a summary of the proposal. The reviewer thought this synopsis was so accurate and succinct that he just used this instead of writing his own.

Example 3

The following abstract is from a project seeking federal funding to research virtual organizations as sociotechnical systems:

Project Overview

Open communities create complicated issues for organizations and researchers because they are more complex than simply technology-enabled groups; they are a mix of power and knowledge, liberty and enlightenment, progress and intervention. As design and development evolves within open communities, new affordances present new possibilities, and organizations must balance "contributions to" and "differentiation from" the open community for reasons of cost, resource management, and time to market. Organizational participation in open communities is timely in light of recent analyses by the Linux Foundation indicating that 75 percent of kernel contributions are by paid developers. In this proposal, we build on principles of public sharing and collaboration using the Linux open-source community as our basis for understanding open communities. The focus of this project is why organizations participate with open communities, how they participate with open communities, and what we should be teaching our students regarding open community participation. We apply action research as a methodological approach within which a quantitative field study will be conducted. Action research supports our dual goal of developing a solution to a practical problem which is of value to the people with whom we are working, while at the same time developing theoretical knowledge of value to an academic community involved in research and pedagogy.

Intellectual Merit

Participation with open communities is a real option for many organizations. We provide an in-depth and broad examination of how organizations participate with open communities with respect to contributions and differentiation. In the project, we focus on building intellectual merit across two fronts:

1) *Practical Intellectual Merit*: The findings will be available to organizations interested in developing their participation with the Linux open community. The findings will be linked to existing business practices as tractable recommendations for improved participation for both new organizations and those currently engaged with the Linux open community.

2) *Academic Intellectual Merit*: The findings will be available to researchers interested in theoretical and pedagogical frameworks associated with open communities. The project is differentiated from a broad suite of academic publications by examining the interface between an organization and an open community, and not just an open community itself. By differentiating, opportunities exist for publication of both theoretical and pedagogical frameworks.

Broader Impacts

We aim to make the findings available beyond the organizations and research communities associated with this project. From a practice perspective, we have built numerous access points from which nonparticipating organizations of the project can gain access to the findings in the form of publishing, workshops, and blogs. The findings can aid participation with open communities for organizations who are not currently active in open communities. As open communities provide real options for leveraged development and support, the proposed research could prove useful for organizations seeking lower-cost technology solutions. As cost and access can inhibit technology adoption, open communities promote the philosophy of we all give a little; we all get a lot. From increased and improved participation in open communities we hope to see broader adoption of the public sharing and collaboration technologies they promote. From an academic perspective, we are not limited to the dissemination of findings to the field of information systems and seek to make advancements across fields. The academic findings can prove valuable to both computer science and management disciplines, and efforts will be made to contribute to these fields. Finally, we aim to continue to refine and improve science, technology, engineering, and mathematics (STEM) curriculum. In doing so, we aim to provide exposure to emerging issues in STEM topics and encourage these topics to continue to grow across universities in general and the University of Westerland specifically. University of Westerland, like other universities, is "dedicated to the recruitment, retention, and advancement of a diverse student body, faculty, staff, and administration." As universities make strides in advancing diverse campuses, we hope that projects like the one proposed here can increase the exposure of STEM disciplines to increasingly diverse student bodies.

Not only does this project summary address separately the two merit review criteria of the National Science Foundation, namely, intellectual merit and broader impacts, but it also highlights for reviewers that two types of intellectual merit will be addressed: practical and academic. This degree of precision caught the attention of reviewers.

Example 4

The following is a project abstract written by a university faculty member seeking fellowship support from a nonprofit organization to conduct research on the topic of female mortality disadvantage in India:

> Millions of infant girls die in India due to gender bias in childhood investment. Combined with aborted unwanted female fetuses, they are known as India's missing girls. Prior research has only examined national trends in missing girls. This study contends that the more inferior the status of mother in a patriarchal family, the higher is the mortality risk faced by daughters. India's National Family Health Survey will be

used to: (a) estimate the risk of a girl child becoming a missing girl, and (b) demonstrate the association of this risk with four indicators of mother's status in the family.

This project abstract was particularly challenging to develop: the grantmaker's fillable form limited it to 600 characters with spaces! Nevertheless, in a mere 99 words, it touches on the problem, objective, methods, and outcomes.

WRITING TIPS FOR PROPOSAL ABSTRACTS

1. Don't write the abstract until you have completed the proposal.
2. Unless otherwise indicated, limit your abstract section to between 250 and 500 words.
3. Include at least one sentence each on problem, objectives, methods, and outcomes.
4. Use major headings in the abstract: Problem, Objectives, Methods, and Outcomes.
5. Write to the level of expertise of the audience, whether specialists or generalists.
6. Limit use of technical jargon, acronyms, and abbreviations to only those that are truly essential.
7. Seek out prepositional phrases—often beginning with "of" and "by"—and see whether the sentence can be revised to be shorter with more punch.
8. Use action verbs instead of forms of "be" and "have" whenever possible.
9. Do not cross-reference to tables, charts, maps, or illustrations in the proposal narrative; the abstract should be able to stand on its own.
10. Make time to polish your abstract; because abstracts are often the first thing that reviewers read, they establish the mindset for understanding the entire proposal.

REJECTION REASONS

Weak proposal abstracts have caused reviewers to raise the following concerns:

1. The applicant raises points in the abstract that are not explained in the proposal narrative.
2. The abstract was unclear and raised questions at the outset that were subsequently confirmed upon reading the narrative. This proposal simply is not well reasoned.
3. The applicant ignored the 100-word limitation on the abstract. In fact, the entire proposal is rather verbose.

GRANT GAFFES

A grant gaffe typical to abstracts occurs when the abstract is written prior to the proposal narrative. The annotated example in Exhibit 82 is taken from a government proposal to increase the number of first-generation, low-income, and diversity students who pursue higher education. As you can see, the abstract is pretty vanilla, offering no real specifics about the need for the project or the outcomes to be realized. This might be considered "prewriting," where ideas were simply being put down on paper (or the computer), rather than an executive summary of the entire project.

A real education means learning what you live and living what you learn. That's what we hope to impact with "College Bound." Beginning in 6th grade, students and parent will begin to cultivate a seven-year plan with the aim of increasing college matriculation. Having just traveled by bus three hours round trip to visit the closest university in 5th grade, the possibility of higher education will have been revealed to them. Using the College Bound program's special software, families will forecast classes for their child's future as well as explore careers and colleges. School counselors will also work closely with families in order for all involved to understand the higher education process, along with the hard work that it takes to get there.

The lack of attention to document design—headings, boldface type, and bulleted lists to create emphasis—stands out. It is not immediately apparent to reviewers that the abstract even attempted to touch on each of the major sections of the proposal. At the micro level, reviewers begin to experience dissonance as soon as the second sentence: it is unclear to whom the "we" refers. It is further unclear why the second sentence describes a project serving 6th–12th grade students but the third sentence describes a field trip in which 5th graders participate. At the macro level, reviewers struggle with a paragraph that proposes a "solution"—increasing college matriculation—without describing the "problem" situation.

College Bound will be offered free of charge to all students throughout middle school and high school, with an emphasis on first-generation, low-income and diversity students. The program walks students through life purpose planning and principles of success as well as connects students to their communities through community service. High school students will explore civic engagement opportunities and learn to meet the criteria, apply for, and receive scholarships. Of the $1.25 million in scholarships available to students from Ramsey High School, students who have participated in the College Bound program earned 37% of the total scholarship dollars. We are grateful for the scholarship support but are frustrated that awards represent only 15% of students (38/253).

The second paragraph continues to describe the project, namely the target audience to be served and key program activities. And yet, the paragraph lacks detail. Reviewers do not know how many students are in grades 6–12; the percentages who are first generation, low income, and/or of diversity backgrounds; and, the number who are targeted to be served by the proposed project. Ironically, the specific details in the final two sentences focus on money (i.e., scholarships) as an end in itself rather than as a means to the desired end (i.e., increasing college matriculation), which undermines the other humanistic appeals in the abstract.

GRANT GAFFES

EXHIBIT 82

Of the five paragraphs in the abstract, this third one is the most powerful. It includes important statistical information that begins to document the frequency and severity of the problem. It speaks with the details federal reviewers are trained to look for in a proposal. However, paragraphs three, four, and five are much shorter and less interconnected than paragraphs one and two. The tone of the whole abstract should be more along the lines of this paragraph—logical and factual—than the outwardly humanistic appeals of, "We're good people doing good things, please give us money."

While reviewers will surely agree that trusting relationships are important to students' educational success, the fourth paragraph of the abstract continues to communicate in generalities. It does not identify sample workshop topics, nor quantify the number or duration of contacts that will be held and allow these bonds to begin to forge. The second sentence, for example, could be enhanced greatly with the addition of a mere 11 words to read: "Through a series of monthly, hour-long workshops with age-appropriate interactive exercises, such as role-playing activities on self-control, College Bound teaches students that all actions have consequences."

The fifth paragraph continues to appeal directly to reviewers' emotions. The first two sentences of this paragraph, however, seem to be more self-reaffirming rather than an effort to persuade the sponsor to invest in the proposed project. This abstract is full of passion, but it is short on specifics. Future iterations of the abstract may bring greater balance to the appeal to logic versus the appeal to emotion.

On our most recent senior survey, nearly 95% of high school students indicate their intent to pursue higher education immediately after graduation. In reality, the average over the past six years is closer to 35%. Clearly a disconnect exists between plans and practice. Also disconcerting is that of students who do go on to college, only 18% graduate within six years.

With the benefit of time, adults know the key to success is self-discipline; too many of our students do not understand this concept. Through a series of workshops and interactive exercises, College Bound teaches students that all actions have consequences. Community leaders welcome the opportunity to present these workshops. Trusting relationships are essential in supporting students throughout their educational experience; the long-term impact of encouraging words can never be underestimated.

We are doing good things. We want to do great things. With grant support, College Bound can break down the barriers that prevent students from pursuing higher education; students will see firsthand that through learning and hard work, they can change how they live.

GRANT GAFFES

EXHIBIT 82 (Continued from page 217)

STARTER SENTENCES

Greater than 90 percent of your abstract should be sentences lifted from your proposal narrative. Nevertheless, the following sample sentences might help jumpstart writing your abstract:

1. Community Eats, the only food bank in west central Ohio, invites your investment of $xx,xxx to alleviate hunger in Seneca County.

2. Obesity in the United States has become epidemic: more than one-third of adults and approximately one-fifth of children are obese. North Carolina ranks #16 in the nation with the percentage of adults and children who are obese and overweight.

3. In partnership with the University of Noodlenoggin, the Center for Big Brains aims to increase the mathematics and reading achievement of Native American students in grades 4–8.

4. The Community Health Rankings recently bestowed a dubious honor on Cook County: the worst possible community health score in the state. Residents suffer from high rates of cardiovascular disease, type 2 diabetes, cancer, and premature death.

5. The purpose of this pilot program is to engage, educate, and encourage African American teens to make healthy decisions about sexual health behaviors.

6. The Central School District seeks a grant of $xx,xxx to enhance the teaching skills of K-12 educators who work with children with disabilities.

7. According to a recently completed general preservation assessment survey, environmental monitoring is required immediately to preserve the library's special collections, which include a significant number of pre-1600 and pre-1700 imprints. The goal of this project is to improve the environmental climate surrounding these rare materials through training and the purchase and installation of environmental monitoring equipment.

8. Social inequality and income growth varies considerably more across households in developing economies than conventional economic factors can explain. The researchers undertaking this interdisciplinary research project hypothesize that environmental, social, cultural, and historical variations interact with economic factors to. . .

9. With foundations in three existing campus service/leadership programs, the "First Year Student Program" is a new initiative that integrates citizenship and scholarship through these primary goals: (1) Improve retention rates and academic success of first-generation and low-income students who transfer from two-year institutions; (2) Develop a peer network that enables students to serve as agents of civic engagement to respond effectively to local community issues; and (3) Foster a deep appreciation of democratic values and citizenship among students.

10. Griffin College requests $xx,xxx to improve teaching about Islam in the Independent School District. This grant will enable yy in-service teachers to participate in a comprehensive graduate seminar series on Islam, broadening their knowledge of beliefs and practices and helping them translate that knowledge into improved classroom instruction for zz,zzz students. Curriculum planning for the seminar series will begin in September 2014, with the seminars and the ensuing dissemination to the wider education community to be completed by December 2015.

Clip File Action Item # 19
Abstracts

Following are some action items to build your Abstracts clip file:

- Gather sample abstracts of successfully funded proposals, regardless of subject matter.
- Collect examples of document design principles that will enhance your abstract: use of headings, white space, and layout.

PART IV
The Final Steps

At this point in the proposal development process, you have identified potential sponsors (Chapters 2–3) and selected one who might be interested in supporting your project (Chapter 4). It's now time to put your thoughts and ideas on paper—or the computer screen.

Establish some reasonable writing objectives. Don't try to do everything at once. Chunk it up. Whether you are writing a grant or your first novel, successful writers stress the importance of getting the first draft down on paper as quickly as possible, even if you would not want to share it with anybody. It doesn't have to be good, just down—in writing.

Successful grantseekers estimate they spend 25 percent of their time writing the first draft and 75 percent of their time editing it. Editing is a multistage process: edit for only one feature at a time. The multiple loops through the proposal ensure that all elements are presented with punch and persuasion.

Chapters 5 through 15 offer many key questions that you should be asking yourself as you write a particular proposal section. Additionally, review the examples for ideas on approaches to take and reflect on the grant gaffes and rejection reasons for things to avoid.

In Part IV, our attention turns to the final steps. Chapter 16 focuses on creating your first draft and then doing a thorough job of editing. Once your first draft is written, you can spend the bulk of your proposal writing time editing and polishing your document. The latter portions of Chapter 16 offer numerous editing suggestions. You want to edit with "tunnel vision"; that is, keep your focus on only one feature per pass through the entire draft, such as clarity of sentences, punctuation, organization, or document design.

Remember that no matter how many times you have cycled through the draft looking for specific linguistic glitches, you are apt to miss something. It is extremely difficult to edit your own copy; you end up reading what you intended to write instead of what is actually written. Accordingly, recruit someone with good linguistic intuitions to provide an objective, second pair of eyes on your text.

Finally, Chapter 17 discusses the next steps—after your proposal has been submitted. We describe the review process, including site visits, and dealing with grant decisions. In the grants arena, there are no guarantees of funding. Recognize, however, that a "no" from a sponsor does not mean they will "never" fund you; rather, it may mean "not right now." Based on sponsor feedback, you may consider reviewing and resubmitting your proposal in a future cycle. Persistence pays.

CHAPTER 16
Writing and Editing Techniques

No grantsmanship will turn a bad idea into a good one, but there are many ways to disguise a good one.
—*William Raub*

OVERVIEW

As a proposal writer, your job is to "out-imagine" the reviewers.

You need to present your best ideas persuasively. There are many ways to disguise a great idea, as Dr. Raub notes. All too often, proposals do just that—they cleverly mask, albeit unintentionally, a novel idea that reviewers ultimately reject. As a proposal writer, your job is to write a highly readable proposal, one that is persuasive, stylistically appropriate, and free of jargon. In Chapter 16, you will learn the following:

- Tips for starting to write and for writing collaboratively.
- Strategies for identifying hot buttons in RFPs.
- A process for systematically editing proposals.
- Simple tools to help you find and fix weak sentences.
- The value of paying attention to document design considerations.

Your proposal should analyze a significant problem, propose an effective solution, and communicate your credibility. A well-written proposal will always have a competitive edge. Skill in proposal writing cannot compensate for a weak project, but it can provide the extra measure of quality that distinguishes a high-quality proposal from its competition.

PROPOSAL WRITING TIPS

Are you ready to start writing? Before your turn on your computer, ask yourself these questions:

1. Do I have an experienced and well-credentialed project director? (Chapter 4).

2. Have I had preproposal contacts with program officers, past grant winners, and prior reviewers? (Chapter 4).
3. Do I have a clearly focused and innovative idea? (Chapter 7).
4. Do I have access to data that will document the frequency and severity of the problem my organization wishes to address? (Chapter 7).
5. Have I developed my idea in detail? (Chapter 7).
6. Have I compared the application guidelines with the reviewer's evaluation form? (Chapter 10).
7. Do I have active buy-in from project collaborators? (Chapter 14).

If you have seven "yes" answers, then you may be ready to write, but not before. The agony of staring at a blank computer screen—it's a feeling all grant writers have experienced. Just how should you get started? Your mental preparation should remind you that the first draft is for getting down, not for getting good. Type anything, even if it doesn't make sense. Eventually some cohesion will emerge and you can later delete the garbage copy.

As you begin to write, you will occasionally grope for the perfect word or phrase. If so, insert a *** at the place where you experience trouble and keep on going. When you have completed the first draft, activate your word processor's find command and let it identify the fill-in-the-blank places.

Don't try to do all of your writing in one setting, or in an intensive manner. You lose the benefit of two processes that are important to persuasive writing. One is the perspective that can come only with percolation time. If you back away from the project for 24 hours, you will have a clearer view when you return to it. The second process is that of testing a limited part of the project against the overall project structure. That happens when you force yourself to consider only one segment of the project at a time. Work on your idea in small pieces.

If you're still stuck, take a break. Over the years, we've informally surveyed grant writers about the strategies they use to overcome writer's block. The most common answer is that they take a break. What we've found interesting is what they do when they take a break. Billie takes a walk. Courtney prefers a quick yoga practice to dislodge words. Sam reviews prior successful grants. Susan prefers munching down prewashed baby carrots. Mike creates an outline from the RFP and pastes the review criteria into the outline in a different color to help focus the writing task. Caroline prefers to grin and bear it; she says those awful minutes of sitting are actually part of the writing process that allows her brain to synthesize complex information. Pat says when her brain turns to guacamole, she talks to someone who has no understanding of her project, thereby forcing her to explain it in understandable language. Steve prefers to play solitaire on the computer while he thinks it through. Griffin changes mediums until inspiration strikes, writing longhand on paper and dictating ideas into his smart phone. If none of these suggestions work for you, remember the worst thing you write is better than the best thing you never write.

Successful grantseekers emphasize the importance of quickly completing the first proposal draft, so that most of their writing time is actually spent on editing—polishing the proposal. Write your first draft quickly and spend much more time on editing and revising. Experienced grant writers usually submit their ninth or tenth draft for proposal review. If you are submitting draft number 3 (or 4 or 5), you are at a competitive disadvantage. Your editing skills will make the difference between a "good" proposal and a "great" one.

Collaborative Writing

Sometimes, several writers will collaborate to develop a grant proposal. This occurs when time is short, the project is sizeable, or multiple areas of expertise are required. To produce a coherent proposal, one person must be designated as the lead writer. Experience shows that the leadership skills of the head writer will determine the coherence and persuasiveness of the final proposal draft. All writers should work from an agreed-upon outline. Writing assignments must be delegated and deadlines established. Segments must be exchanged for review and comment. Revisions must be made in a timely manner to meet established deadlines.

Often people writing proposal sections on collaborative grants are in different locations. Proposal drafts can be prepared in a word processor and swapped via e-mail or shared in cloud storage. When writing a proposal draft, use "Track Changes" (Microsoft Word) or "Compare" (WordPerfect) commands to strike through words that should be deleted and add new copy in a different color type. This way, it is easy to identify precisely changes that have been made between an original and edited text. Later, you can accept or reject the proposed changes, as you wish. Other tools to write and edit documents are Dropbox (www.dropbox.com) and Google Drive (http://drive.google.com).

Avoid overreliance on a committee when writing. While you should seek reactions to proposal drafts from many readers, one person should be responsible for writing the proposal and have the authority to make final decisions when inevitable contradictory suggestions emerge. Further, not all committee members will share your timeline responsibilities; failure to get timely feedback demoralizes proposal writers, especially when writing under deadline. Use a committee to critique your proposals, but let it be known clearly where the "buck stops."

ADVANCED PROPOSAL WRITING TIPS

Computational linguistics uses computer science techniques to analyze and synthesize language. You don't have to be a computer scientist or a linguist to use some existing available tools to help you work smarter, not harder, to increase your proposal persuasiveness. Two specific online tools that you can use for free include:

- Word Frequency Counter (http://writewords.org.uk/word_count.asp)
- Phrase Frequency Counter (http://writewords.org.uk/phrase_count.asp)

One major computational linguistic application involves analyzing the frequency of word occurrence. Before you start writing your proposal, you should scrutinize the application guidelines. Commonly, the grant opportunity announcement contains the "heart" of what the grantmaker is looking for and information about how to apply. Words and phrases will be emphasized repeatedly in the Request for Proposal (RFP) and preproposal contact—they are sponsor hot buttons. These primary concerns affect the shape of a project's structure and implementation processes. Hot buttons are not always stated as evaluation criteria, yet may appear as recurring themes, such as accountability, collaboration, communication, cost effectiveness, outcomes, participation, replication, and sustainability. The word and phrase frequency counters can help you pinpoint sponsor hot buttons.

The tools are exceptionally easy to use. Block copy the RFP and paste it into the frequency counters. Clicking "submit" will then produce an ordered list of words and phrases that appear in the text from most to least frequently occurring. As you review the list, ignore little words like prepositions and articles. Instead, concentrate on the nouns, verbs, adjectives, and adverbs that appear repeatedly. These higher frequency words and phrases may form the basis for themes to develop in your proposal that will appeal to sponsor hot buttons. Of note, while you can set the phrase counter to search for long strings, usually two- or three-word strings will reveal the hot button phrases that you will want to sprinkle throughout your narrative.

After you've finished a complete draft of your proposal, you should block copy the narrative and paste it into the frequency counters. Clicking "submit" will, once again, produce an ordered list of words and phrases that appear in the text from most to least frequently occurring. The hot button words and phrases that you identified in your RFP analysis should also be appearing with considerable frequency in your proposal. While there is no magic number of times that the themes should appear, experience suggests one or more times per page of the narrative. This advanced writing tip helps you establish a level of trust and understanding with the sponsor because you are communicating to them directly that you share the same values.

GENERAL EDITING SUGGESTIONS

Put your initial draft aside for 24 hours before editing to give you a fresh perspective. Edit copy that is double- or triple-spaced; this format invites you to make changes. Be completely brutal with your first draft. Nothing should satisfy you. Delete. Substitute. Rearrange. Insert. Be especially critical of the first few paragraphs. You probably had not warmed up at that stage. Read aloud for content and style. When it comes to detecting errors, the ear is more efficient than the eye. Don't be the only one to proofread and edit your work. The odds of spotting errors increase with each new pair of eyes. Don't view editing as a time waster, even when time is tight. Your credibility is at stake whenever you send out a proposal.

As you begin to edit, cycle through the proposal many times, each time looking for something different.

Experienced grantseekers follow a four-step editing process, which looks at content, clarity, mechanics, and design.

Content and Organization

Did you include all of the content information in the order requested in the application guidelines and on the reviewer's evaluation form?

Be sure you didn't leave out major parts that could help reviewers gain a better understanding of your proposal. Did you include a persuasive need statement, measurable objectives, process and outcome evaluation measures, table of contents, page numbers, and appropriate appendixes, including résumés? Does your proposal present a logical flow of ideas?

Clarity

Is all of the necessary content clear and persuasive?

Purge each phrase of extraneous words. Weed out unnecessary words. Choose concrete words instead of abstract ones whenever possible. Make sure technical terms, jargon, and abbreviations are defined. Avoid vague adjectives. Is your average sentence length about 15–20 words? Does your proposal flow smoothly with appropriate use of transitional words, sentences, and paragraphs?

Mechanics

Is your proposal structurally unblemished?

Ensure your writing is mechanically flawless by checking the following: punctuation, spelling, pronoun agreement, verb agreement, numbers, paragraph length (1.25 inch maximum), omitted words, word choice, and passive constructions.

Design

Does your proposal look inviting to read?

Look at your proposal for appearance. Have you used adequate white space, distinctive headings and subheadings, and lists to invite skim reading? Are margins at least one inch? Have appropriate devices been used to indicate proposal structure: headings, bullets, numbers, bolding, indentations, and spacing?

Do not sacrifice proposal design in favor of including more text. Rather than reducing type size or eliminating white space, edit sentences for clarity, eliminating extra words wherever possible.

INITIAL EDITING TIPS

Below you will find a number of editing tips that are usually overlooked in the initial proposal drafting. Collectively, these suggestions can significantly strengthen your proposal.

Headings

Headings and subheadings act like a table of contents placed directly in your proposal text; that is, at a glance they reveal the main ideas and the organization of your proposal to the reader. Ask your program officer for a copy of the reviewer's evaluation form, and use those same headings and subheadings in your proposal. If a reviewer's evaluation form is not available, use headings and subheadings that are specific to your proposal. Generic headings such as "Introduction," "Background," "Materials," "Methods," "Results," "Conclusions," and "Recommendations" are not unique to your proposal. Short, specific headers such as these will have more impact on your readers:

- **The Problem: Overcoming Distance Barriers**
- **Eliminating the Shock Waves**
- **Our Credentials: 125 Years of National Experience**
- **Benefits of Youth Programming**
- **Capabilities: 75 New Volunteers**

Specific headings give reviewers an overview of your entire project, even if they are merely skimming your proposal. Note that the headings are in a different type style (Arial Boldface in the above examples) than the proposal text (Times New Roman in this paragraph).

Levels of Organization

You can use vertical and horizontal white space to create up to three levels of organizational headings. Do not use more than three levels of headings because you may lose the reader in the structural detail of your proposal. Effective use of white space sets off headings and enhances readability.

- Level one headings should be centered, sans serif type face (e.g., Arial), all capital letters, and 12-point boldface font; double spaced before further text follows.
- Level two headings should be left justified, sans serif type face (e.g., Arial), keywords capitalized and italized, 12-point boldface font. Single space before further text follows.
- Level three headings should be indented, serif typeface (e.g., Times New Roman), keywords capitalized, and 12-point boldface font. Punctuate and continue with paragraph copy.

Exhibit 83 is an example of all three levels of headers:

Level one headings signal new topic areas, whereas levels two and three indicate subtopics within level one. The headings should be concise but informative. Too few or too many headings challenge the reviewer to recognize the proposal structure.

THIS IS A LEVEL ONE HEADING

The rest of the proposal would continue here.

This Is a Level Two Heading

The rest of the proposal would continue here.

  This Is a Level Three Heading. The rest of the proposal would continue here.

Note the spacing between the three heading levels. This visual chunking strategy is highly readable and facilitates reviewer skimming.

LEVELS OF HEADINGS

EXHIBIT 83

Line Length and Margin Width

Lines approximately 65 characters long are preferred from the standpoint of readability. Physiologic studies of the eye suggest this line length is comfortable to read without inducing fatigue. The line length relates to the standard one-inch margins used in proposals. While smaller margins allow more words per page, the proposal narrative becomes too difficult to read.

References and Bibliographies

All too often, the documentation of key proposal points is left to the last minute and assembled in a hurried fashion. A better alternative is to develop your citations as you write, something that is easy to do when you have convenient and simple systems for organizing and displaying your supporting documents. While many good commercial software programs exist for publishing and managing bibliographies, citations, and references, we often use the free, open-source program from Zotero (www.zotero.com). Zotero can display bibliography materials according to 17 different style manuals.

There is no one "right" style manual to follow. Checking with the program officer or reviewing prior successful proposals may offer some clues. Perhaps the most important consideration is consistency of style, something easily accomplished with bibliographic software, which has the added advantage of one-click software to insert citations in the text as well as generate a reference list or bibliography at the end of the proposal.

One final reference citation tip: Some grant writers prefer to use a superscript numbered citation when documenting a statement in the proposal narrative, such as, "Research[1] shows that focus groups are an effective approach to gather patient reported outcomes." While the superscript notation approach is a space saver, it forces the reviewers to break their reading fluency and jump to the reference list to learn the citation before returning to the narrative and continuing to read. Inserting the author and year, avoids the fluency break: "Research (Smith and Wesson, 2012) shows that focus groups are an effective approach to gather patient reported outcomes." This version is more convenient for the reviewer but does consume a bit more space, for which tight editing can overcome this constraint. Remember, you are writing for the reviewer, not for yourself.

Sentence Length

While sentence length varies, limit each sentence to 15 words or less on the average. If you have any sentences over 30 words, they are too long to track easily. Hold your draft copy in your hand and walk around the room at a fast pace while reading it aloud. If you have to fight for breath in the middle of any sentence, it is too long.

Too Long: The elastic fabric surrounding the circular frame whose successive revolutions bear you onward in space has lost its pristine roundness.

Better: You have a flat tire.

Sexist Language

Use nonsexist language to prevent excluding others. Instead of "chairman," consider "chair" or "chairperson." Change "man hours" to "staff hours." "Policeman" can become "police officer." Replace "mankind" with "humanity" or "people."

Pronoun problems with "s/he" or "his or her" can usually be avoided by shifting the entire sentence to the plural form: "they" or "them." Write with a sense of dignity, equality, and appropriateness for both sexes.

Sexist: Every participant will complete his evaluation form at the end of the program.

Nonsexist: Participants will complete their evaluation forms at the end of the program.

Transitional Words and Phrases

Transitional expressions—words and phrases that signal connections among ideas—can help you achieve coherence in your writing. Each expression is a signal to the reader that explains how one idea is connected to the next. Business writers suggest that the use of transitions makes the difference between average and persuasive copy. Common transitional words and phrases can indicate:

- *Addition*: also, in addition, again, and, and then, too, besides, further, furthermore, equally important, what's more, next, then, finally, likewise, moreover, first, second, third, last, indeed, more precisely
- *Comparison*: similarly, likewise, in like manner, in the same way, in comparison
- *Concession*: after all, although this may be true, at the same time, even though, of course, to be sure, certainly, naturally, granted

- *Contrast*: but, yet, however, on the other hand, nevertheless, nonetheless, conversely, in contrast, on the contrary, still, at the same time, after all, although true, and yet, in spite of, notwithstanding
- *Example*: for example, for instance, thus, as an illustration, namely, specifically, in particular, incidentally, indeed, in fact, in other words, said differently, that is, to illustrate, of note
- *Location*: in the front, in the foreground, in the back, in the background, at the side, adjacent, nearby, in the distance, here, there
- *Restriction*: despite, contrary to, although, while, provided, in case, if, lest, when, occasionally, even if, never
- *Result*: therefore, thus, consequently, so, accordingly, due to this, as a result, hence, in short, otherwise, then, truly, that caused, that produced
- *Sequence*: first, firstly, second, secondly, third, thirdly, next, then, finally, afterward, before, soon, later, during, meanwhile, subsequently, immediately, at length, eventually, in the future, currently, after a short time, as soon as, at last, at the same time, earlier, in the meantime, lately, presently, since, temporarily, thereafter, thereupon, until, when, while
- *Summary*: as a result, hence, in short, in brief, in summary, in conclusion, finally, on the whole, to conclude, to sum up, thus, therefore, as a consequence, at last
- *Time*: now, later, meanwhile, since then, after that, before that time

Transitional Sentences and Paragraphs

To ensure that your proposal reads smoothly and fluently, use transitional sentences and paragraphs. They blend separate proposal segments into one continuously flowing copy. Insert them wherever you are making major content shifts within your proposal. These overview paragraphs provide signals that the current ideas are shifting to something else; often they summarize what was just read and foreshadow what is coming next.

1. A transitional bridge from a problem section to a solution section in the proposal:

> In sum, a combination of school and community poverty, health disparities, and shortage of health care providers are preventing children from leading healthy lifestyles. School-based health centers can bridge these gaps in order to provide comprehensive primary and preventive health care to this medically underserved community.

This transition paragraph reminds reviewers of the problems as a prelude to discussing solutions.

2. An introductory statement to a methodology section:

> This section summarizes our plans and is supplemented with concise statements that provide the motivation behind this plan of action.

This sentence does two things: it foreshadows for the reviewer what the upcoming proposal section is all about, and it alerts the reviewer that the rationale for selecting this particular methodology section will be explained, an important inclusion that is often overlooked.

3. A proposal section that helped establish the credibility of the project codirectors:

> One added value of the codirectors is that they have experienced the challenges of managing multifaceted projects; they know what works and doesn't work. Based on this experience, and a concern that reviewers might feel the codirectors are already "overextended," considerable thought has gone into this carefully crafted project organizational structure, which includes strategic highly trained professionals as key support personnel.

This section tells the reviewers that the key project personnel are not only experienced project managers, but also are not overcommitted.

4. A proposal section that alerts the reviewer to the structure of the methodology section:

> Each of these activities is written in a way that is consistent with the agency scoring system.

This sentence signals the reader that the proposal writers obtained a copy of the reviewer's evaluation form from the program officer and follow it in their discussion of the methods section, thereby simplifying the reviewer's task.

5. These proposal writers had a pretty good idea who their competition might be and wanted to position themselves favorably against their competition:

> Our plan of activities is built on a careful reading of the RFP priorities, and of activities of the existing center at the XYZ Institute. While their activities are appropriate, we believe we have the infrastructure in place that enables us to aim higher.

In a very professional manner, this section says "we're better than our competition."

Verb Choice

Use action verbs instead of forms of "be" and "have" whenever possible. Persuasive proposals typically contain no more than 25 percent of passive voice sentences. Although passive-voice verbs add variety to your sentence structure, your proposal becomes dull, weak, hard to read, and filled with useless words if you use too many passives. Passives are a form of the verb "to be" and a past tense form of another verb.

Passive: The homeless are little appreciated by people today.

Active: Today, people don't appreciate the homeless.

Passive: By the year 2020, half of this population is projected to be 75-plus, according to the Census Bureau.

Active: The Census Bureau estimates one-half of the elderly will be over age 75 by the year 2020.

When you write in passive sentences, readers often "rewrite" the sentence into an active form, thereby slowing reader comprehension. When editing, use your computer's find command to locate forms of "be" and "have." Convert passive to active sentences whenever possible, but do not feel guilty about using some passives.

Voice

Once you have started to write, you need to make decisions regarding whether you will write using first person ("I," "we," "me," "us") or third person ("he," "she, "the PI," "they") language.

First Person: I will summarize the research findings before asking for questions.

Third Person: He will first summarize the research findings before asking for questions.

The trend in grant writing is toward the more informal approach, meaning first person usage. That said, since preferences still vary among grantmakers, you may wish to ask during your preproposal contact (See Chapter 4), "Are most of the proposals you receive written in first or third person?" If they have a preference, they will express it; if not, the choice is yours. Your grant writing intent should be to send a familiar document because a familiar document is a friendly document.

White Space

Use white space to break up long copy. Ample white space makes your proposal appear inviting and user friendly. In addition, white space gives readers a visual clue to the structure of your proposal. That is, in a page full of print, a block of unprinted lines, or white space, stands out immediately. White space can indicate that one section is ending and another is beginning, or that an idea is so central to the proposal that it needs to be set off by itself. Judicious use of white space breaks your proposal into smaller, manageable "chunks" of information. Some grant writers recommend that up to 50 percent of each page should be white space. To open up white space in your proposal, consider these suggestions:

- Indent five spaces at the start of new paragraphs.
- Limit paragraph length to an average of eight single-spaced lines (or no longer than the distance between the first and second knuckle on your index finger).
- Insert a blank line of space between minor proposal segments.
- Insert two blank lines of space between major proposal segments.

Finally, when writing proposals, demonstrate the capability to carry out the proposed activities and stress the impact of the project on others. For example, one effective corporate proposal started out:

Fifty-one percent of the community, 58 percent of the company's future workers, and 62 percent of the firm's potential stockholders are represented by the applicant.

Needless to say, when set off with white space, this caught the eye of the contributions committee.

TECHNICAL EDITING TIPS

Acronyms

They permeate our existence—we hear them and use them nearly every day. Acronyms are convenient because they allow us to abbreviate multiword terms into a single understandable term. "Sport Utility Vehicle" becomes SUV. "Cable News Network" becomes CNN. "Best Friends Forever" becomes BFF. "Oh My God" becomes OMG.

While shortened versions of words are important space savers, be sure to define your acronyms. When writing grants, abbreviations can mean different things to specialists in different areas. Consider the following examples:

- ADA—to an oral health professional it means "American Dental Association," while to a special education teacher it refers to the "Americans with Disabilities Act."
- BOD—to an executive director of a nonprofit agency it means "Board of Directors," while to a technology specialist it refers to "Bandwidth on Demand."
- CAP—to an environmental specialist it means "Clean Air Plan," while to a social service professional it refers to "Child Abuse Prevention."
- DNR—to a health professional it means "Do Not Resuscitate," while to a conservationist it refers to the "Department of Natural Resources."
- ERA—to a politician it means "Equal Rights Amendment," while to a grant administrator it refers to "Electronic Research Administration."

The first time you use an acronym in a grant proposal, always write out the complete term, followed by the abbreviated form in parentheses. For example, "Sunshine Day Care (SDC) has been servicing the needs of inner city children for over 100 years." In long proposals, however, you can help your readers greatly by repeating the full term periodically—about every third page—so that they do not have to search back to the first time it was used to find its meaning.

Not sure if your acronym has multiple meanings? Check out the Acronym Finder (www.acronymfinder.com), a searchable database of more than a million acronyms and abbreviations.

Color

While high resolution graphics look attractive in proposals, many grantmakers do not reproduce the color in your proposals as they are distributed to reviewers. Generally, you should not rely on colorized visuals to make your proposal arguments. Check with your program officer before including, for example, a line graph showing different colors. Too, remember that some reviewers may be color blind.

Writing Traps

Even skilled proposal writers fall into common writing "traps" that confuse reviewers.

Original: "In fact, we conduct surveys of our clients on a regular basis"
Revision: "In fact, we regularly survey our clients."

The revised sentence solved two problems: the verb-noun trap (conduct surveys) and the prepositional phrase (on a regular basis). The verb-noun trap often occurs when we want our writing to sound very formal or "business-like." This often means that we use more words than necessary. In particular, we use a weak verb and a noun, when the verb by itself is stronger. Some weak verbs include: conduct, perform, and made.

Vary Your Punctuation

Don't limit yourself to periods and commas: that's monotone speech on paper. For example, use questions, especially when you really have one.

"How many of the oldest old adults live alone?"

Then go on to answer the question in your gerontology proposal. It draws the reader in to the paragraph. It controls emphasis; it replaces the hand gestures and voice inflections used in speaking.

Use colons: they point to more useful information about what you just said. Colons are "arrows" that come at the end of sentences.

The elderly face one major barrier to health care: cost.
The elderly face three barriers to health care: cost, transportation, and red tape.
The elderly face one major barrier to health care: service providers are spread out in too many different locations.

You may use the colon to point to a single word, a list, or another complete sentence. Use colons when you want to control emphasis in your proposal.

Use dashes—a remarkably handy way to emphasize important ideas. Dashes tell the reader you are adding something more about what you've just said—an example, an elaboration, or a contradiction. Once regarded as too informal for grant writing, dashes are now fully accepted. They give the reviewer a slightly more informal feel than a colon does.

The elderly face one major barrier to health care—cost.

The elderly face three barriers to health care—cost, transportation, and red tape.

The elderly face one major barrier to health care—service providers are spread out in too many different locations.

You can also use dashes to set off useful information in the middle of a sentence.

Mr. Jones had a heart attack—and a quadruple bypass—two months ago.

Use semicolons; they are more formal than colons and dashes. Grant writers use semicolons much less today than several decades ago. Semicolons separate equal grammatical units. Semicolons are "pivots" that have similar grammatical units on each side, whether those units are independent clauses, dependent clauses, or phrases. Semicolons do not separate unequal units, e.g., an independent clause from a dependent clause.

Cost is one major barrier to health care for the elderly; access to transportation is another hurdle.

This project has the support of many different organizations: Midwest University, a major academic institution; Journey House, a leading community based organization; the Department of Health and Human Services, a county government health unit; and, New Horizons, a citizen's activist group.

Limit Comma Usage. Of all punctuation marks, the comma is the easiest to misuse. Readers generally prefer a style in which commas are kept to a minimum. Too many commas, even when used correctly, can lead to sentences that are hard to read, especially as reviewers skim read often. Edit and rewrite sentences to eliminate excessive commas. The following example reduces a sentence with five commas down to two commas:

Original: Truly, your support, along with that of others, will make a difference in the lives of all the children, parents, and families who participate in this program.

Revision: Your support will make a difference in the lives of over 100 children, parents, and family members per year who participate in this innovative program.

Experiment with these punctuation marks, and others you know: the results will be dramatic.

Sick Sentences

Sick sentences often come about when we write without first conceptualizing the whole project. Here's a concrete example of a sponsor's question, an applicant's response, and our analysis:

Sponsor: Describe how the problem is an advanced and innovative telecommunications-based project and effort to educate the state's residents about the benefits of technology applications.

Applicant: (1) As far as I know, there are no other homebound programs that use telecommunications in this way. (2) There will be obvious advantages for students who cannot come to school if they can still be linked to the school setting. (3) I would estimate that between 15 and 20 students who are confined to their homes will benefit from this project each year. (4) Once we have the project up and running, we will happily share our idea with other school districts and will encourage them to come visit our program to see it work.

Our Sentence-by-Sentence Analysis:
(1) Question: No other programs in the local area? The state? The nation? Which sources did you check to see if any other similar programs existed?
Suggested Improvement: "A review of state K–6 instructional technology programs over the past five years reveals that no homebound programs use telecommunications in this way."
(2) Question: What are these "obvious" advantages?
Suggested Improvement: "Homebound students who are linked to school settings via telecommunications will benefit in two ways: a sense of involvement and increased self-esteem."
(3) Question: Why the shift from the singular pronoun "I" in sentence three to the plural pronoun "we" in sentence four? Is this an individual or collaborative effort?
Suggested Improvement: "This innovative telecommunications project will touch the lives of an estimated 15–20 homebound students annually."
(4) Question: How long will it take to get the project up and running? How do you intend to share information with how many other school districts? How many site visits will you host?
Suggested Improvement: "After the pilot year, we will disseminate a project executive summary, including 'lessons learned,' to 12 local schools in the county. We expect to host site visits from ABC and XYZ Elementary Schools, who also have large numbers of homebound students."

Expressing Action

We were once asked this technical editing question: "Which of three ways is best to express action in your proposals?"

A. "A literature review was conducted."
B. "We conducted a literature review."
C. "I conducted a literature review."

He added: "I assume the passive is uncool; my hunch is that the *I* sounds solo and uncollegial, and that the *we*, implying the involvement of wise and skilled associates, is best. Which sounds cool?"

Our first answer: We pointed out that even with 391 collaborators, we'd write from the point of view of your university as the single point of contact. So, given your three choices, the sentence could be "XYZ University conducted a review." However, we thought there was an even better answer.

Our final answer: We saw no need to emphasize the word *conducted?* An alternative and more powerful sentence could read:

"A thorough review of the literature over the past 10 years revealed. . . ."

This sentence gets away from the action taken and focuses on the results of that action.

Describing Visuals

Including graphs, charts, or tables in your proposal allows you to illustrate information that may be too complex to present in narrative format. However, include graphs, charts, or tables only if they are essential to the central body of the proposal; complicated displays disrupt the reader's fluency.

Make reviewers' jobs easier by describing where in the proposal they should look to find graphs, charts, or tables, rather than simply numbering each illustration. The following are examples of original and revised sentences:

Original: See Exhibit 3.

Revision: Exhibit 3 on page 12 illustrates the proportion of philanthropic giving to health, education, and the arts.

Original: Table 4-2 gives details about chronic health conditions in our state.

Revision: The table below, "Chronic Health Conditions in Our State," details rates per condition per thousand.

Original: We've included a graph that compares enrollment data from the last three years.

Revision: The graph on the following page compares enrollment data from the last three years.

All three revisions help focus the review on the information to which they should pay attention. The titles should be placed just above the visuals and describe concisely what they represent. Box the visuals to set them off rather than "bleed" onto the page.

Plotting Multiple Map Locations

Occasions arise when grant writers want to plot multiple locations on a map. For example, you may wish to establish a food bank service in six local churches and show the location of each site on one map.

Currently, Google Maps only allows you to plot one location. To plot multiple locations, go to http://gmaps.kaeding.name. Scroll down to the box where you can enter one street, city, state, and zip code per line. Click "Submit Query" and you will find your multiple locations "pinned" on Google Map. You can even add descriptive comments on each location, e.g., a specific address, "test site #1," or "Food Bank # 2."

Use of Latin Words

One common mistake that proposal writers make is the use of italics in Latin words or phrases. Three examples are *et al.*, *i.e.*, and *e.g.*.

The Latin designation et al. means "and others" and is used in bibliographic citations such as "Smith et al., 2009." Years ago, style manuals expressed a preference for italicizing Latin abbreviations. This is no longer the case, as the Chicago Manual of Style points out. Some stylists even recommend deleting the period after "al," but we are not prepared to deviate that far from our Latin roots. So, follow this rule: no italics or underlining and one period after the second word: et al.

Two additional Latin abbreviations that frequently occur in grant proposals are "i.e." and "e.g." To the untrained eye, they are interchangeable. In reality, their meanings are slightly different.

The abbreviation "i.e." comes from the Latin phrase *id est* and means "that is." It allows you to clarify a preceding statement by restating or expanding upon an idea.

We will disseminate project results locally and nationally (i.e., at the annual Teacher Educator

Conference on campus and at the Biennial Conference on Education in Washington, DC).

The abbreviation "e.g." comes from the Latin phrase *exempli gratia* and means "for example." It allows you to clarify a preceding statement by force of example.

> At the end of the academic year, students will be required to produce a final product (e.g., a written report, a science project, or art exhibit) as a way of demonstrating what they have learned.

As you write your grant proposals, use "i.e." and "e.g." carefully: the parenthetical explanations that follow can describe exactly what you "will" do or provide examples of what you "may" do. Note that our use of "i.e." and "e.g." did not use italics, only periods after each of the two abbreviation letters.

ADVANCED EDITING TIPS

Simple tools exist to help you find and fix weak sentences. In addition to the spelling and grammar checker in your word processing program, three other tools that are available to you right now are readability statistics, the "find" command, and line numbering. These tools are often underutilized, if they are used at all when editing proposals. The outcome will be shorter narrative copy as you look for ways to increase persuasiveness and, simultaneously, meet taxing page limitations.

Readability Statistics

Analyzing the frequency of word occurrence can facilitate your proposal writing. Analyzing readability statistics can facilitate your proposal editing. Readability tools are built into word processing programs such as Microsoft Word and WordPerfect, and others are available for free online use, such as StoryToolz (www.storytoolz.com).

Once you have completed a draft of your proposal, you can examine its readability, the extent to which it is clear regarding grade level of difficulty, sentence structure, and word usage. The readability statistics in Microsoft Word, for example, provide three sets of values:

1. *Counts*: number of words, number of characters, number of paragraphs, and number of sentences.
2. *Averages*: averages for number of sentences per paragraph, words per sentence, and characters per word.
3. *Readability*: number of passive sentences, Flesch Readability Ease, and Flesch-Kincaid Grade Level.

StoryToolz, on the other hand, provides a more detailed analysis using four readability values:

1. *Reading Levels*: Flesch-Kincaid Grad Level, Automated Readability Index, Coleman-Liau, Flesch Reading Ease, Gunning Fog Index, Laesbarhed Index Formula, SMOG Index, and Average Grade Level.
2. *Sentence Information*: number of characters, number of words, characters per word, syllables per word, number of sentences, words per sentence, number of short sentences, number of long sentences, number of paragraphs, sentences per paragraph, number of questions, number of passive sentences, and longest sentence, shortest sentence.
3. *Word Usage*: number of "to be" verbs, number of auxiliary verbs, number of conjunctions, number of pronouns, number of prepositions, and number of nominalizations.
4. *Sentence Beginnings*: pronouns, interrogative pronouns, articles, subordinating conjunctions, conjunctions, and prepositions.

Regardless of the readability statistical tool you use, you must decide which indices are most useful for you. In our experience, the grade level indices provide comparable values; we look at them to see if the grade level values appear appropriate for the reviewers. Among the sentence information, we pay particular attention to the words per sentence (target: 25 words), sentences per paragraph (target: 8–12), number of passive sentences (target: under 25 percent), and longest sentence (target: under 50 words). In terms of word usage, we aim to keep the number of "to be" verbs small because they are usually embedded in passive voice sentences. We also examine the use of prepositions because they represent potential places to reduce sentence length. Finally, we minimize the use of the six sentence beginnings values to keep persuasive punch in the sentences by starting out with a strong subject/verb combination. All of these recommendations should be interpreted flexibly and will vary depending on your reviewers. Higher readability statistics might be found, for example, in basic science research proposals to federal agencies compared to service delivery proposals to local community foundations.

"Find" Command

A powerful tool in your word processing program that can help increase the persuasiveness of your proposal is your "search" or "find" command. With it, you can quickly locate and edit sentences waiting to be tweaked. The following examples illustrate the types of problems to search out:

Verbs Hiding Inside Nouns. Locate sentences where verbs hide inside of nouns. Such words often end with "ance," "ants," "ence," "ents," and "tion."

Original Sentence:	Dr. Calder will conduct an investigation of the leading causes of Type 1 diabetes.
Revised Sentence:	Dr. Calder will investigate the leading causes of Type 1 diabetes.
Original Sentence:	Theresa will perform an evaluation of the program's effectiveness.
Revised Sentence:	Theresa will evaluate the program's effectiveness.
Original Sentence:	The board of directors made a decision to support his new research endeavor.
Revised Sentence:	The board of directors decided to support his new research endeavor.
Second Revision:	The board of directors supports his new research endeavor.

Words like "conduct," "perform," and "make" combine with nouns and become weak verbs when the verb form of the noun communicates the same idea more persuasively. Verbs pack the persuasive punch in proposals.

Weak Words. As writers, we are all guilty of using weak words. One word used a lot with little impact is "very." In an early draft of a recent proposal, we wrote, "This is a very important idea." The word "very" tells little about the significance of the idea. We rewrote the sentence to read, "This idea is crucial."

Another weak word often used is "good." "That is a good idea" could be rewritten as "That concept is valuable."

The same holds true for "regular." "The project director will hold regular meetings with collaborators" can be revised to say, "The project director will

hold monthly teleconferences and quarterly in-person meetings with collaborators."

Search out those weak words, or better yet, delete words like "very," "good," "regular," and "important" from your spell checker dictionary. Reason: each time you spellcheck a document, your word processor will point out the offending words as misspelled, and you'll have a chance to change them.

Double Negatives. Although double negatives are widely used in colloquial speech, avoid using them in your proposal writing. Double negatives are an awkward way of reinforcing a negative meaning. Moreover, reviewers who skim read proposals may miss the second negative, thus altering your intended meaning.

To eliminate double negatives, find incidences of "not" and "un," and then revise the sentences accordingly. Consider the following:

Original:	Physicians are not unfamiliar with asthma protocols, yet they continue to underdiagnose this chronic health condition.
Revised:	Although physicians are familiar with asthma protocols, they continue to underdiagnose this chronic health condition.
Original:	It is not uncommon for youthful victims of violence to experience feelings of sadness, loneliness, and isolation.
Revised:	Youthful victims of violence frequently experience feelings of sadness, loneliness, and isolation.

Since the use of double negatives in a sentence cancel each other out, use the positive form instead.

Subjective Adjectives. Principal investigators and project directors must establish their credibility. But how much is too much? How do you communicate your credibility to reviewers without overdoing it?

Below, we list three original sentences from proposals we've been asked to edit, followed by our suggested revisions:

Original:	We have been extremely successful in adapting instructional materials to communicate engineering and information technology issues to undergraduate students.

Revision: We have 10 years of experience in adapting instructional materials to communicate engineering and information technology issues to science undergraduate students.

Original: The PI and his research team have had remarkable success developing teaching materials dealing with information technology.

Revision: The PI and his research team of four science educators have developed eight multimedia information technology teaching materials in the last five years that have been adopted in 50 universities.

Original: Furthermore, the PI has a strong affiliation with an online educational resource laboratory.

Revision: Additionally, the PI has an established track record of collaboration with an online educational research collaboration; we signed our memorandum of understanding in 2011, and it has led to 12 joint projects in the area of undergraduate instructional materials.

The biggest problem in these braggadocio sentences is a misuse of adjectives. The PI used subjective adjectives (extremely successful, remarkable success, strong affiliation) instead of objective adjectives. Especially with federal proposals, you want reviewers to draw the conclusions after you present the objective facts. Each revision above shifted from the subjective to the objective use of adjectives.

That and Which. That and which are two words often misused. We'll avoid here the technical writing perspectives on restrictive and nonrestrictive clauses and simply say "which" commonly requires a comma and "that" doesn't.

Scientists understand *that* basic research does not yield immediate results.
Basic research, *which* does not yield immediate results, is important to the future of science. Linus Pauling, *who* helped develop the polio vaccine, was a Nobel Prize winner.

That and *which* refer to things and animals, whereas *who* refers to people.

"Only." To avoid ambiguity, the word "only" should be placed immediately before the word or phrase it modifies. Varying the placement of "only" can change the meaning of a sentence. Consider:

Example 1: Only Midwest University offers tuition support to its students. (No other universities offer support to students.)

Example 2: Midwest University only offers tuition support to its students. (No other type of support is available.)

Example 3: Midwest University offers tuition support only to its students. (Students must attend Midwest University to be eligible for support.)

Use "only" correctly so the reviewer doesn't have to figure out what you mean. Find out where the word "only" occurs in your proposal and be sure it is properly placed to ensure its intended meaning in the sentences.

"There is/are" and "Here is/are." Sentences that begin with "There is" and "There are" are often weak structures. They prevent the verb from carrying a full sentence load.

Original: There is no easy solution to this problem.

Revision: The problem is not solved easily.

Experienced grant writers often use sentence starter phrases such as "there is/are" and "here is/are" to quickly generate first draft copy. However, since those structures are weak, use the find command to strengthen the sentences during proposal editing.

Original: As we begin our fifth year, there are several problems facing our agency.

Revision: As we begin our fifth year, three problems face our agency: increasing service demand, decreasing resources, and an inadequate infrastructure.

Linking Verbs. Linking verbs join the subject and predicate in sentences. While they bond the two major parts of a sentence, linking verbs also rob color, energy, and force from the sentence.

Original: Our agency has two types of clients it serves.

Revision: Our agency serves two types of clients.

Notice that linking verbs stand alone and are not joined by other verbs.

Original: Mrs. Smith is a volunteer in our clinic.

Revision: Mrs. Smith volunteers in our clinic.

Linking verbs are forms of "to be" (be, being, been, am, is, are, was, were) or "to have" (has, have, had). Sometimes these verb forms appear with other verbs, such as "She was applying" or "He had traveled." Used that way, they are helping verbs, not linking verbs. Limit yourself to using no more than 30 percent of linking verbs in your proposal sentences.

"Make" Verbs. A common offender of the verb phrase is the use of the word "make" (present tense) or "made" (past tense). Examples follow in Exhibit 84. Use your find command to locate and revise "make" and "made" verb constructions.

Prepositions. Use your computer find command to seek out prepositions: about, above, across, after, at, before, by, during, for, from, in, of, on, over, since, to, until, with. Often, you can revise the sentence and save a word or two.

Original: Community forums are small, informal educational programs offered by our organization at neighborhood centers, churches, and community-based organizations.

Revision (saves two words): Our organization hosts community forums, small informal educational programs at neighborhood centers, churches and community-based organizations.

Original: Curriculum vitae of the core staff are included in the appendix.

Revision (saves four words): Curriculum vitae are included in the appendix.

Original: Nationally, respiratory conditions are the most prevalent chronic health problem experienced by children, as reported by the Department of Health and Human Services.

Revision (saves two words): Nationally, the Department of Health and Human Services reports respiratory conditions as the most prevalent childhood chronic health problem.

Line Numbering

When editing proposal drafts, experienced grant writers use the line numbering feature, whereby each line of text is numbered consecutively. That way, it is an easy matter to pinpoint where questions exist when critiquing text, thereby saving editing time. This tool is particularly valuable when drafts are shared with colleagues, whether they are serving as an objective fresh set of eyes or as collaborative partners with a stake in the project. You can also use line numbers proactively, channeling the focus of your colleagues to specific sections of the narrative: "I appreciate your holistic feedback on the draft, but in particular I need to know whether the section between lines #806–#1229 makes sense."

PROPOSAL APPEARANCE

Although you will obviously spend much time working on the content of your proposal, you should also

Instead of	Rewrite as
• make a decision	• decided
• made a modification	• modified
• make a determination	• determined
• made a revision	• revised
• make a recommendation	• recommend
• made a suggestion	• suggested
• make a judgment	• judged

CONVERTING NOUNS TO VERBS

EXHIBIT 84

pay attention to its appearance or design. Experienced proposal writers believe appearance may account for as much as one-half of your overall proposal evaluation. Just as clothing is important in the business world for establishing initial impressions, so, too, is the appearance of your proposal as it reaches the reviewer's hands. The proposal should "look" familiar to the reader. A familiar proposal is a friendly proposal. Look at the printed materials issued by the sponsor. When appropriate, use the same type size and style, layout, white space, and headings as they do.

A good proposal design reduces the likelihood of reviewer errors and misunderstandings about the proposal. As a consequence, you will simplify the reviewer's job. A well-designed proposal makes even complex information look accessible and gives the reviewers confidence that they can master your proposal information.

Use these design tips to create visual chunks of information that can be quickly noticed and absorbed.

- Visual devices like headings and white space help reviewers see your proposal structure.
- Use white space to make difficult subjects easier to comprehend by breaking into smaller units.
- Use white space as an active design element to communicate user friendliness to readers as opposed to a cluttered, tightly packed page that intimidates the readers.

- Major headings should normally appear at the top of a page.
- Never leave a heading on the final line of a page.
- The most effective positions for headings and captions are left-hand outside columns because the outsides of pages are noticed first.

As you learn about your reviewers and consider proposal appearance, try to anticipate which of the following reading styles the reviewer is likely to use: skimming, search reading, or critical reading. Recall that your earlier prospect research from a past reviewer or program officer identified the likely manner in which your proposal would be reviewed. Reviewers skim proposals when they have many pages to read in a very short time. Reviewers search proposals when they are following an evaluation sheet that assigns points to specific proposal sections. Reviewers always critically read proposals, especially when the reading occurs in the time luxury of a mail review. Exhibit 85 shows some of the writing techniques that are particularly appropriate for different reading styles.

Sample Edited Proposal

A sample edited proposal is provided as Exhibit 86. Note the comments in the call out thought bubbles, which exemplify many of the specific writing and editing tips outlined previously.

Reading Style	Writing Technique
Skim reading	• White space • Headings and subheadings • Ragged right margins • Graphs, charts, illustrations • Keywords
Search reading	• Bold type • Lists and examples • Table of contents • Page numbers • Appendixes
Critical reading	• Transitions • Type style • Type size • Line spacing • Case

READING STYLES AND WRITING TECHNIQUES.

EXHIBIT 85

Today's Date

Mr. Lee K. Wallet
Executive Director
Deep Pockets Fund
P.O. Box 17971
Anytown, WI 53017

Dear Mr. Wallet:

Our House, a nonprofit community-based agency providing quality educational and recreational opportunities for Anytown's southside, invites your investment in a $25,320 project to prevent drug and gang involvement among "at-risk" youth.

Our House, a recent winner of Anytown's Community Development Award, utilizes a self-help philosophy to encourage the growth and development of individuals, families, and a health community. Three years ago, Our House began participating in a federally funded program to prevent the recruitment of at-risk youth into gang and drug activity. During this time, Our House helped more than 120 misguided youth find their way back to being fully functional members of the community. However, dollar-conscious politicians have systematically reduced government funding of critical drug and gang prevention programs. More immediately, neighborhood youth centers, including Our House, face an emergency situation because the government, without notice, terminated federal support funds 14 months ahead of schedule. Consequently, Our House must identify new and creative ways of continuing to provide quality prevention programs at minimal expense.

Our House: Anytown's Southside Neighbor. Established in 1973, Our House is located in the heart of Anytown's southside neighborhood. Unquestionably, Our House is in one of the most ethnically diverse areas in Anytown. Neighborhood demographics consist of:

- 54% Hispanic
- 23% Caucasian
- 14% African American
- 5% Native American
- 4% Asian

In addition to being one of Anytown's most diverse neighborhoods, it is one of Anytown's most desperate. The southside neighborhood accounts for over one-quarter of all county AFDC cases, nearly one-third of all General Assistance cases, and over one-fifth of all Children's Court referrals for abuse, neglect, and teen births.

For over one-quarter of a century, Our House has provided health alternative activities for Anytown's southside youth. However, Our House can attend to only a limited numbers. With more than 100 children per square block, it is virtually impossible to provide quality education and recreational opportunities for everyone. Consequently, Our House is currently focusing its efforts on Anytown's "at-risk" youth population.

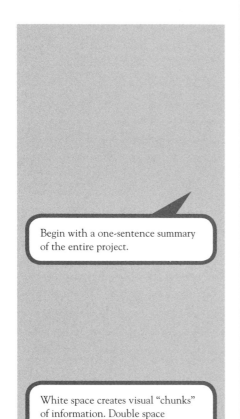

Begin with a one-sentence summary of the entire project.

White space creates visual "chunks" of information. Double space between proposal sections.

Headings are specific to the proposal and help readers to skim or search for details.

SAMPLE EDITED LETTER PROPOSAL

EXHIBIT 86

Problem: Prevalence of Gangs and Drugs. Without a doubt, Anytown has its share of gangs. In fact, gang membership currently averages 4,000 participants operating in 20–30 gangs. Furthermore, studies indicate:

- Gang members are 15 years old, on average
- 52% of gang members used alcohol in the preceding month
- 72% of gang members have an average GPA of 1.73, "D"

In addition, law enforcement agencies witness that there is a significant link between gangs, drugs, and violence. But perhaps the most revealing assessment of gang activity in Anytown was made by the Juvenile Court Assistant District Attorneys when they asserted that membership in gangs was a way of identifying oneself.

At Our House, we recognize this need to "fit in." Furthermore, we recognize that many adolescents turn to gangs, drugs, and violence as a means of combating boredom and loneliness. Our House provides adolescents with health alternatives to gang life. More importantly, the youth who participate in Our House's programs report increased levels of respect, self-esteem, positive peer involvement, and more positive attitudes and behaviors. In other words, at Our House they find a real sense of purpose and belonging.

Solution: Youth Programs. Our House currently services over 120 "at-risk" youth and adolescents between ages of 10–16. These "at-risk" youth include those failing in school, in children's court on minor offenses, causing neighborhood disturbances, or having trouble socializing at home.

Our House, together with a local consortium of churches and residential leaders, has designated a Neighborhood Strategic Plan (NSP) to improve the overall quality and safety of the southside neighborhood community. NSP addresses the particular strengths and weaknesses of the community and outlines policies and procedures for social improvement. Our House has taken a leading role in this project by establishing a safe haven where youth and adolescents can get away from the stresses and pressures of street gang life and actively cultivate personal growth through specific programming.

- Educational: after-school and ESL tutoring
- Cultural: computer programming, drawing, painting, field trips
- Recreational: basketball, volleyball, pool, Ping-Pong
- Employment: summer work opportunities.

More importantly, because students are involved in educational and recreational activities, they gain a new sense of personal identity; consequently, they no longer turn to gangs, drugs, and violence for identification and recreational purposes.

Capabilities: Encouraging Responsible Life Decisions.
Last year alone, there were over 11,500 youth participant visits to Our House's educational and recreational facilities. That averages out to over 200 participant visits each week. In the past three years, Our House has had many distinguishing educational and recreational successes.

Our House's educational programs have had remarkable participation. In three years, 71 students have earned GED certification—more than any other community-based program in Anytown!

> Arial type style headings match those used in the sponsor's printed material.

> Times Roman type style matches that used in the sponsor's printed material.

> Bulleted list conveys information simply and quickly. List is set off with white space above and below.

SAMPLE EDITED LETTER PROPOSAL

EXHIBIT 86 (Continued from page 238)

Participation in Our House's recreational programs has more than tripled since its inception three years ago. Specifically, youth and adolescents are active in at least one of three unique Rec Center Programs:

- **The Hang Tough Club**–a drug and alcohol prevention club for teens
- **Girls in the House**–a special club for addressing the needs of girls and young women
- **Youth Opportunities Initiative**–a teenage gang prevention club

The goal of each of these programs is to provide youth and adolescents with the skills, foresight, and habits necessary for them to make responsible life decisions. More concretely, as a result of obtaining a more positive self-image, youth and adolescents attend school more regularly, earn better grades, and employ more effective coping strategies in their lives.

Since this project is still in its formative years, Our House will continue to track the progress and success of these programs to evaluate their effectiveness. Specifically, we will calculate the number and frequency of youth participating in these programs; we will also gather program improvement suggestions from youth and adolescents, their educational and religious leaders, and private consultants. These suggestions will be used to implement any necessary changes in youth programming and determine the feasibility of expanding our services to include other at-risk adolescents.

Budget Request: $25,320. With the demonstrated concern that the Deep Pockets Fund has shown for community revitalization programs, Our House requests a grant in the amount of $25,320. Quite frankly, without fiscal government support, this project extends beyond Our House's financial boundaries. Accordingly, we must now reach out for assistance in what surely is a vital service to Anytown's southside community. In effect, by investing 72¢/day in each of the 120 adolescents who participate in Our House's at-risk youth programs, you will be empowering many youth and families to better combat the issues of gangs, drugs, and violence.

Your support really will make a significant difference. The Deep Pocket Fund will be directly aiding hundreds of children and adolescents who are in desperate need of quality educational and life-skill opportunities, and at the same time, you will be making a significant contribution to gang and drug prevention in Anytown. Please contact Lindy Ross, Development Coordinator at Our House, at (414) 867–5309 to answer questions or provide additional information.

Sincerely,

Karen Tilly
Executive Director

P.S. Please come visit Our House and see this important project yourself!

Enclosures:
    Attachment A: Budget
    Attachment B: IRS 501(c)(3) Certification

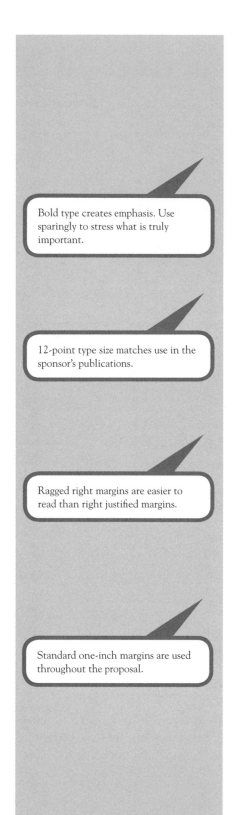

Bold type creates emphasis. Use sparingly to stress what is truly important.

12-point type size matches use in the sponsor's publications.

Ragged right margins are easier to read than right justified margins.

Standard one-inch margins are used throughout the proposal.

SAMPLE EDITED LETTER PROPOSAL

EXHIBIT 86 (Continued from page 239)

THE FINAL EDIT

You're nearly ready to send the proposal to the sponsor. It's time for one last pass through all proposal details to make sure everything is complete. Double-check these major last minute items.

Binding

For small to medium-size proposals (less than 30 pages), staple the proposal once (using a heavy-duty stapler) along the vertical margin of the upper left-hand corner of the proposal. Do not bind serially along the left-hand margin or use "slip-on" binders. Both procedures make it difficult to open up the proposal and read the inside pages. Use a large binder clip for larger proposals, making sure your agency name and page number is a heading on each page.

Electronic Submission

If you submit your proposal electronically, especially via Grants.gov, ensure that you have met all requirements, including a DUNS number and SAM registration. If not, allow two weeks to complete all eligibility requirements.

Mailing Day

Unless you have a specific deadline date, mail your proposal so it arrives on a Tuesday or Wednesday. Most people receive less mail on those two days, so your proposal will be better noticed. If you do have a specific deadline date, check to see whether it is a receipt date or a postmark date.

Mailing Envelope

Mail the proposal in a manila envelope large enough to accommodate the proposal without having to fold or bend it, even if you have a short letter proposal. It'll be more distinctive than those with folds in the paper.

Page Numbering

Place page numbers in the top right or bottom center of the pages of your proposal. Start numbering with "2" on the second page of your proposal; do not number the first page. Some electronic submission programs automatically superimpose their page numbers regardless of how you handle pagination. In such cases, the numbers usually appear at the bottom of the page. As a result, if you do include page numbers, post them in the upper right-hand corner of your proposal to avoid being "stamped over" by their software programs.

Paper Size

Use the standard 8.5- by 11-inch paper unless the sponsor indicates otherwise.

Paper Color

Use white paper. Do not use colored paper for the proposal text or as a divider between proposal sections.

Paper Weight

Use a twenty-weight bond paper, a moderately high-quality, reasonably priced paper that will photocopy or print nicely in laser printers.

Paragraph Style

Indent your paragraphs five spaces because the additional white space increases readability.

Proofreading

Proofread and proofread your proposal. Proofread your proposal several times in multiple readings, looking for different features on each reading. As you proofread, look at mechanics and format.

Are words spelled correctly, especially proper names? Are there any missing words? Did any words get transposed due to sloppy cutting and pasting? Are sentences grammatically correct? Are sentences punctuated properly? Is there any missing punctuation? Are words properly capitalized? Are apostrophes used appropriately? Are all numbers and computations accurate?

Know your common mistakes. Make one proofreading pass looking exclusively for your common errors, e.g., pronoun-antecedent agreement. Have three different people proofread, including at least one reader who has not been involved with the writing of the proposal.

Use your computer spell checker but recognize it will not pick up certain types of errors, e.g., misuse of "there" for "their," "assure" for "ensure," or "principle" for "principal." Existing grammar checkers are of some value but are still in their linguistic infancy.

To proofread word by word, start from the end of the proposal and read backward. By doing this you are not influenced by the syntax; you must read each word independent of the others.

To spot the extra spaces sometimes accidentally inserted between two words, turn the proposal upside down and read the spaces; spacing errors quickly reveal themselves. You can also use your computer's find command: search for instances of two spaces together.

Increase the size of your proofreading copy on your computer or photocopy machine; mistakes show up more easily in larger print. Do your proofreading from a doubled-spaced copy.

Ask others to proofread as well. When asking a content specialist, provide specific guidance, e.g., Is the content clear? Is it easy to follow? What is missing from the proposal? What should be deleted? How can I make the proposal more persuasive? Beyond asking a content specialist, ask someone to read the proposal who lacks knowledge of the subject matter but has an eagle-eye for grammar. Ask your writing specialist for specific advice, e.g., Find any typos? Any cludgy sentences? Headings and subheadings okay? Appropriate use of white space? Do proposal sections easily transition from one part to another? What would make the proposal easier to read? Technical terms defined? The point to remember: when you ask others for feedback, you will get better-quality responses if you tell them what to look for.

Title

Select an interesting, descriptive title: 10 words or less. Avoid cutesy titles or tricky acronyms on the cover page.

> *Poor*: Extinguishing Apollo's Flame
> *Better*: Expanding Fire Protection Services in Dallas

 ## Clip File Action Item # 20
Complete Proposals

While each suggestion in this chapter represents a potential clip file action item, perhaps the starting point is to have on-hand complete examples of successful proposals. They become important reference points as one considers such things as organization, structure, and level of detail. The best way to obtain copies of successful proposals is to swap with past grant winners.

CHAPTER 17
Grant Review and Funding Decisions

The way to avoid criticism is to do nothing.

—Steve Ross

OVERVIEW

This final chapter discusses what happens once your proposal is submitted. At a minimum, it will be subjected to administrative assessment by program officers and technical evaluation by grant reviewers. It may pique enough interest such that the sponsor wishes to conduct a site visit. Finally, after what can feel like an interminable amount of waiting, the sponsor will make a funding decision. Understanding a sponsor's grant processes can help improve your odds for a positive outcome. In Chapter 17, you will learn the following:

- The value of simultaneous submissions to multiple sponsors.
- Site visit survival strategies.
- Planned options for handling grant decisions.
- The importance of being persistent.
- How to become a grant reviewer.

This chapter closes with suggestions of follow-up actions you should take, whether or not your proposal is funded. The review and constructive criticism of your proposal—not you—can only strengthen your idea. Beginning grantseekers with eggshell egos can take the advice of a Fortune 500 CEO, Steve Ross, and do nothing, but, obviously, that won't get you funded.

MULTIPLE SUBMISSIONS

Your completed proposal represents an important piece of intellectual property. To receive full value from your efforts, you should submit your proposal to multiple sponsors. This will increase your chances of getting funded.

Beginning grantseekers sometimes wonder if it is ethical to submit a proposal to more than one sponsor at the same time. Our answer is "Yes, it is ethical, provided you advise all grantmakers of your actions." Failure to let sponsors know of your actions would be deceitful—and that is unethical.

Implications

"Will making multiple submissions hurt your chances of getting funded?" ask beginning grantseekers. While the question is understandable, in practice making multiple submissions will not jeopardize the likelihood of getting your proposal funded. In fact, it could help because sponsors with similar interests often form close communications networks among themselves. Grantmakers with similar interests talk to each other. Co-funding sometimes happens; that is, several sponsors may contribute partially to the total project cost. Furthermore, engaging in multiple submissions communicates to sponsors that you are seriously committed to your project and that you are willing to exert considerable effort to secure funding.

When submitting multiple proposals, present similar but not identical versions; that is, each version should be tailored to meet the varying interests of sponsors as determined by feedback from your preproposal contacts (Chapter 4). Sponsors expect you will submit similar proposals to other grant makers. You should name the other sponsors in your transmittal letter. For example, your letter might include a sentence like this:

A similar version of this proposal is currently under consideration by the Pain Management Foundation; Mr. Guillermo Sainz, 414–234–6789, is the point of contact.

or

A similar version of this proposal will be will be submitted to the Chronic Pain Association within the next month; preliminary communications have been held with Ms. Rocio Witt, 414–987–6543.

Budget Considerations

If you submit multiple proposals, how much money should you ask for? The total amount you need from multiple sponsors? Partial amounts from each of several sponsors? For example, assume you identified five potential sponsors and want to request support for a $50,000 project. It would be very difficult to get all five sponsors to agree to contribute $10,000. Getting five sponsors to collaboratively support your project is akin to trying to herd cats. Rather, ask all five sponsors for $50,000 each. Funding from any one of them could support your project.

On rare occasions, you may have an "embarrassment of riches" problem whereby several sponsors want to fully fund the same project. To solve this problem, you have two main options. First, you may accept both awards and increase the size or scope of your project, assuming you can handle such a project increase and both sponsors agree. If you expand the project size, you should keep the budgets separate and not comingle the funds. Second, you may delay the start date from the second sponsor in order to increase the length of the project period; each sponsor will profit by the funds from the other sponsor. In essence, consider making your project bigger or longer before rejecting offered grant dollars. Usually, sponsors will be flexible in implementing your project, once they decide it merits funding.

REVIEW MECHANISMS

Your preproposal contact revealed how your proposal will be reviewed. The review process varies considerably. Your proposal may be reviewed internally by existing staff members or referred externally for evaluation. The external review may be done by mail (print or electronic), panel meetings (in-person or teleconference), or a combination of the two. You need to know how your proposal will be reviewed and by what type of individual because your proposal should be written to the level of expertise of the reviewer. This audience analysis will help you determine the amount of detail you need to include in your proposal. For instance, if your proposal will undergo mail review by a technical specialist in your field, you will need considerable detail and documentation in your proposal.

On the other hand, if your proposal will be reviewed by generalists who are also reading 15 other proposals in a three-hour panel review (where they might be able to spend a maximum of 20 seconds per page reviewing your proposal), you would write with all the organizational and skimming mechanisms at your disposal. With an electronic review, your proposal may lose some special features like bolding or italics; as a result, document design considerations (Chapter 16) become critical.

The National Institutes of Health is an example of a federal agency that relies on outside specialists to conduct panel review meetings. In fact, they use a two-tier approach to the proposal review process. The first level of review has specialists evaluate the content or merit of the proposal. The second level of review examines the proposal's relevance to the agency mission. The National Institutes of Health two-tier approach is illustrated in Exhibit 87.

Of note, for informational purposes only, NIH publishes a roster of the individuals who serve as reviewers for various study sections: www.csr.nih.gov/committees/rosterindex.asp. While it would create a conflict of interest scenario if you contacted these individuals directly, you should conduct prospect research on these individuals to get a better understand of their values glasses. This will help you write more persuasively. For instance, your literature review (or methodological approach) may reflect best practices in the field and include strategic citations, as appropriate, of articles published by members of the review committee. In other words, by recognizing reviewers' expertise in research-based approaches to advancing health, you enhance the credibility of your own project.

The job of reviewers is to ask questions about your proposal. Regardless of whether your proposal is being reviewed by a public or private agency, five basic areas are covered, at a minimum:

1. Scope of work
2. Personnel
3. Facilities
4. Track record
5. Budget information

Experienced proposal writers often conduct proposal review sessions within their organizations prior to formal submission.

Electronic Reviews

In an effort to streamline operations and become more eco-friendly, some public and private grantmakers accept applications electronically. Practically speaking, this means that sometimes you will submit a PDF (Portable Document Format) file via e-mail; other times you will write your proposal in a word processing program and subsequently copy and paste responses into the sponsor's fillable text box forms online; and in a number of cases, you will upload grant documents via a secure portal on the sponsor's Web site. More interesting, however, is the unintended consequence of the shift to electronic submission systems; namely, the impact on how grant reviewers read proposals.

When it comes to reading proposals, reviewers tend to fall into two camps: new school and old school. Old school reviewers tend to print out hard copies and use red pens, highlighters, and sticky notes to annotate the proposals with their thoughts and reactions when applications are submitted electronically. They may rearrange pages to see concepts side-by-side; for instance, they may pull the budget from the end and move it next to the project timeline to ensure that cost items match up with planned activities.

New school reviewers often read proposals on their computers, skimming at first and then circling back as necessary. They use technology to their advantage. Beyond text highlighting and comment box features of software programs, they conduct keyword searches to find details. For example, as reviewers dive into a proposal during a panel discussion, they may question:

• Did the applicant include "milestones"?
• Does the project ensure access for "underrepresented groups"?
• Who is the "project coordinator"?
• How much cash and in-kind "matching support" has been committed?
• What are the intended "long-term outcomes"?

New school reviewers can conduct keywords searches in an effort to locate quickly the answers to these questions. That is, of course, assuming that the applicant used the same vocabulary as the sponsor. A challenge could arise when the proposal relies on synonyms to address sponsor hot buttons rather than employing a bit of professional plagiarism.

The message is clear: particularly with electronic reviews, keywords from the application guidelines and reviewer evaluation forms should be repeated throughout the narrative. "Benchmarks" are important, but not when the RFP (Request for Proposals) asks for "milestones." "Cost sharing" can be an incentive to win a grant award, but not when reviewers are searching for evidence of "matching support." "Transformational results" are impressive, but not when sponsors expect significant "long-term outcomes." Strategically lifting words and phrases directly from an RFP and reviewer's evaluation form can help demonstrate to sponsors that you speak the same language and share the same values.

MINDSETS OF PROGRAM OFFICERS

Program officers are the individuals who are charged with administering a sponsor's grant programs. As part of their duties, they cultivate in potential applicants' innovative solutions to challenging problems that are consistent with the sponsor's organizational values and funding priorities. In many instances this means treading carefully, providing encouragement for potential applicants to submit their ideas while at the same time not guaranteeing that a project will be funded.

Program officers have intimate behind-the-scenes knowledge of the sponsor's grant processes and often have a direct influence in the process, though they may not admit to it. For instance, program officers may be responsible for identifying and selecting grant reviewers as well as assigning proposals to reviewers; among the reviewers, they know who the "tough graders" are and can make assignments accordingly.

To gain an understanding of their views and mindsets, we interviewed two former program officers, one who worked at a federal agency and one who worked at a national private foundation. Both have since shifted over to the "other side of the desk" and are now involved in writing proposals and helping others write them. Because both have broad perspectives on grantseeking, we think you'll find their responses to the following four questions particularly valuable. Their insights may even have direct implications for the writing of your next grant proposal.

Question #1: What's your most memorable experience? What made it memorable?

Private Foundation Program Officer: In the proposal review process, it's always a challenge to discern among great ideas. Applicants have their livelihood on the line, their reason for being—and based on their written proposals, I had to make a judgment on the merit and fundability of their ideas.

One memorable experience occurred when an applicant thought that their organizational history and connection to a foundation board member could override good proposal development. They identified an important problem and proposed an innovative solution, but didn't articulate a convincing strategy for making change happen.

Although the board member who supported the applicant was disappointed that I did not recommend them for funding, he supported my position because I had carefully documented all of the shortcomings of the proposal. Although my rejection letter initially discouraged the applicant, subsequently they used it as an outline of issues to address in a revised proposal. They submitted their revised proposal a year later and got funded.

Federal Program Officer: There were several memorable experiences. One that I had nearly every day was talking to prospective applicants on the phone about the science behind their applications. Such conversations were usually the intellectual high point of the day for most program officers at the NIH. Love of the science in our fields is one reason we choose science administration as a career.

Another, more intense version of intellectual stimulation concerned the scientific meetings I organized for experts in a specific area. These meetings discussed the "state-of-the-science" in that area and they often resulted in recommendations to the institute to sponsor RFAs to help promote progress in the field. Through the meetings I was able to help advance the science by providing a forum for discussion of new ideas and, by using recommendations generated by the scientists at the meeting, I was able to garner more funding for RFAs in these areas.

Question #2: What were the things you looked for in selecting grant recipients?

Private Foundation Program Officer: Successful grant applicants described projects that fit within the foundation's guidelines, identified a real problem, and articulated a strategy for making change happen. Very few proposals were funded without preproposal contact and development.

The best grantees weren't overly solicitous, but they kept me informed. They put me on e-mail and traditional mailing lists. About once a month they sent a brief e-mail update, or when there was something substantial to report, for example, a relevant journal publication or the résumé of a newly hired key project person. In a sense, they included me as a collaborative team member.

Federal Government Program Officer: In the NIH system, program officers have limited influence in the selection of grant recipients. Approximately, 95 percent of all individual project grant applications are awarded based on priority scores given to the application by peer review committees. The remaining 5 percent, involving the funding of applications beyond the priority score cutoff (called *out-of-sequence funding*), were selected by a complicated administrative process.

First, program officers selected high scientific quality applications near the funding cutoff score that appeared to fill a programmatic need within their scientific areas of responsibility. Next, the program officers had to argue their case for funding these applications before two different internal groups: one at the division level and the other at the institute level. These groups decided whether to list these projects for out-of-sequence funding. Money always runs out before all the recommended projects are funded.

Due to my experience at NIH dealing with this out-of-sequence funding, I recognized the extreme importance of faculty making sure that their program officers understand the significance of their projects. I recommend to my faculty that they communicate with the program officers at funding agencies and explain to them the importance of their projects in a larger context. I call it "building enthusiasm" for their application.

Question #3: What were some common problems you experienced with grantees?

Private Foundation Program Officer: Perhaps the most common problem was not keeping me in the communication loop. In one instance, after receiving their award, the grantee had no contact with the foundation for two years, and then they only came back for renewal funding. In another case, a grantee did not tell me about some key staff who left the project. I didn't appreciate learning about these personnel changes from discussions with other organizations. And when new project personnel came on board, I expected to be introduced to them.

Another challenge was that some smaller nonprofit grantees, who perhaps did not understand foundation relations, would forget to invite me to their project functions. One grantee failed to invite me to the conference that we funded!

Federal Government Program Officer: I encountered four major problems. (1) Applicants that did not follow the printed directions. (2) Applicants that did not clearly address in revised applications the criticisms of peer reviewers in summary statements of previous applications. (3) Applicants who have submitted repeatedly the same application project but who have received only minor change in priority scores. Hint: these applicants need to move on to another project. (4) Grantees who submitted unusable progress reports. By "unusable"

I mean either none was submitted or what was submitted was too long or technical to be understood by a nonspecialist in the field. NIH program officers used these progress reports to build their own annual progress reports for their units, which in turn are used by NIH to support funding from Congress.

Question #4: What kinds of things could grantees do to make your life easier?

Private Foundation Program Officer: Grantees make my life easier by keeping me in the communication loop. Let me know about changes in the project. Don't wait until the end of the project period to report significant changes in personnel, finances, and management. The foundation expects that you'll make some changes, so you're not asking for permission as much as you are keeping me up-to-date.

In the grant progress report, use the same budget format as was submitted in the original proposal, and add a column to show a comparison of "projected" versus "actual" expenditures. Discrepancies between projected and actual are acceptable, but explain those differences. The foundation allows some cost shifting among categories; however, be sure to secure approval first.

Grantees should also meet due dates for grant progress reports, especially for renewal awards. While you might not like writing these reports, I need this information to justify requests for continuation funding to the foundation board. Collecting information on an ongoing basis to document accomplishments will make it easier to develop a grant progress report.

Federal Government Program Officer: (a) Follow the directions in the application kit. (b) Make sure that you are contacting the appropriate NIH program office. For example, don't contact the National Cancer Institute if you have a question about digestive diseases. It is relatively easy to get to the appropriate contact place if you look at the missions of the various NIH units. (c) Do some homework about the NIH applications and review system so that program officers will not need to go over the basics for the millionth time. (d) Write short (two page) progress reports designed to be read by the nonspecialist.

While these opinions represent only two from among many past and current program officers, their responses are not atypical in our experience. Noteworthy among the points they raise:

1. Engage in preproposal contact.
2. Follow application guidelines.
3. Preproposals are helpful.
4. Submit excellent, not just good ideas.
5. Suggest ways your project will impact people.
6. Recognize that part of the program officer's job is sometimes saying "no."
7. Know when to move on.
8. Keep program officers in the communication loop.

Program officers can influence funding decisions, although they sometimes deny it. Persistence pays.

KEY QUESTIONS TO ANSWER

Does the proposal do the following:

1. Show sufficient understanding of sponsor guidelines and priorities?
2. Address well-documented problems in need of solution?
3. Show a good approach to the problem?
4. Have an efficient time schedule?
5. Indicate probable outcomes?
6. Identify key personnel and their assignments?
7. Provide sufficient information to evaluate key personnel?
8. Deal with all clearance requirements?
9. Propose a reasonable budget?
10. Identify the probable project impact?

SITE VISITS

Occasionally, the sponsor may wish to conduct a site visit as a part of the evaluation process. This visit is a good sign that you are on their "short list" of potential grantees. The purpose of the site visit is to see firsthand your organization—its environment and people. Site visits are held when reviewers feel they need information available only at the proposed project site. Information gathered in a single day by a team of reviewers can decide the fate of an application that may have taken months to prepare. Think of a site visit as a "quality control" measure for the sponsor, a way for the sponsor to run a credibility check on you, your organization, and your idea.

Site Visit Questions

While the number of and nuances in questions that site visit teams could ask is theoretically limitless, site visit questions tend to fall into five interrelated categories. Questions often address sponsor concerns about project design, project mechanics, leadership, evaluation, and finances, as the following examples illustrate:

Project Design

1. How does this project fit in with your organizational mission?
2. Please elaborate on how the internal staff and collaborators have been involved in the development of the proposal and will be engaged throughout the project.
3. Please clarify which geographic areas will be targeted for intervention. Please explain why those specific areas and organizational sectors have been targeted.

Project Mechanics

1. Please discuss anticipated project barriers and how they will be overcome during the granting period.
2. Please discuss plans to share findings and lessons learned with external audiences and elaborate on whether the potential exists for the project to serve as a model for other communities locally, regionally, and/or nationally.
3. Please discuss how proposed effort levels for the project director and codirector will be sufficient to oversee fiscal responsibilities, staffing, reporting, and data collection and analysis as well as participate in key project activities and soliciting funds for financial sustainability.

Leadership

1. What has been your history of collaboration among project partners?
2. Please provide some examples of how community representatives and the target population are involved in leadership and decision-making processes. How will you ensure this level of involvement continues during the implementation and expansion phases?
3. When and how do you plan to secure greater support and participation from the business community? Elected officials? Policy makers? Media? Other stakeholders?

Evaluation

1. Please elaborate on the measures of success. What data will illustrate that efforts of the coalition were essential to the activities and

outcomes? How will your coalition assess and manage these data?

2. Please clarify whether the evaluation tools, such as meeting evaluation forms, stakeholder attitude assessments, and participant satisfaction surveys already exist with established reliability and validity characteristics or will need to be developed as well as implemented during the project period.

3. Does institutional capacity exist, e.g., data systems and collaborative arrangements, which would enable you to compare outcomes for a population who participated in the intervention with outcomes for a population who did not participate? If so, please describe.

Financial

1. Please clarify plans for securing the required match and identify the proportion of cash and in-kind contributions.

2. Please confirm that institutional capacity exists to clearly document that all matching funds are designated solely for the proposed project.

3. What will happen to this proposed project if it is not selected for grant funding?

Site visits represent a double-edged sword. Your site visitors will come armed with questions, and a poor showing on your part may doom the application. On the other hand, site visits give you a golden opportunity to make up for weaknesses in an application and meet with specialists in the field.

Site Visit Survival Strategies

If you are involved in a site visit, you should prepare properly. First, bring all potential project personnel together and review in detail the components of your proposal. Ask the sponsors if they have a particular agenda they wish to follow or if they want to see any special background documents. Arrange a private room for them to meet in and conduct interviews. Your job is to show them, not snow them, that your idea and organization are indeed credible.

To survive a site visit, follow the three "Rs."

- **Review.** Have everyone reread the proposal, understand, and be able to articulate their contributions, both to your organization and the project.
- **Rehearse.** Conduct practice site visits. The most common mistake in a site visit is for project team members to be unfamiliar with proposal details. It

is for this reason that a "dress rehearsal" is crucial, even to the extent of asking outside colleagues to come in and hold a practice site visit. Recently, a few grantmakers have opted to conduct virtual site visits using Skype or a similar video conferencing technology. This is a cost- and time-saving move on their part. You should conduct your dress rehearsal under the same conditions.

- **Respond.** Follow the established agenda. Stay on schedule. Don't bombard reviewers with lots of new information. Do provide copies of any specific documents that are requested. Do provide plenty of time to answer reviewers' questions. Give reviewers a "Take Away" folder that includes the agenda, proposal abstract, contact information for all key participants, any requested documents, written answers to any specific questions raised, and a list of other related projects.

Site Visit Example

Successfully managing site visits is, in large part, a matter of paying attention to many details. The following nuts-and-bolts example came from a recent full-day site visit from a national foundation. A proposal had received favorable initial reviews, and now four site visitors wanted to see the applicant organization firsthand and discuss in greater detail some aspects of the proposed project.

The sponsor provided three weeks' advanced notice of the site visit date. They asked the applicant to develop an agenda for the day, which would include a short presentation of the proposal, answers to specific follow-up questions, and time for questions and answers with the project's collaborative partners. A great deal of preparation behind the scenes was done to ensure that the site visit went smoothly. Here's an outline of what happened—and when:

Two Weeks Before the Visit.

- Review the sponsor's specific follow-up questions
- Identify key participants—internal staff and collaborative partners
- Confirm participant availability
- Have all participants review the original proposal
- Reserve a conference room for the presentation
- Begin to develop the presentation
- Begin to develop the agenda for the day
- Offer to coordinate hotel and travel accommodations for out-of-town site visitors

One Week Before the Visit.

- Finalize the agenda
- Send the agenda to the sponsor and participants
- Send a map and driving directions to the sponsor and participants
- Contact the sponsor and participants to identify any special dietary restrictions
- Share the presentation with key participants for critique and input
- Discuss participants' roles and responsibilities during the presentation
- Practice

One Day Before the Visit.

- Print name tags
- Hang up signs directing site visitors and participants to the conference room
- Order continental breakfast, box lunches, and afternoon snacks
- Copy handouts: (1) agenda, (2) participant list, (3) PowerPoint presentation slides, and (4) answers to specific follow-up questions
- Check technology—laptop, data projector, Internet, PowerPoint, remotes
- Make sure the conference room is clean and has an adequate number of chairs
- Have a final dress rehearsal for the presentation
- Get plenty of sleep

During the Visit.

- Look good. Feel good. Think good. Do good.
- Smile

One Day After the Visit.

- Send a thank you note to the sponsor
- Send a thank you note to key participants

During the actual site visit, the reviewers asked questions to assess project leadership, accountability, involvement, and communication. Some of their actual questions follow:

- Could you describe your vision for this project?
- Have you secured buy-in from project personnel?
- Do you anticipate ongoing evaluation and feedback during the project: with project participants? With project personnel? With collaborating institutions?
- Do you anticipate that labor shortages will be a problem for staffing this project?
- Have you had difficulties with staff turnover?

- Who will be responsible for data entry?
- Are project personnel familiar with mobile technology devices?
- Can data systems communicate across partnering institutions?
- How do you deal with language and cultural issues?

Since the project under review involved multiple institutions, the site visitors asked questions of project partners about the nature of the collaborative relationships. These questions get at intangible characteristics such as energy, passion, trust, commitment, and ownership.

- How does this project fit in with the work that you do?
- How often do you interface with the project director and lead applicant institution?
- Have there been previous alliances among your institutions?
- Could you describe the planning process: who was involved? Why does it work so well? What would you do differently?
- Do you see any barriers or challenges to this collaboration that need to be addressed?
- Do you feel the need for formalized administrative and management structures?

The preparation and attention to detail paid off: the proposal was funded.

DEALING WITH GRANT DECISIONS

Plan Ahead

Planned reactions become planned options. How do you plan to behave if your proposal is funded? Rejected? What are your options? When you have a powerful itch, it is almost unbearable waiting to get it scratched! Having to wait to get what you want demands patience and tolerance—unless you have planned options. Patient people turn to other activities to meet other needs while they are waiting for grant decisions. These activities keep them strong and in control. Strong people wait a lot. It may take many months before the decision on your proposal is made.

Sometimes while you are waiting for a funding decision, you may be asked to supply further information or respond to specific questions from your potential sponsor. Do this in a timely manner, for it means your proposal is under active consideration. Your clip file may be able to provide the requested information.

If You Were Funded

At some point, you will find out if your proposal was successful. Whether your proposal was funded or not, you should do some follow-up work. For example, if you were successful with a proposal, you should request a copy of the reviewer comments, if allowed by the sponsor. Ask the program officer about common mistakes others make in implementing grants so you don't fall into the same trap. Inquire how you can be a good steward of their money. Ask your sponsors what attracted them to your proposals. The answer provides insights about your organizational uniqueness. Add those uniqueness statements to your clip file and use them in your next grant proposal. Clarify the submission deadlines for technical and financial reports; you can keep your program officer very happy if you submit your reports on time. Invite your program officers to visit you. Add them to your organizational public relations list for news releases about your agency.

If You Were Not Funded

If you were not funded, don't take it personally. Many factors can cause a proposal to be rejected: amount of competition, available budget, geographic distribution, and closeness of match to priorities. Often, these factors are beyond your control. If the sponsor declined your proposal, thank them for reading the proposal and ask what can be done to improve it. Request verbatim written reviewer comments, not summary comments, which are less specific. If you can't get reviewer comments, then request a "debriefing" to go over your proposal over the phone or in person. Learn how your proposal could be more competitive. Ask if you should reapply next year. Use this as an opportunity to build bridges with the sponsor for the next submission cycle. Periodically send them a photocopy of articles or publicity with the "Thought you might not have seen this and might be interested" approach. Invite them to your agency to get to know you better. Avoid the "You only love me at submission time" syndrome.

If You Were Approved but Not Funded

It's a rather inglorious message when you learn that you were "approved, but not funded," a reality in grantseeking. This letter of disappointment often uses these words:

> Your application was sufficiently meritorious to warrant a recommendation for approval, but in terms of available funds and the competition

for them, it did not receive a priority score high enough to be funded.

This "close-but-no-cigar" communication amounts to a near miss. Usually, it is "good news" information, for it suggests that the reviewers were attracted to your proposal but were concerned about some procedural issues, as opposed to finding the proposal inherently flawed. To leverage this situation to your advantage, ask the program officer for verbatim reviewer comments, not just summary remarks. Once you learn what the precise issues of concern were to the reviewers, you need to decide whether you should revise and resubmit your proposal to this sponsor or seek another funding source. To make this decision, you need three pieces of information: probability estimates, proposal weaknesses, and timeframes.

Probability Estimates. Call the program officer and find out where you are on the "alternate" list: first, tenth, or whatever? Ask how far down the "pay list" the agency has gone in past competitions? Ask about their probability estimate of you getting funded: 10 percent, 50 percent, or 80 percent?

Proposal Weaknesses. Ask for the program officer's reactions to the written reviewer comments; of the weaknesses cited, which ones were the most significant? Are they easily fixable?

Timeframes. Find out when the next review cycle is. Are you better off to withdraw the proposal, revise, and resubmit it as opposed to leaving it in the "hopper?" How soon will the program officer know if additional grant funds might become available?

If you decide to revise and resubmit, your revision should cite the concerns of previous reviews, itemizing them one-by-one and offering appropriate responses, whether you have made changes to accommodate their concerns or rejected their concerns for solid reasons, which you spell out. (See Exhibit 89.)

THE LANGUAGE OF REJECTION LETTERS

Rejection letters from government agencies usually include comments about concerns raised by the reviewers. You are entitled to this feedback and should request it, if it does not accompany your rejection letter. Private foundations, on the other hand, vary in the extent of their communications. To illustrate, one private foundation provides you with a successful proposal when they turn yours down. Another private foundation commonly provides a funding source book to help you identify alternative sponsors when they reject you. A few private foundations will write detailed rejection letters, spelling out the reason for turndown.

The most common experience for private foundations is to get the "form letter" rebuff. The rejection language in four typical foundation letters reads as follows:

- We regret that we will be unable to contribute as the funds available to us are, unfortunately, not sufficient to assist all the worthy organizations that come to us for support.
- Due to numerous requests for gifts and grants and limited funds, we regret we are not in a position to be of assistance to you. We were pleased to have the opportunity of reviewing the proposal, and only regret we will not be able to provide support for your organization.
- We regret to inform you that the foundation is not in a position to provide a grant for your program.
- We have received your request to our foundation. In reviewing your proposal, it appears your project is beneficial to certain segments of the community. However, in view of the numerous requests we receive, our limited funds, and the direction in which foundation funds are applied, it appears we cannot be of assistance.

Occasionally, a reasonable amount of time elapses and you don't hear anything from a foundation: no funded or declined feedback. This is probably due to the fact that most foundations lack a support staff to handle such communications; at best, they can only communication with their grantees. When faced with this situation, you should first attempt to call and see when funding decisions can be expected. If you cannot connect via phone, successful grantseekers usually wait a maximum of one year before sending a letter requesting that their proposal be withdrawn from further consideration. The language of that letter might include something like the following example.

> On February 2, 2017, we submitted a proposal to you titled, "STAR Parent Training Program." Through a fortunate combination of circumstances, we now have the necessary resources to carry out this project. Accordingly, we ask that you withdraw this proposal from further consideration. Since you value the importance of parent training, we will keep you posted on our major project outcomes. Perhaps, some future occasion will warrant submission of a different proposal to you.

In most cases, corporations decline grants in a manner similar to foundations; that is, they usually send some short letter announcing their decision without any elaboration of key reasons. A follow-up telephone call may provide further insights. If no response is forthcoming after a reasonable timeframe, then you may wish to submit a withdrawal letter, like noted above.

RESPONSE TO REJECTION LETTERS

Getting rejected is the first step to getting funded. Rejection letters present an opportunity to build good will with a future potential sponsor. Consider sending them a letter like the following in those instances when your proposal is declined. This letter contains model paragraphs for use with corporations or foundations:

> Thank you for your letter informing us of your decision regarding our request for support the STAR Parent Training Program. We are, of course, disappointed that the Healthy Baby Foundation cannot support the project. We recognize, however, that there are always more requests than funds, and we are sympathetic with the difficult responsibilities of foundation officers.
>
> As I reflect on the many achievements of our organization and on the challenges yet to be addressed, I am hopeful that the foundation will be able to give future consideration to support for us if we submit a different proposal. As a nonprofit organization, we must rely on the generosity of those who value our mission.
>
> We appreciate your consideration of our request. You and your colleagues of the foundation have our cordial good wishes and our esteem for the conscientious work you do.

In contrast with foundations and corporations, it is not necessary to respond to rejection letters from government agencies for two reasons. First, government funding is more dependent on the merit of the idea and less on their relationship with you. Second, many government agencies are mandated to respond to any communication received from citizens; your letter to them means they must write back to you. In essence, responding to their initial rejection letter simply makes more work for them, instead of building a relationship.

Persistence Pays

Like so many things in life, the first "no" is not necessarily the final "no." With federal grants, it is often possible to obtain reviewer comments, revise your proposal, and resubmit. Your funding chances usually improve with resubmissions. In fact, many successful federal proposals are rejected the first time they are submitted. Accordingly, initially declined proposals are revised on the basis of reviewer feedback and resubmitted with a greater likelihood of funding. Lack of prior success is not a solid reason for not trying again.

At the National Institutes of Health, records show that over one-half of those who apply eventually get funded, if they are persistent and obtain rewrite suggestions from their program officers. Another federal agency reports that the mathematical odds of getting first-time funding are one chance in six. Those who are initially rejected but then revise their proposal resubmit it to improved odds: one chance in three for funding. If the second submission is rejected, the odds improve to one chance in 1.5 for a third, revised submission—decent funding chances. Most successful grantseekers switch to a different sponsor after the third declination.

In the world of grantseeking there are no guarantees. Even resubmitting a revised proposal a second or third time is not an assurance of funding. Why? Because review panels change personnel and perspectives. A proposal feature acceptable to one review panel may be unacceptable to another. In reality, this is beyond your control. Successful grantseekers minimize the possibility of changing standards by flagging those components in the revised proposal that respond to concerns of a previous review panel. In this way, you let the current review panel know you have taken previous concerns seriously and attempted to follow through.

Two examples of responses to reviewer comments in a revised application are presented in Exhibit 88 and Exhibit 89. In these instances, in addition to revisions in the proposal narrative, the sponsor permitted a cover page to be included where reviewer comments and responses could be summarized point-by-point. Exhibit 88 shows the applicant taking an aggressive stance, challenging directly the credibility and competence of grant reviewers. Clearly, the reviewer comments were interpreted as personal attacks and the response was used to counterattack. The hostile tone of the cover page effectively turns reviewers off to the rest of the proposal, irrespective of whether the review panel this second time around consists of the same members, all new members, or a combination thereof. Exhibit 89, on the other hand, strikes a much different tone: it reflects confidence, optimism, and deep appreciation. The applicant's cover page responses demonstrate that thoughtful consideration was given to each reviewer comment. The applicant sets a positive mindset for reviewers as they read the revised submission.

More broadly, a four-part model can be used to craft your opening to a proposal resubmission.

1. **Introduce Your Response**: "In responding to our three reviewer critiques, we've substantially revised our research context and approach. Summary feedback was extremely valuable in preparing this revised proposal. Direct responses to reviewer concerns are described below."

Reviewer comments and responses are incorporated below.

Reviewer: It is not clear whether or not the challenges of gaining access to some very sensitive protected health information have been adequately considered.
Response: This comment reveals a reviewer who is ignorant of common practice and is parlaying that ignorance into damaging speculation. We have been engaging in this type of work with myriad partners for three decades. This is simply a nonserious and subprofessional review.

Reviewer: The proposal would be strengthened if it addressed sustainability directly. How will this program continue?
Response: This is an astonishing comment. There is no call in the RFP to address sustainability. The RFP does not offer any support for a reviewer to use this as a criterion.

Reviewer: Is there a known number or percentage of individuals who report difficulties or delays or inadequate health insurance?
Response: Did the reviewer even read the application? Specific data about the proportion of individuals reporting difficulties and delays and inadequate health insurance is included on pages 3–4.

EXAMPLE OF HOW NOT TO RESPOND TO REVIEWER COMMENTS IN A REVISED APPLICATION

EXHIBIT 88

We appreciate the thorough review of our previous proposal and reviewers' detailed feedback. Incorporating their recommendations clearly strengths this proposal. This document contains point-by-point responses and modifications based on reviewer comments.

Reviewer: The proposal lacks a strong link between cultural competence in the health care workforce and reducing health disparities among the target population.
Response: In the revised proposal we cite several references that suggest culturally congruent care may be one mechanism for addressing health disparities. The proposed project is the first in a series of projects we would like to conduct to better establish this link between culturally congruent care and patient health outcomes.

Reviewer: A tension exists in the narrative because the proposal really addresses the health care workforce, not the public health workforce that is described.
Response: This is a point well taken. We have revised the proposal to refer specifically to nursing practice.

Reviewer: Clarify which aspects of the project will be sustainable and which will require additional funding.
Response: There are two expected outcomes: one is improvement in the cultural congruence of nursing practice and the other is provision of a template for decision making so that participating sites can continue these processes beyond the life of the grant. The replication manual will provide health care facilities a framework for communication on an ongoing basis. The online training will remain available as well. The coordinator position will be folded into internal budgets.

EXAMPLE OF HOW TO RESPOND TO REVIEWER COMMENTS IN A REVISED APPLICATION

EXHIBIT 89

2. **Summarize General Concerns**: "All reviewers thought the topic was highly significant but stressed that important changes were necessary. Accordingly, problems and solutions are stated more clearly, specific aims are better focused, and the research design now justifies the experimental approach for each aim."

3. **Cite and Respond to Specific Reviewer Concerns**: "The first reviewer was concerned about the apparent lack of coworkers and limited resource description. In response, the PI has now hired an experienced laboratory supervisor with a background in cellular biology and two advanced graduate students."

4. **State Your Conclusion**: "In this revised proposal, a wealth of new evidence existed that the proposed experiments will produce useful and publishable information. Moreover, reviewer concerns have been addressed and the proposal is now presented with a distinct focus on the specific aims. The PI, along with an expanded research group, is uniquely postured to carry out the proposed project."

This four-part model is particularly useful with federal grant resubmissions because grant written feedback will be available. You can flag changes, as appropriate to sponsor resubmission policies, so that the scholarly critique of the original application led to a substantially revised and enriched proposal. Feedback from private foundations is more likely to be verbal than written. In rare instances, minor tweaks may be sufficient in cases where your proposal was judged to be mechanically flawed but conceptually sound. More likely, however, is that major changes will be necessary. In addition to reworking the intellectual heart of the narrative, be sure to give your proposal a new look and feel: consider changing the title and rewriting completely the opening pages. This facelift will help drive home the point to reviewers, some of whom may have read the original submission, that the revised application is decidedly different and improved.

Rejection Reasons

Some years ago, the federal government studied 353 research proposals that had been rejected in order to identify some common proposal mistakes. Their review of the rejected proposals yielded the following findings:

- 18 percent failed to number the pages
- 73 percent provided no table of contents
- 81 percent had no abstract
- 92 percent didn't provide résumés of proposed consultants
- 25 percent had no résumé for the principal investigator
- 66 percent included no project evaluation plan
- 17 percent failed to name the project director
- 20 percent provided no list of objectives

These are easily correctable mistakes, pitfalls you should avoid. Some people may make these mistakes out of ignorance about the proposal writing process. Probably more people make these mistakes out of time pressure and haste. As you write your proposal, you should allow sufficient time to attend to these format issues as well as to your proposal content. Both content and format are important. Collectively, they speak to your overall credibility.

GETTING GRANTS: THE LONG-TERM VIEW

In this book you have been introduced to the basic reference tools for identifying funding sources. From these potential suspects, you have seen the importance of engaging in preproposal contact in order to maximize the "fit" between your idea and the sponsor's interests. You have read the clip file suggestions that will help you establish your own grants system for developing proposals while saving valuable time. You have dissected the components of public and private proposals. You have seen in this chapter the importance of being persistent; if you get turned down the first time, revise and resubmit your proposal based on feedback from your reviewer.

We conclude with one final tip: become a grant reviewer yourself. The "inside look" is very helpful later when you are ready to prepare your next grant. How do you get to be a federal grant reviewer? It's usually a self-nomination process. Once you identify a grant program for which you'd like to become a reviewer, tweak your résumé to show related skills and experiences and send it to the program officer, along with a cover letter expressing interest. It might look like this:

> You and I share something in common—an interest in serving multiple handicapped children.
>
> I'm writing now because depending on how you are reviewing your grant proposals, there is a possibility my expertise and experience may be of value to you.
>
> As you review the enclosed résumé, you will note the following:
>
> - Six years of experience in the delivery of rehabilitation services to multiple handicapped children.
> - Hands-on experience with children who have two or more of the following disabili-

ties: hearing, vision, speech, intellectual, emotion, and motor control.
> - Extensive interactions with diverse rehabilitation professionals.
> - A bachelor's degree in special education.
>
> I'll call you in two weeks to see if you'd like more information or have special application forms to fill out.

Many federal agencies and programs actively seek reviewers and welcome your volunteer efforts. Occasionally, sponsors will respond with a simple form you will need to fill out so they can enter demographic information in their reviewer database. Some federal agencies and programs, such as the ones listed in Exhibit 90, allow you to register online directly.

Typically, federal proposal reviewers are selected either on the basis of having received a prior grant from that agency or through a self-nomination process. It is usually not necessary to have a PhD and publish 20 books to become a reviewer. A NEH program officer told us recently they use approximately 10,000 reviewers annually to critique submitted proposals; there is a 100 percent turnover of panelists every year.

The process in becoming a reviewer for a private foundation is not standardized. Some private foundations use a peer review process similar to federal sponsors and others have a closed system, relying exclusively on program staff and board members to make funding decisions. We suggest you contact the program officer and ask whether they use external reviewers. If so, volunteer by sending your customized résumé.

In essence, being a reviewer significantly increases your chances of getting funded. When serving as a reviewer, you will learn many things to do—and not do—as you write your next proposal. Update your résumé so it reflects the values of the grantmakers for which you wish to review, showing in particular that you understand the target problem and audience. Then send it to the program officer following their instructions.

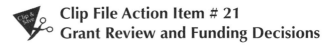 **Clip File Action Item # 21**
Grant Review and Funding Decisions

Build your Grant Review and Funding Decisions clip file by including the following items:

- Administration on Intellectual and Developmental Disabilities
  http://addreviewer.org/
- Corporation for National and Community Service
  www.nationalservice.gov/egrants/peer_review.asp
- Department of Labor
  www.doleta.gov/doc/grant_panelist.cfm
- Health Resources and Services Administration
  https://grants.hrsa.gov/webreview/
- Institute of Museum and Library Services
  www.imls.gov/reviewers/default.aspx
- National Endowment for the Humanities
  https://securegrants.neh.gov/prism/
- National Institute of Food and Agriculture
  www.csrees.usda.gov/business/prs.html
- National Institutes of Health
  http://grants.nih.gov/grants/peer/becoming_peer_reviewer.htm
- National Science Foundation
  www.nsf.gov/bfa/dias/policy/merit_review/reviewer.jsp
- Office of Community Services and Office of Public Health and Science
  https://rrm.grantsolutions.gov/
- Office of Justice Programs
  https://www.bja.gov/FAQDetail.aspx?ID=191
- Office of Postsecondary Education
  http://opeweb.ed.gov/frs/index.cfm
- Office of Safe and Drug Free Schools
  www2.ed.gov/about/offices/list/osdfs/peerreview.html
- Substance Abuse and Mental Health Administration.
  www.samhsa.gov/Grants/emailform/index.aspx

FEDERAL PROGRAMS ACCEPTING APPLICATIONS ONLINE FOR GRANT REVIEWERS

EXHIBIT 90

- Sample letters to program officers requesting verbatim reviewer comments, whether your proposal was funded or rejected.
- Sample letters to program officers acknowledging their declination notice.
- Lists of questions asked by program officers during site visits.

- Lists of grant programs where you could serve as a reviewer.

You have hundreds of tips on successful grantseeking and efficient, time-saving suggestions to implement them.

Now, go write your best grant ever!

Bibliography

Anderson, Cynthia. *Write Grants, Get Money*. Columbus, OH: Linworth Publishing, 2008.

Arizona Guide to Grants & Giving. Glendale, AZ: Arizona Human Services, 2003.

Avery, Caroline D. *The Guide to Successful Small Grants Programs When a Little Goes a Long Way: Feature Case Studies of Foundation Programs*. Washington, DC: Council on Foundations, 2003.

Barbato, Joseph. *How to Write Knockout Proposals: What You Must Know (And Say) to Win Funding Every Time*. Medfield, MA: Emerson & Church Publishers, 2004.

Barber, Daniel M. *Finding Funding: The Comprehensive Guide to Grant Writing*. Long Beach, CA: Bond Street Publishers, 2002.

Bauer, David G. *The "How To" Grants Manual: Successful Grantseeking Techniques for Obtaining Public and Private Grants*. Lanham, MD: Rowman & Littlefield Publishers, 2011.

Bishop, Wendy and David Starkey. *Keywords in Creative Writing*. Logan: Utah State University Press, 2006.

Bowers-Lanier, Rebecca. *The Nurse's Grant Writing Advantage: How Grantwriting can Advance your Nursing Career*. Indianapolis, IN: Sigma Theta Tau International, 2012.

Brewer, Ernest W. *Finding Funding: Grantwriting from Start to Finish, Including Project Management and Internet Use*. Thousand Oaks, CA: Corwin Press, 2001.

Brinkerhoff, Robert O., Dale M. Brethower, Terry Hluchyj, and Jeri Ridings-Nowakowski. *Program Evaluation: A Practitioner's Guide for Trainers and Educators*. Boston: Kluwer-Nijhoff, 1983.

Brophy, Sarah S. *Is Your Museum Grant Ready?: Assessing Your Organization's Potential for Funding*. Lanham, MD: AltaMira Press, 2005.

Brown, Larissa G. *Demystifying Grant Seeking: What You Really Need to Do to Get Grants*. San Francisco, CA: Jossey-Bass, 2001.

Browning, Beverly A. *Grant Writing for Dummies*. NJ: Wiley & Sons, 2011.

Browning, Beverly A. *Grant Writing for Educators: Practical Strategies for Teachers, Administrators, and Staff*. Bloomington, IN: National Education Service, 2005.

Browning, Beverly A. *How to Become a Grant Writing Consultant: Start-up Guide for Your Home-based Business*. Chandler, AZ: Bev Browning & Associates, 2001.

Burke, Jim, and Carol Ann Prater. *I'll Grant You That: A Step-by-step Guide to Finding Funds, Designing Winning Projects, and Writing Powerful Grant Proposals*. Portsmouth, NH: Heinneman, 2000.

Burke, MaryAnn. *Simplified Grantwriting*. Thousand Oaks, CA: Corwin Press, 2002.

Burke Smith, Nancy, and E. Gabriel Works. *Complete Book of Grant Writing*. Naperville, IL: Sourcebooks, Inc., 2006.

Cambron, Jeff, Carolyn Pense, and Emily White, eds. *Grant Funding for Elderly Health Services*. Manasquan, NJ: Health Resources Publishing, 2008.

Carlson, Mim, and Tori O'Neal-McElrath. *Winning Grants Step by Step*. San Francisco: Jossey-Bass, 2008.

Catalog of Federal Domestic Assistance. Available at www.cfda.gov, updated semiannually.

Celebrity Foundation Directory. New York, NY: Foundation Center, 2012.

Chronicle of Philanthropy. Available at www.philanthropy.com, published biweekly.

Clarke, Cheryl A. *Storytelling for Grantseekers: The Guide to Creative Nonprofit Fundraising*. San Francisco, CA: Jossey-Bass, 2001.

Clarke, Cheryl A., and Susan P. Fox. *Grant Proposal Makeover: Transform Your Request from No to Yes*. San Francisco, CA: Jossey-Bass, 2006.

Coley, Soraya M., and Cynthia A. Scheinberg. *Proposal Writing: Effective Grantsmanship*. Thousand Oaks, CA: Sage Publications, Inc., 2007.

Corporate Foundation Profiles. New York, NY: Foundation Center, 2002.

Corporate Giving Directory. Washington, DC: Taft Group, 2006.

Crum, Nina, ed. *Grant Funding for Elderly Health Services*. Manasquan, NJ: Health Resources Publishers, 2003.

Directory of Corporate Affiliations. Available at www.lexisnexis.com/dca.

Dove, Kent E., Alan M. Spears, and Thomas W. Herbert. *Conducting a Successful Major Gifts and Planned Giving Program: A Comprehensive Guide and Resource*. San Francisco: Jossey-Bass, 2002.

DuBose, Mike, Martha Davis, and Anne Black. *Developing Successful Grants: How to Turn Your Ideas into Reality*. Columbia, SC: Research Associates, 2005.

Edles, L. Peter. *Fundraising: Hands-on Tactics for Nonprofit Groups*. NY: McGraw-Hill, 2006.

Faruqi, Saadia. *Best Practices in Grant Seeking : Beyond the Proposal*. Sudbury, MA: Jones and Bartlett Publishers, 2011.

Federal Register. Available at https://www.federalregister.gov, published weekdays.

Fortune 500 Companies. Available at money.cnn.com.

Foundation Center's Guide to Winning Proposals. New York, NY: Foundation Center, 2008.

Foundation Directory. New York, NY: Foundation Center, 2012.

Foundation Directory Part II. New York, NY: Foundation Center, 2012.

Foundation Directory Supplement. New York, NY: Foundation Center, 2012.

Foundation Grants to Individuals. New York, NY: Foundation Center, 2012.

Freeman, David F., John A. Edie, and Jane Nober. *The Handbook on Private Foundations*. Washington, DC, Council on Foundations, 2005.

Friedland, Andrew J., and Carol L. Folt. *Writing Successful Science Proposals*. Cumberland, RI: Yale University Press, 2009.

Fund Raiser's Guide to Religious Philanthropy. Washington, DC: Taft Group, 2000.

Geever, Jane C. *Foundation Center's Guide to Proposal Writing*. New York, NY: Foundation Center, 2012.

Gerin, William. *Writing the NIH Grant Proposal: A Step-by-Step Guide*. Thousand Oaks, CA: Sage Publications, 2010.

Gitlin, Laura N., and Kevin J. Lyons. *Successful Grant Writing: Strategies for Health and Human Service Professionals*. New York, NY: Springer Publishing Company, 2008.

Glass, Sandra A., ed. *Approaching Foundations: Suggestions and Insights for Fundraisers*. San Francisco, CA: Jossey-Bass, 2000.

Grants for At-risk Youth. Gaithersburg, MD: Aspen Publishers, 2002.

Grants Register. Chicago, IL: St. James Press, 2007.

Grantseekers Guide to Faith-based Funding. Silver Spring, MD: CD Publications, 2003.

Guide to Community Foundations. Antwerp, OH: Freeman & Costello Press, 2002.

Guide to Funding for International and Foreign Programs. New York, NY: Foundation Center, 2012.

Guyer, Mark. *A Concise Guide to Getting Grants for Nonprofit Organizations*. New York, NY: Kroshka Books, 2002.

Hackshaw, Allan K. *How to Write a Grant Application*. Chichester, UK: Wiley-Blackwell, 2011.

Hale, Phale D. and Deborah Ward. *Writing Grant Proposals That Win*. Boston, MA: Jones & Bartlett Publishers, Inc., 2005.

Hall, Jeremy L. *Grant Management: Funding for Public and Nonprofit Programs*. Sudbury, MA: Jones and Bartlett Publishers, 2010.

Hall, Mary S., and Susan Howlett. *Getting Funded: The Complete Guide to Writing Grant Proposals*. Seattle, WA: Word & Raby Publishing, 2011.

Hall-Ellis, Sylvia D., and Ann Jerabek. *Grants for School Libraries*. Westport, CT: Libraries Unlimited, 2003.

Health Funds Grants Resource Yearbook. Wall Township, NJ: Health Resources Publications, 2004.

Henson, Kenneth T. *Grant Writing in Higher Education: A Step-by-Step Guide*. Boston, MA: Pearson/Allyn and Bacon, 2004.

Henson, Kenneth T. *Successful Grant Writing for School Leaders: 10 Easy Steps*. Upper Saddle River, NJ: Pearson Education, 2012.

Holtzclaw, Barbara J, Carole Kenner, and Marlene Walden, *Grant Writing Handbook for Nurses*. Sudbury, MA: Jones and Bartlett Publishers, 2009.

Johnson, Victoria M. *Grant Writing 101 : Everything You Need to Start Raising Funds Today*. New York, NY: McGraw-Hill, 2011.

Johnson-Sheehan, Richard. *Writing Proposals: Rhetoric for Managing Change*. New York, NY: Longman, 2001.

Kachinske, Timothy, and Judith Kachinske. *90 Days to Success in Grant Writing*. Boston, MA: Course Technology PTR, 2010.

Karsh, Ellen, and Arlen Sue Fox. *The Only Grant-Writing Book You'll Ever Need: Top Grant Writers and Grant Givers Share Their Secrets*. New York, NY: Basic Books, 2009.

Kenner, Carole, and Marlene Walden. *Grant Writing Tips for Nurses and Other Health Professionals*. Washington, DC: American Nurses Association, 2001.

Kepler, Ann. *The ALA Book of Library Grant Money*. Chicago, IL: American Library Association, 2012.

Klein, Kim. *Fundraising for Social Change*. Oakland, CA: Chardon Press, 2001.

Knowles, Cynthia. *The First-Time Grantwriter's Guide to Success*. Thousand Oaks, CA: Corwin Press, 2002.

Lansdowne, David. *The Relentlessly Practical Guide to Raising Serious Money: Proven Strategies for Nonprofit Organizations*. Medfield, MA: Emerson & Church Publishers, 2005.

Levenson, Stanley. *How to Get Grants and Gifts for the Public Schools*. Boston, MA: Allyn & Bacon, 2001.

Liberatori, Ellen. *Guide to Getting Arts Grants*. New York, NY: Allworth Press, 2006.

Licklider, Mary M., and the University of Missouri Grant Writer Network. *Grant Seeking in Higher Education:*

Strategies and Tools for College Faculty. San Francisco, CA: Jossey-Bass, 2012.

Margolin, Judith B., ed. *After the Grant: The Nonprofit's Guide to Good Stewardship.* New York, NY: Foundation Center, 2010.

Martorana, Janet, and Sherry DeDecker. *RFP and Grant Writing Resources.* March 2002. Available at www.library.ucsb.edu/guides/rfps.html.

Maxwell, Nancy Kalikow. *Grant Money through Collaborative Partnerships.* Chicago, IL: American Library Association, 2012.

McGrath, James M., and Laura Adler, eds. *Grant Seeker's Guide: Foundations that Support Social & Economic Justice.* Kingston, RI: Moyer Bell, 2005.

McNabb, David E. *Research Methods in Public Administration and Nonprofit Management: Quantitative and Qualitative Approaches.* Armonk, NY: M. E. Sharpe, 2002.

Mikelonis, Victoria M., Signe T. Betsinger, and Constance E. Kampf. *Grant Seeking in an Electronic Age.* New York, NY: Longman, 2003.

Miner, Jeremy T. "Behind Door #3: The Hard-to-Please Grant Reviewer." *Research Management Review* 18, no. 2 (Fall/Winter 2011), available online at www.ncura.edu/content/news/rmr/docs/v18n2_Miner.pdf.

Miner, Jeremy T., and Lynn E. Miner. *Models of Proposal Planning and Writing.* Westport, CT: Praeger Publishers, 2005.

Miner, Jeremy T., Lynn E. Miner, and Jerry Griffith. *Collaborative Grantseeking: A Guide to Designing Projects, Leading Partners, and Persuading Sponsors.* Santa Barbara, CA: Greenwood Press, 2011.

Miner, Lynn E., Jeremy T. Miner, and Jerry Griffith. "Best– and Worst–Practices in Research Administration." *Research Management Review* 13, no. 1 (Winter/Spring 2003), available online at www.ncura.edu/data/rmrd/pdf/v13n1.pdf.

Mudd, Mollie, ed. *Grants for K-12 Schools.* Gaithersburg, MD: Aspen Publishers, 2001.

National Directory of Corporate Giving. New York, NY: Foundation Center, 2012.

New, Cheryl Carter, and James A. Quick. *How to Write a Grant Proposal.* Hoboken, NJ: John Wiley & Sons, 2003.

Nober, Jane C. *Grants to Individuals by Community Foundations.* Washington, DC: Council on Foundations, 2004.

Orosz, Joel J. *The Insider's Guide to Grantmaking: How Foundations Find, Fund, and Manage Effective Programs.* San Francisco, CA: Jossey-Bass Publishers, 2000.

Paprocki, Steven L. *Grants: Corporate Grantmaking for Racial and Ethnic Communities.* Wakefield, RI: Moyer Bell, 2000.

Patterson Porter, Deborah. *Successful School Grants: Fulfilling the Promise of School Improvement.* D & R Publishing, 2003.

Payne, Mary Ann. *Grant Writing Demystified.* New York, NY: McGraw-Hill, 2011.

Pequegnat, Willo, Ellen Stover, and Cheryl Anne Boyce, eds. *How to Write a Successful Research Grant Application: A Guide for Social and Behavioral Scientists.* New York, NY: Springer, 2011.

Peters, Abby Day. *Winning Research Funding.* Aldershot, UK: Gower, 2003.

Peterson, Susan L. *The Grantwriter's Internet Companion: A Resource for Educators and Others Seeking Grants and Funding.* Thousand Oaks, CA: Corwin Press, 2001.

PRI Directory: Charitable Loans & Other Program-Related Investments by Foundations. New York, NY: Foundation Center, 2010.

Quick, James A., and Cheryl Carter New. *Grant Winner's Toolkit: Project Management and Evaluation.* New York, NY: John Wiley, 2000.

Quick, James A., and Cheryl Carter New. *Grant Seeker's Budget Toolkit.* New York, NY: John Wiley, 2001.

Reif-Lehrer, Liane. *Grant Application Writer's Handbook.* Sudbury, MA: Jones and Bartlett Publishers, 2005.

Robinson, Andy. *Grassroots Grants: An Activist's Guide to Grantseeking.* San Francisco, CA: Jossey-Bass, 2004.

Rosenberg, Gigi. *The Artist's Guide To Grant Writing: How to Find Funds and Write Foolproof Proposals for the Visual, Literary, and Performing Artist.* New York, NY: Watson-Guptill, 2010

Setterberg, Fred, Rushworth M. Kidder, and Colburn S. Wilbur. *Grantmaking Basics II: A Field Guide for Funders.* Washington, DC: Council on Foundations, 2004.

Smith, Nancy, and E. Gabriel Works. *The Complete Book of Grant Writing: Learn to Write Grants Like a Professional.* Chicago, IL: Sourcebooks, 2012

Solla, Laura A. *The Guide to Analyzing Wealth and Assets: Corporations, Foundations, Individuals.* Freeport, PA: L. A. Solla, 2001.

Solla, Laura A. *The Guide to Prospect Research & Prospect Management: Corporations, Foundations, Individuals.* Freeport, PA: L. A. Solla, 2007.

Staines, Gail M. *Go Get That Grant! A Practical Guide for Libraries and Nonprofit Organizations.* Lanham, MD: Scarecrow Press, 2010.

Stanton, Sally, and Laurie Risch, *Grant Writing Made Simple: 87 Tips for Great Grants.* Milwaukee, WI: Crickhollow Books, 2009.

Swan, James. *Fundraising for Libraries: 25 Proven Ways to get more Money for Your Library.* New York, NY: Neal-Schuman Publishers, 2002.

Teitel, Martin. *Thank You for Submitting Your Proposal: A Foundation Director Reveals What Happens Next.* Medfield, MA: Emerson & Church, 2006.

Thompson, Waddy. *The Complete Idiot's Guide to Grant Writing.* New York, NY: Penguin Group, 2011.

Tremore, Judy, and Nancy Burke Smith. *The Everything Grant Writing Book: Create the Perfect Proposal to Raise the Funds You Need.* Cincinnati, OH: Adams Media Corporation, 2008.

Ward, Deborah. *Writing Grant Proposals That Win*. Boston, MA: Jones & Bartlett, 2011.

Wason, Sara D. *Webster's New World Grant Writing Handbook*. San Francisco, CA: Jossey-Bass, 2004.

Weinstein, Stanley. *Capital Campaigns from the Ground up: How Nonprofits Can Have the Building of Their Dreams*. Hoboken, NJ: John Wiley & Sons, 2004.

Wells, Michael K. *Grantwriting Beyond the Basics*. Portland, OR: Continuing Education Press, 2005.

Wholey, Joseph S., Harry P. Hatry, and Kathryn E. Newcomer, eds. *Handbook of Practical Program Evaluation*. San Francisco, CA: Jossey-Bass, 2004.

Yang, Otto O. *Guide to Effective Grant Writing: How to Write a Successful NIH Grant Application*. New York, NY: Springer, 2005.

Yuen, Francis K., and Kenneth L. Terao. *Practical Grant Writing and Program Evaluation*. Pacific Grove, CA: Brooks/Cole Thomson Learning, 2003.

Zils, Michael. *World Guide to Foundations*. München: K.G. Saur, 2001.

Zimmerman, Robert M. *Grantseeking: A Step-by-step Approach*. San Francisco, CA: Zimmerman-Lehman, 2001.

Index

About the Authors

Jeremy T. Miner, MA, is president of Miner and Associates, Inc., a nationwide consulting firm that provides grant-seeking and fundraising services to nonprofit organizations. He is also director of grants and contracts in the Office of Research and Sponsored Programs at the University of Wisconsin–Eau Claire. In addition to developing and administering proposals to public and private grantmakers, he has served as a reviewer for federal grant programs and helped private foundations streamline their grant application guidelines. Miner is an active member of the National Council of University Research Administrators (NCURA) at the national and regional levels, serving on committees, presenting workshops and concurrent sessions, and publishing journal articles. He has presented grantseeking workshops nationally and internationally to thousands of grant-getters. His successful grant writing techniques have generated millions of grant dollars for many nonprofit education, health care, and social service agencies.

Lynn E. Miner, PhD, is founder and a principal in Miner and Associates, Inc., and directs the office in Milwaukee, Wisconsin. He has been an active grantseeker in academic, health care, and other nonprofit environments for the past four decades. He has been affiliated with hospitals and public and private universities as a professor and research administrator as well as holding deanships in the graduate school and in engineering. Along with Jeremy Miner, he authored *Models of Proposal Planning & Writing* (Praeger Publishers) and *Collaborative Grantseeking: A Guide to Designing Projects, Leading Partners and Persuading Sponsors* (Greenwood Press) and coedits *Grantseeker Tips*, a free biweekly electronic newsletter on successful grantseeking, available through www.MinerAndAssociates.com.

Public Grant Web Sites

Web addresses for 50 major public grant information sources.

Name	Web Address
Electronic Funding Information Sources	
Catalog of Federal Domestic Assistance	www.cfda.gov
Congressional Record	www.gpo.gov/fdsys/search/home.action
Faith-Based and Neighborhood Partnerships	www.whitehouse.gov/administration/eop/ofbnp
Federal Acquisition Regulations	https://www.acquisition.gov/far/
Federal Business Opportunities	www.fedbizopps.gov
Federal Register	https://www.federalregister.gov/
Federal Research in Progress	www.ntis.gov
Grants.gov	www.grants.gov
Grantmaking Agencies	
Administration for Children and Families	www.acf.hhs.gov
Administration on Aging	www.aoa.gov
Advanced Research Projects Agency	www.darpa.mil
Air Force Office of Scientific Research	www.wpafb.af.mil/afrl/afosr
Army Research Office	www.arl.army.mil
Bureau of Health Professions	bhpr.hrsa.gov
Centers for Disease Control and Prevention	www.cdc.gov
Centers for Medicare and Medicaid Services	www.cms.gov
Civilian Research & Development Foundation	www.crdfglobal.org
Corporation for National & Community Service	www.nationalservice.gov
Department of Agriculture	www.usda.gov
Department of Commerce	www.commerce.gov
Department of Defense	www.defense.gov
Department of Education	www.ed.gov
Department of Energy	www.energy.gov
Department of Health and Human Services	www.hhs.gov
Department of Homeland Security	www.dhs.gov
Department of Housing & Urban Development	www.hud.gov
Department of Interior	www.doi.gov
Department of Justice	www.justice.gov
Department of Labor	www.dol.gov
Department of State	www.state.gov
Department of Transportation	www.dot.gov
Environmental Projection Agency	www.epa.gov
Food and Drug Administration	www.fda.gov
Institute of International Education	www.iie.org
National Academic of Science	www.nas.edu
National Aeronautics & Space Administration	www.nasa.gov
National Endowment for Democracy	www.ned.org
National Endowment for the Arts	www.nea.gov
National Endowment for the Humanities	www.neh.gov
National Gallery of Art	www.nga.gov
National Historical Publications & Records Commission	www.archives.gov/nhprc/about/
National Institute of Standards & Technology	www.nist.gov
National Institutes of Health	www.nih.gov
National Science Foundation	www.nsf.gov
Office of Naval Research	www.onr.navy.mil
Smithsonian Institution	www.si.edu
State & Local Government Agencies	www.statelocalgov.net
U.S. Agency for International Development	www.usaid.gov
U.S. Institute of Peace	www.usip.org
U.S. Small Business Administration	www.sba.gov